NOMINATING THE PRESIDENT

NOMINATING THE PRESIDENT

Edited by
Emmett H. Buell, Jr.
and Lee Sigelman

The University of Tennessee Press / Knoxville

The paper in this book meets the minimum requirements of the
American National Standard for Permanence of Paper for Printed
Library Materials. ⊚   The binding materials have been chosen
for strength and durability.

Library of Congress Cataloging in Publication Data

Nominating the President / edited by Emmett H. Buell, Jr., and Lee
  Sigelman. — 1st ed.
      p.   cm.
    Includes bibliographical references and index.
    ISBN 0-87049-686-7 (cloth : alk. paper)
    ISBN 0-87049-687-5 (pbk. : alk. paper)
    1. Presidents — United States — Nomination.   2. Presidents — United
  States — Election — 1988.   I. Buell, Emmett H.   II. Sigelman, Lee.
  JK521.N66   1991
  324.5′0973 — dc20   90-43212   CIP

Contents

Tables

Acknowledgments

This is the place where a few words of thanks must somehow serve to express our appreciation for much good advice and valuable assistance. We are especially grateful to our editors at the University of Tennessee Press, first to Cynthia Maude-Gembler for enthusiastically endorsing the project in its initial phases, and then to Tana McDonald for guidance and support during the book's final stages. F. Christopher Arterton, Michael Nelson, Richard A. Watson, David Welborn, and two other readers who preferred anonymity offered useful suggestions and constructive criticisms in evaluating our prospectus and eventual manuscript. The manuscript itself would not have gotten very far without the prompt and generally cheerful assistance of Glenda Nease, Margie Boring, Nelma Higgins, and Barbara Jones, who processed, copied, and mailed off many chapter drafts under tight deadlines. Denison University students Nelson Fox and Keith Rummer helped in final checks of tables and footnotes. Donna Childers and Mary Kay Larimer rendered invaluable assistance in checking page proofs and compiling the index.

We gratefully acknowledge the permission of the American Enterprise Institute for Public Policy to reprint table 2.1 of S. Robert Lichter, Daniel Amundson, and Richard Noyes, *The Video Campaign: Network Coverage of the 1988 Primaries* (Washington, D.C.: American Enterprise Institute, 1988), and table 2 of S. Robert Lichter's "Misreading Momentum" in *Public Opinion* 11 (May–June 1988). We are similarly grateful to Continuum Press for permission to reprint a lengthy passage from Senator Paul Simon's *Winners and Losers* (New York: Continuum Press, 1989).

Introduction: Nominating the President— An Overview

Lee Sigelman

In 1940 a small band of social scientists descended on Erie County, Ohio, to undertake an in-depth study of "votes in the making" in the upcoming presidential election (Lazarsfeld, Berelson, and Gaudet, 1944). Thus began what would ultimately become a massive amount of scholarly literature on voter decision-making in presidential elections—highlighted by Campbell, Converse, Miller, and Stokes's *The American Voter* (1960). Two decades later, journalist Theodore H. White's *The Making of the President 1960* initiated a series of detailed chronicles of specific presidential campaigns and spawned numerous other intensely colorful accounts, including Joe McGinniss's *The Selling of the President 1968*, Timothy Crouse's *The Boys on the Bus,* and, most recently, Jack Germond and Jules Witcover's *Whose Broad Stripes and Bright Stars? The Trivial Pursuit of the Presidency 1988*. Over the years, the intersection of these two bodies of literature, one scholarly and the other popular, has provided readers with a rich store of systematic data and behind-the-scenes glimpses of presidential campaigns.

All of these works focus primarily upon the general election phase of presidential campaigns, by which time the field has been narrowed to the two (or, on occasion, three) remaining contenders and their running mates. However, the general election campaign amounts to only the homestretch in a very long race—the last few months of a competition that drags on for years. Focusing so single-mindedly on these last few months leads to a neglect of the longer-term dynamics involved. Because political scientists are especially likely to fall prey to this tendency, our systematic knowledge of earlier phases of presidential campaigns is still far outstripped by our command of the fascinating anecdotes told and retold by journalists.

In 1987, reflecting on a half-dozen or so book-length treatments of the 1984 election by political scientists (e.g., Abramson, Aldrich, and Rohde, 1987; Nelson, 1985; Pomper, 1985; Ranney, 1985; Sandoz and Crabb, 1985), we lamented this tendency to spotlight the general election to the virtual — or, in a few cases, total — exclusion of the most time-consuming, expensive, and formative portion of the campaign. We decided to try to rebalance the scales through a sustained examination of the politics of the presidential nomination process. We would, we resolved, assemble a team of experts on topics whose coverage we deemed vital to understanding presidential nominations. We would also, we decided, ask these scholars not only to focus on the 1988 nomination campaigns but to (a) consider the events of 1988 against the backdrop of the accumulated "conventional wisdom" concerning nomination campaigns, and (b) where possible, to distill from the 1988 experience portents for future presidential nomination campaigns.

Nominating the President is the product of these efforts. It is an extremely wide-ranging work, treating such disparate topics as specific campaign events like the Iowa caucuses and the Super Tuesday primaries and such broad forces as religion and candidate personality in presidential nominating politics. The authors bring no single political, theoretical, analytical, or methodological perspective to bear on these diverse issues. They do, however, add significantly to our understanding of the 1988 campaigns in particular and presidential nomination campaigns in general because they have taken seriously our injunction to treat the 1988 campaigns as case studies of an evolving process.

In chapter 1, "Win Early and Often," Emmett Buell and James Davis survey the broad strategic environment confronting contenders for the presidential nomination — the considerations the various camps must take into account in plotting the strategies they hope will carry their candidate to the convention rostrum for a rousing acceptance speech. The strategic environment includes the formal "rules of the game," such as the scheduling of primaries and caucuses, modes of delegate selection, and regulations concerning campaign finance. It also includes the "opportunity structure," which in 1988 was fundamentally shaped by the absence of an incumbent from the race and the resulting logjam, in both parties, of contenders with various strengths and weaknesses. Any nomination race will present some surprises: an expected front-runner will stumble out of the blocks, or a laggard will suddenly sprint past the field. But what sometimes seems to the uninitiated observer to be no more than a chaotic and virtually random process governed largely by accident, coincidence, and sheer dumb luck is best understood, as Buell and Davis make clear in the context of the 1988 campaigns, as a process in which those who respond most opportunistically to the strategic environment of the campaign are best equipped to cross the finish line ahead of their opponents.

From virtually that moment in November when the winner of the presidential election is declared, the *next* presidential contest begins to take shape. Politicians from around the country who have previously displayed little or no interest in agricultural policy suddenly develop a burning curiosity about the price of corn, the staple commodity of Iowa, where the first-in-the-nation presidential caucuses are held, and find New Hampshire, the site of the earliest presidential primaries, an absolutely irresistible place to visit. For many years, New Hampshire occupied a unique place in the thinking of campaign strategists, who did everything they could to parlay a fast start there into momentum that would carry through to the nomination. In the 1970s, though, Iowa began to challenge New Hampshire for the place of primacy, and some would claim that Iowa now looms even larger as a strategic concern than New Hampshire. In any event, the wealth of data supplied by Alan Abramowitz, Ronald Rapoport, and Walter Stone in chapter 2, "Up Close and Personal," gives readers a more accurate view of caucus participants than suggested by conventional wisdom. Conventional wisdom depicts the caucuses as dominated by an unrepresentative handful of ideologues and single-issue purists whose sole purpose is to exact promises from candidates, regardless of the consequences in November. Not so, say Abramowitz and associates, who find few ideological extremists or single-issue zealots in their survey of 1988 caucus attenders. For the most part, the authors conclude, Iowa caucus participants are well informed, moderate, and thus well suited to make the first cut of candidates.

Two weeks after Iowa and New Hampshire, the headline event of the 1988 nomination process was Super Tuesday, when twenty states held primaries or caucuses. In chapter 3, "The Best Laid Plans . . . ," Barbara Norrander explains the origins of this mega-event and reveals how it disappointed planners in both parties. The Democrats, who created Super Tuesday, hoped that in 1988 it would launch a moderate southerner and offset the returns from Iowa and New Hampshire. Instead, it revived Jackson and boosted Dukakis as much as Gore. Republicans looked forward to massive crossover voting by Democrats in open-primary states, but Norrander reveals that most defectors were Republicans, at least some of whom cared more about statewide and congressional races than the struggle for their party's presidential nomination. In fact, according to Norrander, one of every four Republican voters in Super Tuesday's southern and border-state primaries cast Democratic ballots. Still another bit of conventional wisdom was that Pat Robertson would win overwhelming support from fundamentalist Protestants in the South. Norrander demonstrates, however, that Bush would have beaten Robertson in Dixie even if the primaries had been restricted to born-again Christians and voters who interpret the Bible as God's literal word.

In "Financing the 1988 Prenomination Campaigns," chapter 4, Clyde Wilcox examines the conventional wisdom concerning one of the most important and problematic aspects of modern campaigns. Wilcox describes the legal setting of campaign finance, especially the Federal Election Campaign Act, which was enacted in response to the notorious excesses of 1972. These reforms have made it imperative for presidential aspirants to gear up early, and they have placed a premium on wide rather than deep early support. They have also led to considerable "front-loading" of campaign expenditures, as candidates attempt to demonstrate early on that they are indeed viable contenders. Wilcox describes the candidates' spending patterns in 1988 and analyzes the effects and noneffects of such spending. In 1988, he concludes, there were significant departures from past patterns. For example, the successful candidates were the ones who relied least on small contributions, and candidates who made especially impressive early showings did not experience the expected surge in contributions. However, certain familiar patterns did recur, especially the front-loading of campaign spending and the correlation between spending and success, at least when several little-known candidates are competing for the nomination.

A unique feature of the 1988 nomination contests was the active presidential candidacies of two "outsiders," neither of whom had ever held public office and both of whom were ordained Baptist ministers. In chapter 5, "Ministering to the Nation," Kenneth Wald analyzes the Jackson and Robertson challenges against the broader backdrop of the role of religion in American political life. While Jackson and Robertson are no more similar politically than they are personally, both campaigns had deeply religious ideological and organizational roots. Indeed, Wald characterizes their campaigns as "lengthy exercises in applied theology." According to Wald, there are important lessons to be learned or relearned from the Jackson and Robertson campaigns: that party reforms have paved the way for outside challenges like those mounted by Jackson and Robertson; that politics and the pulpit can be a potent mixture; that religious congregations can provide an excellent infrastructure for a presidential campaign; and that even seemingly similar religious beliefs can lead to entirely different political appeals. These lessons, Wald argues, are likely to be of continuing importance to the parties, just as, Wald suspects, Jackson in particular is likely to be to the Democrats.

Nomination campaigns are, in many different senses, media events. They are, among other things, staged largely *for* the media, with extraordinary attention being paid to gaining name recognition early in the campaign and to maintaining favorable coverage throughout. And they are conveyed to the public largely *by* the media; these days, when candidates campaign in a certain town, very often their visit consists of nothing more than a hurried press conference at the airport, from which they are whisked away to yet another airport for yet another press conference. In chapter 6, "Meeting Expectations?" Emmett Buell explores candidate coverage during the earliest stage of the nomination campaign. At this point, most people know little about the candidates, whose identities and prospects must still be defined. On the basis of a painstaking content analysis of "exhibition-season" coverage in five major metropolitan newspapers, Buell detects a correspondence between where a candidate stood in the polls and the amount of coverage he attracted. Being taken seriously as a candidate, Buell reports, also strongly influences the nature and extent of "character coverage" and helps determine the volume and spin of "horse-race coverage." Even so, Buell concludes that, at least during the exhibition season, the major newspapers do a better job of covering the campaigns than is commonly supposed.

But what about the television networks, and what about coverage of the nomination campaigns themselves? In "The More Things Change . . . ," chapter 7, Michael Robinson and S. Robert Lichter give mixed reviews to the networks' coverage of the 1988 nomination campaigns. The networks have often been charged with "horse-racism," i.e., ignoring the "real" issues and covering the campaign as if the only issue were who is going to win. In 1988, Robinson and Lichter report, horse-racism was once again evident, and, given prevailing definitions of what constitutes "news," this sort of coverage will almost surely recur in future campaigns. However, "early-bird news," that is, the tendency to exaggerate the importance of early contests and downplay late ones, was present in 1988 only because of saturation coverage of the Iowa caucuses and the New Hampshire primary. Once those two early races were over, the networks generally covered state contests in proportion to their electoral importance. Robinson and Lichter anticipate a continued fading of the "early-bird news" bias in future campaigns. "Surprise journalism," i.e., the tendency to react to a candidate's performance on the basis of how well the candidate was "expected" to do, also took some surprising twists in 1988. But according to Robinson and Lichter, the real story in 1988, with potentially major strategic implications for the future, was the increased importance of "compensatory reporting," that is, the networks' tendency to treat challengers better than front-runners.

The final event in a nomination campaign is the national party convention. In 1988, as in most other recent nomination campaigns, the outcomes of the contests were known well in advance of the conventions. As the nominating process has been "democratized" over the years, the conventions have come to play a less and less decisive role. They cannot, however, be dismissed as inconsequential, as Emmett Buell and John Jackson argue in chapter 8, "The National Conventions," since the conventions serve as a bridge between the nominating and electing stages of the presidential selection process—ratifying the tickets, adopting platforms, and seeking to join together what the nomination campaigns have torn asunder. The latter in particular is often a greater challenge for the fissiparous Democrats, and 1988 proved to be no exception, as the general election campaign would make obvious.

Finally, in "Evaluating the New Nominating System," the concluding chapter of this volume, Wayne Shannon draws on the preceding chapters to assess the presidential nominating system as it actually operates against the benchmark of what he considers an ideal nominating system. Shannon poses several crucial tests. Does the nominating system produce candidates who are, by dint of experience and personality, well qualified to become president? Does it permit, or even encourage, the parties to engage in coalition building? Does it reduce information costs for voters? Does it encourage widespread participation in party affairs? And does it discourage the selection of candidates with limited electoral appeal? On virtually all of these tests, Shannon assigns low grades to the current system of presidential nominations. While others may disagree with some of his assessments, Shannon's discussion has the potential to structure ongoing considerations of reform in the presidential nominating system.

References

Abramson, Paul, John Aldrich, and David Rohde. 1987. *Change and Continutiy in the 1984 Elections*. Rev. ed. Washington, D.C.: CQ Press.

Campbell Angus, Philip E. Converse, Warren E. Miller, and Donald E. Stokes. 1960. *The American Voter*. New York: John Wiley.

Crouse, Timothy. 1972. *The Boys on the Bus: Riding with the Campaign Press Corps*. New York: Random House.

Germond, Jack W., and Jules Witcover. 1989. *Whose Broad Stripes and Bright Stars? The Trivial Pursuit of the Presidency 1988*. New York: Warner Books.

Lazarsfeld, Paul F., Bernard Berelson, and Hazel Gaudet. 1944. *The People's Choice.* New York: Duell, Sloan & Pearce.

McGinniss, Joe. 1969. *The Selling of the President 1968.* New York: Trident Press.

Nelson, Michael, ed. 1985. *The Elections of 1984.* Washington, D.C.: CQ Press.

Pomper, Gerald M. 1985.*The Election of 1984: Reports and Interpretations.* Chatham, N.J.: Chatham House.

Ranney, Austin, ed. 1985. *The American Elections of 1984.* Durham, N.C.: Duke University Press.

Sandoz, Ellis, and Cecil Crabb. 1985. *Election 1984.* New York: NAL.

White, Theodore H. 1961. *The Making of the President 1960.* New York: Atheneum.

1. Win Early and Often: Candidates and the Strategic Environment of 1988

Emmett H. Buell, Jr.
James W. Davis

In 1988, as in past election years, the Democratic and Republican presidential nominations were decided in a context of resources, delegate-selection rules, state laws, momentum, and what Machiavelli called "fortuna." To have any prospect of success, every presidential aspirant had to formulate a plan that made sense in this strategic environment. A comprehensive strategy, like Hamilton Jordan's for Jimmy Carter in 1976, had to take account of delegate-selection rules in each state, pinpoint likely sources of funds, identify supporters, match probable resources against likely rivals, hatch a plausible scenario for winning or doing well enough in critical early contests, and, in the event of initial success, offer a plan for the long march to the nominating convention. Even the most improbable of long-shots had to suggest at least one or two early contests where success seemed possible.

The foremost "given" in the strategic environment of 1988 was that Ronald Reagan could not seek renomination. For the first time in two decades, the presidential nomination in both parties was officially wide open, and at least twenty aspirants seriously considered running. But only a few had the name recognition, personal organization, or fund-raising capacity to sustain a national campaign. Some—like Governor Bill Clinton and Senator Dale Bumpers of Arkansas, Senator Sam Nunn of Georgia, Governor Mario Cuomo of New York, former Senator Paul Laxalt of Nevada, Congresswoman Pat Schroeder of Colorado, Ohio Governor Richard Celeste, and former United Nations Ambassador Jeane Kirkpatrick—assessed the strategic environment and decided that 1988 was not their year. Former Senator Gary Hart of Colorado and Senator Joseph Biden of Delaware withdrew after media exposés destroyed their capability in a year of intense "character" scrutiny.

This chapter is concerned with the strategies of twelve candidates who formally entered and stayed in the race at least through the Iowa caucuses, and with Gary Hart, who returned to the fray hoping to rebuild his reputation.

The Strategic Environment

In order to understand candidate strategies and their eventual success or failure in 1988, let us examine the strategic environment in greater detail. Table 1.1 lists the most important concerns facing any candidate contemplating a race for the Democratic or Republican presidential nomination.

More Primaries Than Caucuses in 1988

First, candidates had to chart their course through a maze of formal rules governing voting, scheduling, and allocation of delegates. Primaries rather than caucuses dominated this terrain, with the Democrats scheduled to hold thirty-seven and the Republicans thirty-eight. According to Rhodes Cook (1989: 28), 66.6 percent of all delegates to the Democratic convention in Atlanta eventually were selected as a result of voting in the 1988 primaries, compared to only 17.9 percent chosen in caucus-convention procedures. "Superdelegates" made up the remaining 15.5 percent.[1] On the

Table 1.1 **Questions Facing Candidates Considering a Presidential Nominating Race**

Formal rules of the game:
Which states hold primaries? Which hold caucuses?
Which states hold earliest contests?
How much front-loading?
How are delegates selected?
How much fund-raising and federal matching funds?
Is an incumbent president seeking renomination?
What is the cost of losing?
How many rivals for the nomination?
Resources of candidate and rivals:
Name recognition and reputation?
Prior government experience?
Fund-raising sources?
Theme and issues of campaign?
Ability to interest news media?
Prominent supporters in key states?
Strength of organization?

Republican side, primaries accounted for an even larger share of convention delegates, 76.9 percent, while the remaining 23.1 percent won their positions in caucuses and conventions.[2]

Letting voters in primaries select the great majority of delegates to presidential nominating conventions is a fairly recent development in American politics. Presidential primaries of any type were not used until the early 1900s, when, in a Progressive mood, numerous states followed the lead of Florida, Wisconsin, and Oregon and legislated their own. Between 1912 and 1968, never fewer than twelve nor more than twenty states held some type of presidential primary. Only in 1916 did the Democrats use primaries to select more than half of all their delegates to a presidential nominating convention. The average number of Democratic convention delegates selected in primaries throughout the period was 40 percent. Republicans averaged 42.9 percent between 1912 and 1968, picking half or more of their delegates in the primaries of 1916 and 1920 (Davis, 1980: 42).

Even though primaries became a common method of selecting delegates during this time, relatively few delegates thus chosen were actually bound to support candidates in the manner now firmly established in the rules and practices of both parties. Writing in an era very different from today, Paul T. David and associates (1960: 252–53) estimated that less than 10 percent of Democratic and less than 5 percent of Republican delegates selected in primaries were bound by any instruction to vote for a particular candidate at the nominating convention. And, although delegates committed to "favorite sons" or to no candidate at all had started to drop in number well before 1972 (Reiter, 1985: 25–27), one or the other bloc was often big enough to exercise considerable power at pre-reform conventions. Elaine Kamarck (1987: 278) estimates that 72 percent of all Democratic delegates in 1952 went to their convention uncommitted to any candidate. The unaffiliated figure was 39 percent in 1956, 31 percent in 1960, and 29 percent in 1968. In the pre-reform era, according to Kamarck (1987: 279), "delegates were elected first and their presidential preferences determined second."

In 1968 Vice-President Hubert Humphrey won the Democratic nomination without formally entering any of fifteen primaries. Indeed, Humphrey did not become a candidate until after the New Hampshire and Wisconsin primaries had helped convince Lyndon Johnson not to seek another term. Despite his late start and avoidance of those primaries still open to him, Humphrey probably had the nomination in his grasp just before the California primary in June (Polsby, 1983: 23–24). Meanwhile, his rivals Robert Kennedy and Eugene McCarthy had battled each other in highly publicized but hardly decisive primaries. Under 1968 rules, winning the preference vote in a primary did not necessarily entitle a candidate to all or even most of a state's convention delegates. Party regulars took full advantage of this situation in certain primary states to slate mostly Humphrey delegates even though Kennedy and McCarthy had won most of the preference vote (Crotty, 1983: 26). Humphrey supporters also prevailed in numerous caucus-convention states where Democratic party rules did not require advance notice of meetings, regular meeting times or places, quorums, or selection of delegates in the same year as the presidential election (Crotty, 1983: 29–30).

Already divided by Vietnam, the war on poverty, and racial tensions, Democrats convening in Chicago to pick their 1968 standard-bearer split further over whether Humphrey's nomination was fairly won. What came out of this tumultuous convention has been exhaustively described elsewhere (especially by Shafer, 1983). Here it is enough to say that a reform era was launched during which the Democrats, in remarkably short time and with surprisingly little resistance, transformed their presidential nominating process from one controlled by state party leaders to one dominated by political activists, candidates, campaign consultants, and the news media. Secret caucuses, casual proceedings, and reliance on the party faithful soon passed into history. Reform forced state parties to open their doors to all self-proclaimed Democrats, to ensure the presence of women and hitherto less-represented minorities among the delegates slated, and to select the delegates according to the preference vote. After 1968, most delegates went to Democratic conventions firmly bound to candidates, the nomination decided well before the first session came to order.[3]

Once reform began to take hold, Democrats in many states concluded that the easiest path of compliance lay in replacing caucuses with primaries.[4] States holding Democratic presidential primaries jumped from fifteen in 1968 to twenty-two in 1972. Thirty states conducted Democratic primaries in 1976, thirty-five in 1980, and twenty-five in 1984 (Crotty and Jackson, 1985: 16).

As noted earlier, Republicans were hardly unfamiliar with presidential primaries. Even so, in conjunction with the reform-impelled rise in Democratic primaries, the number of states hosting Republican primaries also increased—from fifteen in 1968 to twenty-one in 1972, thirty in 1976, thirty-four in 1980, and thirty in 1984 (Crotty and Jackson, 1985: 16). Since legislation was often necessary to change from state caucuses to primaries, and since Democrats controlled most legislatures, the new laws often pushed Republicans into adopting primaries as well. Yet Nicol Rae (1989: 128–29) maintains that, even without the statutory stick, state Republican leaders "would not have wanted to permit the Democrats to gain the registration advantages and media attention that would have been exclusively theirs had the GOP refused to hold a primary on the same day." Thus primaries came to dominate the reformed presidential nominating politics of both parties.

Early Contests and Front-loading

The second great concern to candidates contemplating a presidential nominating effort in 1988 was the timing, spacing, and concentration of primaries and caucuses. Which states go first, how much time separates each event, and how many primaries and caucuses take place on the same day are critical strategic questions for front-runners and long-shots alike.

Even though Republican caucuses in Michigan, Hawaii, and Kansas preceded those in Iowa (the Michigan process began in August 1986), the news media clearly regarded Iowa's precinct caucuses as the first real test of the 1988 nominating process. Iowa has enjoyed this status since 1972, when its Democrats scheduled their precinct caucuses before the New Hampshire primary in an attempt to space out each stage of their caucus-convention process (Winebrenner, 1987: 37–40). Iowans have been unwilling to part with their priority ever since.

Although somewhat diminished by Iowa, New Hampshire still takes great pride in holding the nation's first presidential primary. State law requires that the primary be held at least one week before any "similar election" and contains a "trigger" clause allowing New Hampshire officials to select an even earlier date should any other state schedule its primary on the day initially set aside for New Hampshire. After protracted conflict with the national party in 1984, New Hampshire and Iowa Democrats won understandings that they would be the first to vote, that no other state would share the media spotlight on the days reserved for them, and that both contests would be held before any others on the Democratic calendar (Buell, 1987a). South Dakota and Minnesota put this agreement to the test in 1987 by rescheduling their events for February 23, 1988—the date set aside for New Hampshire. When national party threats failed to force South Dakota and Minnesota back into their old time slots, New Hampshire rescheduled its primary for February 16 and Iowa changed from February 16 to February 8.

Starting the process in Iowa and New Hampshire has had important consequences for presidential nominating politics. Perhaps most obvious is the chance each small state gives to dark-horse candidates. Long-shots often stake everything on Iowa or New Hampshire in hopes of upsetting the front-runner or making an impression sufficient to generate publicity, poll ratings, and money to stay in the race. An unexpected win in either state can treble poll standings and open thousands of checkbooks, as Gary Hart discovered in 1984. The stakes are equally high for front-runners. Back-to-back wins in Iowa and New Hampshire can make a front-runner seemingly unstoppable, but a defeat in either place immediately raises grave questions about the candidate's future. Losses in both may prove fatal even though only a handful of delegates have been selected.

In recent election years only eight days have separated voting in the two states. Thus Iowa has had an undeniable impact on the following week's New Hampshire primary, perhaps mattering more than all the personal campaigning of the candidates and get-out-the-vote efforts of their organizations (Moore, 1985). Still, Iowa's impact is mediated by all manner of situational factors, not the least of which are journalistic "hype" and "spin" (Robinson, 1985). At any rate, one factor has become fairly constant. By going first, Iowa or New Hampshire gets more news coverage than any other state (or regional) contest in the nominating process, much more than the number of delegates at stake would otherwise predict (Matthews, 1978; Adams, 1987; Buell, 1987b).

The next concern in the 1988 strategic environment is the occurrence of so many caucuses and primaries in the month following New Hampshire. Compared to the fast and crowded track of the seventies and eighties, the typical primary calendar of earlier years seems downright leisurely.

Take 1960, another year in which no incumbent president sought renomination. New Hampshire kicked off with its first-in-the-nation primary on March 8. Wisconsin followed almost a month later on April 5. The season ended with primaries in California and South Dakota on June 7. All told, sixteen states held primaries, seven of these had primary election days all to themselves, no more than three primaries took place on the same day, and April 26 was the first time two states held primaries on the same day (Davis, 1980: 326–29).[5]

Table 1.2 shows how much things had changed twenty-eight years later, when thirty-six states held presidential primaries over a period only three weeks longer than in 1960. The most dramatic development was scheduling as many primaries on the same "Super Tuesday" in March as had been held in all of 1960. The enormity of this mega-primary precluded extensive personal campaigning in every state, and nearly every campaign relied almost entirely on television and radio advertising to reach voters and caucus participants. Airport press conferences and other symbolic stops in as many media markets as possible constituted most of the actual campaigning in Super Tuesday states.

Super Tuesday was but the most dramatic example of "front-loading," or early scheduling of caucuses and primaries in hopes of exerting greater influence on nominations. James I. Lengle (1987) has documented a steady

Table 1.2 **1988 Schedule of Democratic and Republican Primaries**

Date	Both Parties	Republicans Only
February 16	New Hampshire	
February 23	South Dakota	
March 1	Vermont	
March 5		South Carolina
March 8	Alabama, Arkansas, Florida, Georgia, Kentucky, Louisiana, Maryland, Massachusetts, Mississippi, Missouri, North Carolina, Oklahoma, Rhode Island, Tennessee, Texas, Virginia	
March 15	Illinois	
March 20	Puerto Rico	
March 29	Connecticut	
April 5	Wisconsin	
April 19	New York	
April 26	Pennsylvania	
May 3	District of Columbia, Indiana, Ohio	
May 10	Nebraska, West Virginia	
May 17	Oregon	
May 24	Idaho	
June 7	California, Montana, New Jersey, New Mexico	
June 14	North Dakota	

SOURCE: *Congressional Quarterly Weekly Report* 46 (July 19, 1988): 1894–95.

NOTE: Democratic primaries in Vermont, Idaho, and North Dakota were advisory or nonbinding, as were GOP primaries in Virginia and Montana. Texas Democrats selected 119 district-level delegates in a primary, and 64 statewide delegates in a three-tiered process beginning with precinct caucuses on March 8.

shift to earlier nominating contests in both parties. According to his calculations, the Democrats in 1980 held nineteen of their fifty-six caucuses and primaries by the second week in March, thereby selecting 29 percent of their convention delegates. In 1988 thirty contests would pick 43 percent of all the Democratic delegates by the same time. On the Republican side, fourteen caucus-convention and primary states chose 20 percent of all the delegates by the second week in March 1980. In 1988, he estimated, twenty-four states would select 46 percent of all the GOP delegates by this point (Lengle, 1987: 264).[6]

So much front-loading has led to the elimination of most candidates by the end of March. As we shall see, along with winner-take-all rules, it forced an early conclusion of the 1988 Republican race. To appreciate these dynamics and their importance to candidate strategies, we must first understand the specific methods of delegate selection in each party.

Democratic and Republican Selection of Delegates

When it comes to the actual rules for selecting delegates, the two parties are not much alike. Reform nationalized the Democrats to an unprecedented degree, bringing state parties into compliance with myriad national party regulations. Yet Republican state parties have lost little of their traditional autonomy in the GOP nominating process. The upshot is different rules for different parties.

Table 1.3 details the delegate-selection rules used by Democrats in all fifty states and the District of Columbia in 1988. One sees at a glance that

Table 1.3 **1988 Democratic Delegate-Selection Rules for Fifty States and District of Columbia**

Open Primaries	Closed Primaries	Open Caucuses	Closed Caucuses
Proportional Representation			
Alabama	California	Idaho	Arizona
Arkansas	Connecticut	Maine	Delaware
Indiana	Kentucky	Michigan	Hawaii
Mississippi	Louisiana	Minnesota	Iowa
New Hampshire	Nebraska	North Dakota	Kansas
Rhode Island	New Mexico	South Carolina	Nevada
Tennessee	Oklahoma	Utah	Texas
Texas	Oregon	Vermont	Wyoming
Virginia	South Dakota	Washington	
Wisconsin	District of Columbia		
Bonus Proportional Representation			
Georgia	Florida		Alaska
Massachusetts	New York		Colorado
Missouri	North Carolina		
Montana			
Ohio			
Loophole			
Illinois	Maryland		
New Jersey	Pennsylvania		
West Virginia			

SOURCE: Rhodes Cook, *Race for the Presidency* (Washington, D.C.: Congressional Quarterly Press, 1987), 3.

NOTES: Texas is listed twice, as an open primary and as a closed caucus, both under proportional representation, because both methods were used to select delegates. The New Hampshire, Rhode Island, Massachusetts, Ohio, New Jersey, and West Virginia primaries were open to independents but not to registered Republicans. All other open primaries allowed Republican as well as independent participation. By the same token, Iowa and Maine excluded Republicans from their otherwise open caucuses.

most Democratic caucus and primary states employed proportional representation. Ten states added a "bonus" factor, and five conducted so-called "loophole" primaries where voters directly elected delegates. According to Jerry Calvert (1988: 5), 41.7 percent of the 4,161 delegates to the 1988 Democratic convention were selected in proportional representation contests, 20 percent in bonus caucuses and primaries, and 11.8 percent in loophole primaries. (The remaining 26.5 percent were pledged party and elected officials and superdelegates.)

The goal of pure proportional representation is to give candidates the same percentage of delegates as they have won of the popular preference vote. However, like virtually all other practitioners of proportional representation, the Democrats have made their method more complex by requiring thresholds, or minimum percentages of the popular vote necessary to win any delegates. Delegates are chosen by congressional or legislative district, so thresholds apply to every district in a state using proportional representation in its caucuses or primary. Ever higher thresholds pose ever more insuperable obstacles for obscure, poorly funded, or otherwise unlikely candidates while aiding already advantaged front-runners. Under complicated rules established in 1976 and later modified for 1980 and 1984 by Democratic reform commissions, some states had district thresholds well above 20 percent. Jesse Jackson repeatedly complained about such levels before, during, and after the 1984 nominating race. (He did so again four years later.) After negotiations with Jackson and Hart, both getting ready for another run, the Democratic Fairness Commission settled on 15 percent as a uniform threshold for all 1988 primaries and caucuses using proportional representation.

New Hampshire's Democratic primary illustrates how proportional representation would work in 1988. Of the twenty-two delegates representing New Hampshire at the Atlanta convention, twelve (six in each congressional district) were to be chosen as a result of the preference vote in the February primary. Only candidates winning at least 15 percent of the vote in a district were entitled to any of its six delegates, and how many each got would be determined on a proportional basis.

Under the bonus version of proportional representation, delegates still would be awarded by congressional district to candidates garnering 15 percent or more of the popular vote. An extra delegate would be awarded to the plurality winner of the popular vote in each district.

Even more complex was the loophole primary, where voters would be asked not only to express a presidential preference but also to choose individual delegates. In West Virginia's first congressional district, for example, this meant not only voting for Dukakis or Jackson, as it turned out, but also picking six candidates for convention delegates from eighty-two names listed on the ballot (Calvert, 1988: 39).[7] A loophole primary becomes a winner-take-all affair when a candidate captures every delegate in every district. In any event, only candidates winning at least 15 percent of the delegates at the district level were entitled to compete for remaining at-large delegates and for the pledged party and elected officials (Cook, 1987a).

To turn to Republican methods of choosing delegates, table 1.4 reflects the variety one would expect from a sustained tradition of state party autonomy. This tradition is most obvious in the final category of state contests, where the particulars of delegate selection were left to the participants to determine. A similar arrangement would be inconceivable under present Democratic rules. More often than not, the method adopted was some version of winner-take-all (Calvert, 1988: 17). In Michigan and Hawaii such latitude set the stage for ferocious rules disputes between the Bush and Robertson campaigns (Cook, 1988).

Some similarity to Democratic methods can be seen in the proportional representation primaries of thirteen states and the District of Columbia. Still, only the Kentucky, Massachusetts, Missouri, and Tennessee primaries used the same 15 percent threshold adopted by the Democrats. No fixed threshold obtained in Connecticut, the District of Columbia, North Dakota, and Oregon.[8] In the remaining GOP primaries using proportional representation, thresholds ranged from 5 percent in Idaho to 20 percent in Rhode Island and South Dakota.

GOP direct election primaries also bore some resemblance to Democratic loophole contests. In Nebraska, New Jersey, and West Virginia it was possible for the designated delegates of one candidate to win every district and the at-large race as well. In Illinois, New York, and Pennsylvania voters picked the delegates for each district while state party committees chose the at-large delegates. At-large delegates in the last three states were to be formally uncommitted; the same held true for delegates chosen in Pennsylvania districts (Cook, 1987a).

Thirteen other states would choose most or all of their delegates in winner-take-all primaries. California loomed as the biggest prize, its 175 delegates going to the plurality winner of the statewide preference vote. The method in Florida, Georgia, Maryland, Ohio, Oklahoma, South Carolina, and Wisconsin awarded all delegates in each district to the plurality vote victor and all at-large delegates to the plurality winner statewide. Indiana used the same method at the district level but did not formally bind its at-large delegates to any candidate. Alabama and Texas preferred a more complicated process wherein a candidate would get three delegates for every district carried by outright majority. Similarly, winning more than half of all votes statewide entitled a candidate to all of the state's at-large

Table 1.4 **1988 Republican Delegate-Selection Rules for Fifty States and District of Columbia**

Open Primaries	Closed Primaries	Open Caucuses	Closed Caucuses
	Proportional Representation		
Arkansas	Connecticut		
Idaho	Kentucky		
Massachusetts	North Carolina		
Missouri	Oregon		
New Hampshire	South Dakota		
North Dakota	District of Columbia		
Rhode Island			
Tennessee			
	Winner-Take-All		
Alabama	California		
Georgia	Florida		
Indiana	Louisiana		
Mississippi	Maryland		
Ohio	Oklahoma		
South Carolina			
Texas			
Wisconsin			
	Direct Election		
Illinois	Nebraska		
New Jersey	New York		
West Virginia	Pennsylvania		
	Method Determined by Participants		
	New Mexico	Iowa	Alaska
		Maine	Arizona
		Michigan	Colorado
		Minnesota	Delaware
		Utah	Hawaii
		Vermont	Kansas
		Virginia	Montana
		Washington	Nevada
			Wyoming

SOURCE: Rhodes Cook, *Race for the Presidency* (Washington, D.C.: Congressional Quarterly Press, 1987), 3.

NOTES: Alabama and Texas rules called for a winner-take-all system if a candidate wins a majority of the preference vote statewide or in every congressional district. Otherwise, delegates would be chosen under proportional representation with thresholds of 15 percent in Alabama and 20 percent in Texas. In districts without a majority winner, the plurality winner would receive two delegates, the runner-up one. Open contests in Massachusetts, New Hampshire, Ohio, South Carolina, New Jersey, West Virginia, Iowa, and Maine excluded registered Democrats. All California delegates were awarded on a statewide winner-take-all basis determined by preference-vote plurality.

delegates. In districts where no candidate received a majority, the plurality vote winner would get two delegates and the closest rival one. If no candidate won a statewide majority, the at-large delegates would be apportioned to those candidates getting over a threshold (15 percent in Alabama, 20 percent in Texas).

Although arcane, rules for delegate selection are often crucial in determining who wins the nomination, how soon, and how convincingly.[9] Some scholars perceive a causal relationship between Democratic reforms and Democratic defeats in every presidential election since 1968 except one. Proportional representation methods of selecting delegates have been especially criticized in this connection. According to Nelson Polsby (1983) and Elaine Kamarck (1987), proportional representation helps prolong divisive races well beyond the point of achieving meaningful unity at the nominating convention. As Kamarck (1987: 297–98) notes, proportional representation encourages some candidates to stay in the race because they can continue winning delegates even while losing primaries and caucuses. The point is relevant to early front-runners as well as to losers bent on taking their "cause" to the convention. Early front-runners can absorb the loss of later primaries as they continue to pick up delegates. Candidates who enter late or start slowly are unlikely to overtake an early leader because even winning big state primaries probably will not yield enough delegates to block the nomination. Consequently, early contests eliminate all but one or two rivals to early front-runners, thus increasing the latter's chance of nomination, albeit in a process almost certain to send the nominee "limping and wounded into the general election" (Kamarck, 1987: 306).

Some Democrats have come to agree with this diagnosis and to urge deregulation of their nominating process so that it more closely resembles that of the Republicans. In effect, this is an argument for winner-take-all primaries. Looking at how winner-take-all rules worked for the Republicans in 1976 and 1980, Kamarck stresses the significance of momentum (1987: 299): "It is as important to maintain momentum in the middle of a process as it is early on." The candidate who builds momentum early and sustains it throughout a winner-take-all race will wrap up the nomination well before the convention, but one who loses big state primaries in April and May must fight for delegates right up to the convention—as Gerald Ford was compelled to do in 1976—and might well lose the nomination altogether. In short, winner-take-all rules accentuate momentum, whatever its particular manifestations.[10]

Campaign Finance

Last but hardly least in our list of formal rules are those governing campaign finance. Money is not the only factor in winning the nomination, but it now costs about $20 million to sustain a truly national effort. Since chapter 4 examines preconvention campaign finance in great detail, our discussion need point up only the most salient connections to candidate strategies.

To have any chance of winning, most candidates must start raising money two or three years before the nominating convention. This generally means forming personal political action committees (PACs), like George Bush's "Fund for America's Future" or Richard Gephardt's "Effective Government Committee," to pay for the candidate's first forays into key states, to build the beginnings of a national campaign organization, and to contribute to candidates for other offices likely to be appreciative later. The next step is to establish exploratory committes for the purpose of raising enough money to qualify for federal matching funds.

Under the system created by an amended Federal Election Campaign Act (FECA), candidates who raise a minimum of $100,000 in twenty states ($5,000 per state with no donation more than $250) are entitled to matching federal funds. Of all the candidates who have sought the Democratic and Republican presidential nominations since passage of the FECA in 1974, only former Texas Governor John Connally refused to accept federal money and its accompanying regulations. (Pat Robertson toyed with the idea in 1988.) Since federal cash constitutes a third or more of all receipts for preconvention campaigns (Sorauf, 1988: 191), few candidates are likely to refuse it, despite the law's limits on individual contributions and spending in early state contests.

In some ways matching funds are a boon to long-shot candidates because they enable a Bruce Babbitt or a Pierre du Pont to make a credible effort, at least in Iowa and New Hampshire. (Low FECA limits on how much can be spent in these contests also help dark horses.) On the other hand, matching funds aid front-runners because the more money a candidate raises, the more is matched.

In planning a run for their party's nomination, candidates must take account of the connections among scheduling of contests, delegate-selection rules, momentum, fund-raising, and provision of federal money. The quest for individual contributors impels an early start. Small wonder that in 1985 Gephardt visited thirty states and Jack Kemp twenty-five (Taylor, 1986). The importance of Iowa and New Hampshire obliges all candidates to visit them earlier and more often than other states, as performance in these critical contests directly affects fund-raising for Super Tuesday. Front-loading compels candidates to spend most of their money early in the race and is all the more reason for front-runners to adopt a knockout strategy. As previously noted, winner-take-all rules facilitate such a plan while proportional representation does not. Yet even proportional representation cannot save a candidate who gets below 10 percent of the vote in two consecutive primaries, thus forfeiting matching funds (unless able to win 20 percent in the next primary). And, as is the case with early building of a delegate base, front-runners in a proportional representation system need to raise all the cash they can as soon as possible to remain competitive in the event of later setbacks.

Opportunity Structures for 1988 Candidates

Having sketched the strategic environment's legal and institutional features, we can now discuss the political backgrounds and resources of the 1988 candidates. Our account is informed by the work of Joseph Schlesinger (1966), John Aldrich (1980), and others who have studied connections between "opportunity structures" and political ambition. The first basic assumption in such research is that politicians rationally assess the risks of seeking higher office and desist when the cost is too high and success seems too unlikely. A second assumption is that politicians follow a "ladder of ambition," moving from office to office in logical progression.

Opportunity in American presidential politics traditionally has depended largely on one's experience in government and one's political base. In his analysis of presidential backgrounds, Stephen Hess (1988: 39) points to a tradition of early beginnings in electoral politics, with nonmilitary men running before turning thirty. Although lower rungs in the ladder of office seeking have changed over time, according to Aldrich (1987), experience in important government positions has almost always been a necessary condition for nomination. Historically, presidents have come from the ranks of senators, state governors, vice-presidents, and, particularly in the last century, generals (Hess, 1988; Nelson, 1987; Davis, 1987: 55–60). All have been white males, and most have hailed from major states.

Of the 1988 candidates, four of the seven Democrats and three of the six Republicans held public office when they formally entered the race. Governor Michael Dukakis of Massachusetts, Vice-President George Bush, Senator Robert Dole of Kansas, and Senator Paul Simon of Illinois were most faithful to "ambition theory" in moving up the ladder of presidential opportunity. Dukakis had served in the state legislature before winning a gubernatorial term, lost the renomination, and came back to win two consecutive terms as governor. Bush started in the House, lost two Senate campaigns, headed the Central Intelligence Agency, served as ambassador to China, and failed in a bid for the 1980 GOP presidential nomination before election and reelection as Reagan's vice-president in 1980 and 1984. After recovering from World War II wounds, Dole served in the Kansas House and as a county prosecutor before election to the U.S. House for four terms. He captured a Senate seat in 1968. Like Bush, Dole knew something of defeat, having lost the 1976 general election as Ford's running mate and having failed in his own attempt at the 1980 GOP nomination. Simon had served in both houses of the Illinois state legislature, four years as lieutenant governor, ten years in the U.S. House, and two years of a Senate term when he announced his presidential candidacy. His only defeat was in 1972, when he lost the Illinois gubernatorial primary.

Among the remaining candidates, Hart was most remembered for losing the 1984 Democratic nomination and for having served as Colorado's senior senator. Senator Albert Gore of Tennessee had served four terms in the House of Representatives before winning election to the Senate in 1984. Gephardt and Kemp were in the running despite historically poor odds of moving directly from the House of Representatives to the White House. Alexander Haig had served as secretary of state under Reagan and previously as NATO commander but had gained earlier notoriety in the Watergate White House. Babbitt and du Pont were little-known ex-governors of small states; du Pont had also served three terms in Congress.

Though familiar to millions, Jackson and Robertson had never served in public office. In his defense, Jackson made much of his past as a protest leader and his 1984 campaign experience, thus embodying Richard Rose's (1987) argument that American presidential candidates learn to campaign rather than govern. Robertson's response was to lay claim to a worldly background. Both were further anomalous for getting into politics as ministers of the gospel. Finally, Jackson broke new ground in 1984 as the first "serious" African-American candidate for a major party's presidential nomination.[11]

Only Hart, Kemp, and Gephardt actually gambled an existing office on their presidential chances. Hart acted consistently with Aldrich's proposition (1980: 33) that candidates free of other responsibilities can wage longer and more continuous campaigns than their rivals in office. He therefore avoided the risks and distractions of a 1986 reelection fight by resigning his Senate seat. Kemp, having irked his Buffalo constituents by spending so much time on the presidential campaign trail, gave up any chance of renomination for his House seat but continued to serve throughout his bid for the White House. In contrast, Missouri Democrats allowed Gephardt to try for the presidency and, having withdrawn in time, to seek reelection to the House. (House Democrats elected him majority leader in 1989.) Neither Kemp nor Gephardt answered many roll calls during his presidential exertions. The burdens of office fell even more heavily on Governor Dukakis, who made a brave show of keeping up with statehouse matters while on the presidential campaign trail but still came under severe criticism for neglecting his duties. Senator Dole was equally taxed; his responsibilities as minority leader kept him in Washington while Bush barnstormed in Iowa and the South. Dole even contemplated giving up the leadership to allow more time for presidential campaigning. Like Gephardt and Kemp, Gore and Simon missed many Senate votes while seeking higher office. Free of such obligations, the others had plenty of time to campaign. As vice-president, Bush was afforded not only the time but also many of the regal trappings of executive office to impress voters.

A political base and free time are only two of the factors defining a candidate's opportunity structure. Others are national name recognition and standing in the polls. Poll ratings strongly correlate with how much attention the news media pay to candidates (Adams, 1985) and how much money candidates are able to raise (Sorauf, 1988) during the "exhibition season" leading up to Iowa. Since the advent of scientific polling, early front-runners in the Gallup poll have nearly always won the GOP nomination, with Barry Goldwater in 1964 being the only clear exception. The Democrats have proven less predictable, nominating Adlai Stevenson rather than early poll leader Estes Kefauver in 1952, McGovern instead of Muskie or Humphrey in 1972, and Carter over Humphrey or almost anyone else in 1976.

Table 1.5 reports the standings of every 1988 candidate in early national surveys by three different organizations. Some candidates like Babbitt and du Pont rated well below sampling error, and the polling periods noted here did not fully overlap. Even so, certain patterns stood out in the results of all three firms. First, the signs were consistently dismal for Babbitt, Gore, du Pont, Haig, and Robertson, none of whom broke into double digits in any poll during the early period. Second, even though Gephardt, Simon, and Kemp did break the double-digit barrier at least once, none could have drawn much comfort from his standing. Third, the Democratic field lost most of its coherence when Hart departed in May. True, Jackson and Dukakis led the pack in his absence, but at no point during the summer and fall of 1987 did either consistently attract the support of more than a quarter of Democrats expressing a preference. And in every poll the percentage of undecideds and those picking someone not in the race exceeded the support given Jackson or Dukakis. Indeed, in some early polls the combined total of Jackson and Dukakis supporters was less than of those undecided or wanting somebody not in the race. Everett Ladd (1987: 4) warned that it was "silly" to make very much of the Democratic race at that point. The same was decidedly not true of the Republican race, where Bush led Dole by a wide margin in every poll of GOP identifiers and likely primary voters. No other Republican got so much as half of Dole's support in any poll.

In sum, the Republican field had a clear favorite, a runner-up, and four long-shots. An erratically populated Democratic field had no solid favorite after Hart's withdrawal, one nominal front-runner unable to attract significant white support, another candidate unable to get above 20 percent, and several even less credible possibilities.

Although high name recognition is better than low name recognition in presidential politics, some 1988 candidates paid a price for public visibility. The cost for Jackson and Robertson was exceedingly negative evaluations of their fitness for the presidency. Favorably or otherwise, 88 percent of the respondents in an early ABC/*Washington Post* poll expressed opinions on Jackson as a potential leader of the free world (*The Polling Report*, 1987a: 2–3). Nearly two-thirds were able to assess Robertson's capabilities. And, though not taken seriously, Haig enjoyed greater recognition than any other candidate except Bush, Hart, Jackson, and Dole. Seventy-one percent commented on his qualifications. Dukakis at this point had made so little of an impression that 59 percent could not express a judgment on his presidential potential. Poll data for the remaining candidates exhibited more of a correlation between preference ratings and evaluation of competence. Looking first at long-shots, 69 percent of the ABC/*Washington Post* respondents could not evaluate Gore's qualifications, 62 percent had no clue about Babbitt and du Pont, 54 percent could not judge Gephardt, 53 percent blanked on Simon, and 48 percent had the same difficulty with Kemp. Conversely, only 6 percent had no opinion of Bush and 23 percent no handle on Dole.

Thus some candidates were well known and strongly supported (Bush and Dole); others were well known but notorious (Jackson, Robertson, and Haig) with varying degrees of support; still others were largely unknown and weakly supported (Babbitt, Gephardt, Gore, Simon, du Pont, and Kemp); and at least one (Dukakis) enjoyed more support than would have been expected from the general unfamiliarity with his record and positions. (Hart joined the notorious group upon rejoining the race.) Some candidates enjoyed considerable latitude in developing their strategies and themes while others had little freedom of movement.

Democratic Strategies and Campaign Themes

The early Democratic front-runner was Hart, an obvious candidate for having nearly knocked Mondale out of the 1984 race. Despite frequent press attention to unpaid debts from his 1984 campaign, he led all other likely Democrats in early 1987 polls, including New York's much-mentioned

Table 1.5 1987 National Poll Standings of Democratic and Republican Candidates

Candidate	ABC/*Washington Post* January–December			CBS/*New York Times* January–November			Gallup June–October		
	High (%)	Low (%)	Mean (%)	High (%)	Low (%)	Mean (%)	High (%)	Low (%)	Mean (%)
Democrats									
Babbitt	5	1	2.9	5	1	2.0	2	1	1.7
Dukakis	18	4	11.5	13	8	10.2	14	11	12.7
Gephardt	10	1	5.6	5	3	3.7	7	3	5.2
Gore	6	1	4.6	7	5	6.2	8	5	7.0
Hart	46	30	37.7	N.A.	N.A.	N.A.	N.A.	N.A.	N.A.
Jackson	27	12	19.4	25	14	18.2	22	17	19.0
Simon	13	4	8.6	10	6	8.0	8	7	7.2
Republicans									
Bush	54	35	44.5	48	33	38.6	47	39	41.5
Dole	30	20	26.0	23	15	19.4	22	18	20.0
du Pont	3	1	1.8	6	1	2.1	3	1	2.0
Haig	5	3	4.2	7	2	3.7	7	4	5.2
Kemp	11	5	7.0	10	5	7.0	10	4	7.7
Robertson	8	5	6.5	7	3	5.6	8	5	6.2

SOURCES: *The Polling Report* 3: 12 (June 15, 1987); 3: 22 (November 9, 1987); 3: 23 (November 23, 1987); and 3: 24 (December 14, 1987).
NOTE: Seven ABC/*Washington Post* polls for Babbitt, Gephardt, and Jackson; six for Dukakis; five for Gore and Simon; four for Hart; six for each Republican. Seven CBS/*New York Times* polls for each Republican; four (beginning in May) for each Democrat. Hart data collapsed with "other/not sure." Four Gallup polls for all candidates except Hart, who was not in the race during this polling period.

Cuomo, and beat both Bush and Dole in March NBC/ *Wall Street Journal* "trial heats" (*The Polling Report*, 1987b: 4–5). With the mountains of his adopted state in the background, Hart formally announced his candidacy on April 13. Several weeks later, however, *Miami Herald* reporters observed him spending a weekend with a Florida model while his wife was elsewhere. The story quickly grew into a raging controversy with the promise of fresh revelations. Long dogged by rumors of womanizing, Hart could not effectively respond and formally withdrew on May 8. But inactivity and lost opportunities evidently pained Hart more than further humiliation by the press, for on December 15 he astounded political pundits by rejoining the race.

Before the Donna Rice episode destroyed his candidacy, Hart's strategy was to do well in Iowa and New Hampshire, hold his own on Super Tuesday, and eventually prevail in subsequent primaries. Super Tuesday would narrow the field to Jackson, Gore, perhaps one or two others, and himself (Runkel, 1989: 18).[12] Hart's chief rivals in Iowa likely would be Gephardt and Simon, both midwesterners from neighboring states but still relatively unknown. A Hart win in Iowa would probably finish them both whereas coming in second would eliminate at least one. In New Hampshire his main competitor was Dukakis of next-door Massachusetts. A Hart win there would probably knock Dukakis out of the race, for New Hampshire was the prologue to any future the governor might have in the South. On the other hand, owing to Dukakis's seeming advantage in New Hampshire, Hart would suffer no disgrace by finishing a close second. Conversely, barely besting Hart in his own backyard would help Dukakis little.

New Hampshire posed an even more critical test for the resurrected Hart. If he could not win here, pundits declared, he could not win anywhere. High poll ratings immediately after rejoining the race gave him a slender basis for hope in Iowa, but now his tiny organization lacked the means to mobilize caucus participants. Earlier Hart had campaigned on "new ideas" themes of industrial policy, military reform, and "enlightened engagement" in foreign affairs. He still articulated these views upon rejoining the race, but the Hart theme now most reported by the news media was a plaintive "let the people decide."

Most speculation about the immediate impact of Hart's return concluded that it had helped Dukakis by inflating the value of his now almost certain victory in New Hampshire. The Dukakis strategy all along had called for placing among the top two in Iowa, winning New Hampshire, prevailing in selected Super Tuesday states, and eliminating his remaining competitors in the war of attrition to follow. After considering a top aide's assessment of the strategic environment, Dukakis made a much-publicized pilgrimage to Iowa one year before the caucuses. He formally declared his candidacy on April 29, 1987. No rival could match his war chest, much of it gotten from proud Greek-Americans responding to the Dukakis theme of immigrants and dreams. "Good jobs at good wages," "managerial expertise," and the "Massachusetts Miracle" were other Dukakis messages.

Iowa was the key to everything for Simon, Gephardt, and Babbitt. Simon has since described his own plan (1989: 21):

> Our strategy was relatively simple: Carry Iowa. Build a strong enough base in New Hampshire so that with the win in Iowa I could either carry New Hampshire or run such a strong second to Dukakis that he would emerge badly damaged as a candidate. If that happened, I would carry Minnesota and South Dakota and have significant momentum going my way into Super Tuesday. On Super Tuesday I would carry at least one-third of the delegates because of momentum and because of the base of support we had in many of these states. If the first four states delivered as planned, then the public support that would emerge from key figures in the South and around the nation would have a significant impact on Super Tuesday. And after Super Tuesday we moved to states where I was the natural candidate. Well before the June 7 primaries in California, New Jersey, New Mexico, and Montana, I should have it virtually wrapped up.

According to Simon (1989: 21), Gephardt's plan was not "dramatically different" from his own. But neither candidate appreciated the extent to which Iowa would distract him from other contests. Indeed, Gephardt invested more in Iowa than any other candidate, visiting all ninety-nine counties and spending more than a hundred days in the state before the caucuses. With Iowa increasingly viewed as a game with only one winner, Gephardt abandoned the South and Simon neglected New Hampshire. As for themes, Gephardt fashioned a message of outrage intended to resonate with farmer and worker frustrations in a depressed economy. "It's your fight, too!" Gephardt avowed as he called for retaliatory trade legislation and farm production controls. Simon cast himself as a "traditional Democrat," "not a neo-anything," ready to expand domestic spending and care for the elderly and less fortunate. Still, he hedged by endorsing a constitutional amendment to balance the federal budget. Simon also made the most of favorable appraisals of his integrity at a time when other reputations suffered.

Attempting to overcome his lack of recognition and to stake out distinctive positions, former Arizona Governor Babbitt risked all on Iowa and a theme of candor about reducing the federal deficit. Perhaps more than any other Democrat, he used the televised debates to reiterate this message and to point up the reluctance of his rivals to grasp the nettle of tax hikes and spending restraints. In one debate he dramatically rose to his feet while challenging the courage of his opponents to stand up for necessary tax increases. (None did.)

At first Iowa also figured in the plans of Senator Gore, at thirty-nine the youngest candidate of either party. By the fall of 1987, however, he had embarked on a high-risk strategy of bypassing Iowa to concentrate on the South. He also had effectively written New Hampshire off by the time Hart rejoined the race in December 1987.[13] Endorsed by numerous southern politicians and saving his cash for Super Tuesday, Gore used the televised debates to distance himself from rivals by blaming their brand of liberalism for the Democratic predicament in presidential elections. After failing to rise in the Iowa polls, Gore began questioning the value and representativeness of the Iowa caucuses. He crossed the Rubicon in a November 7 speech to Iowa Democrats: "There is something wrong with a nominating process that gives one state the loudest voice and then produces candidates who cannot even carry that state" (Cook, 1987b: 2919).

In televised debates Gore repeatedly characterized himself as a "mainstream Democrat" who believed more strongly in national defense than his rivals did. By endorsing the 1983 Grenada invasion and the Reagan administration's policy in the Persian Gulf, Gore aimed his Super Tuesday appeal directly at the "Reagan Democrats" of the South, whites who had voted Republican in one or both of the last two presidential elections despite their party identification. Of course, this appeal hinged on them turning out to vote in the first place, then voting in Democratic rather than Republican contests, and, finally, voting for him. What Gore had in mind after Super Tuesday was not clear. According to one veteran chronicler of presidential campaigns (Drew, 1989: 168), there was no serious plan for the remaining caucuses and primaries, and Gore squandered his resources accordingly.

No candidate in either party paid more attention to formal rules than Jesse Jackson did. Jackson in 1984 had thundered that high thresholds had denied him a "fair share" of the delegates (10 percent for 19.5 percent of the primary vote). He also inveighed against loophole primaries and superdelegates. Though hardly mollified by party tinkering with the 1988 rules, Jackson was more than satisfied with the scheduling of Super Tuesday.

A quick review of recent history and a glance at the March 8 lineup are enough to explain why Jackson had cause for celebration. In 1984, as Cook (1987c: 2385) has noted, Jackson's best primary states had been scattered across the Democratic calendar from March to May. Indeed, aside from the South Carolina caucuses, he won only the District of Columbia primary on May 1 and the Louisiana primary four days later. His base of black voters thus dispersed, Jackson never collected enough delegates to threaten Mondale. This was all to change in 1988, when the moderate and conservative architects of Super Tuesday handed Jackson a remarkable opportunity by bunching all the southern primaries into one early mega-event. Now scheduled for March 8 were six of Jackson's nine best 1984 primary states—Louisiana (43 percent for Jackson), Maryland (26 percent), North Carolina (25 percent), Tennessee (25 percent), Georgia (21 percent), and Alabama (20 percent). To sweeten the pot, Arkansas, Mississippi, and Virginia were also scheduled to vote on Super Tuesday, having replaced their Democratic caucuses with primaries. In 1984 Jackson had won between 17 and 32 percent of the delegates in these states. Ranked by black percentage of 1980 population, eight of the top ten states in the nation would hold Democratic primaries on Super Tuesday. And this time Jackson would have no rival with Mondale's appeal to black voters. Moreover, proportional representation would be used to select the delegates in Alabama, Arkansas, Louisiana, Mississippi, Tennessee, and Virginia. Georgia and North Carolina would employ the bonus method. Only Maryland would hold a loophole primary. Thus Super Tuesday mattered no less to Jackson than to Gore, and, unlike Gore's base, Jackson's was solid.

Race also determined the benchmark Jackson wanted the news media to use in judging his Iowa and New Hampshire performances. Given the paucity of blacks in either state, he insisted, even 10 percent must be considered a "victory" for him. By the same token, Jackson expected his rivals to split most of the white vote until fairly late in the game. Meanwhile he would fashion a "rainbow coalition" of blacks, economically distressed workers and farmers, the elderly, the underemployed, feminists, gays, and foreign-policy dissidents. (As it turned out, Jackson's white support would come mostly from the affluent and college-educated; see Pomper, 1989: 44–45.) Winning preference vote and delegate pluralities in several early primaries would broaden his appeal to mainstream Democrats and make his candidacy credible. By building early momentum and taking full advantage of proportional representation, Jackson hoped to go to the convention with more delegates than anybody else, if not an outright majority.

Republican Strategies and Campaign Themes

No less than for Gore and Jackson, Super Tuesday was crucial to the strategy of Vice-President Bush. Although sometimes distracted by a prolonged struggle in Michigan and by straw-poll losses to Robertson, Bush kept to a basic plan: finish at least second in Iowa, take New Hampshire, and effectively decide the nomination with wins in South Carolina and the Super Tuesday states. If all went according to plan, the nomination would be sewed up in April. And, if Iowa or even New Hampshire did not follow the script, the South would serve as a "fire wall" against adverse momentum.

Republican scheduling and delegate-selection rules made this scenario highly plausible. Between them, South Carolina and the eight southern states holding winner-take-all primaries on Super Tuesday would award up to 465 delegates to the plurality or majority winner in their congressional-district and statewide voting. With still other primary and caucus states to be heard from on March 8, the Bush campaign expected to reap most of this rich harvest.

Abundant poll data gave Bush every reason for optimism. According to a March 1987 poll taken for the *Atlanta Journal-Constitution*, 53 percent of the likely Republican voters in twelve southern states picked him against 17 percent for Dole, the nearest rival. A second *Journal-Constitution* poll six months later showed no appreciable change (*The Polling Report*, 1987c: 4). And, in a Scripps-Howard survey taken about the same time in most of the same states, 48 percent named Bush as their first choice for the nomination, 20 percent preferred Dole, and no more than six percent backed anyone else (*The Polling Report*, 1987d: 8).

Bush also led the pack in fund-raising and would eventually take in the maximum ($23 million plus $4.3 million in fund-raising costs) allowed by law. His money men collected about $11 million in Texas, California, Florida, New York, and Ohio alone. Particularly noteworthy were $1,000-per-head functions across the nation where Bush managers held costs to an unusually low twenty cents on the dollar (Babcock and Morin, 1988). Such successes made possible a vigorous advertising campaign in Iowa, the Boston–New Hampshire area, and selected media markets in Super Tuesday states.

Bush's main themes were his record of accomplishment and his loyal service as Reagan's vice-president. The Reagan connection cost him support in Iowa but was invaluable in New Hampshire and the South, even after much press attention to Bush's role in the Iran-contra affair. Loath to repudiate any part of the Reagan record, Bush was at first the only Republican candidate to endorse his chief's Intermediate-range Nuclear Forces (INF) treaty with the Soviets. (Dole finally did so after much hedging and studying of the Iowa polls.) Though progressive in his INF stand, Bush sought the approval of his party's right wing with an unequivocal declaration against tax increases and a statement of support for a constitutional amendment against abortion.

As the race took shape, Bush sought the endorsement of governors in key states. Three would prove especially important in the battle to follow: John Sununu would salvage Bush's New Hampshire effort in the difficult week after Iowa, Carroll Campbell would play a vital role in whipping both Dole and Robertson in South Carolina, and strong support from James Thompson's organization in Illinois would help finish Dole off after Super Tuesday.

Bush's most serious rival in 1988 was Dole of Kansas. Since losing the 1980 GOP presidential nomination, Dole had rebuilt his reputation with impressive performances as Senate Finance Committee chairman and as Republican leader. Washington elites lauded his expertise, "pragmatism," and "courage" on the deficit, and some polls showed him drawing more support than any other Repbulican from Democrats and independents.

To become the nominee, Dole depended on early midwestern victories, especially in Iowa, where he usually led Bush by a comfortable margin. With even-earlier Kansas in the bag, Dole expected his Iowa momentum to overwhelm Bush in New Hampshire. Bush defeats in Kansas, Iowa, New Hampshire, South Dakota, and Minnesota might crack the southern "fire wall." If so, opportunity beckoned in Illinois and other midwestern primaries after Super Tuesday. Dole's most common themes were pragmatic leadership and "I'm one of you," a play on his humble beginnings and a deliberate contrast to Bush's princely upbringing. On November 9, 1987, he was the last candidate in either party to make his bid official. Standing on a flag-bedecked platform in his hometown of Russell, Kansas, Dole characterized the federal deficit as America's most pressing problem, touted his record of leadership in Congress, and urged compassion for the disabled and less fortunate.

Yet even as he spoke, Dole's campaign was beset with difficulties. Despite successful fund-raising, his national headquarters seethed with internal feuding while field operations in New Hampshire and the South lagged behind Bush efforts. Part of the problem seemingly originated with the candidate, who reportedly could not delegate meaningful responsibility to others. In any event, as 1987 drew to a close, Dole had offered few specifics to substantiate his deficit theme, and his floundering organization appeared poorly positioned to seize the moment if the Iowa and New Hampshire scenario came true.

Owing to their common strategy of claiming greatest fidelity to the Reagan revolution and of winning over the Republican right, du Pont and Kemp can be discussed together. As the darkest horse in the Republican stable, du Pont was the first candidate in either party to make his formal announcement, on August 16, 1986. Kemp waited until the next April, but, except for Haig, he declared six months earlier than any remaining GOP rival.

Both du Pont and Kemp sought to separate Bush from Reagan in the minds of conservatives by disputing the vice-president's ideological bona fides. Both regarded Bush as vulnerable in Iowa and New Hampshire, and each banked on finishing among the top three in Iowa and perhaps second in New Hampshire. Under what the *New York Times* called his "best case scenario," du Pont would emerge as the alternative to the new front-runner after twin defeats in Iowa and New Hampshire eliminated Bush. The Kemp campaign harbored similar hopes. Yet neither du Pont nor Kemp had much of a campaign beyond Iowa and New Hampshire, and if Bush survived, third place in the first two contests seemed unlikely to spark momentum anywhere else. A belated endorsement by the *Manchester Union-Leader* gave du Pont some basis for hope in New Hampshire, and Kemp's standing in the polls there finally moved up a few points after he unleashed television spots attacking Bush and Dole.

Known to millions as the genial host of the "700 Club," a television program on his own Christian Broadcasting Network (CBN), Robertson planned to capture the nomination with an insurgent strategy perhaps best described as "onward Christian soldiers." A well-trained and lavishly funded "invisible army" of charismatic Christians would defeat or diminish Bush and the others in straw polls and early caucuses. These successes would build momentum for the South—Robertson's home turf—where opportunity abounded in vast numbers of socially conservative, fundamentalist whites, many of them former Democrats or previously inactive in presidential politics. Mobilizing even a fraction of this enormous population might make the difference in open GOP primaries in South Carolina, Alabama, Arkansas, Georgia, Mississippi, Tennessee, and Texas.

Robertson had been preparing a political career for some time, a development increasingly evident in his television evangelism as CBN and his other business ventures prospered during the seventies. He began mobilizing charismatic Christians for grass-roots political activity in 1981 with the formation of the Freedom Council. Six years later, with Robertson's presidential bid well underway, the council claimed upwards of fifty thousand members, many reportedly organized at church, precinct, county, and congressional-district levels in eleven states.

Robertson's campaign began with a challenge to his viewers in 1986. If three million registered voters would sign petitions asking him to seek the 1988 GOP nomination, he would run. One year later, the signatures reportedly obtained, Robertson formally declared his candidacy on October 1, 1987, at the site of his former dwelling in Brooklyn's Bedford-Stuyvesant district. It was while living here that Robertson had undergone the religious experience that launched his career as a minister.

His reception on that October day, like so many in his campaign to follow, ran the spectrum of emotional reactions from adoration to revulsion. His reputation had preceded him, and, depending on the sympathies of onlookers, it was the record of a celebrity given to making profound or outlandish statements. On the "700 Club" and in numerous publications, he had described the Anti-Christ as a twenty-seven-year old man, called on God to cure assorted illnesses, reviewed his own conversations with

God, and mused on the inevitability of nuclear war as foretold in the Bible. This last line of commentary had been excoriated by liberal critics as "Armageddon theology." Repeatedly heckled by "militant gays" in his Bedford-Stuyvesant speech, Robertson asked the audience to join in a quest to restore family values, reduce the rate of teenage pregnancies, improve public schooling, and achieve prosperity and dignity for Americans in every walk of life (King, 1987; Robertson, 1987). In future speeches, he would promise to appoint only conservatives to high-level posts in the executive branch if elected, brand birth control as genocide, question Reagan's anticommunism, insist that AIDS is spread through the most casual contact, and maintain that Cuba bristled with Soviet missles. Adverse publicity would attend each claim, as it would the revelations that his first child had been conceived out of wedlock, that his résumé had been partly fabricated, and that he had not been a "combat veteran" of the Korean war, as claimed. On the day he declared his candidacy, however, Robertson trailed only Bush in fund-raising and was second to no rival in the dedication of his supporters.

Clearly the candidate most contrary to the tenets of "ambition theory" in 1988 was General Haig. Though experienced, articulate, and certainly ambitious, he had no notable following in the party, very little money and no base in any state or region. True, he hoped his military experience would appeal to southern conservatives, but first Haig had to do well enough in Iowa or New Hampshire to have a Dixie campaign. By October 1987, however, he had written Iowa off and staked everything on New Hampshire. According to Haig's campaign manager, the strategy was to become a "viable contender" by placing third or fourth in New Hampshire: "Our aim is to wind up with a delegate total that will make Haig not only competitive, but a key player in a brokered convention" (Weinraub, 1987). Unfortunately for Haig, few in New Hampshire took his candidacy seriously. Consistently last or next to last in the polls, he withdrew from the race in the final week of the New Hampshire campaign.

1988 Primary and Caucus Outcomes

The foregoing discussion of candidate strategies revealed not only different plans for winning the nomination but enormous variation in the resources informing such plans. Bush represented one extreme with his lengthy record, high poll ratings, abundant funding, big organization, and other advantages. With such resources, anything less than a detailed strategy to capture the nomination would have been wasteful. Haig embodied the other extreme, with his meager resources and primitive plan to match. Let us now determine what happened to each candidate in this contest of unequals, beginning with the Democrats.

The Democrats: Dukakis Wins a Protracted Struggle

Governor Dukakis eventually captured the Democratic nomination in a grueling marathon that progressively narrowed the field to Jackson and himself. Of the thirty-seven Democratic primaries, Dukakis won twenty-two, Jackson seven, Gore five, Gephardt two, and Simon one. As for caucuses, Dukakis won twelve, Jackson seven, Gore two, and Gephardt one.[14]

A sound strategy, abundant funds, exploitation of the rules, momentum (erratic at first but later sustained), and some good fortune gave Dukakis the nomination. More or less according to plan, he finished third in Iowa and won New Hampshire resoundingly, as was essential to satisfy high media expectations. Success followed immediately in the Maine and Minnesota caucuses. And on Super Tuesday, Dukakis led the pack in the Florida, Massachusetts, Rhode Island, and Texas primaries as well as in the Hawaii, Idaho, and Washington State caucuses. With Babbitt and Hart out of the race, Simon and Gephardt seemingly spent, and the field effectively narrowed to Gore, Jackson, and himself, Dukakis hoped to build unstoppable momentum by taking Illinois and Michigan. Major defeats in both states not only stalled him but inspired fresh speculation of a brokered convention. Yet Dukakis soon bounced back with wins in Connecticut and Wisconsin that eliminated Simon and ended talk of Jackson as the possible nominee. New York is generally acknowledged to have decided the Democratic race by narrowing the field to Dukakis and Jackson (Cook, 1989: 52) and by dramatizing the limits of Jackson's support (Pomper, 1989: 46). After New York, Dukakis won every remaining contest except the District of Columbia primary. Final wins in the California, New Jersey, Montana, and New Mexico primaries put him over the top in delegates needed to nominate.

In chronicling the failure of Dukakis's rivals, let us recall Iowa's importance to Gephardt and Simon. After a seesaw battle of poll ratings with Simon and Dukakis, Gephardt finally pulled ahead in January and was pronounced the Iowa winner even though returns showed Simon a very close second. Unfortunately for Gephardt, news media preoccupation with events in the Republican race reduced his Iowa impact, and he accordingly finished sixteen points behind Dukakis in New Hampshire. Although the victor in South Dakota, Gephardt could not match Dukakis or Gore in Super Tuesday's media battle.[15] He carried only Missouri on March 8, and, after a last hurrah in Michigan, departed the race in time to reclaim his House seat. Since Iowa was his launching pad, Simon's trajectory thereafter was downward: third in New Hampshire, third in Minnesota, and a distant fourth in South Dakota. At this point Simon fashioned a new strategy: abandoning the South, concentrating on Illinois, and hoping for a brokered convention. Victory in Illinois would improve his prospects in Wisconsin, New York, and subsequent states where he thought his base strong (Simon, 1989: 33). Simon won Illinois but lost badly in Wisconsin on April 5. He "suspended" his campaign two days later.

Two other candidates depending on Iowa or New Hampshire were Babbitt and Hart. After running fifth in Iowa and sixth in New Hampshire, Babbitt gracefully withdrew. Hart finished dead last in both states but did not make the obvious official until March 11.

Having prepared the news media for a poor Iowa outing, Gore suffered little by landing at the bottom with Hart. Running fifth in New Hampshire, however, guaranteed a test of his southern strategy. On Super Tuesday, Gore won the primaries in Arkansas, Kentucky, North Carolina, Tennessee, and Oklahoma, as well as the Nevada caucuses, and may have encouraged future candidates to bypass Iowa or even New Hampshire. Anyone contemplating such a strategy would do well to remember Gore's fate after Super Tuesday, when he took his distinctly regional campaign to the Midwest and East: 5 percent in Illinois, 2 percent in Michigan, 8 percent in Connecticut, 17 percent in Wisconsin, and 10 percent in New York. Probably hurt more than helped by Mayor Edward Koch's support in New York, Gore suspended his candidacy on April 21.

Jackson was no less successful than Gore in persuading the press to buy his interpretation of early results. Thus having "survived" Iowa with 9 percent, New Hampshire with 9 percent, South Dakota with 5 percent, and Minnesota with 19 percent, Jackson moved confidently into the South where Super Tuesday was supposed to launch his candidacy. And so it did with primary wins in Alabama, Louisiana, Georgia, Mississippi, and Virginia, as well as in the South Carolina and Texas caucuses. Although second to Simon in Illinois, Jackson still won twice as many votes there as Dukakis.

Jackson's greatest triumph followed on March 26 in Michigan, where the Democratic caucuses were open to any registered voter who showed up. An inspired get-out-the-vote drive helped Jackson overcome his deficit in state polls and beat Dukakis soundly—53 to 29 percent in the preference vote, seventy-four to fifty-five in delegates. Michigan stunned pundits and party elites into taking Jackson more seriously. Three days after his Michigan upset, Jackson breakfasted with Clark Clifford and other Democratic elders to receive assurances of support in the event of his nomination.

Yet, even as this "power breakfast" was getting underway, returns from Connecticut indicated that Dukakis was on the comeback trail. This turn of events became brutally apparent to the Jackson campaign on April 5, when Dukakis won the Wisconsin primary and the Colorado caucuses. Reportedly the Wisconsin defeat (28 percent to 48 percent for Dukakis) was especially painful for Jackson (Colton, 1989: 199) since he had strongly supported Kenosha auto workers against Chrysler and moved large audiences throughout the state with his impassioned rhetoric. On primary election day, however, Kenosha voted for Dukakis. More bad news followed in crucial New York, where Jackson was continually reminded of his 1984 "Hymietown" remark and other difficulties with Jews, and in Pennsylvania, where Dukakis took 163 of 178 delegates on the ballot in a loophole primary. On May 3 Jackson won his final 1988 contest, the District of Columbia primary, with 80 percent of the vote. On the same day, however, Dukakis got 70 percent in Indiana and 63 percent in Ohio. At this point, according to Pomper's estimates (1989: 42–43), it was no longer mathematically possible for Jackson to win the nomination. Still he continued to campaign all the way to Atlanta. There, as in San Francisco four years earlier, his demands and fulminations dominated news coverage of the convention, distracted the delegates, and probably hurt the Democratic nominee's chances in the fall election.

Before ending this discussion of Jackson's 1988 bid, a few summary statistics should be noted. First, by almost any measure, he did substantially better in 1988 than in 1984. This time he won 29.1 percent of the 23,230,525 votes cast in Democratic primaries. In 1984 he had gotten 19.5 percent of 17,020,259 votes (*Congressional Quarterly Weekly Report*, 1988a: 1892; Pomper, 1985: 19). Most, though hardly all, of this increase can be attributed to greater support among whites. On the other hand, five of his seven primary victories were on Super Tuesday in southern states with large black electorates. According to a CBS/*New York Times* poll (Rosenbaum, 1988) taken on Super Tuesday, 91 percent of the black voters in fourteen southern and border states marked their ballots for Jackson, as opposed to 7 percent of whites and 21 percent of Hispanics. His two other primary victories were in Puerto Rico and the District of Columbia, where the electorates were also predominantly nonwhite.

Why did Dukakis win the Democratic nomination in 1988?

Part of the answer is that no rival matched his war chest at any point in the process. According to the Federal Election Commission data reported in chapter 4, Dukakis eventually took in more than $19 million in individual contributions and received an additional $9 million in matching funds. Jackson was a distant second with $12 million in individual receipts and about $6 million in matching funds.

As previously noted, money alone does not win presidential nominating campaigns, but it does make possible all manner of things conducive to victory. An amply funded Dukakis organization made continual use of tracking polls in key states, often adjusting campaign spending when fresh intelligence suggested more efficient applications. When such polls disclosed that television advertising had achieved its desired effect in Florida, for instance, the Dukakis staff cut further media buys there and shifted the balance to other states (Wertheimer, 1988). Similarly, the campaign switched funds from media market to media market in Texas after polls pointed up soft spots.

Fortuitous scheduling unquestionably helped Dukakis in several ways. First, of course, he had a decided advantage in New Hampshire, where his big win greatly diminished Gephardt's Iowa victory. Second, holding the Massachusetts and Rhode Island primaries on Super Tuesday meant he would not be shut out on March 8, whatever the outcome in Dixie. Finally, friendly Connecticut voted only three days after Michigan and thus helped revive his campaign at a critical time.

Dukakis also took full advantage of formal rules of delegate selection, as is apparent in table 1.6. True, he dominated every type of event except closed caucuses, but closer inspection of the table discloses important variations in the degree of Dukakis success by category of contest.

Loophole primary states were clearly the happiest hunting grounds for Dukakis. Of five such events, he won four, including delegate-rich Pennsylvania, where his slate prevailed in twenty-one of twenty-three congressional districts (Calvert, 1988: 25). Indeed, according to Calvert's estimates (1988: 26) Dukakis won 61.5 percent of the delegates listed on the ballot in these states while his own preference vote was only 49 percent. Conversely, Jackson got 29.7 percent of the preference vote but only 14.2 percent of the delegates.

Dukakis also benefited from the bonus system. Table 1.6 shows him winning five of eight primaries employing this method whereas Jackson carried one. According to Calvert (1988: 26), Dukakis picked up 54 percent of the delegates in these states for 43.3 percent of the vote. Jackson again fared poorly in comparison — 29.9 percent of the delegates for 28.5 percent of the vote.

Things were more even in the proportional representation primaries, where Dukakis won at least a plurality of the preference vote in ten of twenty such contests. As table 1.6 reveals, it made no difference to Dukakis whether the primary was open or closed. All told, again according to Calvert (1988: 26), Dukakis collected 43.8 percent of the delegates for 39.4 percent of the vote, while Jackson netted 35.2 percent of the delegates for 30.2 percent of the vote.[16]

Finally, in addition to his remarkable self-discipline and tactical ability, Dukakis got some good breaks. The Donna Rice affair demolished the early front-runner, who otherwise might well have beaten him in critical New Hampshire. Most news organizations chose not to interpret his Iowa showing as a genuine loss. An ill-timed Jackson letter urging Manuel Nori-

Table 1.6 **Democratic Primary and Caucus Outcomes, by Winning Candidate**

Open Primaries	Closed Primaries	Open Caucuses	Closed Caucuses
Proportional Representation			
Alabama (J)	California (D)	Idaho (D)	Arizona (D)
Arkansas (Go)	Connecticut (D)	Maine (D)	Delaware (J)
Indiana (D)	Kentucky (Go)	Michigan (J)	Hawaii (D)
Mississippi (J)	Louisiana (J)	Minnesota (D)	Iowa (Ge)
New Hampshire (D)	Nebraska (D)	North Dakota (D)	Kansas (D)
Rhode Island (D)	New Mexico (D)	South Carolina (J)	Nevada (Go)
Tennessee (Go)	Oklahoma (Go)	Utah (D)	Texas (J)
Texas (D)	Oregon (D)	Vermont (J)	Wyoming (Go)
Virginia (J)	South Dakota (Ge)	Washington (D)	
Wisconsin (D)	District of Columbia (J)		
Bonus Proportional Representation			
Georgia (J)	Florida (D)		Alaska (J)
Massachusetts (D)	New York (D)		Colorado (D)
Missouri (Ge)	North Carolina (Go)		
Montana (D)			
Ohio (D)			
Loophole			
Illinois (S)	Maryland (D)		
New Jersey (D)	Pennsylvania (D)		
West Virginia (D)			

SOURCES: Rhodes Cook, "The Nominating Process," in *The Elections of 1988*, ed. Michael Nelson (Washington, D.C.: Congressional Quarterly Press, 1989), 54; Gerald M. Pomper, "The Presidential Nominations," in *The Election of 1988*, ed. Gerald M. Pomper, et al. (Chatham, N.J.: Chatham House, 1989), 40–41; "1988 Democratic First-Round Caucus Results," *Congressional Quarterly Weekly Report* 46 (July 9, 1988): 1895.

NOTE: "D" indicates a win by Dukakis, "Ge" by Gephardt, "Go" by Gore, "J" by Jackson, "S" by Simon.

ega to give up power in Panama was widely publicized just before the Wisconsin primary, thus provoking criticism of Jackson's "grandstanding" in foreign policy and probably costing him some votes. And Mayor Koch backed Gore rather than Dukakis in New York, an endorsement that hurt Gore far more than Dukakis.

Bush Wins the Republican Nomination Early

Bush effectively captured the nomination on Super Tuesday after a rough start in early caucus states, especially Iowa, and after rallying in New Hampshire. Dole's collapse just before the Wisconsin primary gave Bush three months to rebuild party unity before his nomination in New Orleans, not an unimportant undertaking since the more united party has won every presidential election in the last quarter century (Wattenberg, 1988: 18). Bush won thirty-seven of the thirty-eight GOP primaries, losing only South Dakota to Dole. He also won caucuses in Michigan, Nevada, and Colorado and tied Dole in Wyoming. Dole won the Kansas, Iowa, and Minnesota caucuses. Robertson was victorious in the Hawaii, Alaska, and Washington State caucuses.

As previously noted, the Republican race started with precinct delegate elections in Michigan eighteen months before Iowa's first-in-the-nation caucuses. Initial reports from Michigan indicated that a Kemp-Robertson alliance had upset Bush, but, after lengthy rules disputes, Bush eventually ended up with most of the delegates. Robertson greatly embarrassed Bush in an Iowa straw poll, thus prompting a showdown in Florida's straw poll, which the Bush campaign won after an all-out effort.[17] More bickering over the rules delayed the Hawaii caucuses until February 4, when Robertson activists overwhelmed party regulars. Meanwhile Dole won virtually every vote when fellow Kansans caucused one week before Iowa.

For all the rancor associated with the earliest clashes, the race really began on February 8 with the Iowa caucuses. Michigan had come too soon and confused too many to rival Iowa for domination of the early news agenda. Dole's winning of 98.7 percent in Kansas was too much of a good thing, for the press took virtually no notice of his local triumph. Hawaii attracted no more attention than earlier straw polls. Iowa moreover was the first event truly contested by all of the GOP candidates (though Haig eventually pulled out). Finally, Iowa offered a compelling drama of Bush against Dole. The plot in this case took an interesting turn when Bush strategists sought to wring advantage out of running second in the Iowa polls by casting their man as the underdog. This lowered expectations for Bush while putting Dole even more on the spot. Now he had to win Iowa convincingly to remain credible. But the same ploy created a firm expectation of nothing less than second for Bush. So, when Robertson finished a strong second and Bush a feeble third in Iowa, the vice-president suddenly found his candidacy in grave peril.

With only one week of compaigning left in New Hampshire, Dole rapidly rising in state polls, and some pundits already administering his last rites, Bush undertook a desperate handshaking tour of the southern counties and unleashed television spots accusing Dole of tax-raising proclivities. Reportedly Governor Sununu advised these steps, and, in any event, lent Bush his full support in New Hampshire's final frantic days. Bush got a critical weekend break when Dole's people failed to counter his tax ads. He beat Dole the following Tuesday, 38 to 29 percent. Kemp came in a distant third at 13 percent, du Pont got 11 percent, and Robertson 9 percent. Du Pont promptly withdrew, Dole blundered badly by snarling at Bush on the "NBC Nightly News," and Robertson blundered even worse by agreeing that he had to win the South Carolina primary on March 5 to remain viable.

Bush made the most of his advantages in the South. Helped by New Hampshire momentum, his association with Reagan, a vastly superior organization, abundant cash, and careful planning, he swept South Carolina and sixteen other primaries on Super Tuesday, including all nine of the southern and border states holding winner-take-all contests. Of the 465 delegates selected in winner-take-all primaries, Bush won 448 or 96 percent (Calvert, 1988: 30–31). All accounts agree that Super Tuesday decided the race for Bush (Calvert, 1988: 30; Cook, 1989: 42; Pomper, 1989: 58). Kemp withdrew on March 10. Although Robertson did not formally exit until May 16, his campaign effectively ended on Super Tuesday.

Now facing hopeless odds but still driven by obvious loathing for Bush, Dole moved on to Illinois, where he called for Lincoln-Douglas–style debates. Bush disdained the challenge, made effective use of Governor Thompson's support, and trounced Dole in the preference vote, 55 to 36 percent. Although his aides subsequently conceded defeat in statements to the press, Dole refused to withdraw until just before the Wisconsin primary. His withdrawal removed Bush's last organized opposition, and, on May 1, the nomination was mathematically decided (Pomper, 1989: 59).

Even more so than in the Democratic race, the candidate with superior resources and best positioned to exploit delegate-selection rules won the nomination. Among his greatest advantages was a close association with Reagan, who remained popular in New Hampshire and the South. Kemp, in accounting for his own defeat, reportedly said that he could beat Bush or any other GOP rival but not Ronald Reagan. Du Pont's explanation (1988: 11) was that he had been a candidate of change at a time when voters did not want change: "They simply were going to vote for George Bush because he carried the flag for the Reagan administration." Subsequent studies may reveal an inverse correlation between Dole's primary vote and Reagan popularity. In any event, as it turned out, Dole was no less a regional candidate than Gore; he was a winner only in early midwestern states. Robertson's insurgency failed in no small part because most fundamentalist Christians voting in Republican primaries preferred Bush. Like Jackson, Robertson did best in caucuses where his avid supporters were numerous enough to make the difference. Today, however, winning the nomination depends on winning primaries early and often.

Coda: The 1992 Strategic Environment

In what ways will the 1992 nominating process resemble that of 1988? On the Republican side, the renomination of President Bush without serious opposition seems almost certain. The most interesting question for the GOP will be Bush's choice of a running mate, a decision he rather than the convention will make. Republican caucus and primary turnout will be comparatively light in any event, and pundits will find more parallels to 1984 than to 1988.

The Democrats, as usual, are harder to forecast. Bush's high poll ratings, together with favorable economic conditions, apparently discouraged the early formation of a Democratic field. No likely candidate, not even Jesse Jackson, had launched a visible effort by July 1990. Still, the chief lesson of 1988 and earlier nominating struggles of the reform era remains valid: early efforts are essential to raising the enormous funds and building the state organizations essential to success in so front-loaded and prohibitively expensive a process. If another crowded field does materialize, many a candidate will suffer for starting so late.

However many Democrats eventually run, the process in 1992 will differ in important respects from 1988. Owing to the withdrawal of several southern states, Super Tuesday probably will be a smaller affair, perhaps on the scale of 1984.

Another major difference will be the use of straight proportional representation with a standard 15 percent threshold in every state's Democratic precinct caucuses and presidential primary. Hoping to win his rival's good behavior at the 1988 convention, Dukakis agreed to back Jackson's demand that loophole and bonus primaries be abolished for the 1992 nominating process. Each candidate's delegates dutifully voted for these changes, which have since been upheld by the DNC.

Straight proportional representation has not been universally acclaimed by Democratic elites. Immediately after the convention vote, for example, Ohio Democratic party Chairman James Ruvolo denounced Dukakis and Jackson for excluding Democratic officials from their talks (Curtin and Embrey, 1989). More discontent surfaced in a memorandum, circulated among "Democratic friends," in which Robert Beckel and Thomas Donilon argued that straight proportional representation would encourage multiple and prolonged candidacies likely to embroil the convention in factional strife and undermine the eventual nominee's chances. "Why hamper a nominee who may have a winning message for the general election campaign," Beckel and Donilon (1989: 2) asked, "with an unnecessarily drawnout nomination fight which serves little purpose except to increase the nominee's negatives and delay preparation for the general election?" Even DNC approval did not silence critics within the party. Writing in a magazine published by the Democratic Leadership Council (DLC), Al From (1990: 22) criticized DNC ratification of rules that would "allow the loser— like Ted Kennedy in 1980 and Jackson in 1988— to harass the nominee all the way to the convention."

Though proportional representation may indeed have the consequences predicted by Beckel, Donilon, and other "mainstream" Democrats, their argument is blind in at least two respects. First, front-loading and the prohibitive costs of campaigning will bring down many a candidate whatever the precise method of delegate selection. Second, and especially concerning candidates like Jackson who stay in the race regardless of money problems, the argument falsely assumes that formal rules will determine not only who wins but who lines up behind the winner. As Beckel and Donilon (1989: 3) put it in their memorandum, "there must be a process whereby the runners-up in the nomination fight end their individual efforts and get behind the common effort." But this assertion begs the question of ideological, racial, and other cleavages retarding such unity even under winner-take-all rules. In any event, Kennedy and Jackson bedeviled nominees under rules very much like those Beckel and Donilon wish to preserve.

Finally, attacking "unfair" rules is an established tradition in presidential nominating politics, going back to the congressional caucuses of the early 1800s. Many a convention has since been enlivened by ferocious battles over rules, and, because rules never treat candidates equally, future battles are inevitable. And so presidential nominating politics remains a mixture of the predictable and the unexpected, the systematic and the erratic, the arcane and the obvious.

Notes

The authors gratefully acknowledge the assistance of Richard L. Thompson in providing essential information on 1992 Democratic rules changes.

1. "Superdelegates" are party and elected officials uncommitted to candidates in the Democratic race. They include governors, Democratic National Committee (DNC) members, and most Democratic members of Congress. In 1984, 568 superdelegates as well as 305 party and elected officials who were pledged to specific candidates participated in the San Francisco convention.
2. A caucus-convention process requires several steps to complete and generally begins with precinct caucuses, meetings where participants make a public show of support for their presidential candidates. The main point of precinct caucuses is to elect delegates to a convention at the county or congressional-district

level. Some states hold separate county and congressional-district conventions. In any event, delegates are eventually elected to attend a statewide convention at which a still smaller number are finally chosen to attend the presidential nominating convention. All three or four steps typically take several months to complete and are time-consuming for participants. Voting in presidential primaries requires no more time than it does in any other election, and, as in other elections, the ballot is secret. Turnout is understandably higher in primaries than in caucuses. According to Calvert (1988: 18), average turnout of the voting-age population for the 1988 primaries was 24 percent, contrasted with 2 percent for the Republican caucuses and even less for Democratic caucuses.

3. According to Byron Shafer (1988), owing to long-term changes in American politics, conventions had lost their chief function of actually picking presidential nominees by 1960. Earlier statements of the same point may be found in Davis (1983) and Reiter (1985). See chapter 8 in the present volume.

4. On this point, see James I. Lengle and Byron Shafer (1976: 26) and Nicol C. Rae (1989: 128).

5. The 1960 and 1988 primaries differed in other important respects as well. Aside from Democratic superdelegates, uncommitted delegates are no longer chosen in any appreciable number, and favorite sons are unlikely to emerge even in a protracted race, as Governor Cuomo demonstrated in 1988. In 1960, however, only uncommitted delegates were picked in the New Jersey primaries. This was also true of Republican primaries in the District of Columbia, West Virginia, and South Dakota. Favorite sons topped the Democratic ballot in Ohio, Florida, and California (Davis, 1980: 326–29).

6. Lengle's data slightly understate the extent of 1988 front-loading because he expected Minnesota and South Dakota to adhere to their 1984 dates rather than move up to February 23.

7. According to Calvert (1988: 39), more than half the voters in the West Virginia loophole primary did not indicate whom they wanted as delegates.

8. At least in Oregon the lack of a fixed threshold was not the same as no threshold at all. Calvert (1988: 16–17) noted that candidates had to "qualify" for at least one delegate in a district by winning enough popular votes. In a district where three delegates were at stake and 10,000 people voted, a candidate had to win at least 33.3 percent or precisely 3,334 votes.

9. In this connection see Lengle and Shafer (1976), Pomper (1979), and Geer (1986).

10. See Bartels (1988) for the most extensive analysis of momentum in presidential nominating campaigns to date.

11. Rep. Shirley Chisholm of New York preceded him in 1972 as the first black candidate for the Democratic nomination.

12. According to Susan Casey, who spoke for the Hart campaign at the Kennedy School's conference of campaign managers on the 1988 campaigns, Hart's strategy called for finishing first, second, or even third in Iowa and/or New Hampshire. While second might have been acceptable in either, third—especially in New Hampshire—would have probably killed Hart's chances in the South.

Casey also claimed that Hart expected the field after Super Tuesday to number as many as five, including himself. Since no more than eight Democrats were ever in the race, and given the "winnowing" effects of Iowa and New Hampshire as well as Super Tuesday, this estimate of remaining rivals, if serious, was unrealistically high.

13. We are indebted to Gregory G. Lebel for information on this point. Lebel had played a prominent role in Hart's 1984 campaign and was much involved in his 1988 New Hampshire effort when Hart first withdrew. Lebel then joined the Gore campaign but soon found himself at odds with the national campaign over inattention to New Hampshire. In a December 5, 1989 letter to Buell, Lebel wrote that the Gore campaign had decided to abandon New Hampshire as well as Iowa at the point when Hart got back in the race in December 1987. Lebel soon reenlisted in the Hart campaign.

14. Readers will no doubt have noted that thirty-seven Democratic primaries and twelve caucuses add up to nine more states than the present fifty. The apparent discrepancy is explained by some states holding advisory primaries as well as caucuses. Vermont, Idaho, and North Dakota followed this procedure, and Texas Democrats used a hybrid primary-caucus system. Note also that Puerto Rico was included among the thirty-seven Democratic primaries and that American Samoa, Democrats Abroad, and the Virgin Islands were included in the count of Democratic first-round caucuses.

15. William Carrick, Gephardt's campaign manager, later explained that his candidate got no financial "bump" out of winning Iowa and had only $1 million to spend on media advertising for Super Tuesday. Unlike Dukakis, who had targeted selected states in a "four corners" strategy (Texas, Florida, Washington State, and Maryland), Gephardt attempted to compete throughout the South on Super Tuesday. It was, Carrick conceded, a $4 million strategy with only $1 million on hand (Runkel, 1989: 174–75). Gore had a similar strategy but much more money to carry it out. According to his campaign manager, Gore began airing spots on February 7 in twenty-five to thirty southern media markets and was able to sustain this media effort for the next thirty days (Runkel, 1989: 177–78).

16. For slightly different data on the same point see *Congressional Quarterly Weekly Report* 46 (1988b): 1800.

17. Hardly based on random sampling and completely unrelated to delegate selection, straw polls nonetheless offer an early opportunity to embarrass rivals, flex organizational muscle, and grab a few headlines. Typically hosted by state or local parties and limited to paid ticket-holders, straw polls can consume limited resources best saved for contests where the votes truly count, as several Democratic candidates discovered in 1984. Having learned from experience, the Democrats agreed not to hold straw polls in the early days of their 1988 race.

18. The DNC has since adopted the Dukakis-Jackson agreement on proportional representation. At its March 23–24, 1990, meeting in Indianapolis, the full DNC upheld an earlier vote by its Rules and Bylaws Committee to require simple proportional representation with a 15 percent threshold in every presiden-

tial primary and caucus in 1992. The DNC also went along with the Rules and Bylaws Committee's recommendation to restore superdelegate status to 363 DNC members. Jackson reportedly did not oppose this action because upwards of 100 of his supporters had been added to the DNC since 1988 (Taylor, 1990).

References

Adams, William C. 1985. "Media Coverage of Campaign '84: A Preliminary Report." In *The Mass Media in Campaign '84: Articles from Public Opinion Magazine*, ed. Michael J. Robinson and Austin Ranney. Washington, D.C.: American Enterprise Institute for Public Policy Research.

———. 1987. "As New Hampshire Goes . . ." In *Media and Momentum: The New Hampshire Primary and Nomination Politics*, ed. Gary R. Orren and Nelson W. Polsby. Chatham, N.J.: Chatham House.

Aldrich, John H. 1980. *Before the Convention: Strategies and Choices in Presidential Nominating Campaigns*. Chicago: University of Chicago Press.

———. 1987. "Methods and Actors: The Relationship of Processes to Candidates." In *Presidential Selection*, ed. Alexander Heard and Michael Nelson. Durham, N.C.: Duke University Press.

Babcock, Charles R., and Richard Morin. 1988. "Bush's Campaign Cup Runneth Over." *Washington Post National Weekly Edition* (May 23–29): 6–7.

Bartels, Larry M. 1988. *Presidential Primaries and the Dynamics of Public Choice*. Princeton, N.J.: Princeton University Press.

Beckel, Robert, and Thomas Donilon. 1989. "The Rules for 1992." Memorandum circulated to "Democratic friends" (March 29).

Buell, Emmett H., Jr. 1987a. "First-in-the-Nation: Disputes over the Timing of Early Democratic Presidential Primaries and Caucuses in 1984 and 1988." *Journal of Law & Politics* 4 (Fall): 311–42.

———. 1987b. "'Locals' and 'Cosmopolitans': National, Regional, and State Newspaper Coverage of the New Hampshire Primary." In *Media and Momentum: The New Hampshire Primary and Nomination Politics*, ed. Gary R. Orren and Nelson W. Polsby. Chatham, N.J.: Chatham House.

Calvert, Jerry W. 1988. "Rules That Count: Voter Choice, Party Rules and the Selection of National Convention Delegates in 1988." Unpublished paper presented at annual meeting of American Political Science Association, September 1–4.

Colton, Elizabeth O. 1989. *The Jackson Phenomenon: The Man, the Power, the Message*. New York: Doubleday.

Congressional Quarterly Weekly Report. 1988a. "Primary Recap: The Aggregate Vote" (July 9): 1892.

———. 1988b. "How States Allocated Democratic Delegates in 1988" (July 2): 1800.

Cook, Rhodes. 1987a. *Race for the Presidency: Winning the 1988 Nomination*. Washington, D.C.: Congressional Quarterly Press.

————. 1987b. "Gore's Big Risk: Center-Right May Not Show." *Congressional Quarterly Weekly Report* 45 (November 28): 2919–2922.

————. 1987c. "Bids of Jackson and Robertson Are Uphill, But Bear Watching." *Congressional Quarterly Weekly Report* 45 (October 3): 2383–87.

————. 1988. "GOP's View of Delegate Rules Invites Procedural Shenanigans." *Congressional Quarterly Weekly Report* 46 (February 6): 249.

————. 1989. "The Nominating Process." In *The Elections of 1988*, ed. Michael Nelson. Washington, D.C.: Congressional Quarterly Press.

Crotty, William. 1983. *Party Reform*. New York: Longman.

————, and John S. Jackson III. 1985 *Presidential Primaries and Nominations*. Washington, D.C.: Congressional Quarterly Press.

Curtin, Mike, and George Embrey. 1989. "State Chairmen Should Call Shots, Ohio Leader Says." *Columbus* (Ohio) *Dispatch* (May 2): 6B.

David, Paul T., Ralph M. Goldman, and Richard C. Bain. 1960. *The Politics of National Party Conventions*. Washington, D.C.: Brookings.

Davis, James W. 1980. *Presidential Primaries: Road to the White House*. 2d ed. Westport, Ct.: Greenwood Press.

————. 1983. *National Conventions in an Age of Party Reform*. Westport, Ct.: Greenwood Press.

————. 1987. *The American Presidency: A New Perspective*. New York: Harper & Row.

Drew, Elizabeth. 1989. *Election Journal: Political Events of 1987–1988*. New York: William Morrow & Co.

du Pont, Pierre. 1988. "What I Learned in Cedar Rapids: Pete du Pont Discusses His Presidential Campaign." Interview with Adam Meyerson in *Policy Review* 45 (Summer): 10–13.

From, Al. 1990. "The Myth of Unity." *The Mainstream Democrat* 2 (May): 22, 24.

Geer, John G. 1986. "Rules Governing Presidential Primaries." *Journal of Politics* 48 (November): 1006–25.

Hess, Stephen. 1988. *The Presidential Campaign*. 3d. ed. Washington, D.C.: Brookings.

Kamarck, Elaine C. 1987. "Delegate Allocation Rules in Presidential Nomination Systems: A Comparison Between the Democrats and Republicans." *Journal of Law & Politics* 4 (Fall): 275–310.

King, Wayne. 1987. "Robertson, Returning to Brooklyn Home, Enters Race." *New York Times* (October 2): 12A.

Ladd, Everett C. 1987. "Polls Help Map Political Terrain But Hold Pitfalls." *Christian Science Monitor* (November 6): 3–4.

Lengle, James I. 1987. "Democratic Party Reforms: The Past as Prologue to the 1988 Campaign." *Journal of Law & Politics* 4 (Fall): 233–74.

Lengle, James I., and Byron Shafer. 1976. "Primary Rules, Political Power, and Social Change." *American Political Science Review* 70 (March): 25–40.

Matthews, Donald R. 1978. "'Winnowing': The News Media and the 1976 Presidential Nomination." In *Race for the Presidency: The Media and the Nominating Process*, ed. James D. Barber. Englewood Cliffs, N.J.: Prentice-Hall.

Moore, David. 1985. "The Death of Politics in New Hampshire." In *The Mass*

Media in Campaign '84: Articles from Public Opinion Magazine, ed. Michael J. Robinson and Austin Ranney. Washington, D.C.: American Enterprise Institute for Public Policy Research.

Nelson, Michael. 1987. "Who Vies for President?" In *Presidential Selection*, ed. Alexander Heard and Michael Nelson. Durham, N.C.: Duke University Press.

The Polling Report. 1987a. 3:12 (June 15). Washington, D.C.

———. 1987b. 3:7 (April 6). Washington, D.C.

———. 1987c. 3:20 (October 12). Washington, D.C.

———. 1987d. 3:18 (September 14). Washington, D.C.

Polsby, Nelson W. 1983. *Consequences of Party Reform*. New York: Oxford University Press.

Pomper, Gerald M. 1979 "New Rules and New Games in Presidential Nominations." *Journal of Politics* 41 (August): 784–805.

———. 1985. "The Nominations." In *The Election of 1984: Reports and Interpretations,* ed. Gerald M. Pomper et. al. Chatham, N.J.: Chatham House.

———. 1989. "The Presidential Nominations." In Gerald M. Pomper et al., *The Election of 1988: Reports and Interpretations*. Chatham, N.J.: Chatham House.

Rae, Nicol C. 1989. *The Decline and Fall of the Liberal Republicans from 1952 to the Present*. New York: Oxford University Press.

Reiter, Howard. 1985. *Selecting the President: The Nominating Process in Transition*. Philadelphia: University of Pennsylvania Press.

Robertson, John. 1987. "Evangelist Robertson Enters Presidential Race." *Boston Globe* (October 2): 1A.

Robinson, Michael J. 1985. "Where's the Beef? Media and Media Elites in 1984." In *The American Elections of 1984*, ed. Austin Ranney. Durham, N.C.: Duke University Press.

Rose, Richard. 1987. "Learning to Govern or Learning to Campaign?" In *Presidential Selection*, ed. Alexander Heard and Michael Nelson. Durham, N.C.: Duke University Press.

Rosenbaum, David E. 1988. "Blacks, Years after Selma, Share in Jackson's Victory." *New York Times* (March 10): 1A.

Runkel, David R., ed. 1989. *Campaign for President: The Managers Look at '88*. Dover, Mass.: Auburn House.

Schlesinger, Joseph A. 1966. *Ambition and Politics: Political Careers in the United States*. Chicago: Rand McNally.

Shafer, Byron E. 1983. *Quiet Revolution: The Struggle for the Democratic Party and the Shaping of Post-Reform Politics*. New York: Russell Sage Foundation.

———. 1988. *Bifurcated Politics: Evolution and Reform in the National Party Convention*. Cambridge, Mass.: Harvard University Press.

Simon, Paul. 1989. *Winners and Losers: The 1988 Race for the Presidency—One Candidate's Perspective*. New York: Continuum.

Sorauf, Frank J. 1988. *Money in American Elections*. Glenview, Ill.: Scott, Foresman.

Taylor, Paul. 1986. "Kemp and Gephardt: Image-Building in Iowa." *Washington Post National Weekly Edition* (March 17): 6.

————. 1990. "Democrats Invite California to Set '92 Primary in March." *Washington Post* (February 15).

Wattenberg, Martin P. 1988. "The 1988 and 1960 Elections Compared: What a Difference a Candidate-centered Politics Makes." Unpublished paper presented at annual meeting of American Political Science Association, September 1–4.

Weinraub, Bernard. 1987. "Haig's Aides Insist They Are in a Real Campaign." *New York Times* (October 21): 7A.

Wertheimer, Linda. 1988. "Dukakis' Secret to Success: He Wouldn't Budge." *Washington Post National Weekly Edition* (June 20–26): 23–24.

Winebrenner, Hugh. 1987. *The Iowa Precinct Caucuses: The Making of a Media Event.* Ames: Iowa State University Press.

2. Up Close and Personal: The 1988 Iowa Caucuses and Presidential Politics

Alan I. Abramowitz
Ronald B. Rapoport
and Walter J. Stone

The Iowa caucuses have developed a bad reputation among students of American presidential elections since the 1970s, and their image did not improve in 1988. As in previous years, pundits criticized allowing a small and atypical state to exert so much influence on the rest of the nominating process. Not only is Iowa said to be unrepresentative of the nation, but turnout for the caucuses seldom exceeds 15 percent of the state's registered voters (Schier, 1980; Hutter and Schier, 1984; Stone, Abramowitz, and Rapoport, 1989). Moreover, when the field is left to so few participants, a small number of enthusiastic and dedicated supporters can determine the outcome (Keeter and Zukin, 1983; Polsby, 1983; Winebrenner, 1987).

Ever since 1976, when victory in Iowa catapulted Jimmy Carter from obscurity into front-runner status, presidential aspirants have campaigned countless hours and spent enormous sums competing for the state's handful of delegates.[1] More important than the delegates themselves, of course, are the publicity and associated fund-raising benefits usually derived from winning or doing "better than expected" in this first-in-the-nation vote. Highly favorable coverage usually boosts a candidate in the crucial New Hampshire primary, and success in New Hampshire often creates an almost unstoppable momentum. On the other hand, defeat or doing worse than expected in both states is often fatal to candidacies (Orren and Polsby, 1987).

Iowa gained its priority in the nominating process by accident rather than design. National Democratic rules changes in 1969 required each state party to separate the stages in its delegate-selection process by at least thirty days. Moreover, all stages of a state's delegate-selection process had to occur during the first six months of the election year. To follow these injunctions and comply with state law requiring statewide party conventions no later than mid-May, Iowa Democrats were impelled to schedule their first phase of delegate selection, the precinct caucuses, no later than January 24, 1972 (Squire, 1989: 1–2). Thus for essentially parochial reasons Iowa Democrats revised their caucus-convention calendar and inadvertently preempted the New Hampshire primary by several weeks. Once first, Iowa has never relinquished its priority. True, the 1988 GOP race began in August 1986 with caucuses in Michigan, and Republican caucuses in Hawaii and Kansas also preceded those in Iowa. Even so, the Iowa caucuses were the first nominating event contested by every serious candidate of both parties. So far as the national news media were concerned, the race began in Iowa (Lichter, Amundsen, and Noyes, 1988).

Jimmy Carter was the first presidential candidate to fully appreciate the importance of Iowa's priority. Devised by principal aide Hamilton Jordan three years before the caucuses, Carter's strategy called for an all-out effort in Iowa. Months of tireless campaigning paid off on January 19, 1976, when Carter led all other Democratic candidates with 28 percent of the delegates, even though 37 percent remained uncommitted (Squire, 1989: 9). Having previously discounted Carter as a long shot, network television news now hyped him as the man to beat. Iowa gave George Bush a similar push in 1980, when he upset Ronald Reagan, but "mighty mo" soon ran out for Bush in New Hampshire. Gary Hart's distant second in the 1984 Democratic caucuses helped to propel him past Walter Mondale in New Hampshire and to nearly cinch the nomination on Super Tuesday.

Despite Iowa's enormous importance in the contemporary nominating system, there is considerable confusion about how the caucus-convention process actually works. Compounding the problem are the different procedures used by Democrats and Republicans.

Each Republican caucus is open to any resident of the precinct who will be of voting age on general election day in November. Shortly after the meeting starts, the chair conducts a straw poll of participant preference for the various presidential candidates. Results are announced to the news media and often satisfy media questions about who won and lost. The straw poll may have little relationship to the election of candidate supporters as delegates to county Republican conventions in the spring, a more telling indicator of each campaign's strength. In any event, once delegates have been elected, the caucus takes up local party business.

Iowa Democrats follow a more complicated procedure, in which participation is restricted to registered party members (even though registration is allowed right up to the beginning of the caucuses). Rather than simply vote for delegates, the Democrats form "affinity groups" in different parts of the meeting place either to support particular candidates or to remain uncommitted. Any group comprising less than 15 percent of those present—the minimum threshold to elect a delegate to the county convention—is then permitted to disband so that its members can join more viable groups. Lengthy negotiations often follow as leaders of the different groups work out allocation of the delegates. Finally the reformed groups are counted and delegates allocated accordingly, with each group actually choosing its delegate or delegates (Balzar, 1988; Oliphant, 1988).

These were the procedures contested by almost every major candidate for the Republican and Democratic nominations in 1988. Most pundits from the very beginning regarded Vice-President George Bush and Senator Robert Dole of Kansas as the leading GOP contestants. As caucus day approached, however, the news media began paying more attention to the possibility of an upset by Pat Robertson's "invisible army" of conservative evangelicals. Congressman Jack Kemp of New York and former Governor Pierre du Pont of Delaware also campaigned hard in the state. Former Secretary of State Alexander Haig soon abandoned Iowa after polls gave him little chance of finishing in the top four and put all his emphasis on New Hampshire.

The principal Democratic contenders were Congressman Richard Gephardt of Missouri, Senator Paul Simon of Illinois, and Governor Michael Dukakis of Massachusetts. The Reverend Jesse Jackson also made a strong effort in Iowa, hoping to add alienated blue-collar workers and farmers to his "rainbow coalition." With blacks comprising less than 1 percent of the voting-age population, however, the Jackson campaign set its goal as breaking into double figures—10 percent or more. Former Arizona Governor Bruce Babbitt staked his long-shot candidacy almost entirely on Iowa. After a belated effort in the state, Senator Albert Gore, Jr., of Tennessee effectively wrote the caucuses off and concentrated his energies on the Super Tuesday South. Gore signaled this shift by attacking the Democratic caucuses as unrepresentative of party supporters nationwide and unduly influential in deciding presidential nominations.

The Iowa Caucus Survey

Seeking to understand the behavior of 1988 caucus participants, we conducted a mail survey of citizens attending the precinct caucuses on February 8. Our first step was to draw a sample of fourteen counties, with the probability of selection based on county population. We then sampled ten Democratic and Republican caucus sites in each county. Names and addresses of all caucus participants at each site were obtained from state Democratic and Republican headquarters, and an interval sample was taken from the party lists. The Democratic sample included 1,064 participants, the Republican sample 892; the party breakdown of 54 percent Democratic and 46 percent Republican in our sample was identical to that of all caucus attenders. Each member of the sample received a questionnaire in the mail during the first week of March, a postcard reminder one week later, and, for those not responding to the first questionnaire, a follow-up letter and duplicate questionnaire in early April. The ultimate return of usable questionnaires was 541 for the Democrats and 428 for the Republicans, or 51 and 48 percent respectively.

Our questionnaires asked respondents to disclose their candidate preferences at the time of the February caucuses. The results allow comparison of their preferences with the actual choices of all Iowa caucus participants. Table 2.1 shows some overrepresentation of Dukakis and Bush supporters and slight underrepresentation of other campaigns. Perhaps Dukakis and Bush activists responded more readily because their candidates still were running strong when our questionnaires went out, whereas most rival campaigns had collapsed or were clearly in trouble at this point. In any event, every candidate's supporters were adequately represented among our respondents. Table 2.1 reveals a close correspondence between survey and actual caucus results, with an average difference of only 4 percent for Democrats and 2 percent for Republicans.

Table 2.1 **Original Candidate Preferences of Iowa Caucus Survey Respondents Compared with Actual 1988 Caucus Results**

	Survey (%)	Caucus Results (%)	Difference (%)
Democrats			
Dukakis	28	22	+6
Gephardt	27	31	−4
Jackson	8	9	−1
Simon	23	27	−4
Others, uncommitted	13	11	+2
Totals	100	100	
Ns	541	126,000	
Republicans			
Bush	23	19	+4
Dole	36	37	−1
Kemp	11	11	0
Robertson	21	25	−4
Others, uncommitted	9	8	+1
Totals	100	100	
Ns	428	108,838	

SOURCES: Survey results from Iowa caucus survey; caucus results from *Congressional Quarterly Weekly Report* 46 (July 9, 1988): 1895, 1897.

We also asked our respondents about their personal characteristics and backgrounds, past political activities, reasons for attending the caucuses, ideological and issue positions, and views of the presidential candidates.

Caucus Participants

Table 2.2 compares the social backgrounds of the Democratic and Republican caucus attenders in our survey, who in certain respects were atypical of the entire Iowa electorate and who differed importantly among themselves by party.

Table 2.2 **Social Characteristics of Iowa Caucus Survey Respondents**

	Democrats (%; total N = 541)	Republicans (%; total N = 428)	Combined (%; total N = 969)
Age			
17–29	5	14	9
30–39	12	22	16
40–49	10	15	12
50–59	20	22	21
60+	53	26	41
Sex			
Male	52	51	51
Female	48	49	49
Race			
White	96	99	97
Black	2	1	2
Other	2	0	1
Religion			
Protestant	52	81	65
Catholic	36	12	25
Jewish	2	0	1
Other, none	10	8	9
Born-again Christian	20	44	30
Fundamentalist	16	36	24
Education			
High school or less	48	28	40
Some college	24	27	25
College graduate	15	31	22
Post-college	13	14	13
Occupation			
Farmer	8	10	9
Teacher	15	13	14
1987 family income			
Less than $20,000	32	19	26
$20,000–$39,999	41	40	41
$40,000 or more	27	41	32

Looking first at socioeconomic status, both groups were more affluent and educated than Iowans generally, but Republican participants were much better off than their Democratic counterparts. These partisan differences were hardly unexpected, given long-standing differences between Democratic and Republican electoral coalitions.

Important differences of religion also stood out in the comparison of Democrats and Republicans. Catholics, for example, were three times more numerous among Democratic attenders, while "born-again" and "fundamentalist" Christians were more than twice as prevalent among Republican participants. No doubt the heavy Catholic presence among Democrats is at least partly a remnant of the New Deal coalition, while increased evangelical involvement in the GOP may have resulted largely from Robertson's campaign.

Still another big difference was the age distribution of Democratic and Republican caucus participants. Even though relatively few young people took part in either party's precinct caucuses, youth was particularly absent on the Democratic side. An astonishing 53 percent of the Democrats in our survey were sixty or older, while only 17 percent were thirty-nine or younger. Among Republicans, 26 percent were sixty or older and 36 percent younger than forty. This dramatic difference may reflect a general shift to Republicans among younger Iowans since Ronald Reagan's election in 1980. Persistence of this pattern into the 1990s has obvious and ominous implications for the Democratic party.

There were also noteworthy similarities between Democrats and Republicans in our survey. Women made up about half of the participants in the caucuses of both parties; virtually all respondents were white; farmers were a sizable group in both parties, but teachers were even more numerous — an indication of the growing involvement of teachers' associations in presidential nominating politics.

Interest-Group Representation

Another topic of interest in our survey was respondent involvement in organized interest groups. Organizations representing business, labor, agriculture, and other economic interests have long influenced both parties. In recent years, however, feminists, pro- and anti-abortion groups, environmentalists, and other "new politics" groups have penetrated the parties and altered their agendas. Students of the parties often regard these newcomers as inflexible zealots unwilling to compromise for the party's sake.

Table 2.3 shows that single-issue and ideological groups had limited sway over the 1988 Iowa caucus attendees in our survey. Two types of data are reported in this table — the percentage of each party's caucus participants

Table 2.3 **Group Affiliations of Iowa Caucus Survey Respondents**

	Democrats (%)	Republicans (%)	Combined (%)
Group			
Farm	25	29	27
Business	22	32	26
Labor union	34	12	24
Environmental	20	12	16
Public interest	18	12	16
Teachers	17	14	16
Anti-abortion	9	17	13
Evangelical	2	14	7
Conservative	1	14	7
Women's rights	9	3	6
Liberal	10	3	6
Civil rights	7	2	5
Most important group			
Farm	16	20	18
Labor union	27	4	17
Business	10	24	16
Anti-abortion	7	13	10
Teachers	9	8	9
Environmental	10	5	8
Public interest	7	6	7
Evangelical	0	11	5
Liberal	6	1	4
Conservative	1	6	3
Women's rights	3	1	2
Civil rights	4	0	3

NOTE: Ns are same as in Table 2.2.

who belonged to various groups, and the proportions citing each group as most important to them politically. According to these responses, traditional economic interests still dominated each party. More Democrats belonged to labor unions, farm organizations, or business groups than to single-issue or ideological groups, though many had ties to environmental groups. They also cited unions, farm organizations, business associations, and environmental groups as their most important affiliations. A surprising finding was the small membership in women's groups and the apparent unimportance of such groups to Democratic members. Democrats in fact were as likely to associate with an anti-abortion as with a women's rights group and were twice as likely to cite an anti-abortion group as most important to their politics.

More Republican caucus attenders in our survey belonged to business and farm associations than to any other group. The third most prevalent affiliation was with anti-abortion groups, while membership in conservative and evangelical organizations tied with teachers' associations for fourth. Basically the same pattern held for groups identified as most important in the political lives of respondents: business, farm, anti-abortion, and evangelical were the top four.

Evidently, Republican caucus participants in 1988 were more involved in "new politics" groups than were their Democratic counterparts. The difference may result at least partly from Robertson's success in mobilizing conservative evangelicals. On balance, however, more Republicans were associated with traditional economic interest groups than with single-issue or ideological organizations. Still remaining is the question of how much these groups influenced behavior in the caucuses.

Partisanship and Political Activity

Interest groups are often viewed as competitive with political parties (Berry, 1984). As already noted, many of our respondents belonged to one or more interest groups. Indeed, the average Democrat in our survey reported 1.7 interest group memberships, the average Republican 1.6 affiliations. Even so, our Iowa caucus participants exhibited strong party loyalties. Table 2.4 discloses that about half of each party's caucus attenders claimed to be strong partisans, and that more than 90 percent of those voting in the 1984 general election had supported their party's nominee. Since only a quarter of all American adults consider themselves strong partisans, it is likely that the Iowa caucus participants were more partisan than the national electorate or even the voters of their own state.

Given these partisan differences, it was no surprise to find Republican caucus participants viewing President Reagan much more favorably than their Democratic counterparts. Yet it was also widely reported in the news media that Reagan was less popular among Republicans in Iowa than in New Hampshire, the Super Tuesday South, and most other places. Our survey lends credence to this view, for more than a third of our Republican respondents expressed either neutral or negative feelings about the president.[2] Iowa Democrats naturally were even more critical of the Reagan presidency.

In addition to exhibiting strong party loyalties, many caucus participants took an active part in party affairs. Nearly two-fifths of the Democrats and one-third of the Republicans in our survey said they worked for their party "year after year, win or lose," whether or not they liked the nominee or the issues. More than a quarter of each party's caucus attenders served on local party committees. Many also reported prior experience in local, gubernatorial, and congressional campaigns. Forty-nine percent of the Democrats, for example, had been involved in U.S. Senate campaigns, as had 37 percent of the Republicans.

Table 2.4 **Party Identification and Activism of Iowa Caucus Survey Respondents**

	Democrats (%)	Republicans (%)
Party Identification		
Strong Democrat	48	0
Weak Democrat	26	0
Independent Democrat	21	1
Independent	4	4
Independent Republican	1	17
Weak Republican	0	25
Strong Republican	0	53
Party activism		
Serve on local party committee	30	27
Regularly active in party affairs	38	32
Length of party involvement:		
Less than 5 years	35	46
5–10 years	14	17
10–20 years	19	15
More than 20 years	32	22
1984 presidential vote		
Mondale	84	5
Reagan	13	89
Evaluation of Reagan		
Positive	7	62
Neutral	17	24
Negative	73	12

NOTE: Ns are same as in Table 2.2.

Interested in the motivations of caucus attenders, we asked our respondents to rate the importance of four standard reasons for participating in their party's precinct caucuses: helping the party, representing a group or organization, supporting a particular candidate, and concern about the issues. Table 2.5 reports the results.

The most important reasons picked by Democrats and Republicans alike were concern about the issues and supporting a particular candidate. Still, substantial majorities on both sides also rated party support at least somewhat important, and this motivation clearly outweighed representation of some group or organization as a reason for attendance. Indeed, only 2 percent of all Democrats and Republicans listed interest-group representation as their most important reason for caucus attendance. Evidently the direct influence of interest groups on their members participating in the caucuses was quite limited.

Ideology and Issue Positions

Table 2.5 shows the importance of issues in the list of possible reasons for participating in either party's precinct caucuses. Sixty-four percent of the Democrats and 61 percent of the Republicans maintained that concern about issues was a "very important" reason for their attendance. Moreover, 45 percent of the Republicans and 39 percent of the Democrats cited issue concerns as the single most important reason for their caucus activity. These findings lend plausibility to contentions that ideological and single-issue activists now dominate the caucus-convention process. An allied fear is that candidates will stake out extreme positions to win over such activists while alienating moderates whose support is needed in the general election (Kirkpatrick, 1976; Polsby, 1983). A key assumption here is that the great majority of single-issue or ideological activists are also extremists.

Were the 1988 precinct caucuses dominated by single-issue and ideological zealots? The comparison of ideological and issue stands of caucus attenders in table 2.6 enables us to conclude that relatively few extremists participated in either party's caucuses. Moreover, each party's participants

Table 2.5 **Incentives for Respondent Participation in 1988 Iowa Caucuses**

	Democrats (%)	Republicans (%)	Combined (%)
Political Party			
Very important	40	29	35
Somewhat important	39	41	40
Not important	21	30	25
Candidate			
Very important	62	60	61
Somewhat important	31	33	32
Not important	6	7	7
Issues			
Very important	64	61	63
Somewhat important	29	31	30
Not important	7	8	7
Interest group			
Very important	15	12	13
Somewhat important	25	24	25
Not important	60	64	62
Most important incentive			
Candidate	41	43	42
Issues	39	45	42
Party	18	11	15
Interest group	2	2	2

NOTE: Ns are same as in Table 2.2.

held diverse opinions on a wide range of issues. In short, we found little evidence of a system overwhelmed by ideologues or single-issue fanatics.

Let us begin our consideration of table 2.6 by looking at the sharply different ideological views of Democratic and Republican caucus attenders. Liberals outnumbered conservatives by more than three-to-one among Democrats, while conservatives overwhelmed liberals among Republicans by more than sixteen-to-one. Arrayed on a seven-point scale measuring self-designated liberalism-conservatism, with 1 most liberal and 7 most conservative, the mean Democratic score was 3.2, the Republican average 5.4. Compared with party identifiers in the national electorate, Iowa caucus participants were more ideologically polarized (Stone, Abramowitz, and Rapoport, 1989).[3]

Table 2.6 **Ideology and Issue Stands of Iowa Caucus Survey Respondents**

	Democrats (%)	Republicans (%)	Combined (%)
Ideology			
Extreme liberal	5	0	3
Liberal	30	0	17
Moderate liberal	19	5	13
Moderate	25	12	19
Moderate conservative	10	26	17
Conservative	6	47	24
Extreme conservative	0	9	4
None, don't know	6	2	4
Favoring			
Abortion ban	40	53	46
More defense spending	20	51	34
Affirmative action	63	34	50
Balanced-budget amendment	61	81	70
Aid to contras	9	53	29
Aid to farmers	48	42	45
Higher tariffs	62	45	55
Strategic Defense Initiative	11	52	30
School prayer	48	64	55
Tougher environmental regulation	91	71	82
Most important issue			
Balanced-budget amendment	22	36	28
Abortion	13	24	18
Defense spending	15	11	13
Environment	15	4	10
Tariffs	11	4	8
Contra aid	6	6	6
Farm aid	6	4	5
Strategic Defense Initiative	5	4	4
School prayer	2	5	4
Affirmative action	4	2	3

NOTE: Ns are same as in Table 2.2.

Polarization is much less evident when we turn to issue stands. Here the main message of table 2.6 is that neither party was monolithic on issues. Despite their greater ideological consensus, Republican caucus attenders usually divided more on specific issues than did their Democratic counterparts. For all ten issues surveyed, the average Republican breakdown was 50 percent conservative and 35 percent liberal. Democrats averaged 61 percent liberal and 28 percent conservative on the same ten issues.

Party differences were most pronounced on aid to the Nicaraguan contras and the Strategic Defense Initiative (SDI), two highly publicized issues on which the Reagan administration had clashed repeatedly with congressional Democrats, including several seeking the 1988 Democratic nomination. Our respondents exhibited much less of a party gap on domestic issues like the balanced-budget amendment, federal aid to farmers, and restrictive trade policies. The importance of agriculture to Iowa's economy notwithstanding, only 5 percent of our respondents cited farm aid as the nation's most important issue. Indeed, as table 2.6 shows, caucus participants in both parties were about evenly divided on this question.

According to pluralities in both parties, reducing the federal deficit was the nation's number-one problem. Further evidence of this sentiment can be seen in the substantial majorities on both sides favoring a constitutional amendment prescribing balanced federal budgets. Next in importance for Democrats were defense spending and the environment; for Republicans, abortion was the second most important issue, defense spending a distant third.

Exposure to the Campaign

A stock criticism of the contemporary nominating system is that the news media provide inadequate information for choosing between the candidates, however voluminous the flow of "horse-race" news. This problem is seen as especially acute for voters and activists in the early primary and caucus states. In any event, it is important to assess the quantity and quality of information given Iowa caucus participants.

In addition to whatever the *New York Times* and other national media report, the local media also provide extensive coverage, especially in the final weeks leading up to the caucuses. We have already noted the high levels of political interest and activity on the part of our respondents, and so it was no surprise to find 68 percent of the Democrats and 54 percent of the Republicans claiming to have paid "a great deal" or "quite a bit" of attention to newspaper articles about the 1988 presidential race. Conversely, only 7 percent of the Democrats and 13 percent of the Republicans revealed having paid little or no attention to such sources. Nearly all of our respondents—92 percent of the Republicans and 84 percent of the Democrats—had been exposed to television or radio advertisements for at least one candidate seeking their party's presidential nomination.

In an era of thirty-second television spots, events contrived for precious seconds of television news coverage, and videotaped candidate pitches, Iowa is one of the few states where most candidates are still obliged to campaign the old-fashioned way. So many candidate visits to this sparsely populated state afford Iowans myriad opportunities to meet the presidential aspirants of one or both parties. Our survey results reflect the truly extraordinary exposure of caucus activists to the 1988 presidential campaigns: 71 percent of the Republicans and 67 percent of the Democrats recalled face-to-face or telephone contact with at least one presidential campaign in their own party. Thirty percent of the total sample reported having met at least one of their party's candidates; 14 percent of the Democrats and 10 percent of the Republicans claimed to have met two or more. Forty percent of the Democrats and 46 percent of the Republicans attended at least one campaign rally or meeting prior to the caucuses. Seventy-eight percent of the Republicans and 73 percent of the Democrats received presidential campaign literature in the mail. These figures are all the more impressive when put in national perspective. According to the national election studies conducted by Michigan's Center for Political Studies, campaign rallies are attended by less than 5 percent of the country's eligible voters. Probably less than 1 percent ever meet a presidential candidate in person.

For all their exposure to presidential campaigns, how much did the Iowans in our survey really know about the candidates? Our survey asked respondents to rate each candidate in four respects—record in government, moral character, television performance, and foreign-policy expertise. The particular instrument employed was a five-point scale, in which 1 indicated "outstanding" and 5 "poor." Table 2.7 reports mean ratings for the leading candidates of both parties.

In addition to perceptions of specific candidate strengths and failings, this table is also interesting for the similarity of Democratic and Republican perceptions. Thus Jackson scored high for television performance and low on government service in both parties. By the same token, Dukakis rated low on foreign-policy expertise but high on government service, Bush high on foreign-policy expertise but mediocre on television performance, and Robertson low on foreign-policy expertise and government service but somewhat better on character. True, substantial partisanship colored these ratings, but unmistakable signs of a common understanding were also evident, as in similarly favorable character evaluations of Simon and Gephardt.

Many students of American politics have decried the heavy reliance of

Table 2.7 **Average Ratings of Candidate Traits by Iowa Caucus Survey Respondents**

Candidate	Democrats	Republicans	Difference
Dukakis			
Record	2.2	2.7	−0.5
Character	2.2	2.6	−0.4
Television performance	2.4	2.7	−0.3
Foreign policy	2.8	3.4	−0.6
Overall	2.2	2.9	−0.7
Gephardt			
Record	2.5	3.1	−0.6
Character	2.4	2.7	−0.3
Television performance	2.5	3.0	−0.5
Foreign policy	2.8	3.4	−0.6
Overall	2.7	3.4	−0.7
Jackson			
Record	3.3	4.2	−0.9
Character	2.5	3.1	−0.6
Television performance	2.1	2.7	−0.6
Foreign policy	2.9	3.7	−0.8
Overall	2.7	3.7	−1.0
Simon			
Record	2.4	3.2	−0.8
Character	2.0	2.5	−0.5
Television performance	3.1	3.5	−0.4
Foreign policy	2.5	3.1	−0.6
Overall	2.6	3.3	−0.7
Bush			
Record	3.9	2.6	+1.3
Character	3.4	2.5	+0.9
Television performance	3.8	2.9	+0.9
Foreign policy	2.8	1.8	+1.0
Overall	3.9	2.4	+1.5
Dole			
Record	2.7	2.0	+0.7
Character	2.7	2.2	+0.5
Television performance	3.1	2.7	+0.4
Foreign policy	2.5	2.0	+0.5
Overall	2.8	2.2	+0.6
Kemp			
Record	3.5	2.7	+0.8
Character	2.9	2.4	+0.5
Television performance	3.5	2.9	+0.6
Foreign policy	3.4	2.8	+0.6
Overall	3.7	2.8	+0.5
Robertson			
Record	4.6	4.1	+0.5
Character	3.4	2.5	+0.9
Television performance	3.7	3.0	+0.7
Foreign policy	4.3	3.7	+0.6
Overall	4.4	3.4	+1.0

NOTE: Scale ranged from "outstanding" (1) to "poor" (5).

modern campaigns on very brief and often highly superficial television spots to inform voters of candidate accomplishments and policy stands. Such a meager diet, it is argued, starves voters of the substance needed for informed choice. The caucus paticipants in our study, however, appeared well informed about candidate backgrounds, personal characteristics, and public-service records. Of the four traits evaluated, moreover, our respondents ranked television performance as decidedly least important. Compared to the fraction of a percent citing television performance as most important, 58 percent of the Democrats and 48 percent of the Republicans put record of government service first on the list. Another 30 percent of the Democrats and 39 percent of the Republicans said moral character was most important. Being telegenic, in short, did not guarantee success in Iowa.

We also endeavored to discover how caucus participants viewed the liberalism-conservatism of each candidate relative to their own ideological location and that of the average American voter. To measure these perceptions we asked respondents to pinpoint these locations on a seven-point scale, in which 1 designated extreme liberalism and 7 extreme conservatism. Between 85 and 96 percent were able to locate the four major candidates of their own party on this scale, and between 70 and 90 percent also positioned the other party's four leading aspirants.

We also uncovered close agreement in respondent location of candidates. Between 69 and 85 percent of all Republicans agreed on the location of each GOP candidate within a three-point range, while between 69 and 81 percent of the Democrats performed the same feat for their candidates.

Table 2.8 reports average locations on this scale for the eight major candidates, the caucus participants, and the typical American voter. Immedi-

Table 2.8 Iowa Caucus Survey Respondents Locate Major Candidates, American Voters, and Themselves on Seven-Point Ideological Scale

Candidates	Mean perception of Democrats	Mean perception of Republicans	Absolute Difference
Dukakis	3.0	2.4	0.6
Gephardt	3.2	2.7	0.5
Jackson	2.0	1.7	0.3
Simon	3.0	2.7	0.3
Bush	5.9	5.2	0.7
Dole	5.3	5.3	0.0
Kemp	6.0	5.7	0.3
Robertson	6.2	6.0	0.2
American voter	4.2	4.1	0.1
Self	3.2	5.4	2.2

NOTE: Scale ranged from "extreme liberal" (1) to "extreme conservative" (7).

ately evident is a remarkable similarity in Democratic and Republican positioning of candidates. (The correlation between average candidate locations was .99.) Both groups viewed Jackson as the most liberal candidate and Robertson as the most conservative. They differed most on Bush, whom Democrats rated nearly as conservative as Kemp and Robertson, while Republicans located Bush slightly to Dole's left. The overall picture, however, is one of substantial agreement between, as well as within, parties. Still another noteworthy finding was the remarkable similarity in each party's perception of the typical American voter as just right of center. This is all the more interesting since Democrats and Republicans in our survey respectively placed themselves considerably to the left and right of typical voters. Evidently their own ideological biases did not prevent respondents from viewing the electorate realistically.

On average, Democratic and Republican respondents viewed the winners of their respective caucuses—Gephardt and Dole—as closest to their own ideological positions. Even so, every major candidate except Jackson was no more than 0.6 of a position from his party's average caucus participant. Jackson stood 1.2 points to the left of the average Democrat. Nearly all major candidates, then, were regarded as centrists within their respective parties. No doubt this perception diminished the importance of ideology as a determinant of candidate choice.

Candidate Choice

Perhaps the most important question that can be asked of caucus participants is why they supported one candidate over another. Table 2.9 discloses relationships between candidate choice and selected socioeconomic characteristics of Iowa caucus attenders. These results indicate that the group appeals of at least some candidates were successful.

Among the Democrats, Gephardt sought farmer and blue-collar support by advocating farm production controls and retaliatory tariffs on foreign imports. Table 2.9 shows him winning 34 percent of all Democratic farmers, more than twice the number supporting any other candidate except Simon. Dukakis, Gephardt, and Simon competed fiercely for the votes of elderly Iowans by speaking out on health care and Social Security. Between them, Dukakis, Gephardt, and Simon won the backing of 85 percent of all Democratic caucus attenders sixty and older. No candidate matched Jackson's passion and eloquence in asking for the support of small farmers and low-income Iowans. Jackson underscored the point by locating his state headquarters in tiny Greenfield. In the end, however, he won little backing from either group. In fact, the poorest Democrats in our survey supported him less than the most affluent did. Jackson also

Table 2.9 Original Candidate Preferences of Iowa Caucus Survey Respondents by Social Background Characteristics

| | Democratic Candidate Supported | | | | | | |
	Dukakis (%)	Gephardt (%)	Jackson (%)	Simon (%)	Other (%)	Total (%)	N
Age							
17–39	16	15	17	36	15	99	89
40–59	28	29	11	17	16	101	152
60 +	33	30	3	22	11	99	262
Sex							
Male	27	30	8	22	13	100	258
Female	30	24	8	24	14	100	244
Religion							
Protestant	25	32	7	24	12	100	259
Catholic	31	26	8	23	12	100	178
Other, none	33	12	16	21	18	100	58
Born again	24	31	11	23	11	100	92
Fundamentalist	32	33	4	17	14	100	80
Education							
High school	31	35	7	18	9	100	225
Some college	28	26	9	23	15	101	112
College degree	21	16	11	33	19	100	144
Occupation							
Farmer	16	34	12	25	12	99	32
Teacher	25	13	7	32	23	100	76
1987 income							
Under $20,000	32	30	7	17	15	101	152
$20,000–$39,999	26	30	9	23	12	100	198
$40,000 +	31	20	9	28	12	100	134

Republican Candidate Supported

	Bush (%)	Dole (%)	Kemp (%)	Robertson (%)	Other (%)	Total (%)	N
Age							
17–39	13	32	18	30	7	100	153
40–59	24	42	5	15	13	99	154
60 +	36	34	8	15	6	99	108
Sex							
Male	24	39	11	16	11	101	212
Female	22	33	11	27	7	100	202
Religion							
Protestant	22	39	9	21	8	99	326
Catholic	35	35	21	2	7	100	46
Born again	10	26	13	45	5	99	166
Fundamentalist	12	30	14	41	2	99	132
Education							
High school	25	34	10	26	5	100	109
Some college	13	36	13	28	11	101	113
College degree	29	38	10	12	11	100	178
Occupation							
Farmer	20	51	3	14	11	99	37
Teacher	27	46	10	15	2	100	50
1987 income							
Under $20,000	20	24	9	41	5	99	76
$20,000–$39,999	19	37	16	22	6	100	157
$40,000 +	28	42	8	11	11	100	161

NOTE: Percentages total horizontally; some rows do not total 100% due to rounding.

targeted young people, but it was Simon—the oldest Democrat in the race—who did best with this group. (Unfortunately for Simon, not many young people took part in the Democratic caucuses.) Simon's emphasis on aiding education also paid off with teachers.

On the Republican side, Dole tirelessly reiterated his empathy with Iowa farmers by touting his influence in the Senate Agriculture Committee, defending farm subsidies, and emphasizing his rural midwestern roots by assuring audiences "I'm one of you." Table 2.9 shows that 51 percent of farmers participating in the Republican caucuses backed Dole. No other group shown in the table supported any candidate by outright majority.

Robertson's efforts to mobilize conservative evangelicals and fundamentalists can also be traced in these data. Not only were Robertson supporters mostly "born again" and "fundamentalist," but, compared to other campaigns, disproportionately female, young, less educated, and less affluent as well.[4]

Some 1988 candidates also sought the backing of formally organized and rather traditional interests such as labor unions, business associations, and farm groups while others deliberately refrained from doing so for fear of being branded the captive of "special interests." Still others, like Kemp and Robertson, campaigned for the endorsements of single-issue and ideological groups.

Table 2.10 shows the relationship between candidate support and membership in the five largest organized groups. Looking first at the Democrats, Gephardt's support among union and farm association members was especially strong, easily surpassing that of Dukakis and Simon, his principal rivals in Iowa. Dukakis's touting of the "Massachusetts Miracle" probably paid dividends among business association members, more of whom supported the Bay State governor than any other Democrat. Dukakis's opposition to the Seabrook nuclear power facility in New Hampshire probably increased his appeal to environmental group members, but Simon was the favored candidate in this quarter. Simon also won over more members of teachers' unions than any other Democrat.

Turning to the Republicans, Dole's appeal to farmers has already been noted, and so his near majority among agricultural group members came as no surprise. Dole and Bush locked up most members of business and education associations while Robertson and Kemp did very well among members of anti-abortion groups. As expected, Robertson got more than half of all evangelical group members.

Though often important in influencing candidate choice, group memberships and demographic facts are not the only determinants of support. True, 51 percent of evangelical group members backed Robertson, but, on the other hand, 49 percent supported some other candidate. A fuller un-

Table 2.10 Original Candidate Preferences of Iowa Caucus Survey Respondents by Interest-Group Membership

Group	Democratic Candidate Supported						
	Dukakis (%)	Gephardt (%)	Jackson (%)	Simon (%)	Other (%)	Total (%)	N
Labor union	26	39	9	16	10	100	143
Agricultural	16	40	10	22	11	99	103
Business	30	24	8	26	12	100	91
Teachers	21	17	8	32	21	99	72
Environmental	22	11	14	33	20	100	80

Group	Republican Candidate Supported						
	Bush (%)	Dole (%)	Kemp (%)	Robertson (%)	Other (%)	Total (%)	N
Business	34	40	7	8	11	100	116
Agricultural	26	48	5	16	5	100	105
Evangelical	8	20	14	51	6	99	50
Anti-abortion	10	24	24	32	10	100	63
Teachers	29	41	8	16	6	100	53

NOTE: Percentages total horizontally; some rows do not total 100% due to rounding.

derstanding of the behavior of Iowa caucus participants requires us to look beyond group affiliations and socioeconomic characteristics to personal beliefs about politics.

We begin this undertaking in table 2.11, which shows how partisan intensity, feelings about Reagan, and ideology correlated with candidate choice in the caucuses of both parties. Let us start with the Democrats, who, for obvious reasons, were not expected to be greatly influenced by Reagan sentiment. Even so, in sharp contrast to every Republican candidate except Bush, all the Democratic contenders lauded President Reagan's Intermediate-range Nuclear Forces (INF) treaty. Gore went beyond this to praise the administration's Grenada invasion in 1983 and more recent policy in the Persian Gulf. As for ideology, even though Jackson was the only true outlier in the Democratic field, many a pundit has called attention to the party's deep divisions and continuing debate over policy directions.

Several Democratic findings shown in table 2.11 are worth noting. First, the relationship of partisan intensity to Dukakis and Gephardt support was the reverse observed for Jackson and Simon. The tally of strong Democrats backing either Dukakis or Gephardt exceeded the combined number for Jackson and Simon. Simon was a match or more for Gephardt and Dukakis among weaker Democrats, however, and beat them both in the struggle for independent Democrats and pure independents. Jackson did better with independents than with Democrats.

Dukakis was the only Democratic candidate whose support varied systematically with evaluations of Reagan's performance. Thirty-five percent of all Democrats giving the president a positive or neutral rating backed Dukakis, compared to 32 percent of those returning a verdict of "below average" and only 23 percent who felt Reagan's presidential performance had been "poor."

A definite pattern resulted from cross-tabulating Democratic candidate choice with ideological differences. The small number of far-left caucus participants went heavily for Jackson and Simon while Dukakis and Gephardt captured almost equally large percentages of the more numerous centrists and conservatives. Liberals divided almost evenly among Dukakis, Gephardt, and Simon. In sum, Simon had the broadest appeal of any Democratic candidate, Jackson the narrowest. Liberals and moderates, not the radical left, held the balance of power in the 1988 Iowa Democratic caucuses.

Turning to the Republican caucuses, it is well to remember that Vice-President Bush was the front-runner in every national poll and in almost every state except Kansas and Iowa. In New Hampshire and the South, Bush's tactic of trading heavily on his association with the president paid off in the polls. In economically depressed Iowa, however, Reagan's rela-

Table 2.11 Original Candidate Preferences of Iowa Caucus Survey Respondents by Political Attitudes

Democratic Candidate Supported

	Dukakis (%)	Gephardt (%)	Jackson (%)	Simon (%)	Other (%)	Total (%)	N
Partisan intensity							
Strong	31	30	8	18	13	100	242
Weak	25	27	8	27	13	100	133
Independent	25	23	10	27	15	100	128
Reagan view							
Positive, neutral	35	29	7	20	9	100	107
Below average	32	29	6	24	9	100	82
Poor	23	26	10	23	18	100	244
Ideology							
Far left	12	8	36	36	8	100	25
Liberal	27	25	10	24	14	100	246
Centrist, right	31	31	4	21	14	101	198

Republican Candidate Supported

	Bush (%)	Dole (%)	Kemp (%)	Robertson (%)	Other (%)	Total (%)	N
Partisan intensity							
Strong	26	37	11	16	10	100	223
Weak	23	38	6	25	9	101	101
Independent	13	35	14	30	8	100	89
Reagan view							
Outstanding	28	28	16	19	9	100	102
Above average	22	33	13	23	9	100	136
Average or below	16	47	6	17	14	100	140
Ideology							
Far right	22	8	22	46	3	101	37
Conservative	22	37	11	20	10	100	190
Centrist, left	31	54	2	5	8	100	73

NOTE: Percentages total horizontally; some rows do not total 100% due to rounding.

tively low popularity was generally thought to hurt Bush. Bush was the only Republican candidate to endorse the president's INF treaty unequivocally, though Dole eventually came around once polls revealed its popularity in Iowa. Du Pont, Haig, Kemp, and Robertson vigorously denounced the agreement in numerous forums, including televised debates, and both Haig and Robertson took the administration to task on other matters. All of Bush's rivals, moreover, made a great deal of the Iran-contra scandal, thus tarring Bush and Reagan with the same brush.

Looking first at the association between Republican identification and candidate support, the clearest configurations in this respect are for Bush and Robertson. Though he trailed Dole in every category, Bush's support dropped progressively with declining partisanship. Robertson's numbers ran just the opposite, as his support nearly doubled as loyalty to the GOP fell off. This was unsurprising given his success in mobilizing religious conservatives who previously had stayed out of politics.

In keeping with conventional wisdom, evaluations of Reagan's White House performance did make a difference in the pattern of Bush support. Of all the caucus participants who thought Reagan had done an "outstanding" job, 28 percent backed Bush. Among those taking a more restrained but still favorable view, 22 percent endorsed Bush. But, of those who rated presidential performance average or worse, only 16 percent turned out for Bush. We did not expect to find Dole running even with Bush among Reagan's biggest fans, but that is what happened. More in keeping with the conventional wisdom, Dole's support picked up as Reagan's favorability fell off.[5] Among Republican caucus participants expressing a neutral or negative view of presidential performance, Dole swamped Bush three-to-one. Kemp's claim of greatest fidelity to the Reagan revolution evidently enjoyed modest success, as can be inferred from his support by Reagan admirers.

Earlier we noted that Republican caucus participants perceived Bush and Dole as moderate or mildly conservative, and Kemp and Robertson as conservative or ultraconservative. Table 2.11 indicates that these perceptions figured in the choice of candidates. Eighty-five percent of the liberal and moderate Republicans in our survey backed either Dole or Bush, compared to 59 percent of the conservatives and 30 percent of the ultraconservatives. Conversely, Robertson captured very nearly half of the ultraconservatives, 20 percent of the conservatives, and only 5 percent of the moderates and liberals. Kemp's support followed the same pattern, though he trailed Robertson in every comparison.

One final point in table 2.11 bears mentioning. Dole's biggest advantage over Bush occurred among moderate and liberal Republicans, even though on average he was regarded as slightly more conservative than the vice-president. We attribute this seeming anomaly to the dissatisfaction of moderate-to-liberal Republicans with the Reagan administration and to their perception of Dole as the only acceptable alternative to Bush.

Campaign Effects

We turn now to the effects of different campaigns on our respondents. The low turnout for caucuses impels campaigns to make an all-out effort at pinpointing and mobilizing supporters. The oft-repeated formula for victory in the Iowa caucuses is "organize, organize, organize." Except for New Hampshire, no other state places a higher premium on personal contact with potential participants. The personal approach may also be essential in enlisting newcomers unaccustomed to the caucus-convention process. Earlier we provided basic information on campaign contact with respondents. Now it is time to observe the effects of such contact on candidate choice.

Table 2.12 explores the relationship between candidate support and different types of campaign contact. Some forms of contact clearly did correlate with the candidates supported, most notably meeting the candidate in person, attending at least one of his rallies, and receiving a call or visit from his campaign. Literature mailings and television advertisements had no consistent connection with candidate choice.

Looking first at the Democrats, without exception a candidate's supporters were more likely to have met him than any rival, and this was particularly true of Jackson people. By the same token, supporters were more likely to have attended their own candidate's rally than any other campaign's, and again the relationship was strongest for Jackson's group. Except for Jackson supporters, the other Democrats had been visited or telephoned by their own campaign more than any other. No such pattern emerged for mailed literature and television exposure. More Dukakis supporters saw spots for Gephardt, Jackson, or Simon than for Dukakis. Gephardt people were more likely to have viewed Jackson and Simon ads than Gephardt spots, and so on.

Basically the same associations observed for Democrats applied to Republicans as well. A candidate's supporters were more likely to have met him than any rival, to have attended his rally than that of any other campaign, and to have been visited or telephoned by his campaign than by that of another Republican candidate. This was especially true for Robertson's "invisible army," many of whom had to be personally contacted to compensate for their previous inexperience in politics. As for the Democrats, there was no discernible relationship between getting literature in the mail or exposure to television advertisements and candidate support. More Bush, Dole, and Kemp supporters viewed the spots of each rival cam-

Table 2.12 Respondent Contact with Iowa Campaigns by Candidate Preference

	Democratic Candidate Supported				
	Dukakis (%) (N = 151)	Gephardt (%) (N = 146)	Jackson (%) (N = 43)	Simon (%) (N = 124)	All Democrats (%) (N = 541)
Met candidate					
Dukakis	17	8	5	4	10
Gephardt	12	26	0	10	15
Jackson	4	6	22	7	8
Simon	10	10	2	18	13
Attended rally					
Dukakis	26	11	5	11	15
Gephardt	13	30	8	19	20
Jackson	14	9	52	16	17
Simon	12	12	8	27	17
Called or visited					
Dukakis	37	35	40	28	33
Gephardt	28	59	52	44	44
Jackson	13	16	45	14	18
Simon	29	39	58	64	43
Received mailing					
Dukakis	37	26	38	36	34
Gephardt	42	52	55	56	50
Jackson	19	23	45	26	30
Simon	41	46	62	56	49
Saw ads					
Dukakis	38	40	45	46	41
Gephardt	56	56	68	68	60
Jackson	64	76	65	78	72
Simon	55	68	68	68	64

	Republican Candidate Supported				
	Bush (%) (N = 98)	Dole (%) (N = 154)	Kemp (%) (N = 47)	Robertson (%) (N = 90)	All Republicans (%) (N = 428)
Met candidate					
Bush	28	11	5	6	14
Dole	9	21	9	2	13
Kemp	8	5	21	1	6
Robertson	2	5	5	29	9
Attended rally					
Bush	46	26	9	8	26
Dole	12	32	12	11	22
Kemp	3	8	21	4	8
Robertson	6	7	16	42	15
Called or visited					
Bush	55	37	28	13	35
Dole	44	54	23	19	41
Kemp	15	15	46	12	18
Robertson	16	14	28	67	28
Received mailing					
Bush	59	58	54	36	54
Dole	58	57	56	40	54
Kemp	35	39	54	31	38
Robertson	35	29	42	68	41
Saw ads					
Bush	58	63	74	82	67
Dole	67	61	79	77	68
Kemp	74	72	72	73	78
Robertson	74	77	74	76	76

paign than saw their own. However powerful a particular ad may be, campaigns in Iowa are ill advised to rely mostly or entirely on television advertising.

Conclusion

Neither winner of the Iowa caucuses went on to claim his party's presidential nomination in 1988. The prize in both parties went to the man who finished third in Iowa and won New Hampshire. So much for the conventional wisdom that Iowa dictates New Hampshire's outcome.

Does the 1988 experience "prove" that Iowa no longer matters, or that this traditional starting point in each party's nominating race can be bypassed with impunity? We think not.

A careful comparison of New Hampshire returns and poll standings reveals an undeniable "Iowa bump" for both Gephardt and Dole. Indeed, at one point during the long week between Iowa and New Hampshire, Dole actually led Bush in several New Hampshire polls (John, 1989). Having barely beaten Simon in Iowa, Gephardt moved past him in the New Hampshire polls to second place. Even so, both Dukakis and Bush put their overwhelming advantages in New Hampshire to good use and checked the Iowa momentum of their respective rivals. Dukakis was well known to New Hampshire Democrats as the governor of a neighboring state, from which many of them had emigrated, and for his stand against the Seabrook nuclear power facility. Mostly dependent on Boston media for news of the world, New Hampshire residents were exposed to a ceaseless flow of information about the Dukakis administration. Dukakis was also the best heeled Democrat and commanded one of the strongest campaign organizations in the state. Adding to his advantage in the fateful week between Iowa and New Hampshire was Gephardt's decision to fight with Simon rather than focus on Dukakis. No rival came close to matching Bush's New Hampshire organization, much of it composed of supporters who had worked in his 1980 campaign. Bush was popular in New Hampshire, in part because Reagan was popular, while Dole's campaign in the state was disorganized. Bush was also assisted by Governor John Sununu in the final days of New Hampshire campaigning.

Though both failed in New Hampshire, Gephardt and Dole undeniably got many more votes than would have been the case had they not won Iowa. Indeed, anything less than victory in Iowa probably would have finished either of them. The real lessons of 1988 are that Iowa's impact may last no longer than eight days, and that candidates must win both Iowa and New Hampshire if they hope to knock their most serious rivals out of the race. Moreover, as Buell and Davis point out in chapter 1, momentum is more easily sustained under Republican than Democratic rules. News media coverage also counts for a great deal, though its spin is often hard to predict. In 1988, for example, media preoccupation with Robertson's second-place finish in Iowa surely diminished Gephardt's New Hampshire momentum. Whatever the bent of national media coverage, so long as Iowa remains first, it will get the inordinate attention that few candidates can resist. At this writing, likely 1992 candidates have already trekked to Des Moines, and so another cycle with Iowa first has begun.

Of course, another cycle also means more "Iowa-bashing," as critics recite the standard litany—too small, white, and elderly to limit the choices of more representative people voting later in much bigger states. In our view this indictment ignores the compensating importance of "up close and personal" screening of candidates. Starting the race in California, Ohio, or some other mega-state would limit the choice to television images, and the initial cut would not be made mostly by well-informed and committed party activists, an astonishing number of whom had met one or more candidates and attended at least one campaign rally.

Contrary to the conventional wisdom that extremists dominate the Iowa caucuses, we found relatively few single-issue zealots and fringe ideologues. Since Iowa gained priority in 1972, moreover, no winner of the caucuses has been an extremist. Edmund Muskie in 1972, Jimmy Carter in 1976 and 1980, Gerald Ford in 1976, George Bush in 1980, Walter Mondale in 1984, Richard Gephardt and Robert Dole in 1988 all succeeded by building strong organizations, contacting activists, addressing major issues, and withstanding close personal scrutiny. Only in New Hampshire are candidates subjected to the same kind of scrutiny before tarmac-and-television campaigning sets in. "Up close and personal," in our view, is a better beginning than remote and impersonal.

Notes

1. Altogether, fifty-eight Democratic delegates were at stake in Iowa in 1988, amounting to 1.4 percent of the national delegate total at the Atlanta nominating convention; the Iowa Republican delegation numbered thirty-seven, or 1.6 percent of all GOP delegates at the New Orleans convention (Cook, 1987: 10).
2. This finding is consistent with other survey evidence of less enthusiasm for Reagan among Republicans in Iowa than in other states. According to CBS/*New York Times* exit polls, for example, 67 percent of all Republican participants in the Iowa precinct caucuses approved of Reagan's performance and 27 percent disapproved. Eight days later, when the same question was asked of voters in New Hampshire's Republican primary, 78 percent approved and 19 percent disapproved. Similarly, 82 percent of all voters in Republican primaries on Super Tuesday gave Reagan a favorable rating while 14 percent dis-

approved. The authors are indebted to the *New York Times* for releasing these data in mailings to selected "poll watchers."

3. According to the 1984 National Election Study conducted by the University of Michigan's Center for Political Studies, the average Democratic party identifier scored 3.7 on a comparable seven-point scale of liberalism-conservatism while the average Republican scored 4.9. Despite the greater distance between ideological locations of 1988 Iowa caucus participants, only 7 percent of all our respondents located themselves at either extreme of the scale. Only 5 percent of the Democrats in our survey took scale positions indicating ultraliberalism, and merely 9 percent of the Republicans chose archconservatism.

4. Our description of Robertson activists also closely matches the findings of the CBS/*New York Times* exit poll of Iowans discussed in note 2, above. According to this survey, 47 percent of all Republican caucus attenders were women, compared to 54 percent of Robertson's supporters. Twenty-eight percent of all Iowans participating in the GOP caucuses were sixty or older, compared to 18 percent of Robertson's supporters. Forty percent of the entire Republican sample reported 1987 family incomes of $35,000 or more, compared to only 25 percent of the Robertson group. Thirty-four percent of the full GOP sample did not get beyond high school; for Robertson supporters this figure was 48 percent.

5. According to the CBS/*New York Times* poll, 83 percent of Bush's supporters, compared to only 56 percent of Dole's, approved of Reagan's performance. As in table 2.11, Dole support was inversely associated with Reagan popularity.

References

Balzar, John. 1988. "Iowa Caucuses: Study in Party Contrasts." *Los Angeles Times* (January 18): 20.

Berry, Jeffrey M. 1984. *The Interest Group Society.* Boston: Little, Brown.

Cook, Rhodes. 1987. *Race for the Presidency: Winning the 1988 Nomination.* Washington, D.C.: Congressional Quarterly.

Hutter, James L., and Steven E. Schier. 1984. "Representativeness: From Caucus to Convention in Iowa." *American Politics Quarterly* 12 (October): 431–48.

John, Kenneth E. 1989. "The Polls—A Report: 1980–1988 New Hampshire Presidential Primary Polls." *Public Opinion Quarterly* 53 (Winter): 590–605.

Keeter, Scott, and Cliff Zukin. 1983. *Uninformed Choice: The Failure of the New Presidential Nominating System.* New York: Praeger.

Kirkpatrick, Jeane. 1976. *The New Presidential Elite.* New York: Russell Sage.

Lichter, S. Robert, Daniel Amundson, and Richard Noyes. 1988. *The Video Campaign: Network Coverage of the 1988 Primaries.* Washington, D.C.: American Enterprise Institute and Center for Media and Public Affairs.

Oliphant, Thomas. 1988. "Why Iowa?" *Boston Sunday Globe Magazine* (February 7): 14.

Orren, Gary R., and Nelson W. Polsby, eds. 1987. *Media and Momentum: The New Hampshire Primary and Nomination Politics.* Chatham, N.J.: Chatham House.

Polsby, Nelson W. 1983. *Consequences of Party Reform*. New York: Oxford University Press.

Schier, Steven E. 1980. *The Rules of the Game: Democratic National Convention Delegate Selection in Iowa and Wisconsin*. Washington, D.C.: University Press of America.

Squire, Peverill. 1989. "Iowa and the Nomination Process." In *The Iowa Caucuses and the Presidential Nominating Process*, ed. Peverill Squire. Boulder, Colo.: Westview Press.

Stone, Walter J., Alan I. Abramowitz, and Ronald B. Rapoport. 1989. "How Representative Are the Iowa Caucuses?" In *The Iowa Caucuses and the Presidential Nominating Process*, ed. Peverill Squire. Boulder, Colo.: Westview Press.

Winebrenner, Hugh. 1987. *The Iowa Precinct Caucuses: The Making of a Media Event*. Ames: Iowa State University Press.

3. The Best-Laid Plans . . . : Super Tuesday 1988

Barbara Norrander

For all intents and purposes, the 1988 Republican race was decided on March 8—"Super Tuesday"—when Vice-President George Bush handily defeated Senator Robert Dole, Pat Robertson, and Congressman Jack Kemp in sixteen of sixteen primaries. Bush's margin over Dole in eleven of these primaries was better than two to one. Though Dole stayed in the race another five weeks, he never again mounted a serious challenge. Robertson's only victory on Super Tuesday came in the Washington State caucuses. His subsequently feeble effort ended May 16. Kemp withdrew two days after Super Tuesday, about the time an Associated Press report credited Bush with 704 of the 1,139 delegates needed for nomination (Cook, 1989: 43).

Super Tuesday also profoundly altered the Democratic race by narrowing the field to Governor Michael Dukakis of Massachusetts, Jesse Jackson, and Senator Albert Gore, Jr., of Tennessee. The Democrats chose more than one quarter of all their pledged delegates on this momentous day. Having carried only his native Missouri on March 8, Congressman Richard Gephardt ceased to be a serious contender. Disappointed in Iowa, New Hampshire, South Dakota, and Minnesota, Senator Paul Simon decided to skip Super Tuesday altogether and concentrate on the Illinois primary. Gary Hart pulled out two days after Super Tuesday.

The creation of this mega-event can chiefly be credited to the dissatisfaction of southern moderates with most Democratic nominees since 1968. Only one Democrat had captured the White House since 1964, and he had been a moderate southerner. No Democrat since Lyndon Johnson had won more white votes than his Republican opponent, and the proportional gap between the total Democratic vote and that cast by southern whites had been 17 percent in 1968, 18 percent in 1972, and 13 percent in 1984 (Wolfinger, 1985: 285).

Many southern Democrats blamed this state of affairs on the reformed presidential nominating system, particularly its emphasis on Iowa and New Hampshire, where liberal activists supposedly forced candidates into extreme stands. They hoped a southern regional primary would diminish these early events and balance the party's choice of nominees. Some southern Democrats wanted to build a springboard for Senator Sam Nunn of Georgia, often mentioned as a candidate but given little chance in Iowa and New Hampshire. It was thought Nunn could win back the "Reagan Democrats" who had abandoned Jimmy Carter in 1980 and spurned Walter Mondale in 1984. Nunn declined to run, however, thus making Gore the candidate of white southerners by default.

Holding an entire region's primaries on the same day was hardly a new idea. Numerous regional primary bills had been introduced in Congress during the 1970s, and additional cluster-primary schemes had issued from academics. Most proposed holding state primaries on one of several established dates, with the specific date determined by state choice or regional assignment (Davis, 1983: 229–35).

All the congressional efforts notwithstanding, regional primaries to date have resulted from the separate actions of different states. Though nothing came of a 1976 push for a western regional primary (Doyle, 1975), Alabama, Florida, and Georgia agreed on a common date in 1980 at the urging of the Carter White House (Stanley and Hadley, 1987). Four years later, the first Super Tuesday was born, when these three southern states voted with Massachusetts, Rhode Island, and four states holding caucuses on the second Tuesday in March.

Super Tuesday 1988 promised to be even bigger. This time every southern and border state except South Carolina and West Virginia had agreed to hold a presidential primary on March 8. Much of the credit for this feat can be given to the Southern Legislative Conference's task force on primaries and caucuses. The task force took the lead in persuading states already holding primaries to reschedule them for Super Tuesday and in convincing state and party officials in Missouri, Oklahoma, and Virginia to replace their caucuses with primaries. The task force also called attention to these changes by issuing press releases.

Southern Republicans were also drawn into Super Tuesday, usually by state laws requiring both parties to hold their primaries on the same day. Many GOP leaders quickly perceived that a regional primary might backfire on the Democrats, especially if it propelled Jackson into the lead. They also hoped white Democrats would take advantage of open primary rules in eight states and cross over to vote in Republican primaries.[1]

In sum, southern Democrats and Republicans alike had high hopes for Super Tuesday. As we shall see, neither side got entirely what it wanted.

Finally, though most attention focused on the South, Super Tuesday also included primaries in Massachusetts and Rhode Island, the Washington State caucuses, and Democratic caucuses in Hawaii, Idaho, Nevada, and American Samoa.

Participation in Super Tuesday Primaries

Obviously what happened on Super Tuesday depended critically on who voted. Although popular participation in the nominating process has greatly increased since 1968, turnout for presidential primaries is still well below the rate for general elections. Turnout in all 1988 presidential primaries averaged 24.4 percent of the population eighteen years and older, about half the general election figure.

This smaller turnout for presidential primaries raises questions of representativeness, particularly if the "selectorate" consists largely of ideologues and issue purists who force candidates into positions bound to fail in November (Ladd, 1978; Lengle, 1981; Polsby, 1983). Recent research, however, has found more similarities between voters and nonvoters in primaries than this argument allows, and, by the same token, fewer differences between primary and general election voters than commonly supposed (Geer, 1988; Norrander, 1989). Still, who votes in this smaller primary electorate is obviously critical to the outcome.

Table 3.1 reports primary turnout for Super Tuesday 1988, and, for the sake of comparison, turnout in the same states holding 1980 primaries.[2] (Owing to lack of Reagan opposition in 1984, 1980 is a more valid comparison.) Despite falloffs in Maryland, Florida, and North Carolina, overall turnout in the South and border states increased 4 percent in Democratic primaries and 5 percent in Republican primaries. Though seemingly small, these gains added three million voters to the rolls. Turnout also rose slightly in Rhode Island but fell ten points in each party's Massachusetts primary.

In states holding primaries before and after Super Tuesday, turnout for the Democrats rose less than 3 percent and fell 8 percent for the Republicans. (Since Republican voting in 1988 was down before — as well as after — Super Tuesday, this decline cannot be fully explained by the collapse of Bush's opposition after March 8.) Finally, despite the 1988 increases, turnout in the Super Tuesday South still lagged behind that of other regions.

Who Defected to Whom?

Did southern Democrats cross over in droves to vote in Republican primaries? Based on the American National Election Study (NES) of Super Tuesday voters, the answer, shown in table 3.2, clearly is no. Looking only

Table 3.1 Presidential Primary Turnout in Super Tuesday States, 1980 and 1988

	Democratic			Republican		
	1980 (%)	1988 (%)	Change (%)	1980 (%)	1988 (%)	Change (%)
Border states						
Kentucky	15	19	+4	10	12	+2
Maryland	25	23	-2	15	17	+2
Missouri	(caucus)	26		(caucus)	23	
Oklahoma	(caucus)	28		(caucus)	21	
Peripheral South						
Arkansas	41	44	+3	(caucus)	11	
Florida	26	24	-2	19	21	+2
North Carolina	27	24	-3	11	14	+3
Tennessee	17	29	+12	12	16	+4
Texas	22	25	+3	15	20	+5
Virginia	(caucus)	15		(caucus)	12	
Deep South						
Alabama	12	21	+9	32	21	-11
Georgia	14	20	+6	19	28	+9
Louisiana	17	27	+10	6	17	+11
Mississippi	(caucus)	29		5	28	+23
Average southern/ border turnout	21	25	+4	14	19	+5
New England						
Massachusetts	33	23	-10	28	18	-10
Rhode Island	8	11	+3	2	5	+3

NOTE: Turnout figures calculated by the author using method described in note 2.

Table 3.2 **Party Identification of Border-State and Southern Primary Voters, Super Tuesday 1988**

	Party Identification		
	Democrat (%)	Independent (%)	Republican (%)
Voted in Democratic primary	54	31	13
Voted in Republican primary	2	14	36
Did not vote	44	56	51
Totals	100	101	100
Number in sample	585	59	609
Chi square		338.98	
Significance		<.001	

SOURCE: American National Election Study of the 1988 Presidential Nominating Process, Center for Political Studies, Institute for Social Research, University of Michigan, November 1988, hereafter cited as 1988 American National Election Study.

NOTE: Independent leaners classified as Democrats or Republicans; "Independent" column does not total 100% due to rounding.

at southern and border-state respondents, the table actually reveals a net gain for the Democrats since only 2 percent of their identifiers voted in Republican primaries while 13 percent of the Republicans voted in Democratic primaries. Another noteworthy finding was higher Democratic than Republican turnout. In short, Super Tuesday prompted no Democratic exodus to the GOP.

Still, none of the above should be interpreted as a denial of recent Republican gains in the South (Wolfinger, 1985; Black and Black, 1987). Voter registration probably has not kept up with this realignment, so many Republican converts may have remained on the Democratic rolls out of habit. Closed-primary rules in some states no doubt prevented the most recent Republicans from changing parties. In any event, table 3.3 shows that 20 percent of the Republicans in the South's closed-primary states were registered as Democrats while only 2 percent of Democratic identifiers were registered Republicans.

So far as open primaries are concerned, however, no great Democratic defection occurred. Table 3.4 shows few Democrats voting in Republican primaries of any kind, open or closed, while 12 percent of the Republican identifiers cast ballots in open Democratic primaries. What explains the attraction of open Democratic primaries to Republicans?

According to Stanley and Hadley (1989), many Republicans voted in open Democratic primaries on Super Tuesday because they wanted to influence outcomes in nonpresidential races going on at the same time. In Arkansas, Missouri, Mississippi, and in one of Louisiana's congressional districts, the presidential primary coincided with primaries for state offices and the U.S.

Table 3.3 **Registered Voters in Border and Southern States with Closed Primaries, by Party Identification**

	Party Identification	
Party Registration	Democrat (%)	Republican (%)
Democrat	94	20
Republican	2	70
Independent	4	10
Totals	100	100
Number in sample	241	262
Chi square	269.89	
Significance	< .001	

SOURCE: 1988 American National Election Study.

Table 3.4 **Effect of Open Primaries on Participation in Border-State and Southern Primaries**

	Democrats		Republicans	
	Open (%)	Closed (%)	Open (%)	Closed (%)
Voted in Democratic primary	55	52	12	13
Voted in Republican primary	3	1	37	35
Did not vote	42	47	51	52
Totals	100	100	100	100
Number in sample	340	245	340	269
Chi square	4.10		.34	
Significance	NS		NS	

SOURCE: 1988 American National Election Study.
NOTE: NS = not significant.

Table 3.5 **Effect of Nonpresidential Races on Republican Voting in Open and Closed Primaries in Border and Southern States**

	Open Primary		Closed Primary	
	Nonpresidential Race?		Nonpresidential Race?	
	No (%)	Yes (%)	No (%)	Yes (%)
Voted in Democratic primary	5	22	13	16
Voted in Republican primary	39	35	38	24
Did not vote	56	44	49	60
Totals	100	101	100	100
Number in sample	191	149	211	58
Chi square	20.75		3.80	
Significance	< .001		NS	

SOURCE: 1988 American National Election Study.
NOTE: Second column does not total 100% due to rounding.

Table 3.6 Ideology and Participation in Border-State and Southern Primaries

	Ideology		
	Liberal (%)	Moderate (%)	Conservative (%)
Voted in Democratic primary	45	38	26
Voted in Republican primary	9	15	26
Did not vote	47	48	49
Totals	101	101	101
Number in sample	303	207	710
Chi square		60.00	
Significance		<.001	

SOURCE: 1988 American National Election Study.
NOTE: Columns do not total 100% due to rounding.

House. Table 3.5 strongly supports this thesis. When an open-primary state had nonpresidential races on the ballot, 22 percent of the Republicans voted in the Democratic contest. When there was no other race, only 5 percent of the Republicans voted in Democratic primaries. Evidently some Republicans were more interested in state and congressional outcomes than in the struggle for their party's presidential nomination.

Ideology and Primary Voting

Party leaders on both sides also hoped to attract most white conservatives and moderates to their respective primaries. Table 3.6 reveals that conservatives divided evenly in their choice of primaries while moderates preferred Democratic primaries by more than two to one. Most liberals voted in Democratic primaries as well. The upshot was an ideologically diverse Democratic electorate and a smaller and mostly conservative Republican coalition.

Race and Primary Voting

As previously noted, a central reason behind the creation of Super Tuesday was to keep moderate and conservative whites in the Democratic party. Table 3.7 shows that 10 percent more whites voted in the Democratic than the Republican primaries, a success of sorts. No one doubted that blacks would shun Republican primaries, but how many would actually vote in Democratic contests remained to be seen. Table 3.7 shows little difference in white and black turnout in border-state and southern primaries on Super Tuesday.

Table 3.7 **Race and Participation in Border-State and Southern Primaries**

	Race	
	Blacks (%)	Whites (%)
Voted in Democratic primary	54	31
Voted in Republican primary	0	21
Did not vote	47	48
Totals	101	100
Number in sample	127	1,113
Chi square	45.52	
Significance	<.001	

SOURCE: 1988 American National Election Study.
NOTE: First column does not total 100% due to rounding.

Religion and Primary Choice

The rise of a new religious right and Robertson's candidacy point up the likely importance of religious influences on primary voting, especially in the Bible Belt. Well known to millions as a religious broadcaster and television faith healer, Robertson hoped to mobilize an "invisible army" of devout, socially conservative, previously apolitical or alienated followers who would overwhelm more traditional Republican voters at the polls. With so many people answering to this description in the South, Robertson looked to Super Tuesday for a major breakthrough.

Table 3.8 reveals that his premise was faulty. If religious conservatives were to aid Robertson, they first had to turn out and vote in Republican primaries. Even though nearly half the southern and border-state respondents in the NES study called themselves "born-again" Christians, they were no more inclined to vote in Republican primaries than were persons of different religious views. Since one of every six born-again Christians was black, and blacks did not take part in Republican primaries, race might be suspected of suppressing a strong relationship. Controlling on race, however, revealed only that born-again whites were no more likely than other whites to vote in Republican primaries. If anything, they were slightly more likely to vote in Democratic primaries.

Another indicator of religious conservatism is acceptance of the Bible as God's literal word. Table 3.8 reveals how biblical views related to participation in the primaries. Among those rejecting divine and literal interpretations, 45 percent voted in Democratic primaries while only 14 percent cast Republican ballots. On the other hand, Democrats also enjoyed a big advantage among Biblical literalists. Most southern and border-state respondents occupied middle ground on Biblical interpretation, and they

Table 3.8 Religion and Participation in Border-State and Southern Primaries

	Born Again?	
	Yes (%)	No (%)
Voted in Democratic primary	34	30
Voted in Republican primary	20	20
Did not vote	47	50
Totals	101	100
Number in sample	590	550
Chi square	1.76	
Significance	NS	

	Interpretation of Bible		
	Literally God's Word (%)	God's Word, but Not Literally (%)	Written by Men (%)
Voted in Democratic primary	32	31	45
Voted in Republican primary	18	21	14
Did not vote	50	49	42
Total	100	101	101
Number in sample	450	687	101
Chi square		8.80	
Significance		NS	

SOURCE: 1988 American National Election Study.
NOTE: Some columns do not total 100% due to rounding.

too were somewhat more likely to vote in Democratic than Republican primaries. With nonvoters included, these group differences were not statistically significant.[3] Thus a key premise of Roberston's strategy went unfulfilled: born-again Christians and Biblical literalists did not choose Republican over Democratic primaries.

To summarize the findings presented so far, several leading expectations about Super Tuesday turnout did not pan out. Rather than Democrats defecting to Republican primaries, most crossover voting went in the opposite direction. Some Republicans voted in Democratic primaries because they had not changed their registration in time, others to influence congressional and statewide nominations. In any event, the rather diverse electorate voting in Democratic primaries on Super Tuesday included whites of all political persuasions, blacks, persons of varying religious views, and one of every six Republicans.

Voting Choice

The Democratic version of Super Tuesday ended in a three-way tie among Jackson, Dukakis, and Gore. A serious contender up to this point, Gephardt carried only Missouri and was instantly written off by the national news media. Neither Hart nor Simon won a single delegate in any Super Tuesday state. Looking first at southern and border-state primaries, Jackson won 27 percent of the preference vote, Gore 27 percent, Dukakis 24 percent, and Gephardt 13 percent. The yield in delegates was 330 for Jackson, 318 for Gore, 259 for Dukakis, and 94 for Gephardt. In New England, Dukakis received 59 percent of the primary vote and picked up another 97 delegates while Jackson's 18 percent of the preference vote netted him an additional 23 delegates. Neither Gore nor Gephardt won any delegates at all in New England from their respective 5 and 10 percentages of the preference vote. Preliminary reports from western caucus states awarded 26 delegates to Dukakis, 15 to Jackson, 7 to Gore, and 1 to Gephardt (*Congressional Quarterly Weekly Report*, 1988: 638).

Table 3.9 attests to Super Tuesday's vastness by identifying the regions where each major candidate ran best. Jackson led the pack in the Deep

Table 3.9 **The Democratic Vote on Super Tuesday 1988**

	Dukakis (%)	Gephardt (%)	Gore (%)	Jackson (%)
Border States				
Kentucky	19	9	**46**	16
Maryland	**46**	8	9	29
Missouri	12	**58**	3	20
Oklahoma	17	21	**41**	13
Peripheral South				
Arkansas	19	12	**37**	17
Florida	**41**	14	13	20
North Carolina	20	6	**35**	33
Tennessee	3	2	**72**	21
Texas	**32**	14	20	25
Virginia	22	5	23	**45**
Deep South				
Alabama	8	8	37	**44**
Georgia	16	7	32	**40**
Louisiana	15	11	28	**35**
Mississippi	9	6	34	**44**
New England				
Massachusetts	**59**	10	5	19
Rhode Island	**70**	4	4	16
Western caucuses				
Hawaii	**55**	2	1	35
Idaho	**38**	1	8	22
Nevada	26	2	**30**	23
Washington State	**44**	1	2	35
American Samoa	**39**	22	0	6

SOURCE: *Congressional Quarterly Weekly Report* 46 (March 12, 1988): 638.
NOTE: Boldface type indicates winning candidate.

South, with its large black population, while Gore was most formidable in the peripheral South and border states. Dukakis dominated in Florida, Maryland, Texas, Massachusetts, Rhode Island, and every western caucus state except Nevada.

No comparable diversity characterized the Republican outcome, for, as already noted, Bush won everywhere except in the Washington State caucuses. In the South and border states, he received 56 percent of the primary preference vote and captured 566 delegates. In New England he won 59 percent of the vote and 45 delegates. Dole trailed far behind, winning only 24 percent of the preference vote and 81 delegates in southern and border-state primaries, 26 percent of the vote and 19 delegates in New England. His best showings were in Missouri, North Carolina, and Oklahoma. (Missouri and Oklahoma bordered his native Kansas, and his wife had been born in North Carolina.) Robertson finished third in every Super Tuesday primary except in Texas and Louisiana, winning only 9 delegates (*Congressional Quarterly Weekly Report*, 1988: 639). Table 3.10 reports the preference vote by state.

Regional variation, however, was hardly the whole story. Earlier refer-

Table 3.10 **The Republican Vote on Super Tuesday 1988**

	Bush (%)	Dole (%)	Robertson (%)
Border states			
Kentucky	**59**	23	11
Maryland	**54**	32	6
Missouri	**42**	41	11
Oklahoma	**37**	35	21
Peripheral South			
Arkansas	**47**	26	19
Florida	**62**	21	11
North Carolina	**45**	40	10
Tennessee	**60**	22	13
Texas	**64**	14	15
Virginia	**53**	26	14
Deep South			
Alabama	**64**	16	14
Georgia	**54**	24	16
Louisiana	**58**	18	18
Mississippi	**66**	17	13
New England			
Massachusetts	**59**	26	5
Rhode Island	**65**	23	6
Western caucuses			
Washington State	24	26	**39**

SOURCE: *Congressional Quarterly Weekly Report* 46 (March 12, 1988): 639.
NOTE: Boldface type indicates winning candidate.

ence was made to substantial Republican voting in Democratic primaries. If Republican identifiers had not voted in open Democratic primaries, or had not passed for registered Democrats in the closed primaries, Gore would have done much worse on Super Tuesday. (Half of all the Republicans voting in Democratic primaries backed him.) Dukakis and Gephardt would also have suffered since each got about the same percentage of Republican as Democratic votes. Jackson, however, would have looked even stronger since his support came mostly from black Democrats, 94 percent of whom voted for him. These findings appear in table 3.11.

Ideological Variations

Ideology mattered more in the Democratic than in the Republican primaries, as is shown in table 3.12. Gore led among conservatives, Dukakis among liberals, and the two tied for pluralities of the moderate vote. Jackson did best with liberals and worst with conservatives, but he still won about as many conservative votes as Gephardt. This ideological diversity helped muddy the Democratic results.

Only faintly ideological relationships turned up in the Republican data. Even though Robertson got most of his votes from conservatives, three times as many conservatives voted for Bush, who also won the lion's share of moderate and liberal Republican votes.

Religion and the Vote

As previously noted, Robertson counted on millions of religious conservatives to make his campaign viable, and, given the religious bent of so many Southern whites, he openly acknowledged that South Carolina and

Table 3.11 **Party Identification and Vote Choice in Border-State and Southern Primaries**

	Party Identification		
	Democrat (%)	Independent (%)	Republican (%)
Dukakis	34	27	33
Gephardt	12	20	9
Gore	26	33	50
Jackson	28	20	8
Totals	100	100	100
Number in sample	265	15	64
Chi square		19.89	
Significance		< .01	

SOURCE: 1988 American National Election Study.

Table 3.12 Ideology and Vote Choice in Border-State and Southern Primaries

	Democrats		
	Liberal (%)	Moderate (%)	Conservative (%)
Dukakis	40	32	31
Gephardt	9	12	16
Gore	22	32	37
Jackson	29	25	17
Totals	100	101	101
Number in sample	119	69	145
Chi square		13.44	
Significance		< .05	

	Republicans	
	Liberal–Moderate (%)	Conservative (%)
Bush	65	59
Dole	33	22
Robertson	2	19
Totals	100	100
Number in sample	51	157
Chi square		9.34
Significance		< .01

SOURCE: 1988 American National Election Study.

NOTE: Republican liberals and moderates combined as one category owing to small *N*s. Some columns do not total 100% due to rounding.

Super Tuesday would make or break his candidacy. Still, as table 3.13 shows, Bush would have trounced him even had the southern and border-state primaries on Super Tuesday been restricted to born-again Christians and biblical literalists. Bush won more than half the born-again vote and led Robertson by 10 percent among literalists.

Religious differences can also be seen in the Democratic returns. Dukakis did much better with voters who had not been religiously reborn and who did not take a literal view of the Bible, while born-again Christians supported Gore much more than voters yet to have this religious experience. Jackson and Gephardt also did best among reborn Christians and Biblical literalists.

The Reagan Factor

A key Bush stratagem in 1988 was to stress his relationship with President Reagan, and conventional wisdom soon embraced the proposition that Bush's support would ebb and flow with Reagan's popularity. (See chapters 1 and 2 for further discussion of this point.) Nowhere was Reagan expected to help Bush more than in the South. Table 3.15 strongly supports

Table 3.13 **Religion and Republican Vote Choice in Border-State and Southern Primaries**

	Born Again?	
	Yes (%)	No (%)
Bush	54	67
Dole	16	33
Robertson	31	0
Totals	101	100
Number in sample	97	98
Chi square	37.81	
Significance	<.001	

	Interpretation of Bible		
	Literally God's Word (%)	God's Word, but Not Literally (%)	Written by Men (%)
Bush	46	71	58
Dole	19	25	42
Robertson	36	4	0
Total	101	100	100
Number in sample	70	122	12
Chi square		39.10	
Significance		<.001	

SOURCE: 1988 American National Election Study.
NOTE: Some columns do not total 100% due to rounding.

this thesis by revealing how the Bush vote in southern and border-state primaries did indeed vary with Reagan affect. The measure employed for this purpose was a "feeling thermometer" scale of 0 to 100 degrees in which 0 indicates the least and 100 the most favorable score. Bush won the support of less than half of all GOP primary voters evaluating Reagan in frigid to lukewarm terms (0 to 74 degrees). Among Republicans holding Reagan in higher esteem, however, Bush won 68 percent of the vote. Fortunately for him, the latter were far more numerous on Super Tuesday.

Affect toward Reagan also figured in Democratic primary voting. Gore's strength rose progressively with warmer Reagan evaluations while just the opposite characterized Dukakis support. Also, Jackson appealed least to voters most favorably inclined toward the president. Table 3.16 documents these relationships.

Conclusions

Super Tuesday's results are not difficult to understand. On the Republican side, Bush won overwhelming support from a comparatively homogeneous primary electorate. Only Republicans unhappy with Reagan backed

Table 3.14 **Religion and Democratic Vote Choice in Border-State and Southern Primaries**

	Born Again?	
	Yes (%)	No (%)
Dukakis	24	42
Gephardt	13	11
Gore	38	27
Jackson	26	20
Totals	101	100
Number in sample	157	151
Chi square	10.99	
Significance	<.02	

	Interpretation of Bible		
	Literally God's Word (%)	God's Word, but Not Literally (%)	Written by Men (%)
Dukakis	21	35	63
Gephardt	15	12	5
Gore	36	31	11
Jackson	29	22	21
Total	101	100	100
Number in sample	112	189	38
Chi square	25.61		
Significance	<.001		

SOURCE: 1988 American National Election Study.
NOTE: Some columns do not total 100% due to rounding.

Table 3.15 **Reagan Evaluations and Republican Vote Choice in Border-State and Southern Primaries**

	Regard for Reagan	
	Low to Medium (%)	High (%)
Bush	37	68
Dole	47	18
Robertson	16	14
Totals	100	100
Number in sample	51	157
Chi square	19.29	
Significance	<.001	

SOURCE: 1988 American National Election Study.
NOTE: Reagan regard measured by 0 to 100–degree "feeling thermometer" where 0 degree is the coldest and least favorable score and 100 degrees the warmest and most favorable. "Low to Medium" category consists of respondents rating Reagan 0 to 74 degrees; high is 75 or more.

Table 3.16 **Reagan Evaluations and Democratic Vote Choice in Border-State and Southern Primaries**

	Regard for Reagan		
	Low (%)	Medium (%)	High (%)
Dukakis	39	31	30
Gephardt	12	11	14
Gore	20	28	46
Jackson	29	31	11
Totals	100	101	101
Number in sample	131	101	103
Chi square		25.95	
Significance		<.001	

SOURCE: 1988 American National Election Study.

NOTE: Reagan regard measured by 0 to 100–degree "feeling thermometer" where 0 degree is the coldest and least favorable score and 100 degrees the warmest and most favorable. "Low" = 0 to 49 degrees, "Medium" = 50 to 74 degrees, "High" = 75 to 100 degrees. Two columns do not total 100% due to rounding.

Dole over the vice-president. Robertson got his votes from a predictable quarter, but religious conservatives were neither a majority of the Republican vote nor a solid bloc for him. Bush owed a great deal to Ronald Reagan's popularity in the region.

Along with proportional representation rules used to award delegates, a more diverse turnout allowed three Democrats to win. The Democratic primary electorate consisted of Republicans as well as Democrats, conservatives as well as liberals, whites as well as blacks, the religiously devout as well as the indifferent. Thus Jackson did well in the Deep South with massive black support, Gore got white votes in Tennessee and the border states, and Dukakis carried Texas barrios, South Florida condos, and urban professionals all over the region (Cook, 1988). Without his primary wins in Massachusetts and Rhode Island and victories in four of five western state caucuses, however, Dukakis would have had much less cause for celebration.

Super Tuesday 1988 disappointed planners in both parties. Though participation in Republican primaries increased, they were not flooded by tides of Reagan Democrats. (In the general election, however, Reagan Democrats became Bush Democrats.) Democratic retention of moderate and conservative whites probably had more to do with closed primaries, sub-presidential races, and a lingering one-party tradition than with appealing candidates. In any event, the Democratic electorate remained as diverse as before. Going into 1992, the party still faces the daunting task of forging a winning coalition for the fall.

Super Tuesday's Future

Super Tuesday 1988 was an experiment that may not be fully replicated in 1992.[4] Its creators were as much committed to change as to the regional primary concept. Convinced that Super Tuesday 1988 could not be worse than its 1984 predecessor, one Democratic state chairman avowed, "if this doesn't work, we'll change it again" (Gailey, 1986: 9). Though this would require new legislative action in some southern states, some of the more dissatisfied states have already begun to act.

Dissatisfaction in the South has been considerable. Some southern politicians are now convinced that subregional primaries spread over three or four weeks would better serve another candidate like Gore, who otherwise will have to wage a northern campaign after Super Tuesday. Voters in Alabama and Maryland complained of being ignored by the candidates, while officials in Arkansas and Kentucky found the March 1988 date too early, too expensive, and too inconvenient. At this writing, Alabama, Arkansas, and Kentucky have already moved their 1992 primaries to May or June, and Virginia may revert to a caucus-convention process after having experienced a disappointing turnout in its 1988 primary. Maryland and Missouri might opt for later dates as well if other states in their respective regions agree to hold mega-primaries. Ohio GOP Chairman Robert Bennett has proposed a regional primary for Ohio, Illinois, Indiana, Michigan, and Wisconsin (Rheem, 1988).

One last lesson of Super Tuesday 1988 is that the presidential nominating process continually changes. The number of presidential primaries doubled between 1968 and 1988, and states have changed their schedules and transformed their events for various reasons—to gain national attention, help a particular candidate, speed up the process, and so on. Super Tuesday was only the latest in a long series of attempts at altering the process, and one would be foolish not to expect more of the same.

Notes

The survey data analyzed in this chapter were collected by the Center for Political Studies and made available by the Inter-university Consortium for Political and Social Research (ICPSR). James Moore's help in collecting election statistics and computing primary turnout rates is greatly appreciated. Thanks also to Emmett Buell, Peter Haas, and Lee Sigelman for helpful comments and suggestions.

1. Each party held eight open primaries in southern and border states: Alabama, Arkansas, Florida, Georgia, Missouri, Mississippi, Tennessee, and Texas. Both parties also held open primaries in Virginia, but only the Democratic contest was binding.
2. A denominator representing normal Democratic and Republican proportions of the state's voting-age population was used to compute primary turnout. Democratic and Republican percentages of the presidential, gubernatorial, and congressional vote, along with party composition for state legislatures, were averaged over five elections to obtain normal Democratic and Republican percentages of the electorate. Compared to other procedures, this method has been found to have the fewest biases (Norrander, 1986).
3. When limited to southern whites, these differences were significant. The options given respondents were: (1) "The Bible is the actual word of God to be taken literally, word for word"; (2) "The Bible is the word of God, but not everything in it should be taken literally, word for word"; and (3) "The Bible is a book written by men and is not the word of God."
4. The legislation enabling Arkansas, Missouri, and Virginia to participate in Super Tuesday was valid only for 1988; new acts may be required for involvement in Super Tuesday 1992 (Southern Legislative Conference, 1988).

References

Black, Earl, and Merle Black. 1987. *Politics and Society in the South.* Cambridge, Mass.: Harvard University Press.

Congressional Quarterly Weekly Report. 1988. 46 (March 12): 638–39.

Cook, Rhodes. 1988. "One Side is Clearer, the Other Still Murky." *Congressional Quarterly Weekly Reports* 46 (March 12): 636–46.

———. 1989. "The Nominating Process." In *The Elections of 1988*, ed. Michael Nelson. Washington, D.C.: Congressional Quarterly Press.

Davis, James W. 1983. *National Conventions in an Age of Party Reform.* Westport, Conn.: Greenwood Press.

Doyle, William. 1975. "Regional Primaries: The Spirit of '76." *State Government* 48 (Summer): 141–44.

Gailey, Phil. 1986. "Southern Democrats Press Plan for Regional Primary." *New York Times* (March 8): 9.

Geer, John G. 1988. "Assessing the Representativeness of Electorates in Presidential Primaries." *American Journal of Political Science* 32 (November): 929–45.

Ladd, Everett C. 1978. *Where Have All the Voters Gone?* New York: W. W. Norton.

Lengle, James I. 1981. *Representation and Presidential Primaries: The Democratic Party in the Post-Reform Era.* Westport, Conn.: Greenwood Press.

Norrander, Barbara. 1986. "Measuring Primary Turnout in Aggregate Analysis." *Political Behavior* 8 (no. 4): 356–73.

———. 1989. "Ideological Representativeness of Presidential Party Voters." *American Journal of Political Science* 33 (August): 570–87.

Polsby, Nelson W. 1983. *Consequences of Party Reform.* New York: Oxford University Press.

Rheem, Donald L. 1988. "Disgruntled with Primaries, Reformers Offer Suggestions: Get Rid of Super Tuesday—or Have Four More." *Christian Science Monitor* (July 28): 3–4.

Southern Legislative Conference. 1988. "Status Report on Super Tuesday in the Southern States." November press release.

Stanley, Harold W., and Charles D. Hadley. 1987. "The Southern Presidential Primary: Regional Intentions with National Implications." *Publius* 17 (Summer): 83–100.

———. 1989. "Super Tuesday Surveys: Insights and Hindsights." Unpublished paper presented at annual meeting of Midwest Political Science Association (April 13–15).

Wolfinger, Raymond E. 1985. "Dealignment, Realignment, and Mandates in the 1984 Election." In *The American Elections of 1984*, ed. Austin Ranney. Durham, N.C.: Duke University Press.

4. Financing the 1988 Prenomination Campaigns

Clyde Wilcox

Long before the first balloting took place in Iowa and New Hampshire, the media were covering another type of contest among the candidates — the race for campaign funds. Newspaper stories in 1987 and early 1988 focused on which candidates had raised the most money, had the most cash on hand, and had incurred the most debt. Implicit in these stories was the assumption that campaign money is vital to winning either party's nomination.

The 1988 prenomination campaign confirmed some of the conventional wisdom about prenomination funding, altered other parts of it, and proved that some of it no longer applied. The conventional wisdom held that presidential candidates spend their money early in the campaign. Front-runners attempt a "knockout" strategy of winning the early contests while long-shot candidates attempt an "early upset" strategy, spending heavily in Iowa and New Hampshire in hopes of capitalizing on a surprisingly strong showing (Sorauf, 1988). Expectations of early spending proved accurate in 1988, especially for the Republicans. Indeed, had George Bush not won the Super Tuesday primaries by such a crushing margin, the three leading Republican candidates would soon have spent the legal maximum with more than half the delegates still to be chosen.

Although the conventional wisdom among political scientists has been that campaign spending does not buy success, the two candidates who won their party's nominations in 1988 raised the largest sums early and had the most cash available throughout the campaign. Campaign spending seems to have mattered in the early contests for Democrats: in Iowa and in most of the Super Tuesday states, the winner was the biggest spender. The exception to this rule was Jesse Jackson, whose percentage of the vote seemed impervious to spending. Among Republican candidates, however, spending mattered little. George Bush won in states where he was outspent by more than two-to-one. These results suggest a modification of the conventional wisdom: campaign spending matters most when little-known candidates contest the nomination, and it matters considerably less when the candidates are well known or when free media provide voters with sufficient information to make up their minds.

In two other areas, the conventional wisdom did not apply in 1988. The conventional understanding of the logic of federal matching funds was that candidates had strong incentives to pursue small contributions, since only the first $250 of each contribution can be matched. By 1988, inflation had erased that incentive, and both Bush and Dukakis funded their campaigns largely through $1,000 contributions.

In past campaigns, candidates who won in Iowa or New Hampshire could expect a surge in funds. Neither Robert Dole nor Richard Gephardt, the Iowa winners, experienced such a surge in 1988, probably because the Super Tuesday primaries occurred before contributors had time to respond. Each of these issues will be more fully explored below.

Money in the 1988 Campaign

In the fall of 1987, Bruce Babbitt spent two days a week on the telephone asking contributors to give or, if they had given before, to increase their contribution to the legal maximum. By the end of October, his campaign had raised only around a million dollars and had only $35,000 on hand. The Babbitt campaign had taken out large bank loans and would have to use its matching funds in January to repay those loans. In contrast, Michael Dukakis's campaign had raised over $8 million in individual contributions and had more than $4 million in cash. Dukakis had no outstanding bank loans and looked forward to a large infusion of cash from federal matching funds.

This disparity in funds affected the way the two candidates campaigned during the last months of 1987. Babbitt channeled all his funds into Iowa while Dukakis already had staff in place in Texas and Florida—the states that allowed him to claim victory on Super Tuesday. Dukakis could afford to fly to Texas between Iowa campaign stops, visiting the key precincts that later brought him victory (Walsh, 1987).

During the nomination campaign, Republican and Democratic candidates raised and spent over $200 million. Four candidates—Republicans George Bush, Robert Dole, and Pat Robertson and Democrat Michael Dukakis—each spent over $25 million of the $27.6 million allowed through their campaign committees. Several candidates had spent additional funds beginning as early as 1985 through political action committees (PACs) unofficially associated with their campaigns.

In 1988, campaign finance professionals predicted that money would play a vital role. Because of the increased front-loading of primaries, and in particular the early Super Tuesday primaries in the South, effective campaigning would require massive media buys. There would be little time for candidates to visit several southern states in the short interval between the New Hampshire primary and Super Tuesday. Campaigning instead would be a war of television advertisements.

The Legal Setting: The FECA

Financial strategies are mapped within the framework of legislation passed in 1974 in response to the Watergate scandal. The 1972 presidential election had been the most expensive in history, with the Nixon campaign spending a record $56 million and the McGovern campaign spending $40 million. The Watergate investigations revealed numerous improprieties, including illegal corporate contributions laundered through foreign banks, large contributions to Nixon from a number of millionaires who were rewarded by ambassadorships, and many unreported contributions.

In response to these revelations, Congress amended the Federal Election Campaign Act (FECA), establishing new rules that radically transformed the financing of presidential prenomination campaigns. This law and its amendments create very different systems of financing the prenomination and general election campaigns.

Prenomination campaigns are financed by private contributions by individuals and interest groups, and by federal monies that match portions of individual contributions. General election campaigns are financed through a federal grant of equal amounts to each party: in 1988 this grant was approximately $46 million dollars. Large sums are spent by interest groups as independent expenditures during general election campaigns, although reported amounts usually exaggerate actual spending (Malbin, 1985; Wilcox, 1988). The law also allows party committees to raise large sums that may be spent in carefully prescribed ways, e.g., statewide get-out-the-vote drives. These funds, popularly referred to as "soft money," probably totaled more than the federal grant in 1988.

The new law, enforced by the specially created Federal Election Commission (FEC), contained several important provisions.

1. The size of contributions by individuals, interest groups, and candidates themselves were limited: individuals to $1,000, interest groups (through PACSs) to $5,000, and the candidates themselves to $50,000 if they accepted federal matching funds. These limits have not increased since 1974, even though they have been effectively halved by inflation.

2. Individual citizens can contribute, through a checkoff on their federal

income-tax forms, $1 toward a federal fund to help finance presidential elections. During the prenomination campaign, candidates can qualify for public matching funds by raising $100,000 in amounts of $250 or less, with $5,000 coming from each of twenty states. Once a candidate has met these criteria, the first $250 any individual contributes to his or her campaign can be matched by money from the federal fund. There is an overall cap (indexed to the Consumer Price Index) on the total amount of matching funds any candidate can receive, although no candidate in 1988 reached that cap.

3. For candidates who accept these matching funds, there are spending limits for each individual state and a separate limit for the entire campaign. The state limits are geared to the state's voting-age population. The spending limits in states with early primaries or caucuses are quite low, since these states—most notably Iowa and New Hampshire—have small populations. The 1988 spending limit in New Hampshire was $461,000—the same as for the District of Columbia and Alaska. The overall spending limit falls considerably below the sum of the state limits. In 1988 this limit was approximately $23 million, with an additional $4.6 million allowed for spending on fund-raising. Both the individual state limits and the overall campaign limit are indexed to the Consumer Price Index. Many observers believe that the costs of campaigning have been increasing at a faster rate, however, and that the limits therefore are more restrictive than they were in 1974.

Consequences of the FECA

One consequence of this legal framework is that it is now imperative that candidates begin to organize and raise money early—a year or more before the start of the primary season. Because of the $1,000 limit on individual contributions, it is essential to develop a long list of potential contributors who may be willing to contribute to one's campaign. This makes it very difficult for candidates to enter the race once it is underway.[1]

Some candidates work on developing their contributor lists for two years or more before the first primary. Many presidential hopefuls form their own PACs to develop and hone lists of donors. PACs also allow candidates to avoid the limits on individual contributions: each supporter can contribute up to $5,000 to the potential candidate's PAC and, after the formation of an official campaign committee, can contribute another $1,000 to that committee. Although no comprehensive information is available on the extent of double contributions, a *Washington Post* analysis suggested that, in the first part of 1987 alone, seventy-six people contributed both to George Bush's PAC and to his campaign committee, and seventy-nine gave to both the PAC and the campaign committee of Robert Dole.

These double donors gave an average of nearly $5,000 to the Bush committees and just over $4,000 apiece to the Dole efforts (Morin, 1988).

Another consequence of the $1,000 limit is to disadvantage candidates whose contributors would be willing to make larger contributions in favor of those candidates able to attract numerous smaller donations. In the 1988 campaign, George Bush, Robert Dole, and Michael Dukakis all received substantial proportions of their funds in $1,000 contributions. If the limit on individual contributions had been higher, the campaigns of these candidates would have raised money more quickly and cheaply.

The FECA amendments also advantage, to a certain degree, less well-known candidates. For example, both Babbitt and Dukakis faced the same limit for spending in Iowa ($775,217), so the huge Dukakis advantage in available cash could not be converted directly into a spending advantage. There are several legal ways to spend considerably more than the limits in the early states, if a candidate has the available funds, but the spending limits do advantage underdogs and may thereby have increased the number of candidates seeking each party's nomination. Hopefuls like Babbitt, Simon, and du Pont might not have been tempted to seek the presidency if the front-runners had been allowed unlimited spending.[2]

Underdogs are advantaged in another important way: federal matching funds enable them to increase their spending in the quest for name recognition and early victory. Candidates can often borrow against their future matching funds, as Bruce Babbitt did in late 1987. Such borrowing is not always done early in the campaigns: for example, borrowing against matching funds sustained the Hart campaign in 1984 and allowed him to capitalize on his momentum after his upset win over Walter Mondale in the New Hampshire primary. In the long run, however, matching funds also benefit front-runners, who receive more total matching funds. By doubling the value of small contributions, matching funds increase financial gaps among candidates. While matching funds in January 1988 provided Bruce Babbitt with nearly $750,000, Michael Dukakis received nearly $3.5 million. Similarly, Pete du Pont received over $2 million in January, but George Bush, Robert Dole, and Pat Robertson each received over $5.5 million.

The overal spending limit also has consequences for the conduct of campaigns. Because of the importance of victories in the early primaries and caucuses, candidates often spend heavily in the first months of the campaign. If no candidate emerges as an early winner, then spending may be curtailed to prevent exceeding the limit. As we will see below, the overall spending limit was not a major factor in the 1988 campaign, but it would have been if Super Tuesday had turned out differently.

Candidate Receipts in 1988:
Where Did the Money Come From?

The major sources of receipts for presidential prenomination candidates are individual contributions, federal matching funds, and loans. Table 4.1 presents the sources of receipts for each of the major candidates in 1988. Although PACs and party committees give substantial funds to congressional candidates, neither is a major source of money for presidential prenomination candidates. For all candidates seeking the presidency, PAC, party, and other committee contributions totaled just over $3 million, approximately 1 percent of total campaign receipts. Richard Gephardt, who received the largest percentage of contributions from political committees, reported committee contributions totaling only 5 percent of his total receipts.

Individual contributions were the major funding source for every candidate. There were considerable differences, however, in the way each campaign went about soliciting individual contributions. Table 4.2 breaks down each candidate's individual contributions by size. George Bush had great success with $1,000-a-plate dinners; one such event in Houston raised $750,000. Michael Dukakis's fund-raiser, Bob Farmer, used a pyramid scheme to solicit funds, calling well-connected Dukakis supporters and asking each to raise at least $10,000 from their friends. By mid-March, the Dukakis campaign had a list of 600 indivduals who had done so, and by the end of May the list had swollen to 900. Individuals who raised $10,000 were named to the campaign's Finance Committee. The next level, the Board of Directors, was reserved for those who raised at least $25,000; through the end of May there were 230 members. Above this level were national cochairmen and "ambassadors"; by mid-March, 130 of these individuals had each raised $100,000 or more. Much of Dukakis's early money came from officials of companies who did business with the state of Massachusetts, a common source of funds for governors who seek federal office (Werth, 1988; Sullam, 1988). An additional 16 percent came from a network of donors who shared the candidate's Greek ancestry (Berke, 1987b). As the Dukakis campaign began to roll up victories, contributions flowed from individuals across the country anxious to back a winner. The Dole campaign also created a team of fund-raisers, each pledged to raise $50,000. Much of Dole's early money came from officials in the insurance, tobacco, agribusiness, and oil industries, and from midwestern supporters.

In contrast to the campaigns of Bush, Dole, and Dukakis, the campaigns of Jesse Jackson, Paul Simon, Jack Kemp, and Pat Robertson relied on small contributions. Jackson solicited funds in black churches and used direct-mail and telephone solicitations to raise additional funds. On the Sunday prior to Super Tuesday, Jackson held a concerted fund-raising

Table 4.1 Sources of Receipts: Presidential Candidates in 1988 (in Dollars)

	Individuals	Matching Funds	Loans	Other	Total
Democrats					
Babbitt	2,290,538	1,015,992	22,500	1,276	3,398,645
Dukakis	19,314,589	9,040,025	0	31,630	28,885,184
Gephardt	6,118,159	2,818,003	0	589,614	9,740,685
Gore	7,789,127	3,670,732	148,865	519,093	12,207,305
Jackson	12,122,222	6,286,857	747,991	88,552	19,347,948
Simon	5,941,404	3,260,431	0	320,011	9,534,276
Democratic totals	58,877,081	27,974,519	912,339	1,560,176	89,675,641
Republicans					
Bush	22,322,312	8,393,092	0	688,373	31,780,694
Dole	16,910,734	7,547,153	0	834,433	26,458,017
du Pont	5,419,184	2,550,952	0	0	8,060,892
Kemp	10,061,894	5,694,610	0	81,985	16,340,436
Robertson	20,260,835	8,946,589	0	5,160	29,743,309
Republican totals	76,356,534	33,664,565	48,450	1,628,231	112,724,082
Grand totals	141,803,732	62,239,197	960,789	3,235,357	209,653,815

SOURCE: 1988 Federal Election Commission press releases and amendments for prenomination period, subsequently referred to as 1988 prenomination FEC press releases.

NOTE: Democratic totals include candidates not shown: Biden, Hart, La Rouche, and Schroeder; Republican totals include Haig, Laxalt, and Fulani. Loans are net loans after repayment.

drive in black churches around the country, a tactic that aroused criticism from his opponents who charged that these contributions were not recorded and could be from supporters who had already contributed the $1,000 limit. Kemp and Simon also raised some of their money through direct-mail solicitations, but the candidate who relied most heavily on direct mail was Pat Robertson. Robertson began with lists of regular contributors to his "700 Club," supplemented with the names of three million people who responded to his call for letters pledging support. Robertson asked his regular contributors to join his "1988 Club" by pledging to give $19.88 per month for his campaign. Many contributors to his television ministry were accustomed to monthly giving, and the campaign claimed that the 1988 Club had forty thousand members.

Direct mail is an expensive way to raise money. Mailings are costly, and the average gifts seldom exceed $25. Early solicitations designed to build lists of regular donors (referred to as "prospecting") often lose money. Jack Kemp's first mailing reportedly lost $200,000, and subsequent mailings cost forty cents for every dollar raised (Blow, 1988). Direct mail works best for candidates who appeal to one of the ideological wings of their party.

Nearly all the candidates relied on allies in Congress to help in raising funds from the member's most committed supporters. A fund-raising tour headed by a prominent senator or representative can often raise $1 million or more. The Dukakis campaign also directly solicited the Democratic delegation in Congress.

These differences in fund-raising strategies are apparent in table 4.2.

Table 4.2 Individual Contributions, by Size

	< $500 (%)	$500–$749 (%)	$750 + (%)
Democrats			
Babbitt	36	11	53
Dukakis	36	19	45
Gephardt	45	19	36
Gore	44	17	39
Jackson	88	4	8
Simon	62	12	27
Republicans			
Bush	23	12	66
Dole	36	12	52
du Pont	46	14	40
Kemp	68	10	23
Robertson	89	3	8

SOURCE: 1988 prenomination FEC press releases.
NOTE: Data shown are through August 31, 1988.

While nearly two-thirds of individual contributions to Bush were of $750 or more, nearly 90 percent of Robertson's and Jackson's were less than $500. Among leading Democrats, Dukakis received the highest proportion of large contributions.[3]

The second most important source of funds was federal matching funds. The Treasury Department distributed over $60 million to all candidates in 1988, including over $600,000 to Lenora Fulani of the New Alliance Party, who became the first black woman to qualify for matching funds, and nearly $800,000 to Lyndon La Rouche, who proclaimed that the queen of England was involved in a drug-smuggling operation. The candidates who raised the most money through individual contributions also received the most federal funds.

Pat Robertson initially announced that he was opposed to government financing of campaigns and that he was uncertain whether he would accept matching funds. His campaign at first asked for a delay in the receipt of federal monies, then announced that his campaign would accept his initial $4.5 million payment but would place the funds in an escrow account for possible later return. Robertson then borrowed against these funds, raising questions as to whether he could legally return the monies or if in fact they had already been used.

Candidates who accept matching funds are bound by the state and total spending limits, but those who refuse federal funds are free to spend unlimited amounts. Despite the potential advantage of refusing such funds, only one candidate, John Connally in 1976, has ever done so. Ronald Reagan, who has repeatedly stated his principled opposition to federal financing of campaigns, is the all-time leading recipient of matching funds. In 1984, he became the first in history to qualify for the federal limit for matching funds, even though he faced no primary opposition. Most reports suggested that the Roberston campaign delayed its decision on matching funds while it considered attempting to raise sufficient funds to exceed the national spending limit in a Southern media blitz on Super Tuesday.

Loans are the third major source of funds for most candidates. The promise of forthcoming matching funds has provided campaigns with a new source of collateral with which to seek bank loans to buoy their campaigns. Although George Bush and Michael Dukakis managed to avoid borrowing money during the campaign, all the other major candidates were forced to seek loans. Pat Robertson, Paul Simon, Albert Gore, Richard Gephardt, and Jesse Jackson all borrowed fairly substantial amounts while Robert Dole and Jack Kemp borrowed more modest sums. The Robertson campaign borrowed $1.5 million in the last quarter of 1987, an additional $5.5 million in January, and $1.9 million in February 1988. By the end of the summer, the Republican candidates had all repaid their outstanding loans while Jackson still owed nearly $750,000 and Gore was slightly over $140,000 in debt.

The lingering debt of these Democratic candidates is nothing new. In 1988, three Democratic candidates still owed money from their 1984 campaign. Although Gary Hart had resolved much of his outstanding debt by the beginning of his renewed 1988 campaign, some of his 1984 creditors sued his 1988 campaign committee for payment. The FEC eventually ruled that 1988 campaign funds cannot be used to repay debts from previous campaigns, but this controversy (coupled with a *Miami Herald* story about excessive contributions to the 1984 campaign) hurt Hart's Iowa campaign.

The Funding Race

Table 4.3 depicts the dynamics of total candidate receipts for the leading candidates. On the Democratic side, Dukakis enjoyed an enormous fundraising advantage during the early months of the campaign. In 1987, he

Table 4.3 **Total Receipts of Candidates over Time (in Dollars)**

	Major Democratic Candidates			
Period	Dukakis	Gephardt	Gore	Jackson
Pre-4/87	0	1,131,289	0	0
6/87	4,670,104	1,129,928	1,418,928	0
9/87	3,464,818	1,196,701	1,282,724	1,043,864
12/87	2,630,607	2,444,845	1,240,235	359,230
1/88	4,319,541	2,129,462	2,053,462	1,278,880
2/88	2,869,466	1,536,789	1,542,926	1,472,332
3/88	3,426,330	2,088,463	3,405,652	3,266,642
4/88	3,439,519	498,365	1,434,538	4,863,034
5/88	3,457,534	138,075	458,847	4,723,243
6/88	2,100,813	162,085	322,459	3,354,866

	Major Republican Candidates			
	Bush	Dole	Kemp	Robertson
Pre-4/87	2,359,004	626,689	0	0
6/87	7,097,267	3,345,878	3,469,568	0
9/87	3,272,099	3,994,992	2,825,210	11,737,936
12/87	6,330,045	6,401,130	3,911,892	4,669,030
1/88	7,233,108	6,767,578	5,723,979	13,290,675
2/88	1,460,525	2,064,180	1,616,900	4,985,321
3/88	2,169,000	2,402,693	604,586	2,319,548
4/88	2,141,760	1,366,886	604,586	2,319,548
5/88	516,047	432,587	449,099	504,220
6/88	287,094	276,017	333,324	329,324

had a better than two-to-one advantage over each of his rivals. Later in the campaign, though, as the competitors narrowed to Dukakis and Jackson, Jackson actually had slightly greater monthly receipts than did Dukakis, enabling Jackson to be competitive to the end.

On the Republican side, the most notable trend is the virtual dead heat in fund-raising among Bush, Dole, and Robertson. All three raised enough to approach the overall spending limit by the end of February, far surpassing the Dukakis campaign. As had been true of previous campaigns, the Republican contenders were more successful than the Democrats in raising large sums quickly.

Tables 4.4 and 4.5 show the sources of the leading candidates' receipts over time. These tables also point up the ability of underdogs like Gephardt and Kemp to borrow early in anticipation of matching funds. Albert Gore borrowed later in the campaign in his all-out effort to win the southern Super Tuesday primaries. Jesse Jackson also borrowed late in the campaign as the race narrowed to two candidates, but also received a sharp increase in individual contributions and, subsequently, in matching funds.

In previous elections, candidates who have done well in Iowa and New Hampshire have sharply increased their receipts. For example, in 1984, Gary Hart saw his individual contributions jump from $342,000 in February to $3 million in March following his New Hampshire victory. In 1988, Gephardt borrowed in an attempt to capitalize on his early success in Iowa but did not experience a sharp increase in individual contributions, probably because of the heavy front-loading of the 1988 primaries; Super Tuesday occurred before most contributors had much time to react to the outcomes of Iowa and New Hampshire.

Where Did the Money Go?

As noted above, the conventional wisdom among practicing campaign professionals is that candidate spending matters greatly, especially early in the campaign. Few Americans are familiar with more than one or two of their party's candidates, and many know little about any of them. Money buys media exposure, which is one of the most important sources of information about candidates. By spending on TV ads, candidates can acquaint potential supporters with the themes of their campaign. Money also buys organization, which helps candidates get their supporters to the polls—an especially important task in low-turnout caucus states.

Of course, money is not the only way to inform voters or build an organization. In previous campaigns, free media coverage also provided an important boost to candidates. Candidates who have won or done unexpectedly well in Iowa and New Hampshire have traditionally been the

Table 4.4 **Sources of Democratic Candidate Receipts over Time (in Dollars)**

Period	Dukakis	Gephardt	Gore	Jackson
Pre-4/87				
Individuals	0	969,915	0	0
Matching funds	0	0	0	0
Loans	0	0	0	0
6/87				
Individuals	4,230,298	987,022	1,370,667	0
Matching funds	0	0	0	0
Loans	0	0	0	0
9/87				
Individuals	3,401,365	986,462	1,182,460	996,407
Matching funds	0	0	0	0
Loans	0	125,000	0	20,000
12/87				
Individuals	2,555,798	1,040,564	1,102,972	347,980
Matching funds	0	0	0	0
Loans	0	1,310,000	1,450,000	0
1/88				
Individuals	802,274	192,687	168,920	619,783
Matching funds	3,493,418	1,910,832	1,852,052	598,021
Loans	0	0	0	50,000
2/88				
Individuals	1,245,586	926,144	995,158	811,656
Matching funds	1,569,597	268,756	352,176	95,520
Loans	0	149,000	0	500,000
3/88				
Individuals	2,380,131	857,052	1,131,906	2,578,675
Matching funds	621,098	161,107	336,312	330,189
Loans	0	698,059	1,450,000	250,600
4/88				
Individuals	1,877,822	75,415	729,916	2,110,032
Matching funds	1,116,005	286,176	387,547	1,688,722
Loans	0	63,807	150,000	966,823
5/88				
Individuals	2,254,963	52,899	119,426	1,526,873
Matching funds	953,121	24,585	270,847	1,481,234
Loans	0	45,847	0	1,515,659
6/88				
Individuals	645,372	13,476	164,396	2,071,192
Matching funds	936,632	58,859	88,053	555,755
Loans	0	32,937	0	595,958

SOURCE: 1988 prenomination FEC press releases.

Table 4.5 Sources of Republican Candidate Receipts over Time (in Dollars)

Period	Bush	Dole	Kemp	Robertson
Pre-4/87				
Individuals	2,283,908	598,626	0	0
Matching funds	0	0	0	0
Loans	50,000	0	0	0
6/87				
Individuals	6,826,045	2,942,930	3,101,656	0
Matching funds	0	0	0	0
Loans	0	0	50,000	0
9/87				
Individuals	3,142,683	3,821,729	2,060,348	11,070,283
Matching funds	0	0	0	0
Loans	0	0	600,000	233,480
12/87				
Individuals	6,003,745	6,041,428	1,923,212	3,132,939
Matching funds	0	0	0	0
Loans	0	0	1,850,000	1,500,000
1/88				
Individuals	744,891	1,141,494	1,031,171	1,277,681
Matching funds	6,374,981	5,566,329	3,893,845	6,455,898
Loans	0	0	750,000	5,526,582
2/88				
Individuals	1,124,390	1,285,943	983,555	2,256,525
Matching funds	237,348	657,096	612,609	795,883
Loans	0	0	0	1,883,308
3/88				
Individuals	1,643,335	931,961	578,389	873,436
Matching funds	247,118	380,928	0	896,551
Loans	0	0	0	410,000
4/88				
Individuals	699,320	201,517	194,796	659,495
Matching funds	1,160,535	609,942	500,093	341,523
Loans	0	0	50,000	0
5/88				
Individuals	40,884	172,215	141,806	172,547
Matching funds	299,792	143,989	285,544	294,870
Loans	0	0	0	0
6/88				
Individuals	29,981	137,015	105,997	168,941
Matching funds	4,211	0	216,841	95,484
Loans	0	0	0	0

SOURCE: 1988 prenomination FEC press releases.

focus of intense media scrutiny, and this free publicity spurred the campaigns of Jimmy Carter in 1976 and of Gary Hart in 1984. Some candidates enter the race with advantages in organizing as well. Pat Robertson was able to rely on networks of charismatic and Pentecostal churches in organizing in caucus states, and Jesse Jackson could rely on black churches and civil-rights groups for organizational efforts. Candidates who receive endorsements of prominent political figures can often rely on their organizations for support. George Bush had the support of a number of important Republican governors (including Governor John Sununu of New Hampshire, a state that gave Bush an early and vital victory), who put their organizations at his disposal.

Political scientists, on the other hand, have generally claimed that money is not a decisive factor in primary election outcomes. Gary Orren (1985), for example, concluded that money affected the conduct but not the outcome of the 1984 Democratic contest between Walter Mondale and Gary Hart. Similarly, Michael Robinson (1984; 1985) argued that media advertising is costly and usually does not work, and that money does not talk in presidential politics. Both of these conclusions are based on the fact that half of the 1984 Democratic primaries were won by the candidate who spent the most, and half by the candidate who did not.

Clearly, there is no simple relationship between money and votes — expenditures of $100,000 do not buy a certain percentage of the vote. Money may help candidates succeed, but success also brings more money, making the relationship between the two difficult to untangle (Sorauf, 1988). Yet it would seem odd to argue that candidates who spend much of their time raising money to buy media time are merely engaging in superstitious behavior. Moreover, we have already seen that the winners in 1988 were the candidates who had the most cash on hand in the early months. How, then, can we reconcile the differing conclusions that practicing politicians and political scientists have reached about campaign spending?

Candidate Spending

Candidates must allocate their spending among many states. In 1988, Albert Gore chose to husband his resources, spending little in Iowa and probably less than his rivals in New Hampshire, in order to mount an all-out effort in the South on Super Tuesday. Richard Gephardt and Bruce Babbitt, on the other hand, spent all their available funds in Iowa, hoping for an early victory to establish their candidacies.

The Federal Election Commission reports the official allocations of each campaign to each state. These data are not entirely reliable, for several reasons. First, the low spending limits in the early states create a great incentive to circumvent those limits, and most campaigns do so. One common tactic is to report money spent for Iowa and New Hampshire as spending in other states. The cars of New Hampshire campaign workers are filled with gasoline in White River Junction, Vermont. Workers spend the night outside Iowa and New Hampshire borders and charge the room and board to those bordering states. Buses are chartered in St. Paul, Minnesota, to transport volunteers into the Iowa caucuses. The Federal Election Commission has established some very specific rules for allocating expenditures. Because most Boston television stations reach substantially more Massachusetts viewers than New Hampshire citizens, the FEC allows campaigns to allocate 85 percent of their paid media on those stations to Massachusetts, although the primary target is clearly New Hampshire voters. Similarly, the FEC has ruled that, if a paid campaign worker stays in a given state for more than four days, his or her salary must be allocated to that state. As a consequence, campaign workers routinely stay in Iowa and New Hampshire for no more than four days, then leave the state for a short time. Bruce Babbitt reported spending near the limit in Iowa and spending additional funds in neighboring Nebraska and Illinois, although he dropped out of the race long before these states selected their delegates. We cannot be certain how much money is really spent in Iowa and New Hampshire, but in 1988 the du Pont campaign openly planned to spend a million dollars in New Hampshire, more than double the legal limit (Babcock, 1988a; Berke, 1987a).

In 1988, the FEC for the first time allowed campaigns to circumvent state limits in a second way. Acting on a request from the Gephardt and Dukakis campaigns, the commission ruled that television advertisements that include an appeal for campaign contributions (even appeals of a single word) may be partially counted as fund-raising costs and therefore not allocated to any specific states. Both campaigns ran televised advertisements in Iowa that included such appeals, and for both candidates only half of this spending appears in official figures. This practice allowed the Gephardt campaign to spend $100,000 more than it would otherwise have been allowed; the benefit for Dukakis was $40,000 (Babcock, 1988b).

Campaigns seek to circumvent state spending limits only in Iowa and New Hampshire. For other states, spending limits are generally sufficiently high and the political importance sufficiently low that no candidates reach the spending cap. In the four elections since the FECA took effect, candidates have reported spending the limit in only three states.

A second problem with campaign spending data is that not all candidate spending is allocated to states. The law allows candidates to report some spending as being associated with their national campaigns, not with specific state elections. Candidates differ in the centralization of their campaigns, and this may affect state spending figures. One campaign may run its phone banks from a central location using WATS lines while another may conduct its phone efforts in each individual state. The first campaign would allocate its spending to the national campaign while the second campaign would include such expenditures in its state totals. There was wide variation in the proportion of spending allocated to states across campaigns. Among Democrats, Gephardt, Gore, and Dukakis each allocated nearly half of their spending to individual states while Jesse Jackson allocated approximately a quarter of his spending to states. Among Republicans, Dole allocated nearly 50 percent of his spending to specific states while Jack Kemp allocated less than 20 percent.

A final problem is that spending figures do not include spending by candidate PACs and tax-exempt foundations. Candidate PACs and foundations are the latest in a series of attempts by candidates to avoid the restrictions on campaign committees. PACs and foundations generally do not target their efforts to specific states, choosing instead to pay the salaries of campaign aides and to help develop mailing lists for the campaign committees. For Republicans, however, PACs played a vital role in financing the efforts of Kemp and Bush in the 1986 Michigan caucuses. Pat Robertson was also active in Michigan, although his campaign relied on a tax-exempt foundation to conduct the campaign.

Despite these limitations, candidate-spending data still tell us about the choices that the candidates made in allocating their funds to individual states, and about the impact of these decisions on election outcomes. Spending by a candidate in any state is obviously constrained by available funds. Table 4.6 shows the cash on hand and total debt (loans plus other debts) of each campaign in each filing period while a candidate was active. Early in the campaign, Dukakis and Bush enjoyed a substantial advantage over their rivals. In every reporting period, Dukakis had more than $1.4 million on hand, and more than twice the needed cash to cover his debts. Only Gore had cash reserves approaching those of Dukakis, in part because of his decision not to spend large sums in Iowa. At the end of January, the Bush campaign had a cash balance of over $9 million, more than twice the Dole total. Interestingly, although Robertson raised as much early money as Bush and Dole, his early spending left him cash poor. At the end of each reporting period, he had a deficit; only at the end of February, after loans of nearly $6 million, did Robertson lead Bush in cash on hand.

Tables 4.7 and 4.8 show spending allocations by each candidate in each

Table 4.6 **Candidate Cash on Hand and Total Debt (in Thousands of Dollars)**

	Period						
	9/87	12/87	1/88	2/88	3/88	4/88	5/88
Democrats							
Babbitt cash	36	87	176	248	—	—	—
Babbitt debt	339	163	340	388	—	—	—
Dukakis cash	431	2,180	4,041	2,920	1,710	1,412	2,027
Dukakis debt	280	625	512	569	697	700	669
Gephardt cash	574	782	172	450	68	—	—
Gephardt debt	267	1,909	820	1,035	1,824	—	—
Gore cash	1,352	894	2,031	342	416	222	—
Gore debt	112	106	84	92	1,552	1,611	—
Jackson cash	35	6	512	428	866	1,430	1,205
Jackson debt	178	452	355	846	954	633	789
Simon cash	332	202	401	761	359	—	—
Simon debt	213	1,187	691	825	615	—	—
Republicans							
Bush cash	4,793	5,704	9,259	6,704	3,645	4,015	3,044
Bush debt	570	434	811	1,123	1,041	853	747
Dole cash	2,215	2,209	4,154	836	374	—	—
Dole debt	496	973	654	716	1,832	—	—
du Pont cash	253	N.A.	564	225	—	—	—
du Pont debt	83	744	59	214	—	—	—
Kemp cash	407	128	446	60	57	—	—
Kemp debt	882	3,514	1,274	765	673	—	—
Robertson cash	263	106	430	7,412	61	—	—
Robertson debt	637	2,094	5,983	8,399	1,437	—	—

SOURCE: 1988 prenomination FEC press releases.
NOTE: Dashes indicate discontinued candidacies.

state. With the exception of Gore, all candidates listed chose to spend up to (or beyond) the limit if they could in Iowa and New Hampshire. The large number of states that held primaries or caucuses on Super Tuesday forced campaigns to make some important decisions. Media experts estimated that a substantial campaign of television advertising for all Super Tuesday states would cost more than $2 million (Rosenbaum, 1988). Although the Republican candidates were willing and able to spend more than their Democratic counterparts, they too faced important choices in allocating their resources.

Among the Democrats, Dukakis and Gore had the most resources to spend on Super Tuesday. Dukakis, Gore, and Gephardt all faced primaries in their home states, and each candidate outspent his rivals in his home state by a substantial margin since none could afford an embarrassing

Table 4.7 Democratic Candidate Spending by State (in Thousands of Dollars)

State	Dukakis	Gephardt	Gore	Jackson	FEC Limit
Alabama	69.7	117.5	226.3	25.5	1,093.9
Alaska	0.0	0.0	0.0	0.5	461.0
Arizona	19.7	0.0	0.9	19.9	909.8
Arkansas	102.4	49.8	123.6	14.5	642.1
California	489.2	1.0	7.3	664.0	7,509.5
Colorado	76.2	1.6	1.9	14.7	893.2
Connecticut	57.6	2.1	78.8	6.0	905.0
Delaware	7.1	0.0	0.0	18.2	461.0
District of Columbia	96.6	0.0	0.0	47.1	461.0
Florida	737.7	307.1	183.5	31.0	3,436.8
Georgia	133.3	142.1	238.6	44.9	1,654.4
Hawaii	8.6	1.7	1.5	7.4	461.0
Idaho	1.8	0.2	13.8	0.0	461.0
Illinois	458.2	61.2	274.6	255.0	3,152.1
Indiana	97.4	0.1	44.0	22.2	1,497.7
Iowa	756.2	732.3	262.0	195.0	775.1
Kansas	41.7	2.8	19.7	0.1	673.1
Kentucky	60.2	1.4	120.4	39.5	1,007.2
Louisiana	27.4	82.8	74.8	28.0	1,159.9
Maine	167.5	30.0	23.5	18.2	461.0
Maryland	244.8	2.7	39.2	19.3	1,257.6
Massachusetts	271.9	181.3	0.4	4.0	1,666.6
Michigan	452.7	463.5	55.1	77.9	2,485.7
Minnesota	546.6	55.2	4.7	24.3	1,156.2
Mississippi	5.3	4.8	90.1	22.3	676.0
Missouri	3.6	282.9	0.4	4.0	1,399.2
Montana	7.4	2.3	0.7	22.7	461.0
Nebraska	115.6	102.3	2.2	14.7	461.0
Nevada	11.5	0.1	28.1	0.3	461.0
New Hampshire	438.7	345.3	437.6	72.9	461.0
New Jersey	392.1	0.0	1.0	369.2	2,154.2
New Mexico	12.5	6.5	0.0	39.5	461.0
New York	937.2	30.7	980.4	825.0	4,965.5
North Carolina	345.0	22.8	355.4	72.2	1,765.1
North Dakota	2.5	1.3	1.1	0.9	461.0
Ohio	169.2	4.7	9.0	216.5	2,930.9
Oklahoma	80.7	87.9	158.7	0.0	877.4
Oregon	48.9	0.5	0.0	35.0	751.6
Pennsylvania	305.0	8.5	16.1	319.5	3,350.5
Rhode Island	13.9	0.7	0.0	2.5	461.0
South Carolina	40.8	9.5	113.5	40.5	916.1
South Dakota	235.1	101.2	100.8	8.7	461.0
Tennessee	13.5	0.9	28.5	12.0	1,329.2
Texas	1,068.7	441.5	936.1	73.5	4,353.7
Utah	5.7	0.0	0.0	2.2	461.0
Vermont	74.4	11.9	0.0	16.2	461.0
Virginia	88.6	1.6	215.8	20.5	1,638.9
Washington State	108.9	0.1	6.4	2.0	1,242.5

State	Dukakis	Gephardt	Gore	Jackson	FEC Limit
West Virginia	50.6	2.0	4.7	22.4	518.9
Wisconsin	310.7	11.0	515.6	20.9	1,304.4
Wyoming	52.0	34.3	89.1	2.0	461.0
Total allocated	9,853.9	3,751.7	5,658.8	3,814.7	
Nonallocated	12,124.2	3,726.0	4,642.0	10,199 ?	

SOURCE: 1988 prenomination FEC press releases.

NOTE: Figures are through August 31, 1988, and are allocations as reported by the candidates. Gephardt and probably all other candidates understated sums spent in Iowa and New Hampshire. Preference vote winners are set in boldface type. Senator Paul Simon (not shown) won the Illinois primary. Dukakis finished second in Alaska, Arkansas, Delaware, the District of Columbia, Kentucky, Michigan, Nevada, South Dakota, and Wyoming. Gephardt came in second in New Hampshire and Oklahoma. Gore took second in Alabama, Georgia, Louisiana, Mississippi, South Carolina, and Virginia. Before the race narrowed to Dukakis and himself, Jackson was the runner-up in Arizona, Colorado, Connecticut, Florida, Idaho, Illinois, Kansas, Maine, Maryland, Massachusetts, Minnesota, Missouri, New York, North Carolina, Rhode Island, Tennessee, Texas (primary), Vermont, and Washington State.

home-state loss. No candidate chose to challenge another in his home state; Gephardt's reported spending in Massachusetts was actually New Hampshire spending.

Dukakis followed a "four-corners" strategy on Super Tuesday by concentrating on states bordering the Deep South (Texas, Florida, and Maryland) and his home state, Massachusetts. Gephardt spent heavily in Missouri, Georgia, Florida, Alabama, and Oklahoma. Gore outspent the other Democratic candidates in Alabama, Georgia, Kentucky, Mississippi, North and South Carolina, Tennessee, and Virginia. Jackson, who had much less to spend than his rivals, targeted his resources on states with the largest black populations.

The Republican candidates spent roughly equal amounts on Super Tuesday, but on different states. Bush outspent his rivals in Arkansas, Florida, Kentucky, and Mississippi; Dole in Alabama, Georgia, Maryland, Missouri, North Carolina, Oklahoma, and Washington; and Robertson in Louisiana, Texas, and Virginia. Each of the Republican candidates spent sizable sums in every Super Tuesday state, and some believe that, had Dole focused on only a few states, he might have done better (Maisel, 1988).

Did this spending matter? For Republicans, it mattered little. George Bush won all but one of the Super Tuesday contests, despite being outspent in twelve of them. He finished first in Alabama even though Dole spent two and a half times as much there. He won in Louisiana after being outspent by approximately $80,000, in Tennessee despite a more than

Table 4.8 Republican Candidate Spending by State (in Thousands of Dollars)

State	Bush	Dole	Robertson	FEC Limit
Alabama	87.6	216.7	194.1	1,093.9
Alaska	3.2	57.6	22.4	461.0
Arizona	3.2	34.7	82.6	909.8
Arkansas	86.0	78.8	60.7	642.1
California	30.1	139.1	301.6	7,509.5
Colorado	101.9	50.4	132.0	893.2
Connecticut	142.7	68.3	9.0	905.0
Delaware	0.1	4.0	4.6	461.0
District of Columbia	0.7	4.7	6.6	461.0
Florida	1,118.4	304.0	692.5	3,436.8
Georgia	252.9	291.1	211.7	1,654.4
Hawaii	85.6	78.6	45.9	461.0
Idaho	16.9	28.8	0.0	461.0
Illinois	797.4	1,097.6	185.5	3,152.1
Indiana	29.6	42.0	90.5	1,497.7
Iowa	773.8	775.8	771.8	775.1
Kansas	0.0	308.7	11.4	673.1
Kentucky	115.2	88.9	83.5	1,007.2
Louisiana	158.1	195.4	239.1	1,159.9
Maine	167.4	135.9	110.6	461.0
Maryland	115.4	274.8	37.4	1,257.6
Massachusetts	905.9	1,003.5	210.7	1,666.6
Michigan	976.3	79.1	411.3	2,485.7
Minnesota	33.3	655.4	157.0	1,156.2
Mississippi	187.9	82.4	128.6	676.0
Missouri	318.6	423.2	86.0	1,399.2
Montana	8.2	2.2	8.3	461.0
Nebraska	2.2	291.3	70.8	461.0
Nevada	18.1	74.2	97.7	461.0
New Hampshire	481.3	461.5	431.3	461.0
New Jersey	0.0	44.3	28.7	2,154.2
New Mexico	6.0	0.2	4.1	461.0
New York	254.3	158.8	156.5	4,965.5
North Carolina	203.5	704.9	163.6	1,765.1
North Dakota	0.7	12.2	2.9	461.0
Ohio	214.9	53.2	110.9	2,930.9
Oklahoma	180.6	306.4	133.0	877.4
Oregon	11.1	53.1	23.9	751.6
Pennsylvania	306.4	73.7	110.9	3,350.5
Rhode Island	65.9	77.6	10.9	461.0
South Carolina	580.5	341.7	360.4	916.1
South Dakota	203.1	352.8	160.3	461.0
Tennessee	116.1	267.5	160.6	1,329.2
Texas	420.5	158.0	960.7	4,353.7
Utah	3.7	10.5	0.0	461.0
Vermont	105.1	139.7	46.3	461.0
Virginia	55.3	75.4	301.5	1,638.9
Washington State	91.7	343.0	100.2	1,242.5

Table 4.8 **Republican Candidate Spending by State (in Thousands of Dollars)** *(continued)*

State	Bush	Dole	Robertson	FEC Limit
West Virginia	2.0	1.8	0.3	518.9
Wisconsin	**139.8**	124.1	19.3	1,304.4
Wyoming	**29.9**	**70.4**	10.5	461.0
Total allocated	10,026.3	10,735.4	7,761.1	
Nonallocated	13,105.7	11,630.2	14,855.1	

SOURCE: 1988 prenomination FEC press releases.

NOTE: Figures are through August 31, 1988, and are allocations as reported by the candidates. Preference vote winners are set in boldface type. Bush and Dole tied in the Wyoming caucuses. Delegates were selected in the New York primary, but no preference vote for candidates was taken. The Oregon, California, Montana, New Jersey, New Mexico, and North Dakota primaries came after Pat Robertson's May 16 withdrawal from the race.

two-to-one spending advantage by Dole, and in Texas despite a more than two-to-one spending advantage by Robertson.

For Democrats, however, spending did seem to matter in the early contests. It is generally believed that Gephardt outspent his rivals in Iowa, largely because of a final media blitz that helped restore his lead. Money mattered little in New Hampshire, where Dukakis benefited from years of free media coverage by Massachusetts television stations. However, in nearly 75 percent of the Super Tuesday primaries and caucuses, the candidate who spent the most won. In all but one of the remaining contests, the candidate who spent the most finished second to Jackson. Of course, it is difficult to disentangle cause from effect, since the candidates chose to spend in states where they had some chance of winning. Nevertheless, it seems clear that spending played a role in the outcome of the Democratic Super Tuesday elections.

After Super Tuesday, the pattern for the Democrats became more muddied. Jackson outspent Dukakis in the key states of Ohio, California, and Pennsylvania but lost each contest. His spending rivaled Dukakis's in New Jersey, where he lost by a substantial margin. In fact, Jackson outspent Dukakis during April, May, and June by more than $3.5 million, but won only one primary (the District of Columbia) and three caucuses in small states and the Virgin Islands. Jackson campaign officials, however, argue that the funds they spent in these later contests did substantially increase the percentage of the vote that their candidate received, even if they did not assure a Jackson victory.

How, then, do we assess the effects of campaign spending? Perhaps the most important consequence of television advertising is to increase the recognition of a candidate. As the Democratic candidates headed into Super Tuesday, most remained unknown to most voters. Television advertising helped inform the voters about the candidates and increased their name recognition. For the less-known candidates in a crowded field, spending was important.

This was not true of Jesse Jackson, whose name recognition was considerably higher than that of any of his rivals. Jackson began the campaign with a constituency. He could count on the support of most black voters and, in states with few blacks, of some white liberals. Many of those who did not support him were not susceptible to persuasion since they viewed him as unacceptable by virtue of ideology, inexperience in political office, or race. Thus Jackson could do well in states where he was substantially outspent by other candidates (including Lyndon La Rouche) but do little or no better in states where he spent more.

On the Republican side, George Bush was easily identifiable as the vice-president and as such was associated with Ronald Reagan, who was quite popular in the South. Bush won where he spent heavily and where he did not. When the Democratic field substantially narrowed after Super Tuesday, a similar phenomenon occurred. After Gore's departure, most Democratic voters became familiar with the two remaining candidates. Dukakis became the candidate running against Jackson, and no amount of Dukakis spending would eat into Jackson's base, just as spending by Jackson could not substantially broaden his base.

The 1988 election thus provides an important new caveat for the conventional wisdom on campaign spending. Television advertising can neither overcome the effects of long-term, free-media exposure in a short period nor erase deep-seated racial attitudes. It can, however, influence outcomes when a number of relatively unknown candidates are running. In early primaries and caucuses with no nationally known candidates, campaign spending is one route to recognition.

Money may also matter in other circumstances. While campaign spending could not buy victory for Robertson in Texas or for Jackson in California, those candidates may have received a higher percentage of the vote because of their spending. To pinpoint the impact of spending on primary election results, we would need access to the polls conducted for the candidates before, during, and after the actual campaigning in a state. We would further need to take into account the free media exposure that the various candidates received in that state. Only then could we determine whether spending influenced vote totals.

The Overall Limit

Although the overall spending limit did not play a decisive role in the 1988 campaign, it was a factor in candidate strategy. Since the passage of the FECA, candidates have been spending greater and greater proportions of their money very early in the election cycle. In 1984, Mondale had spent half of his legal limit by the end of February (Orren, 1985). In the 1988 election cycle, Bush, Dole, and Robertson had each spent a significant percentage of the limit by the end of 1987. Indeed, Pat Robertson's campaign spent nearly half the legal limit in 1987. By the end of February, Robertson and Dole had spent approximately 80 percent of the legal limit.

Table 4.9 shows cumulative spending as a proportion of the overall limit for Bush, Dole, Robertson, Dukakis, and Jackson, along with the proportion of party delegates selected. The Republican candidates spent their money much earlier than did the Democrats; indeed, these charts understate this pattern, since the Republicans also spent heavily through PACs and foundations in Michigan as early as 1986.

Only Bush's Super Tuesday landslide prevented the Republican candidates from spending the limit with more than half of the delegates still to be selected. By the end of March, all three of the campaigns were close to the limit. Bush could have legally spent $4 million in the next three months; Robertson and Dole would have been limited to $2.5 million apiece.

If the outcome of Super Tuesday had been different, all three campaigns would have quickly exceeded their legal spending limit. Each campaign would then have sought to exploit and widen the many loopholes that

Table 4.9 **Candidate Spending as a Percentage of Overall Limits, and Percentage of Delegates Selected, by Period**

Period	Dukakis	Jackson	Delegates
Democrats			
1987	23	8	0
1/88	30	12	0
2/88	45	19	3
3/88	60	27	57
4/88	72	43	76
5/88	81	56	86
6/88	90	62	100

	Bush	Dole	Robertson	Delegates
Republicans				
1987	33	40	48	0
1/88	45	56	69	3
2/88	59	75	79	11
3/88	79	86	85	50
4/88	84	88	89	59
5/88	89	90	90	86
6/88	92	92	90	100

SOURCE: 1988 prenomination FEC press releases.

have developed in the FECA over the years. The rest of the campaign would have been conducted through independent expenditure committees and candidate PACs as surrogates for the candidates' campaign committees. Bush's landslide victory averted a potential disaster for the FECA.

Loopholes

Each new election cycle has introduced new loopholes for candidates to avoid statewide or overall spending limits. In past cycles, these loopholes have been geared primarily at avoiding the state limits in Iowa and New Hampshire, or at allowing excessive contributions from supporters.

In 1980, the Reagan campaign was the first to take advantage of independent expenditures, one legal method to avoid spending limits. In the New Hampshire primary, considered vital after Bush's surprise victory in Iowa, the Reagan campaign fast approached the limit. At this point, several groups took to the air in support of Reagan. Although the original FECA had prohibited such spending, in 1976 the Supreme Court in *Buckley v. Valeo* ruled that independent spending involved free speech and could not be prohibited as long as such spending was truly independent.

During the 1988 campaign, independent expenditures played a less important role. Independent expenditure committees were formed for several major Republican candidates, but the amount spent and the states in which it was spent did not affect the nomination outcome. As the Democratic race narrowed to two candidates, there was some independent spending against each. When it became apparent that Bush and Dukakis would be their party's nominees, Republican-oriented groups began spending on behalf of Bush and against Dukakis.

Often what initially appears to campaign attorneys as a legal loophole is eventually viewed as a violation of the FECA. The Mondale delegate committees in 1984 are a case in point: the Mondale campaign paid a civil fine after the election. In January 1988, several Democratic candidates were involved in a flap over the purchase of computerized voter lists in Iowa and New Hampshire. The Iowa Democratic party sold computerized lists of Democratic and independent voters to candidates for $10,000, and the New Hampshire party sold its list for $7,500. In lieu of direct payment, party committees accepted solicited contributions by individual backers of each candidate. This practice raised the specter of excessive contributions since at least some of those who contributed on behalf of a candidate had already given the legal maximum directly to that candidate. In response to the controversy, Babbitt paid directly for his Iowa list, although the party had already accepted individual contributions as payment.

The most-exploited loophole in 1988 was PAC and foundation activity.

This was not the first time presidential candidates had used PACs as part of their early activity; Ronald Reagan's PAC, "Citizens for the Republic," was instrumental in his 1980 election. Mondale, John Glenn, and Ernest Hollings used PACs as part of their 1984 strategies. Such PACs have generally served three major functions. First, by contributing to congressional and state and local candidates across the country, a PAC helps build support among political figures. Second, by paying the salaries of campaign officials and by paying for the candidate to travel to speak on behalf of other candidates, PACs help lay the groundwork for the real campaign. Finally, by developing direct-mail solicitation lists, PACs ease a candidate's fund-raising costs in the primary elections.

In 1988, PAC activity reached new levels, particularly among Republican candidates, who were faced with an unusual set of incentives. The Michigan Republican party adopted for the 1988 campaign a complicated caucus-convention process in which the first round of delegate selection took place in August 1986. The FECA declares that individual contributions made before January 1 of the year before the general election are not eligible for matching funds, but spending during this period by an official campaign committee would count against the candidate's overall spending limit. These incentives made PAC and foundation activity particularly attractive. Kemp and Bush used PACs to contest the initial balloting in Michigan while Robertson relied on a tax-exempt foundation. Robertson also used a PAC in the early stages of his campaign. Such activity fell outside the scope of FECA spending limits.

In August 1986 George Bush's exploratory campaign committee reported spending just $1,000 in Michigan, but his PAC spent more than $150,000 (Pincus, 1988). Of course, the PAC had spent considerable sums in Michigan in previous months as well, including money for salaries for Bush operatives, rent for offices, payment for phone banks, payment for mailings, and other campaign expenses. The Bush PAC paid for the services of the consultants who later headed his campaign: Lee Atwater, Roger Ailes, and Robert Teeter. Nor was Bush alone in PAC activity. Kemp's PAC also actively contested the Michigan precinct-delegate elections. Robert Dole's PAC was not involved in the early Michigan balloting but was quite active in the Dole campaign, paying the salaries of consultants and staff, and for direct mail, computers, and travel (Morgan, 1988).

Table 4.10 presents the total level of PAC expenditures, along with total direct contributions to federal candidates[4] by the PAC of each candidate. These amounted to considerably more PAC activity in the 1988 primaries than in previous campaigns, especially among the Republican candidates. Although Paul Simon and Richard Gephardt both used PACs as part of

Table 4.10 **PAC Expenditures and Contributions, 1985–88 (in Dollars)**

	Expenditures	Contributions	Percentage Contributed
Democrats			
Gephardt	1,186,224	67,596	6
Simon	465,721	76,286	16
Republicans			
Bush	10,795,937	860,297	8
Dole	7,553,567	419,813	6
Kemp	4,157,478	165,815	4
Robertson	674,095	37,793	6

SOURCE: 1988 prenomination FEC press releases.
NOTE: PAC activity for 1987–88 cycle is through end of primary season unless candidate dropped out of the race. Contributions are to candidates for federal office. Most PACs made additional contributions to candidates at the end of the cycle, and many made contributions to state and local candidates not reflected in the amounts reported above.

their campaigns, their efforts were much more modest than those of the Republican candidates. For Bush and Dole, PAC activity represented an additional 25 percent to 33 percent of the legal spending limit.

In addition to using PACs, several candidates used tax-exempt foundations as part of their campaign strategy. Most visible was Pat Robertson's Freedom Council. The use of foundations has its drawbacks, however, as Robertson's case clearly demonstrates. To qualify for tax-exempt status, such foundations must not engage in partisan political activity. In December 1987 the Internal Revenue Service filed an administrative summons for Robertson's campaign records as part of an investigation of the connections among the Freedom Council, the Robertson Christian Broadcasting Network (also tax-exempt) and the Robertson campaign. By April, former officials of the Freedom Council were on national television detailing how the organization was used as a front for the Robertson campaign. At the time of this writing, the case was still pending.

Conclusion

Money clearly played a role in the 1988 presidential primaries and caucuses, but its role was not simple or straightforward. Michael Dukakis assembled an impressive fund-raising team and had substantially more money in the early contests than his rivals. In the latter stages of the Democratic primaries and caucuses, however, Dukakis came up against the overall spending limit, and Jesse Jackson raised and spent more money. Still, Jackson's funds did not buy him victories, as Dukakis won a string of contests in the final weeks of the campaign.

For the Democrats, spending seemed to matter in the early contests when the public was faced with a decision among seven little-known candidates. In Iowa and on Super Tuesday, the candidates who spent the most generally won. Jesse Jackson was the major exception to this rule; he won or placed well in primaries where he was massively outspent.

Among the Republicans, Bush, Dole, and Robertson each raised considerable sums early in the campaign, and each spent large amounts before the end of 1987, but George Bush enjoyed a sizable advantage in available cash over his rivals at each stage of the contest. Bush's success, however, does not seem to have been related to his spending. He won nearly all the states on Super Tuesday, despite spending considerably less than his rivals in several.

The 1988 prenomination process sheds new light on the conventional wisdom regarding the role of money in campaigns. Money clearly does not directly translate into victory, as Dole and Robertson discovered on March 8. Money does matter, however, for candidates who are not well known and who are running in crowded fields against other unknowns. Spending is not the only way to gain name recognition, nor is it the only way to put together an organization to mobilize support (as Robertson and Jackson demonstrated), but it provides one route to spreading the candidate's message to potential voters.

Notes

My thanks to Emmett Buell, Elizabeth Cook, and Lee Sigelman for helpful comments, to James Lengle for information on delegate selection, and to Bob Biersack of the Federal Election Commission for essential data.

1. Although Robert Kennedy got into the 1968 nominating process late, raising $11 million in only eleven weeks (mostly from big contributors), a similar strategy would not be attempted today because of front-loading and contribution limits. Despite all the speculation about a late entry by Governor Mario Cuomo in 1988, the schedule of primaries and caucuses and the rules of campaign finance made such a bid most unlikely.
2. There are other reasons for larger candidate fields, however, such as changes in party rules, more primaries, and Democratic use of proportional representation. The Democrats had a large candidate field in 1972, before the FECA, despite Muskie's initial lead in the polls.
3. Note that Babbitt also raised a large proportion of his total funds from big contributors. This is not uncommon among candidates making an early exit and who have raised their "seed money" in large contributions.
4. Such totals do not include contributions to, and expenditures on behalf of, state and local candidates.

References

Babcock, Charles. 1988a. "Stretching the Limits in Iowa." *Washington Post* (January 25): 4A.

———. 1988b. "FEC Approves Writeoffs of TV Ads." *Washington Post* (February 26): 10A.

Berke, Richard. 1987a. "Strange Behavior on Campaign Trail Has Roots in Spending Limit Rules." *New York Times* (December 23): 8.

———. 1987b. "Heeding Plato, Greek-Americans Aid in Effort to Raise Money for Dukakis." *New York Times* (December 27): 20.

Blow, Richard. 1988. "Rolling in It." *The New Republic* 198 (March 21): 23–25.

Maisel, L. Sandy. 1988. "Spending Patterns in Presidential Nominating Campaigns, 1976–1988." Unpublished paper presented at annual meeting of American Political Science Association, September 1–4.

Malbin, Michael. 1985. "You Get What You Pay for, but Is That What You Want?" In *Before Nomination: Our Primary Problems*, ed. George Grassmuck. Washington, D.C.: American Enterprise Institute for Public Policy.

Morgan, Dan. 1988. "PACs Stretching the Limits of Campaign Law." *Washington Post* (February 5): 1A.

Morin, Richard. 1988 "Giving Twice—To Candidates and Their PACs." *Washington Post* (February 7): 17A.

Orren, Gary. 1985. "The Nomination Process: Vicissitudes of Candidate Selection." In *The Elections of 1984*, ed. Michael Nelson. Washington, D.C.: Congressional Quarterly Press.

Pincus, Walter. 1988. "Bush's PAC Used to Evade Spending Lid." *Washington Post* (February 7): 1A.

Robinson, Michael. 1984. "The Power of the Primary Purse: Money in 1984." In *The Mass Media in Campaign '84: Articles from Public Opinion Magazine*, ed. Michael J. Robinson and Austin Ranney. Washington, D.C.: American Enterprise Institute for Public Policy.

———. 1985. "Where's the Beef? Media and Media Elites in 1984." In *The American Elections of 1984*, ed. Austin Ranney. Durham, N.C.: Duke University Press.

Rosenbaum, David. 1988. "A Rationing of Resources to Handle Super Tuesday." *New York Times* (February 21): 1.

Sorauf, Frank J. 1988. *Money in American Elections*. Glenview, Ill.: Scott, Foresman.

Sullam, Brian. 1988. "The Cash Campaign." *New Republic* 198 (March 14): 9–13.

Walsh, Edward. 1987. "The More Seed Money, the Better." *Washington Post* (December 5): 1A.

Werth, Barry. 1988. "The Incredible Rolodex." *New England Monthly* 5 (July): 37–46, 92–93.

Wilcox, Clyde. 1988. "Political Action Committees of the New Christian Right: A Longitudinal Analysis." *Journal for the Scientific Study of Religion* 27 (March): 60–71.

5. Ministering to the Nation: The Campaigns of Jesse Jackson and Pat Robertson

Kenneth D. Wald

No one says, "Right on!" to Richard A. Gephardt or "Amen!" to Bob Dole (Clifford, 1987)

"Major" presidential candidates are usually recruited from the ranks of current or former public officials. Despite an occasional urge to cleanse the Republic by bestowing the presidency on outsiders who are "above" politics, Americans seem to prefer candidates with considerable experience in public office. However, this conventional wisdom, like so many truisms, was challenged during the 1988 nomination struggle by the "serious" candidacies of Jesse L. Jackson and Marion G. "Pat" Robertson. Neither candidate had ever served in public office, and both had entered politics by the unlikeliest of routes—the pulpit. In a nation wary of mixing religious enthusiasm with political passion, Jackson and Robertson established themselves as major forces within their respective parties. This chapter explores the candidacies of the two ministers, using them as vehicles to raise larger questions about American politics and the social and political transformations that have encouraged clerical activism in the secular realm.

Religion in American Politics

Government in the United States takes no official notice of religion with its citizens and disavows formal ties with any particular faith. Despite this official separation of state and religion, religion long has been one of the principal social forces in American life and a factor that suffuses politics at many different levels (Wald, 1987). The religious motif has imparted to

American political culture an insistence on public rectitude and the perception of a transcendent national mission, two political orientations that have long amazed and perplexed sensitive foreign observers. Some analysts claim that respect for individual rights, a central tenet of the American political creed, is grounded in a religious view of the equality of all persons before God. Beyond its consensual impact on political culture, religion has also helped to define the political agenda in the United States and to frame the terms in which contentious issues are understood and debated. Through this mode of influence, religion has been a source of conflict and controversy (Platt and Williams, 1988). Finally, religion has helped demarcate electoral coalitions. Candidates and their strategists have often approached the electorate as a set of ethno-religious blocs with distinctive political interests and outlooks.

All these dimensions of "confessional" politics were apparent during the campaign for the 1988 major-party nominations. The concern with candidate "character," manifest in both the wreckage of the Hart campaign over charges of adultery and the withdrawal of Joseph Biden in response to criticism of untruthfulness, derived at least in part from a culture that demands virtue and rectitude of its leaders. Some campaign issues had direct ties to religious values—abortion being the most prominent—while others, such as drug use, were treated largely as matters of personal conduct susceptible to change by moral suasion. The persistence of religious influence was also clear in the degree to which candidates targeted religious communities with distinct and particular appeals. Once notably cool to the social conservatism of his party's right wing, George Bush evinced a level of support for causes calculated to enhance his appeal to that electoral bloc. Michael Dukakis's nationwide campaign was fueled by substantial contributions from the Greek Orthodox and Jewish communities.

But the most direct and visible manifestation of religion in the 1988 nomination campaign was surely the prominence of two ordained ministers, Jackson and Robertson. The religious affiliation of presidential nominees has occasionally been politically significant. In 1960, more than thirty years after the first Catholic had headed a national ticket, John Kennedy still had to struggle with questions about the suitability of a Roman Catholic to hold the nation's highest office. When Jimmy Carter first emerged as a serious contender in 1976, his profession of evangelical piety raised public interest in the phenomenon of traditionalist Protestantism. Both Kennedy and Carter had to satisfy a skeptical public that they would respect the secular character of the state and public policy before they could attain the presidency. Jackson and Robertson presented a more direct challenge to the norm of church-state separation in 1988. Not only were they ministers, but both offered visions of America steeped in the imagery and values of their respective religious traditions. Moreover, the campaigns of the two candidates were rooted in and sustained by a network of churches and religious organizations.

This chapter maps the divergent paths that brought Jackson and Robertson into the 1988 nomination campaigns and then explores the specifically religious dimension of their campaigns for nomination. We then consider the larger social and political forces that accounted for their status as serious candidates for the nomination.

Political and Religious Background

Pat Robertson

Pat Robertson traveled a circuitous route to the 1988 nomination campaign. The son of a conservative Democratic senator from Virginia, Robertson grew up in a gracious home in Lexington, doted on by his deeply religious mother. Remembered as a "precocious, competitive, aggressive" young man (Shribman, 1987), he graduated from a private school in Tennessee and then returned to Lexington to attend Washington and Lee University. Following graduation with honors, Robertson was called to active duty in the Marines. After his service ended, he entered Yale Law School but failed the New York bar examination in 1955. Robertson subsequently had short stints as a junior executive and a partner in an electronics firm. The failure of his business career and other personal reversals prompted Robertson to consider the possibility of a future in the ministry.

Though initially inclined to pursue this ambition in a "fashionable" church, Robertson's plans underwent a dramatic change upon his meeting in Philadelphia with an itinerant evangelist. As Robertson described it, the meeting brought him face-to-face with the emptiness and aimlessness of his life and pointed toward a solution in the form of a wholehearted commitment to Christ as his personal savior. In short order, he resigned from the electronics company and left his pregnant wife and infant son to attend a fellowship camp in Canada. In three subsequent years of study at an evangelical seminary in New York, Robertson "migrated from casual Christian, to fervent evangelical, to pioneering charismatic" (Harrell, 1987: 45).

Upon graduation, with his unconventional religious beliefs keeping him from pursuing most job opportunities, Robertson moved back to Virginia to purchase a dilapidated UHF television station in Portsmouth. Together with some friends and former teachers, he drew up the articles of incorporation for a "Christian Broadcasting Network" (CBN) that went on the air late in 1961. Though subsequently ordained as a minister in the Southern Baptist Convention and appointed assistant pastor in a Norfolk church,

Robertson's attention was consumed by the demands of building CBN. Robertson quickly developed a facility for televison. Together with Jim Bakker, he hosted a talk show known as "The 700 Club." Though Robertson did not actually preach in the manner of Oral Roberts, Billy Graham, or other media ministers, he frequently engaged in prayer, spoke in tongues, and claimed to have healed the sick by direct appeals to God. Through telethons, the purchase of time on other stations, and other fund-raising efforts, Robertson was able to raise sufficient capital to put CBN on a relatively firm financial footing in the roller-coaster world of religious broadcasting. By the time he left to campaign full-time for the presidency, CBN was the fifth largest television network in the United States, with revenues approaching $200 million and access through satellites and cable-television systems to approximately thirty million homes (King, 1988). Under CBN's aegis, Robertson also promoted a massive charitable fund-raising program, "Operation Blessing," and expanded the reach of his ministry with the founding of "CBN University," an assortment of graduate and professional schools.

Robertson inherited the social and economic values of his conservative Virginia environment and followed the path of many white southerners by moving from the Democratic party to a Republican preference. While clearly articulating his conservative political and social views during the early days of CBN, Robertson eschewed direct political involvement—even to the extent of refusing to assist his father's reelection campaign in 1966. Arguing that God had told him that the divine will could not be tied to the fate of any candidate for public office, Robertson was at best a cautious and sporadic participant in the rising evangelical political movement during the late 1970s. Jimmy Carter's election in 1976 filled him with hope about the prospects for the nation under Christian leadership, but he grew disillusioned with Carter's stewardship and was drawn into the circle of evangelicals who organized the 1980 "Washington for Jesus" rally. This gathering of evangelicals to pray for national redemption suggested to him the possibilities of a broad coalition that could not be mustered effectively under rather sectarian and bombastic fundamentalists like the Reverend Jerry Falwell.

Throughout the 1980s, Robertson edged toward direct political involvement. CBN founded and subsidized the Freedom Council, "which had the avowed purpose of involving Christians in the electoral process" (King, 1988), but which was denounced by critics as a political action organization devoted to laying the groundwork for a Robertson presidential bid. In 1986, Robertson declared that he would require pledges of prayer and support from three million registered voters before undertaking a campaign. By September 1987, "Americans for Robertson," a formally constituted political action committee, announced that the requisite signatures had been obtained, and Robertson committed to campaign for the Republican presidential nomination. Hoping to lay to rest public concerns about breaching the line between church and state, Robertson formally resigned both his ordination in the Southern Baptist Convention and his position at CBN.

The Robertson platform included many specific proposals but asserted that "underneath all the programs is moral decay" (*New York Times*, 1988a). The budget deficit, identified as the principal problem facing a new president, was castigated as "stealing from our children" on the part of undisciplined public officials. In foreign policy, he believed that American troubles could be traced to the baleful influence of "the Eastern liberal establishment," which was attempting to move the country "toward a one-world socialist Government." Reliance on government rather than free enterprise similarly accounted for economic problems and poverty. The solution to the AIDS crisis, he asserted, was for people "to practice abstinence and stop shooting intravenous drugs." Welfare programs and the federal tax code were indicted for contributing to family breakup. Educational problems were attributed largely to crime, drug use, and a breakdown in discipline. With the restoration of social order, together with training "in right and wrong and morality," the nation would return to the path of international competitiveness and prosperity.

The Robertson campaign had actually been underway for some time before the candidate announced his entry. Borrowing from Jimmy Carter's "guerrilla" strategy of 1976, the campaign put substantial energy into party gatherings that, while insignificant in themselves, would catch the attention of the mass media and thereby bring national attention to the candidate in the prelude to the "official" nomination period. The momentum provided by the early victories would tide Robertson over until Super Tuesday, it was hoped, when he would be able to capitalize on the social conservatism of his fellow southerners. The strategy paid off during the "invisible" primary season (Berke, 1987; Dionne, 1987). The Robertson campaign first struck in Michigan in August 1986, electing a near majority of delegates to county GOP conventions. A year later, Robertson triumphed in a straw poll of Iowa Republican activists at a fund-raising event. Robertson subsequently won a straw poll in Virginia and placed a close second to Bush in Florida. These events prompted reluctant party leaders and the media to take Robertson seriously and to assess carefully the magnitude of his "invisible army."

Having laid the groundwork by demonstrating a capacity to turn out committed supporters under adverse conditions, these tactics culminated in Robertson's stunning upset of George Bush in the Iowa caucuses on February 8. Garnering 25 percent to finish second behind Robert Dole,

Robertson hoped to capitalize on this success by a similar surprise in New Hampshire but was disappointed by his fifth-place showing on February 20. The South Carolina primary on March 5 posed his best hope to regain momentum, but Robertson's candidacy stumbled badly in the wake of his distant third-place finish, and his hopes were finally dashed by a dismal showing throughout the South on March 8. In what should have been his most fertile environment, Robertson managed no better than a 21 percent share of the Oklahoma vote, distant second-place finishes in two states, and only 13 percent of the votes cast in all the Super Tuesday primary states. A week later, Robertson slipped to less than 7 percent of the vote in the Illinois primary. Though he continued his candidacy through mid-May, winning lightly attended caucuses in Alaska, Robertson amassed fewer than fifty delegates through the primary election process before suspending his campaign.

Jesse Jackson[1]

By 1988, the Reverend Jesse Jackson was a familiar face to the American public, a veteran of one presidential campaign that had already surpassed the expectations of pundits and pollsters alike. Jackson's entry into the 1984 campaign had divided black leaders, many of whom had previous commitments to Walter Mondale. Despite the intense competition with Mondale for his "core" constituency in the black community, Jackson finished a respectable third in 1984, earning almost one-fifth of all votes cast in Democratic primaries and electrifying the convention audience with his impassioned address. He began the campaign for the 1988 nomination soon after the general election of 1984, utilizing the newly founded "Rainbow Coalition" as a vehicle to advance his candidacy.

Jackson defined his constituency as "the damned, the disinherited, the disrespected, and the despised" (Jackson 1987: 3). His commitment to the underclass has been attributed to his own background as the illegitimate son of a teenage mother in Greenville, South Carolina. Despite this unpromising beginning, Jackson achieved early distinction in both academics and athletics, eventually earning a football scholarship to the University of Illinois. Because of what he describes as the discovery of racism on campus, Jackson left Urbana after one year to attend a predominantly black college, North Carolina A&T. Following graduation in 1964, he returned to Illinois as a divinity student at the Chicago Theological Seminary, an institution known for its emphasis on applied theology.

Like many young ministers of his generation, Jackson was drawn into politics through the civil rights movement. As a college student, he had participated in sit-ins to desegregate public facilities. In 1965, he joined

Martin Luther King's march for voting rights in Selma, Alabama. Through contacts made with King and other leaders of the Southern Christian Leadership Conference (SCLC), Jackson returned to Chicago with the task of organizing the city's black ministers on behalf of the SCLC. King eventually asked Jackson to head "Operation Breadbasket," an SCLC movement that used selective boycotts of white-owned businesses to force greater minority employment and to encourage blacks to patronize black-owned businesses. Jackson was also instrumental in organizing open-housing marches in Chicago, marking the SCLC's first sustained foray against Northern racism and its initial encounter with violent attacks from white mobs outside the South. These commitments drew Jackson away from the seminary into full-time work on behalf of civil rights; he was eventually ordained by a church that did not require a seminary degree.

Following King's murder in 1968, Jackson attempted to portray himself as the heir to the leadership of black America. Frustrated by his inability to control the SCLC, Jackson resigned in 1971 to found Operation PUSH (People United to Save Humanity), which he described as an organization dedicated to placing economic issues on the civil rights agenda. Similar to Operation Breadbasket, PUSH pressed white-owned businesses to provide greater opportunities for minority products, employment, and ownership — signing a number of "covenants" to that effect with major corporations. Operation PUSH had a broader purpose, however, in its goal to instill black youth with self-respect. Through rallies, worship services, appeals to the family and community, and radio broadcasts, Jackson exhorted young people to help themselves by foreswearing drugs and other self-destructive pursuits in favor of education. The organization quickly expanded nationwide, the novelty of its self-help philosophy attracting the national media and federal funding.

Leadership of Operation PUSH both ratified and extended Jackson's status as the premier spokesperson for the black community. His personal dynamism, coupled with the institutional base of the movement, brought Jackson repeated speaking engagements around the nation and frequent opportunities to address a national audience through the mass media. By dint of these efforts and remarkably favorable press coverage, Jackson could lay a credible claim to the position once held by King as the principal spokesperson for black political aspirations. His surprising success in 1984 cemented that status and prepared him to enter the 1988 nomination struggle with the unified support of the black community.

Jackson's ascent was not without controversy. During his early days in the civil rights movement, his reported egotism and thirst for publicity provoked repeated conflicts with Martin Luther King, Jr., and prompted charges that he traded on King's martyrdom by inflating his relationship with the great man. Critics of PUSH maintained that it was poorly run, given to extortion, and diverted money donated at great sacrifice to support Jackson's lavish personal life-style. Jackson's leadership was criticized as long on imagination but short on planning, execution, and accountability. Like Robertson, he often propounded dubious propositions as unassailable facts. These charges do not seem to have seriously impaired his standing with the mass of blacks who acclaimed him with enthusiasm.

The stunning withdrawal of Gary Hart from the race in May 1987 left Jackson as the best-known and most strongly supported of the probable Democratic candidates, a legacy of both his 1984 campaign and the widespread public exposure from his years of activism. Even so, Jackson struggled with skepticism about his electability, the breadth of his support base, limited funding, and substantial doubt whether he was qualified for the presidency. Brushing aside these reservations, Jackson enlisted the support of most prominent black politicians in planning his second run for the nomination. After announcing his candidacy formally on October 10, Jackson began a frenetic nationwide campaign that relied heavily on volunteer labor and personal appearances by the candidate rather than paid advertising.

As in 1984, Jackson aligned himself firmly with what he described as the progressive wing of the Democratic party. In domestic policy, he called for substantial increases in government support for education, housing, drug eradication, and job creation — scoring the Reagan administration for its alleged indifference on these issues. To pay for these investments, he proposed raising taxes on top wage-earners and setting aside a portion of public pension funds for urban redevelopment. In addition to his economic populism, Jackson called for fundamental shifts in American foreign policy toward Africa and Latin America and a more evenhanded approach to Middle East negotiations. Though these positions are customarily associated with the liberal agenda, Jackson's emphasis on personal responsibility and the capacity of individuals to change themselves reveals elements of social conservatism, one heritage of his evangelical theology. Nonetheless, he strongly supported abortion rights and consistently condemned discrimination against gay people.

The electoral strategy mapped out by the campaign hoped for respectable showings in the earliest delegate-selection exercises and looked to the Super Tuesday primaries on March 8 to establish Jackson as a bona fide contender for the nomination. The goal was to knit together a diverse coalition including blacks, other racial and ethnic minorities, liberals, women, and working-class whites. These expectations were largely vindicated as Jackson survived the Iowa and New Hampshire contests to finish strongly on March 8.[2] On that critical day, he garnered almost one-quarter of the total vote, captured nearly a third of the delegates, and came in first in five Southern primaries. A second-place finish in Illinois a week later cemented his status as a contender and was followed a week later by the high point of Jackson's run for the nomination, victory in the Michigan caucuses. On March 26, Jackson stunned Michael Dukakis, widely regarded at the time as the front-runner, by taking a clear majority of the delegates at precinct meetings. Unlike the victories in the South and his adopted home state of Illinois, which were won almost exclusively through his appeal to blacks, the Michigan victory suggested that Jackson could make inroads on a predominantly white electorate. Observers were particularly impressed by his ability to draw votes from "upscale" whites.

Prospects that Jackson might actually claim the nomination, a matter of serious discussion in party circles following Michigan, were dashed by consecutive primary defeats in Connecticut, Wisconsin, New York, and Pennsylvania. Jackson dropped further and further behind Dukakis. By the Pennsylvania primary on April 26, when it had become a two-person race, Dukakis essentially secured the nomination with a more than two-to-one victory over Jackson. Though Jackson continued to compete, he finished a distant second to Dukakis in all the subsequent primaries (with the exception of the District of Columbia). At the conclusion of the primary season, Jackson had nearly doubled his 1984 showing by accumulating 6.8 million votes, 29 percent of all votes cast in Democratic primaries. Exit polls indicate that Jackson received over 90 percent of the votes cast by blacks and increased his showing among white Democrats to the range of 10 to 25 percent. Jackson claimed almost 1,200 of the 4,100 delegates at the convention, too few to achieve the nomination but enough to make him a key player in platform negotiations.

The Religious Motif in the Robertson Campaign

Jackson and Robertson brought a distinctive religious tone to the 1988 campaign. While they approached the church-state issue from very different directions, both campaigns can be understood as lengthy exercises in applied theology.

Because he came to national prominence through his religious endeavors, it was perhaps inevitable that Pat Robertson should face intense questions about his view of the relationship between church and state and, more broadly, about the role of religious values in his political agenda. A Southern Baptist, Robertson is heir to the theological tradition of "evangelicalism." Recognized more as a temper than a creed, a tendency than a denomination, evangelicals generally share a faith that stresses the Bible as the authoritative (but not necessarily literal) guide to God's will, the acceptance of God's grace through a conversion experience, and the importance of encouraging others to share in salvation by embracing the opportunity for spiritual rebirth. These views are subscribed to by many Americans and constitute something of a cultural norm in the South.

While in the seminary, Robertson also partook of another theological movement, known today as charismatic renewal, which was not widely accepted by his church and was even less broadly accepted by the American religious community. Charismatic Christians believe in the "baptism of the Holy Spirit," that God's presence is made known in the world through miraculous and direct intervention. The form of that intervention may include prompting believers to communicate in special prayer languages — the spontaneous act of speaking in tongues — or healing the sick through prayer, or prefiguring the future through prophetic passages in the Bible. Whatever the specific manifestation of the "Holy Spirit," this approach emphasizes an active, present, immediate God who can be encountered directly during worship and private meditation. As the charismatic movement spread from the Pentecostal churches to more evangelical and mainline congregants during the 1960s and 1970s, Robertson competed with Oral Roberts, Jim Bakker, and Jimmy Swaggart as its most prominent advocate and expositor. His active involvement in the Full Gospel Businessman's Fellowship, an interdenominational charismatic organization, brought him nationwide speaking engagements before sympathetic audiences as well as contacts that would prove invaluable as a source of campaign volunteers.

Robertson was not the first Southern Baptist to seek the presidency, but his status as a minister clearly distinguished him from fellow Baptists and raised anew public concerns about the degree to which he respected the historic separation between government and religion. The charismatic commitment accentuated this concern. True to his beliefs as a "Spirit-filled" Christian, Robertson reported direct communication with God and Satan, prayed in tongues, claimed credit for instigating cures through faith healing, and asserted success in diverting hurricanes. These views might have been dismissed as a curiosity if Robertson had not sought the presidency. Critics pounced on tapes from old CBN broadcasts showing Robertson in faith-healing activities and quoted his wilder comments from the past — for example, that only pious Christians and Jews were fit for public office, or that genocide might be an acceptable part of God's plan for human redemption. More than one columnist portrayed Robertson as America's Khomeini in waiting.

To cope with these criticisms, Robertson adopted a three-pronged strategy of insisting on his respect for separation of church and state, charging his critics with religious bigotry, and stressing his secular credentials for the presidency. Citing the Bible and his Reformation heritage, Robertson emphasized respect for the individual and free choice as the central influ-ence of religion upon his political outlook. To reporters who raised con-cern about theocracy, Robertson countered with Biblical admonitions that supported preference for local authority over centralized government, op-position to coercion, and belief in the fundamental equality of humankind (Bandy, 1988). The resignation of his ministerial ordination and severing of all ties with CBN were part of the same effort. When questions about his religious beliefs remained the focus of attention or when he was des-cribed as a "television evangelist," Robertson went on the offensive by declaring himself a victim of "religious bigotry," likening the attacks to the concerns about John Kennedy's Catholicism.

The major thrust of the public campaign was to portray Robertson in terms that would reassure a secular audience of his fitness and qualifica-tions for high office. The centerpiece of this effort was a glossy Sunday newspaper supplement asking, "Who Is This Man?" The answers stressed his education at Yale Law School, business and entrepreneurial background as the "founder of a major televison cable network and a university," his role in organizing an international relief effort, and his heritage as the descendant of two American presidents and son of a former senator (Amer-icans for Robertson, n.d.). Subheadings on the inside pages were accom-panied by portraits of Robertson in his roles as "National Policy Leader," international statesman, educator, Korean War veteran, family man, and businessman. His conservative position on "moral issues" such as abor-tion and school prayer was given less prominence than his views on the economic and foreign-policy issues that have traditionally constituted the core agenda of conservative Republicanism. That the word "Christian" did not appear in the insert was part of a design to overcome Robertson's popular image as a "television preacher" and substitute the business and educational qualifications thought likely to appeal to a secular audience (Robertson, 1988).

Robertson's standard "stump speech" likewise stressed balancing the federal budget, eliminating the trade deficit, and restoring education, pri-orities that did not distinguish him from his Republican competitors. Even when raising an apparently "religious" issue like abortion, Robertson at-tempted to frame the debate in essentially nonreligious terms. Thus he invoked the specter of racism in attacking Planned Parenthood for its alleged plans to create a "master race" and contended during a debate that abortion would eventually reduce the number of workers contributing to Social Security trust funds. Similarly, his support for school prayer was couched in terms of fidelity to the heritage of America's founding genera-tion. According to newspaper reports, Robertson supporters were enjoined by the campaign to avoid religious language, disavow theocratic intentions, and discourage public events — such as church rallies — that would call attention to the religious fervor of the Robertson base. When addressing secular audiences, Robertson similarly downplayed the religious themes that predominated in his talks to church-based groups (Decker, 1987).

The attempt to disavow a sectarian thrust to the campaign was never particularly successful because of Robertson's distinctive message and the fundamental dependence of the campaign upon the charismatic community. When he emphasized traditional Republican themes of limited government, low taxes, virulent anticommunism, opposition to drug use, and the like, Robertson could not easily distinguish himself from competing candidates who possessed, in addition, the legislative and executive-branch experience that he lacked. Where Robertson differed was precisely on the "moral issues." Though most of his fellow candidates for the nomination shared his opposition to abortion and supported a larger public role for religious values, Robertson alone gave these issues pride of place. Newspaper accounts of campaign rallies indicate that the call for restoring God to the classroom and stopping abortion motivated Robertson's audience far more than his economic or foreign-policy views. A Florida fundamentalist accurately revealed the basis of Robertson's mass appeal when he identified "the ability to hear from God" as the prime qualification for president and described Robertson as the man possibly ordained by God to "call us to righteousness" in the White House (Buckingham, 1986).

Robertson's politics are inseparable from his religious faith. Addressing a congregation in Dallas, Robertson described his candidacy as the prelude to a massive spiritual revival that would come only from God. To hasten that day, he said, "we need a government that acts in accordance with Biblical principles" (Dahl, 1988). What principles of governance does he find in the Bible? To judge by the specific policy prescriptions Robertson derives from Scripture, government has both a positive and a negative function. In its active role, the state should promote wholesome conduct by prohibiting or discouraging certain forms of behavior condemned in the Bible. In addition to supporting moral purity, the government should not interfere with free enterprise, which he understands as part of God's plan for humankind (Robertson, 1984). Robertson thus combines elements of diverse theological approaches, principally the "Gospel of Prosperity" and an image of God as lawgiver, to formulate his views of the proper role of government in society.

Despite Robertson's denial that he was the candidate of "a small, well-organized minority" and his efforts to attain broad support, the campaign was clearly directed to the evangelical community. Though he entered 1988 with a poll rating in single digits (*Polling Report*, 1988), Robertson began the campaign with a base exceeding that of many better-known candidates: constant exposure to fourteen million viewers of "The 700 Club" and a long list of loyal financial contributors to his ministry. The viewers and contributors were tied into a network of local churches that served admirably as the infrastructure of his local campaign organizations. Robertson relied on this constituency to establish his credibility as a candidate, claiming in an unguarded moment, "I don't have to broaden my base. My political base is . . . the seventy million evangelical Christians in this country" (Reid, 1987). He told reporters that he could win the nomination by attracting support from only a third of the estimated twenty million evangelical voters who identified with the Republican party (Smith, 1987). The front-loading of southern primaries on Super Tuesday was expected to enhance this strategy because Robertson's core constituency was heavily concentrated below the Mason-Dixon line (Morin, 1987). Debates about whether Robertson could mobilize this "invisible army" dominated news analyses in the early stages of the campaign.

Reports from the campaign trail underscored the reliance of the Robertson organization upon volunteers from charismatic churches who had previously been uninvolved in party politics (Morphew, 1988; Straus, 1987). Many activists were drawn to his candidacy as part of the audience for "The 700 Club" or indirectly after contacts from fellow church members who alerted them to the candidacy. Ministers appear to have spearheaded the Robertson movement by serving as local coordinators, promoting voter registration drives, packing rallies with students from church schools, inviting the candidate to speak in church meeting halls, and recruiting congregants to participate in the caucuses and primaries (Balzar, 1987; Straus, 1987). Church directories and the rosters of Christian organizations were mined as sources of volunteers and contributors (Lawton, 1988).

The ethos of the campaign, unmistakably revivalist and emotional, reflected the culture of traditionalist Protestantism. At Robertson rallies, his supporters greeted his entry by lifting their arms "in the charismatic posture of praise" (Rodgers-Melinick, 1987), greeted his declarations with enthusiastic cries of "Praise the Lord" and "Praise God," and invoked the aid of the Holy Spirit (Morphew, 1988). A reporter accompanying Robertson observed that

> the people who show up at a Pat Robertson rally generally pay more attention to the pulpit than to politics. They can recite passages from Leviticus verbatim but cannot say which party their governor belongs to. Their lapel pins say "I found it!" or "Praise the Lord"; bumper stickers quote scripture. (Reid, 1987)

To communicate directly with potential supporters, the campaign borrowed from a technique widely used among fundamentalist preachers: it distributed thousands of audio and video cassettes featuring the candidate's message to the electorate (O'Connor, 1988; Balzar, 1987). The tapes, played in the privacy of the home, proved to be a potent means of reaching and energizing people who were inaccessible through traditional channels. Though disparaged by a critic as forty minutes of "rambling, shined-up George Wallace with a spiritual overlay" (Reeves, 1988), the tape moved at least one viewer to declare, "I feel like the Lord has risen up a candidate" (O'Connor, 1988).

More systematic evidence confirms these anecdotal accounts of Robertson's dependence upon conservative Protestants. Postal surveys of contributors to his fund-raising committee during the prenomination campaign in 1987 found them to be marked by "an intense and distinctive religiosity," "strong self-identification as 'charismatic' Christians," and a "strikingly different agenda" that gave priority to social rather than economic issues (Green and Guth, 1988). A study in a North Florida county found the same pattern among Robertson activists on the local Republican executive committee. Compared to supporters of the other Republican contenders, Robertson advocates "displayed more salient religious attitudes and behavior, were more likely to identify themselves as fundamentalists and charismatics, and relied more on religious sources for political information" (Kiester, 1988: 29). The magnitude of the differences was striking. More than 80 percent of the Robertson supporters (but only 20 percent of his opponents' advocates) were fundamentalist in their theological orientation; half designated themselves as "charismatic," three-quarters as "born-again Christian"; and all but two belonged to sectarian Protestant churches—i.e., independent Baptist, Church of God, Pentecostal, etc. (Kiester, 1988). Large majorities of Robertson activists reported that they relied for political information on the Bible, Christian broadcasting, and the clergy—information sources utilized seldom, if at all, by supporters of other candidates.

Robertson's mass base in the electorate was similarly distinguished by its religious coloration. A CBS poll of caucus participants in Iowa, where Robertson stunned the party with his second-place finish, found that he captured a clear majority of voters who described themselves as fundamentalists or evangelical Christians (Poole, 1988). In New Hampshire, Robertson obtained most of his support "from persons who attend church weekly, from persons opposed to all abortion, and from those who say they are 'born again'" (Turner, 1988). Among likely voters interviewed just before South Carolina's presidential primary, fundamentalist Protestants gave him five times the support of voters from other religious groups (Brody,

1988). All of these findings suggest that Robertson supporters were recruited and mobilized principally through a network of evangelical churches.

What gave this base strength beyond numbers was its level of commitment. By virtue of their belief that Robertson's candidacy was divinely ordained and his message true to the gospel, Robertson's volunteers were widely acknowledged to be the most committed and enthusiastic of all activists. Stories were told of Robertson volunteers braving icy weather, leaving sickbeds, or suspending careers and social lives in service to the candidacy; those who think they are doing the Lord's work are not apt to be deterred by such minor obstacles. Another sign of that dedication was Robertson's phenomenal ability to raise funds, attributable largely to the trust he had engendered with his audience. Provisional data indicate that he was able to raise and spend funds "on a scale we have not experienced before in politics" (Jackson, 1988).

So why did a candidate with such seeming advantages end up doing so poorly once the campaign left Iowa? Why in particular did Robertson perform so modestly not only in New Hampshire but in the more hospitable states of the Bible Belt? No doubt Robertson's losses can be attributed in some degree to the nature of the 1988 campaign. He was running as a politically inexperienced outsider against key Washington insiders, one of whom could capitalize on his eight years of loyal service to an immensely popular president. Experienced local activists, a valued commodity in any campaign, preferred more mainstream candidates. For all its vigor, the Robertson campaign thus had an amateurish cast to it. Robertson faced two additional handicaps. Despite his attempts to appear as a candidate with impeccable secular standing, Robertson was identified primarily as a "television evangelist" at a time when the status of that profession was suspect. Running as a "television minister" would be difficult enough under normal circumstances, but it was doubly so in 1988 during the well-publicized scandals involving the charismatic video ministries of Jim Bakker, Oral Roberts, and Jimmy Swaggart. The religious enthusiasm of Robertson's ardent backers undoubtedly scared off other Republicans and may have inspired a backlash in crucial primary states.

Robertson also suffered from a self-inflicted wound in the form of his penchant for "funny facts." At various points in the campaign, Robertson asserted that Soviet missiles were stationed in Cuba, that his CBN news department had once known the location of American hostages in Lebanon, that George Bush had personally orchestrated the downfall of Jimmy Swaggart, that Nancy Reagan was urging her husband to go soft on the Soviet Union, that the AIDS virus could be spread by casual conduct, and that one-fourth of automobile workers used illegal drugs. Other assertions, such as his claim that Supreme Court decisions lacked status as supreme law, inspired concern about his commitment to long-held norms. Robertson was also damaged by allegations that he had used his father's influence to avoid hazardous duty during his military service and had then falsely claimed combat experience. Doubts about the candidate's veracity were raised by the discovery that Robertson had misled reporters about his wedding date to disguise the conception of his first son outside marriage and had exaggerated his educational and business credentials. These incidents painted Robertson as a candidate given to wild and unsubstantiated statements. He entered the campaign with the most negative poll evaluations among all declared Republicans, and these gaffes drove his "unfavorability" ratings to previously uncharted levels (*Polling Report*, 1988; Hume and Jaroslovsky, 1988).

Even assuming that Robertson had run an exemplary campaign, it is unlikely that he would have captured the nomination. To begin with, Robertson's mass base was too small to make him a top contender. However one defines evangelical Protestants or the charismatic community, they are not sufficiently numerous to win most elections. Robertson's greatest successes occurred in caucuses, which magnify the value of organization and intensity, favoring candidates whose support is deep rather than wide. These conditions, which encourage permeation by small, dedicated groups, are not as helpful in primary elections.

Upon closer inspection, even Robertson's "natural" constituency was not as cohesive as was widely assumed. The other Republican candidates, unwilling to cede the evangelical vote to Robertson, matched his positions on social-policy questions and similarly targeted evangelicals as an electoral bloc. Jack Kemp hired a controversial fundamentalist to coordinate his religious appeals. The competition recognized that the many distinctive subcommunities within evangelicalism do not always get along and frequently diverge politically (Morgan, 1988). Robertson's "charismatic" orientation antagonized fundamentalists like Bob Jones, who preferred ideological soul mate Jack Kemp over the practitioner of what might be such "satanic" arts as speaking in tongues and faith healing (Bandy, 1988). George Bush, not Robertson, earned the endorsement of the Reverend Jerry Falwell, the pioneer of political activism among fundamentalist evangelicals. Attesting to the same political diversity, a straw poll of leaders of the National Association of Evangelicals revealed that Robertson trailed badly behind Vice-President Bush, Senator Dole, and Representative Kemp (Rodgers-Melnick, 1987). Ministers in other evangelical denominations were cool to the prospect of Robertson's candidacy (Harder, 1988; Langenbach, 1988). In the Super Tuesday primaries throughout the South, Robertson appears to have grabbed less than one-quarter of the voters who accepted the "born-again" label (May, 1988). His own Southern Baptists—a predominantly noncharismatic denomination—were reported to have given him less than one-third of their support, reflecting doubts that extended from leading ministers and prominent laypeople to his own Virginia congregation (Guth, 1989; Morgan, 1988; Straus, 1988; King, 1987).

Even the charismatic community, the hardest core of Robertson support, cannot be assumed to have supported his candidacy. Many charismatics are black Protestants or white Catholics with strong traditions of attachment to the Democratic party. Neither group was particularly drawn to the Robertson campaign, the former uninterested in laissez-faire economic policy and the latter skeptical about Robertson's hawkish stand on nuclear weapons. White Protestant charismatics were difficult to rally even to so sympathetic a candidate because of their tradition of political disinterest. Pentecostals see the solution to human problems not in social or political mobilization but in the conversion and salvation of individual sinners. When arrayed against the power of God's miracles, the incremental changes produced by political action do not impress many charismatics as being worth the effort. A minister who abandons spreading the "good news" for political action risks criticism rather than praise. Thus Robertson alienated some of his most ardent theological friends by leaving the CBN ministry for politics, exchanging a sacred calling for a profane charge.

Jackson's Crusade

The novelty of Jackson's campaign for the nomination involved his race. Press discussions focused on whether a black candidate could win the nomination, what Jackson would do if he fell short of the nomination, and how his supporters would react in November without Jackson on the national ticket. Though the issue of race clearly overshadowed religion, the two cannot easily be disentangled in understanding the basis of his mass appeal. The Jackson campaign was permeated by the distinctive style of black religiosity in the United States.

Jackson is a dynamic preacher whose political discourse is grounded in the religious idiom of black America. Unlike Robertson, who favors Biblical injunctions on private virtue, Jackson approaches Scripture as a text emphasizing justice and compassion. He represents the "prophetic" motif in black Protestantism, which evolved largely as a defense against the doctrine of white supremacy (Washington, 1985). The core of this tradition, which traces its lineage to the revolts against slavery, insists on respect for the divine spark in all human beings. Thus Jackson regards poverty, racism, and other social problems as sins that deny the kinship of humankind through its common link to God. The task of progressive politicians, accordingly, is to "restore a moral tone, a redemptive spirit, and a sensitivity to the poor and dispossessed" through creative leadership (Jackson, 1987: xiv). This can best be achieved by awakening individuals of all races and classes to their common interest in a just and humane society.

Jackson habitually frames political issues in moral terms because he believes that people, himself included, are moved primarily by the "heart" and not the "head" (Jackson, 1987: ix). Accordingly, when addressing white and black audiences alike, Jackson called for the restoration of moral commitment in American politics. When asked whether a black man could realistically hope to win the presidency, Jackson did not talk in terms of poll standing but defined his candidacy as a chance for white Americans to show they had progressed beyond racism (Oreskes, 1987a; Painton, 1988a). His specific economic plans to deal with poverty, poor education, infant mortality, and the like were deemed elements in a drive for "economic justice." He found the common moral failing of greed in the corporate executive's willingness to shut down factories and the drug dealer's callous disregard of community life and peace (Crouch, 1988). Both the stock market crash and American support for right-wing dictators were traced to a lust for power.

As part of his belief in the supremacy of the emotional over the analytical, Jackson delivered his message in the style of an evangelist sensing that "The End" is near. His almost reflexive use of religious language and Biblical imagery was apparent to anyone who heard him speak. To describe his campaign, Jackson borrowed freely from such metaphors as Moses leading the exodus, Noah riding out the flood, or, as in his sermon on the eve of Super Tuesday, the central messianic symbol of Christianity:

> We can transform the crucifixion and on Tuesday roll the stone away and on Wednesday morning have a resurrection: new life, new possibilities, new South, new America. (Dahl, 1988)

The same symbols were deployed to characterize the opposition, as when Jackson portrayed Ronald Reagan as Pontius Pilate to the Jesus-like Martin Luther King, Jr.

Like Robertson, Jackson's political rallies could easily be mistaken for religious revivals, which, in a sense, they were. Watching Jackson preach to a black congregation in Iowa, a reporter marveled at the seamless manner in which Jackson portrayed even the mundane act of voter registration in missionary terms (McLeod, 1987). Preaching against drugs in high schools, he called on students who had used illegal substances to admit it publicly in a ritual that resembled the altar call of religious conversion (Painton, 1988a). The soaring rhetoric, resented as demagoguery by some, gained a receptive audience in the black community, which has long been accustomed to a preaching style infusing political issues with religious enthusiasm. Though less accustomed to community leadership by their clergy, mainly white audiences often responded the same way to the forceful preacher. Through his vibrant persona, Jackson stood out in the public mind as caring, trustworthy, decisive, and no less capable than his main rival of capably managing America's world role (*Polling Report*, 1988: 3)

The Jackson candidacy was sustained in large part by the support of his fellow preachers (Frisby, 1988). As a veteran of the civil rights movement and Operation PUSH, Jackson was respected in black religious circles and enjoyed a special status in the nation's largest black denomination, the National Baptist Convention. Ministers had spearheaded the voter registration drives that preceded his first run for the nomination and commanded major leadership roles in the Jackson campaign (Toner, 1983). This pattern carried over to the drive for the nomination in 1988. Under the guidance of a minister designated specifically as the liaison to black religious leaders, ministers put their congregations at Jackson's disposal. Black churches provided him a pulpit, a pool of potential volunteers, and the skeleton of a campaign organization. They also supplied money. When Jackson preached, the host minister would frequently take up a special offering in support of the candidacy. The fifth Sunday in January of 1988 was designated for such campaign collections in black churches nationwide (*New York Times*, 1988b).

The religious issue surfaced in Jackson's campaign in quite another guise—the question of black-Jewish relations. During his 1984 run for the Democratic nomination, Jackson had alienated some Jews by his calls for a more balanced American approach to the Middle East—including his well-publicized embrace of Yasir Arafat—and had antagonized them by his alliance with the anti-Semitic Louis Farrakhan and his characterization of New York City as "Hymietown." Despite his moving plea for forgiveness at the 1984 convention, Jackson recognized that he needed to make amends with this key constituency. As part of his strategy, Jackson endorsed secure borders for Israel, called for increased Jewish emigration from the Soviet Union, promoted conciliation between the black and Jewish communities, disavowed Farrakhan's anti-Semitism, and included several Jews on his campaign team.

Despite these attempts to heal the wounds of 1984, they surfaced repeatedly in 1988. In part, the conflict derived from disagreement on issues such as affirmative action and Jackson's criticism of Israel's ties with South Africa. But these seemed only surface manifestations of conflicts with deeper roots in the growing estrangement between blacks and Jews in the United States. That conflict reached its greatest intensity during campaigning for the New York primary on April 19. The mayor of New York City, Edward Koch, launched bitter attacks on Jackson and opined that Jews would have "to be crazy" to vote for someone with Jackson's record on the Middle East. An organization calling itself the "Coalition for a Positive America" ran full-page advertisments in the *New York Times* spotlighting Jackson's alleged "Arab connection." Similar inflammatory literature was circulated in Jewish communities across the nation.

Although Jackson was endorsed by several prominent Jews, this did not translate into mass support among Jewish voters. In New York, he won only 9 percent of Jewish voters, a substantially smaller share than he received from other white groups. This was particularly remarkable because Jewish voters normally give black candidates much more support than do other whites and accept many of the policy positions enunciated by Jackson during the campaign. The explanation can be traced to Jewish distrust of Jackson the candidate. Whereas 39 percent of all New York Democratic primary voters agreed with the statement, "Jesse Jackson is anti-Semitic," 78 percent of Jews surveyed in New York did so (Skelton, 1988).

The "Jewish issue" aside, Jackson's own religiosity did not figure significantly in public debate. Perhaps because Americans are more accustomed to political activism by black than by white ministers, Jackson's religious roots were less controversial than Robertson's. Jackson may also have allayed concern because he related religion to politics in a manner less likely to give offense. Unlike Robertson, who seemed to claim divine sanction for his candidacy and greeted his Michigan caucus showing with the infelicitous comment, "The Christians won!" Jackson was circumspect about claiming divine support or inspiration for his political agenda. Warning against misuse of religion to buttress particular political agendas, he called instead for religion that impels believers "to seek to do God's will and allow the spiritual Word to become concrete justice . . ." (Jackson, 1987: ix). According to a sympathetic expositor of Jackson's political philosophy, the candidate's reliance on religious principles does not entail the belief that his political preferences are the result of a direct revelation from God (Hatch, 1989: 98). Though Jackson does believe that religious principles support the goals of progressive political action, he acknowledges that the principles are accessible through nonreligious avenues and must be justified in secular terms to make a legitimate claim on public policy.

What Made Pat and Jesse Run?

Let us now return to the mystery stated at the outset of the chapter, the remarkable presidential candidacies of two ordained Baptist ministers altogether lacking the normal credentials of "serious" candidates. Neither had held public office nor was initially regarded as likely to win the nomination. Both began the campaign with substantial negative evaluations in the major polls, a product of their perceived extremism and lack of government experience. Though it is possible to identify candidates who have triumphed over each of these obstacles, Jackson and Robertson faced the additional handicap of widespread public antipathy to mixing the roles of church and state (Associated Press, 1987; *Boston Globe,* 1988). Notwithstanding their respect for religious faith and their strong moralistic inclinations, many Americans perceive the First Amendment as an injunction against sectarian appeals in politics. Nevertheless, Jackson and Robertson were treated with considerable respect by the other candidates. And the press corps, not known for religiosity, periodically attached the term "kingmaker" to both of them. In view of the obstacles confronting them, the two ministers managed to play large roles in the 1988 nomination campaigns of their respective parties.

What does this tell us about American politics? The surprising campaigns by the two ministers highlight at least four interesting features of contemporary nomination politics: the permeability of political parties, the potency of moralistic and symbolic appeals, the value of churches as bases of political action, and the diversity of religious appeals in public life. Each of these factors transcends the particulars of the 1988 campaign for the nomination.

Porous Parties

Jackson and Robertson benefited from changes in the structure of the presidential nominating system that opened up the process to "entrepreneurial" candidates. Prior to 1972, the outcome was weighted in favor of candidates acceptable to party notables. Under the pre-reformed system, candidates needed to curry the favor of state and local party leaders, who controlled the selection of convention delegations, and the large donors who bankrolled campaigns for the nomination. For all but the most politically aware, the nomination phase was largely hidden from public view until the party conventions convened in the summer of presidential election years.

The major changes ushered in after 1968 meant that nominations were effectively decided by the decisions of primary electorates during the winter and spring months. The primaries accorded potential candidates a means to bypass the party elites in favor of direct appeals to voters. In competing for primary votes, candidates from outside the party establishment benefited from federal matching funds awarded to campaigns that raised funds through small contributions from individual donors. These funds enabled outsiders to build state-level organizations essential to mobilizing mass support.

These reforms dictated changes in strategy that were beneficial to candidates with intense but narrow support. Rather than patiently assembling broad-based coalitions among loyal partisans and party leaders, the road to the nomination in the pre-reformed setting, candidates tried to seize the initiative early in the reformed process. The new system put the glare of intense media attention on the earliest stages of the process, making it imperative that candidates concentrate on attracting a respectable share of the participants in the most visible straw polls and delegate-selection exercises. "The candidate's best strategy," according to Nelson Polsby (1983: 67–68),

> is therefore to differentiate himself from the others in the race and persuade more of his supporters to come out and vote. A premium is placed on building a personal organization, state by state, and in hoping that the field becomes crowded with rivals who cluster at some other part of the ideological spectrum, or who for some other reason manage to divide up into too-small pieces the natural constituencies that exist in the primary electorate.

Utilizing the new strategies, Democratic "outsiders" like George McGovern, George Wallace, Jimmy Carter, and Gary Hart scored dramatic successes in post-1968 competition with perennial insiders such as Hubert Humphrey, Edmund Muskie, Henry Jackson, and Walter Mondale. The startling success of Ronald Reagan in 1976 and 1980—when he was not favored by the vast majority of the Republican establishment—demonstrated that the GOP was subject to permeation by the same tactics that worked so well for Democratic insurgents.

These reforms made it possible for Jackson and Robertson to contend seriously for their parties' presidential nominations. The primaries and public caucuses reduced the status of party officials who would have screened out the ministers as fringe candidates under the pre-reformed system. Instead of appealing to elites, Jackson and Robertson could use their communication skills and media experience to reach potential voters and caucus attenders. It has not often been noticed that the skills required to build a major ministry may be directly transferable to politics. Both Jackson and Robertson were masters of the mass media, exhibiting oratorical gifts and a practiced television presence resulting from countless hours before cameras and microphones.[3] With his long history of fund-raising on behalf of the CBN ministry, Robertson was spectacularly successful in this phase of the campaign, raising over $19 million from an estimated 117,000 donors (Green, 1989).

The reforms thus paved the way for insurgent candidates who could mobilize voters to participate in the sparsely attended caucuses and primaries. That Jackson and Robertson were able to exploit the opening more effectively than some better-known aspirants had much to do with the symbolic qualities associated with their religious status. Both generated an intense, even fervent, loyalty from their core constituencies. In the sense that Max Weber used the term to describe leaders who forged deeply emotional ties with their followers, both Robertson and Jackson were clearly *charismatic* figures. Their capacity to ignite passion was seemingly a product of the ministerial role itself. In the Southern Baptist tradition that both Robertson and Jackson inherited, the minister is not merely a learned expositor of the Bible or a church administrator, but someone who has been touched by God, who has received a call to preach.

For a member of the clergy who can persuade parishioners that a political campaign fulfills a divine purpose, religion provides the basis for an electoral appeal that goes well beyond simple self-interest. As a religious writer noted perceptively, Jackson and Robertson supporters resembled one another in ways that transcended race: they were "church-going citizens of moderate means who long for the triumph of good over evil and for the realization of justice in our time" (quoted in Broder, 1988). More than the other candidates, the ministers addressed this longing by enunciating messages that were urgent and unambiguous. Moreover, both ministers came to represent the larger aspirations of their respective communities for public respect and dignity. Indeed, quite apart from their personal qualities as exemplars of religious traditions, Jackson and Robertson were visible symbols that brought pride to their supporters. Robertson's viability was undoubtedly reassuring to those practitioners of traditionalist religion who were disturbed by the "desacralization" of the public square evident in court decisions, declining respect for old-fashioned morality, and other agents of social change (Wald, Owen, and Hill, 1989). To an even greater extent, Jackson's attainment of national eminence meant the world to his black supporters (Barker, 1988; Painton, 1988b; Harris, 1988).

Both candidates proved adept at channeling this passion through politics. At the very least, their intense ties with their constituents, though not broad enough to attract a majority, enabled the two ministers to withstand personal gaffes and defeats that would probably have torpedoed more traditional campaigns. "Jesse Jackson and Pat Robertson don't have to win a thing to keep themselves in the race," noted an envious staffer from the Bush campaign (Oreskes, 1987b). More important, this enthusiasm translated into the willingness of supporters to endure extraordinary hardships in the service of the campaigns. The ability to engender excitement is particularly valuable in bringing supporters to affairs of low public salience.

Not by chance, Jackson and Robertson performed best in caucuses, which demand maximum levels of commitment. Even in primaries, where passion is diluted by the larger size of the electorate, the two ministers galvanized ideological voters and the previously inactive with clarion calls for public action. Considering how well it suited their ministerial talents, the open nomination system might have seemed heaven-sent.

Moral Dimensions of the Presidency

A ministerial background may have helped Robertson and Jackson with potential supporters outside church-based constituencies. James David Barber (1986) has noted that Americans want the president to exhibit a number of potentially contradictory qualities. Presidents should be sources of reassurance in a troubled world, agents of progress, and—the quality most relevant to this discussion—guarantors of legitimacy. More than simple dignity or propriety, the president conveys legitimacy by acting rightfully in the nation's highest office. According to Barber, Americans believe that the chief executive "ought to inspire our higher selves with an example of principled goodness." This concept of moral leadership enables citizens to perceive the office as above politics and its inhabitant as removed from mundane conflicts among lesser individuals. Because people are accustomed to looking to the clergy for moral guidance and generally believe that members of the clergy act with high ethical standards, ministers would appear to have some advantage in satisfying this aspect of the model presidential candidate.

The appeal of ministers as candidates may be augmented by the role of the president as the major symbol of national unity and chief carrier of what has been called the "civil religion." The American civil religion consists of a belief that the nation has been charged with a divine purpose and has a corresponding obligation to uphold higher standards than the rest of humankind (Wald, 1987: 48). Frequently expressed in presidential inaugural addresses and on other patriotic occasions, these sentiments were very much on display during the campaign for the nomination. With his emphasis on the United States as the special recipient of God's bounty, Pat Robertson reflected the "priestly" strain of civil religion which treats the nation as uniquely worthy of citizen support because of its divine favor. Calling on the nation to exhibit godly qualities in its treatment of the poor and downtrodden, Jesse Jackson exemplified the "prophetic" component of civil religion, the mandate for high ethical standards in government action. The broad appeal of such themes was also exemplified in Michael Dukakis's condemnation of the Reagan administration's failure to uphold adequate standards in public office. Though not exclusively a ministerial function, the invocation of civil religious themes is a natural activity for a candidate who is the product of a church environment.

Churches as Campaign Infrastructures

The performance of the ministerial campaigns should also be credited to the organizational resources at their disposal. Both were able to draw on religious constituencies for funding, leadership, organizational support, and emotional sustenance. As "tightly bound" subcommunities, congregations provide a superb infrastructure for the type of campaigns waged in the presidential nominating process (Hertzke, 1988). They encapsulate a larger share of the adult population than any other secondary organization. Their members assemble frequently, which facilitates political education, voter registration, and other methods of mobilization. Congregations provide a supportive community that reinforces underlying political dispositions by both direct indoctrination and informal social interaction (Wald, Owen, and Hill, 1988). More tangibly, churches have meeting rooms and auditoriums that can host political gatherings, bulletins that can solicit volunteers for favored causes, and buses that can be used to transport members to campaign rallies, caucuses, and polling places. The legal restrictions on church-based political activity, weak to begin with, are rarely enforced.

In relying so heavily on churches as nodes of mobilization, the candidates were emulating patterns that long predated the 1988 campaigns. The civil rights movement was built on the base of the black church, and the evangelical political revival was fostered by the growth of conservative churches and the development of national networks among fundamentalist and charismatic congregations. Candidates with special access to religious communities thus have a distinct advantage in gaining entry to the ranks of "serious" contenders for the nomination.

Pluralism

Despite the similarities between the candidacies of Robertson and Jackson, there was a fundamental distinction between them: their emphasis on radically different strains of evangelical Protestantism. As noted above, Robertson understands the political message of the gospel to support the free-enterprise system, militantly oppose communism, and strictly limit permissible sexual conduct. Jackson believes that free enterprise too often leads to poverty and degradation, that militant anticommunism has blinded the nation to the just aspirations of the third world, and that individuals should be free from state compulsion in their sexual conduct. While Robertson justified deployment of the "Star Wars" complex in scriptural terms, Jackson found biblical grounds to condemn it. These policy differences were rooted in fundamentally different ways of linking religion to politics, approaches that overwhelmed the common denominator of evangelicalism.

Jackson and Robertson were not the first two Protestant ministers to disagree about the political message implicit in the Bible. Jackson stands in a long line of theologians and activists who have enjoined the nation to uphold Christian standards by limiting the privileges of capital and fighting against "social" sin. Robertson, though rejecting the apolitical stance of his predecessors, is only the latest exponent of the Gospel of Prosperity through personal righteousness. The same gap has divided believers of other faiths. It stems from the undeniable ambiguity of religious messages regarding political action.

Remarkably, many political observers still view religion as a monolithic force with a singular message. The ministerial campaigns of 1988 should help to undo that assumption. As religion is diverse, so too are its political manifestations.

Conclusion

Of course, the nation eventually said "No, minister"; Jackson and Robertson lost decisively. The political advantages conferred by the ministry were partially offset by liabilities. In a pluralistic society, religious appeals may confine a candidate to a narrow support base. Voters may wonder whether the ministry equips a person with the requisite skills to manage the nation's business. Party elites, still instrumental in campaigns, may be repelled by what they see as fanaticism. These themes were commonly heard in "mainstream" Republican reactions to Pat Robertson. Despite his attempts to establish secular credentials and reassure voters that his goals were fundamentally political rather than religious, Robertson's gaffes and the crusading mentality of his supporters undercut the message. The religious tie proved less damaging to Jackson, who could point to many years of civil rights activism, experience in negotiations with foreign governments and domestic corporations, and a record of public leadership. For both candidates, religion was one resource in an arsenal. A religious base was necessary for Jackson and Robertson to be taken seriously but insufficient to win them nomination.

What of the impact of the ministers on the subsequent presidential campaign? Curiously, the effect of the candidates after Labor Day was inversely related to the fate of their personal campaigns (Wills, 1989: 5–6). Robertson, who returned to rescue a troubled CBN, is unlikely to play a large role in 1992, whereas Jackson's stature as a presidential prospect was enhanced by his strong showing. But, while Jackson all but disappeared from political news during the fall campaign, the moralistic style that Robertson stressed in the primaries was adopted in full measure by the Bush campaign. Claiming some of the same themes that Robertson had propounded, the vice-president's campaign bombarded the public with emotional "hot button" messages that stressed the flag, patriotism, decency, school prayer, Willie Horton, criminality, abortion, and the like. Not until the last weeks of the campaign did the Democratic nominee invoke some of Jackson's major themes from the primaries.

In the long term, the more substantial impact may be Jackson's. Robertson seems to have reinforced public doubts about a minister's suitability for high elective office and prompted Republican resolve to reduce future opportunities for guerrilla campaigning. In contrast, Jackson has managed to encourage the Democratic party to consider reducing the number of so-called "superdelegates" in 1992 and has seen campaign aide Ron Brown assume the national chair of the Democratic party. While falling short of nomination himself, Jackson may have paved the way for another African American to eventually claim the prize. If not the savior of his people, Jackson may yet lay claim to the mantle of Moses. With his fondness for Biblical analogies, that may be some consolation.

Notes

1. In reviewing Jackson's background and experience, I have found especially useful the accounts by House (1988), Maraniss (1987), Purnick and Oreskes (1987), and Vennochi (1987).
2. All election results were obtained from *Congressional Quarterly Weekly Report* 46 (1988).
3. Robertson's television ministry is better known than Jackson's regular Saturday-morning radio broadcasts from Operation PUSH headquarters in Chicago. These programs developed an appreciative audience and honed Jackson's speaking skills (House, 1988).

References

Newsbank is a machine-readable index to newspaper articles. Abbreviations such as "NIN" and "POL" refer to parts of the microfiche collection containing the text of the actual articles.

Americans for Robertson. n.d. "Who Is This Man?" Advertising supplement prepared by Americans for Robertson.

Associated Press. 1987. "Poll Assails Cleric Bids. " *Los Angeles Times* (December 3): 26A.

Balzar, John. 1987. "The Journey from Pulpit to Populist." *Los Angeles Times* (November 25; Newsbank, NIN, 405: D5).

Bandy, Lee. 1988. "Robertson's Politics Rooted in Religion." *Detroit Free Press* (January 31; Newsbank, POL, 23: E10).

Barber, James David. 1986. "The Presidency: What Americans Want." In *Classic Readings in American Politics*, ed. Pietro S. Nivola and David H. Rosenbloom. New York: St. Martin's Press.

Barker, Lucius J. 1988. *Our Time Has Come: A Delegate's Diary of Jesse Jackson's 1984 Presidential Campaign*. Urbana: University of Illinois Press.

Berke, Richard L. 1987. "Gain for Pat Robertson in Later Michigan Tally." *New York Times* (February 15): 16.

Boston Globe. 1988. "Some Leery of Religion, Politics." (February 16): 11.

Broder, David S. 1988. "Church, State and Politics." *Washington Post National Weekly Edition* (January 3): 4.

Brody, Richard. 1988. "Party Alignment of the Southern Christian Right: An Exploration of the *Washington Post* Pre-Primary Poll in South Carolina." Unpublished paper presented at annual meeting of American Political Science Association, September 1–4.

Buckingham, Jamie. 1986. "Should Pat Robertson Run for President?" *Christianity Today* (September 5): 54.

Clifford, Frank. 1987. "Jackson, Robertson Could Decide Party Nominations." *Los Angeles Times* (December 10): 1A.

Crouch, Stanley. 1988. "Beyond Good and Evil." *New Republic* 198 (June 20): 20–23.

Dahl, David. 1988. "Jackson Preaches Politics from Pulpit." *St. Petersburg Times* (March 7): 1.

Decker, Cathleen. 1987. "Religious vs. Secular Appeal: Robertson Tailors His Message to Audiences." *Los Angeles Times* (November 23): 1.

Dionne, E. J., Jr. 1987. "Robertson Victory in Ballot Shakes Rivals in G.O.P. Race." *New York Times* (September 14): 1.

Frisby, Michael K. 1988. "Black Clergy Play Key Role in Tuesday Vote." *Boston Globe* (March 6): 22.

Green, John C. 1989. "A Look at the 'Invisible Army': Pat Robertson's Campaign Contributors." Unpublished paper presented at annual meeting of American Association for the Advancement of Science, January 14–19.

Green, John C., and James L. Guth. 1988. "The Christian Right in the Republican Party: The Case of Pat Robertson's Supporters." *Journal of Politics* 50 (February): 150–68.

Guth, James L. 1989. "A New Turn for the Christian Right? Robertson's Support from the Southern Baptist Ministry." Unpublished paper presented at annual meeting of American Association for the Advancement of Science, January 14–19.

Harder, Kathleen. 1988. "Pastors and Political Mobilization: 'Preaching Politics.'" Unpublished paper presented at annual meeting of American Political Science Association, September 1–4.

Harrell, David Edwin. 1987. *Pat Robertson: A Personal, Political and Religious Portrait*. New York: Harper and Row.

Harris, Ron. 1988. "Jackson's Successes Inspire Black Hopes." *Los Angeles Times* (April 24): 1.

Hatch, Rodger D. 1989. "Jesse Jackson in Two Worlds." In *Religion in American Politics*, ed. Charles W. Dunn. Washington, D.C.: Congressional Quarterly Press.

Hertzke, Alan. 1988. "Jackson, Robertson and the Politics of Community: Religious Mobilization and the 1988 Presidential Campaign." Unpublished paper presented at annual meeting of International Political Science Association, August 28–September 1.

House, Ernest R. 1988. *Jesse Jackson and the Politics of Charisma*. Boulder, Colo.: Westview.

Hume, Ellen, and Rich Jaroslovsky. 1988. "Republican Rift: Robertson's Candidacy Threatens a Deep Split in GOP for November." *Wall Street Journal* (March 4): 1.

Jackson, Brooks. 1988. "If Robertson Campaign Exceeds Spending Limits, the Question Apparently Would Be: So What?" *Wall Street Journal* (February 29): 52.

Jackson, Jesse L. 1987 *Straight from the Heart*. Philadelphia: Fortress Press.

Kiester, Kirk D. H. 1988. "The Christian Right Enters Electoral Politics: Robertson Activists in the Alachua County Republican Executive Committee." B. A. honors thesis, University of Florida.

King, Wayne. 1987. "Robertson's Ex-Church Uncertain on Candidacy." *New York Times* (October 12): 11.

———. 1988. "Pat Robertson: A Candidate of Contradictions." *New York Times* (February 27): 1.

Langenbach, Lisa. 1988. "Evangelical Elites and Political Action: The Pat Robertson Presidential Candidacy." Unpublished paper presented at annual meeting of American Political Science Association, September 1–4.

Lawton, Kim. 1988. "Iowa Christians and the Race for the Oval Office." *Christianity Today* (January 15): 50–55.

Maraniss, David. 1987. "Jackson: Playing to the Camera." *Washington Post* (December 27): 1A.

May, Lee. 1988. "Robertson Hears No Sour Notes of Defeat." *Los Angeles Times* (July 27; Newsbank, NIN, 276: E13).

McLeod, Don. 1987. "Pulpit Tones on the Stump." *Washington Times* (July 27; Newsbank, NIN, 276: E13).

Morgan, Dan. 1988. "Evangelicals a Force Divided." *Washington Post* (March 8): A8.

Morin, Richard. 1987. "Robertson's Supporters Are a Group Within a Group." *Washington Post National Weekly Edition* (December 21): 37.

Morphew, Clark. 1988. "Supporters Pray Right Is Might in '88 Campaign." *St. Paul Pioneer Press-Dispatch* (Janaury 31; Newsbank, 1988, NIN, 42: C5).

New York Times. 1988a. "A Strong Warning That Moral Decay is Basic Trouble Facing the Nation." (January 14): 12.

———. 1988b. "Jackson to Pass the Plate at Churches Sunday." (January 28): 9.

O'Connor, Sheilah. 1988. "Robertson Uses Video for Message." *Memphis Commercial Appeal* (January 17; Newsbank, NIN, 14: D10).

Oreskes, Michael. 1987a. "Jackson Makes Bid in Democratic Race." *New York Times* (September 8): 8.

———. 1987b. "Jackson and Robertson: 'Bookends' of '88 Race." *New York Times* (November 17): 11.

Painton, Priscilla. 1988a. "Jackson Electrifies Voters with Promise to Fight Drugs." *Atlanta Constitution* (March 13): 14A.

———. 1988b. "Some Fear Loss by Jackson Could Dash Hope He Has Brought to Downtrodden." *Atlanta Constitution* (April 21): 1A.

Platt, Gerald M., and Rhys H. Williams. 1988. "Religion, Ideology and Electoral Politics." *Society* 25 (July–August): 38–45.

Polling Report. 1988. "Campaign Update" 4 (February 8): 6.

Polsby, Nelson W. 1983. *Consequences of Party Reform.* New York: Oxford University Press.

Poole, Isaiah J. 1988. "Robertson Marches on Northeast." *Washington Times* (February 10; Newsbank, POL, 23: E2).

Purnick, Joyce, and Michael Oreskes. 1987. "Jesse Jackson Aims for the Mainstream." *New York Times Magazine* (November 29): 28.

Reeves, Richard. 1988. "Can the Republicans Stand Pat?" *Atlanta Constitution* (February 11): 23A.

Reid, T. R. 1987. "Robertson's Christian Soldiers Are Marching to Political Fray." *Washington Post National Weekly Edition* (October 12): 16.

———. 1988. "Urgent Message." Americans for Robertson circular sent to contributors, January 15.

Robertson, Pat. 1984. *Beyond Reason: How Miracles Can Change Your Life.* New York: Bantam Books.

Rodgers-Melnick, Ann. 1987. "Pat Robertson's Soul Search." *Fort Myers* (Florida) *News-Press* (November 1: Newsbank, NIN, 405: D8).

Shribman, David. 1987. "Robertson's Conversion from Rakishness to Faith Culminates in His Crusade for the White House." *Wall Street Journal* (October 6): 70.

Skelton, George. 1988. "Tally Breaks Sharply along Racial Lines." *Los Angeles Times* (April 20): 1.

Smith, Hedrick. 1987. "Those Fractious Republicans." *New York Times Magazine* (October 25): 30.

Straus, Hal. 1987. "A High-Tech Campaign Measures Robertson's Grass-Roots Success." *Atlanta Journal* (November 14; Newsbank, NIN, 405: D3).

———. 1988. "Clergy Convert to Robertson for S.C. Vote." *Atlanta Constitution* (March 1): 1A.

Toner, Robin. 1983. "Black Clergymen Playing Key Role in Politics Today." *Atlanta Journal* (December 4; Newsbank, POL, 55: F14).

Turner, Robert L. 1988. "The Gospel According to N.H." *Boston Globe* (January 3): 77.

Vennochi, Joan. 1987. "Jackson: His Style Stirs Adoration and Antipathy." *Boston Globe* (December 28): 21

Wald, Kenneth D. 1987. *Religion and Politics in the United States.* New York: St. Martin's Press.

Wald, Kenneth D., Dennis E. Owen, and Samuel S. Hill, Jr. 1988. "Churches as Political Communities." *American Political Science Review* 82 (June): 531–48.
———. 1989. "Evangelical Politics and Status Issues." *Journal for the Scientific Study of Religion* 28 (March): 1–16.
Washington, James Melvin. 1985. "Jesse Jackson and the Symbolic Politics of Black Christendom." *Annals of the American Academy of Political and Social Science* 480 (July): 89–105.
Wills, Gary. 1988. "Introduction: A Moral Derailing." In *The Winning of the White House 1988* ed. Donald Morrison. New York: New American Library.

6. Meeting Expectations? Major Newspaper Coverage of Candidates During the 1988 Exhibition Season

Emmett H. Buell, Jr.

The first and longest phase in each new cycle of presidential nominating politics is the "exhibition season," which begins shortly after the last presidential election and ends more than three years later with the Iowa caucuses.[1] Candidates use this time to raise money, organize their campaigns, and formulate the messages they hope will appeal to activists and voters in the caucuses and primaries to follow.

Success in these endeavors depends partly on the national news media. At no point in the presidential selection process do citizens know or care less about the candidates and issues than during the long exhibition season. Most people learn about presidential campaigns haphazardly, acquiring "bits and pieces" of information from the media (Neuman, 1986: 18). Sparse coverage does little to increase public familiarity with candidates, and moderate coverage accomplishes little more than superficial name recognition. But substantial coverage with much repetition of information is instrumental in establishing a candidate's identity (Patterson, 1980: 110). Thus the selection, focus, number, repetitiveness, and timing of news stories are important to characterizing the candidates, setting the agenda, and "priming" potential voters (Iyengar and Kinder, 1987; Graber, 1989), though media influence will vary significantly according to the predispositions and outlooks of readers and viewers (Bartels, 1988; Entman, 1989).

Pundits generally agree that the presidential nominating process has been transformed since World War II. Owing largely to the rise of television and more recent reforms in selection of delegates and campaign finance, power and influence have shifted from party leaders to the candidates, their campaign consultants, and the press. Experts do not agree on whether more power for the press has been good for the process. John P. Sears, a well-known campaign consultant, reportedly argues that journalists should acknowledge their status as the "new bosses," and openly promote the candidates they think most qualified (Broder, 1987: 279). Among the many expressing a contrary view is Thomas E. Patterson (1989: 94), a leading scholar of campaign journalism, who maintains that the news media now organize public choice more than the parties do, a function for which the media are ill suited.

Senator Edward M. Kennedy took a similarly dim view of the press during the 1988 exhibition season. Noting that front-runner Gary Hart and Senator Joseph Biden were driven from the race before one vote had been cast, Kennedy charged that the news media had fastened on personalities and the "horse race" while neglecting substance and historical context: "If the focus was not on who's ahead in surveys, endorsements, money, and Iowa trips," he asserted (1987: 21), "attention would have to be paid to what the candidates are saying—not about each other—but about principles, problems, and possible solutions."

Several 1988 candidates reiterated this view during the exhibition season. Among them was Congressman Richard Gephardt, who decried greater coverage of scandals than of "the differences of principle and policy that should be at the center of the public debate" (Blake, 1988). In the same vein, Jesse Jackson complained that there was more media interest in his once having taken a painkilling drug than in his present proposals to halt the flow of narcotics into the United States (Political Notebook, 1988a).

Not even journalists maintain that the press plays a neutral role in the presidential nominating process. News organizations cover the exhibition season according to their own commercial priorities and subjective estimates of which contests and candidates are most newsworthy. As a consequence, some candidates get extraordinary coverage while others get relatively little. News reports typically highlight conflict among the candidates, pay more attention to the horse race than to issues of public policy, and provide relatively little information about the personal backgrounds and public records of aspirants. According to the literature on preconvention news coverage, these generalizations hold for all media, whether television or print (Marshall, 1983; Robinson and Sheehan, 1983; Graber, 1989).

The exhibition season is mostly a newspaper story, especially in its earliest months (Broder, 1987: 280). Unless attracted by scandal or other dramatic events, television and newsmagazine coverage is sporadic until shortly before the Iowa caucuses. The earliest part of the season proceeds at a fairly leisurely pace, allowing reporters to follow a campaign for several days before writing about a candidate's message and reception. The tempo quickens as the election year approaches, and candidates crowd more and more events into longer and longer days. By this point, the race has become mostly a television event, as evidenced by the forests of boom microphones and cameras encircling the top candidates at every campaign stop.

In Michael Robinson's phrase, this chapter is about "press behavior" rather than "press impact." My chief objective is to describe how five of the nation's most important newspapers—the *Atlanta Constitution*, the *Boston Globe*, the *Chicago Tribune*, the *Los Angeles Times*, and the *New York Times*—covered selected aspects of the early campaigns for the Democratic and Republican presidential nominations. Specifically, which candidates got the most newspaper coverage, and why? What did these newspapers report about the personal lives and character crises of candidates? How frequently and substantively did the newspapers report the issue stands and campaign themes of candidates? And, finally, how consistently did they evaluate the preliminaries of each party's "horse race"?

Data Base

Three criteria governed selection of the newspapers analyzed in this research. First, by reputation alone, each one ranks among the country's leading newspapers. Each employs widely acclaimed political reporters, maintains bureaus in numerous locales, and dominates its own circulation market.[2]

Second, each newspaper relied chiefly on its own correspondents for coverage of the 1988 preconvention campaigns. By November 1987, for example, eight *Los Angeles Times* reporters were already following the story in Iowa and New Hampshire (Palmer, 1987). Of 533 exhibition-season news stories, feature articles, and news notes published in the *New York Times*, the paper's own staff wrote 90.8 percent; comparable figures for the other papers were 88.9 percent in the *Globe*, 81 percent in the *Tribune*, 80.4 percent in the *Los Angeles Times*, and 74.9 percent in the *Constitution*.

The final basis for selection was region, an obvious factor owing to the caucus and primary schedule of both parties. The *Constitution* was picked for its likely emphasis on Super Tuesday, the *Globe* for extensive coverage of the New Hampshire primary, and the *Tribune* for Iowa emphasis. The *Los Angeles Times* added western balance to the sample, and the *New York Times* a national as well as a northeastern regional view.

The data base of this research consisted of 2,591 news items about the 1988 presidential campaigns published in the five newspapers over a nineteen week period—from October 1, 1987, through February 8, 1988, the day of the Iowa caucuses. Content analysis of these news items entailed close reading and coding of 297,236 lines of newsprint.[3] As table 6.1 shows, there

Table 6.1 **Exhibition-Season Coverage of Five Major Newspapers, by Type of News Item and Print Lines**

News Items	Atlanta Constitution	Boston Globe	Chicago Tribune	Los Angeles Times	New York Times	All Five Newspapers
Stories/features						
Items	407	495	220	325	427	1,874
Print lines	51,933	69,733	30,123	58,519	60,965	271,273
Short notes						
Items	148	338	23	94	92	695
Print lines	3,651	10,437	599	3,111	2,775	20,573
Transcripts						
Items	6	2	0	0	14	22
Print lines	1,282	55	0	0	4,053	5,390
Total items	561	835	243	419	533	2,591
Total lines	56,866	80,225	30,722	61,630	67,793	297,236

were three types of news items: stories or feature articles, briefer notes, and transcripts of candidate speeches or interviews. Stories and feature articles generally were longer and more substantive than notes, averaging between 128 and 180 lines, while note length ranged from 25 to 33 lines. Except in the *Globe*, where both items were speech fragments, the average speech or interview transcript was 213 lines in the *Constitution* and 289 lines in the *New York Times*.

Unequal Coverage of Candidates

A virtual certainty during the exhibition season is that some candidates will get much more press than others. With a few notable exceptions in recent years, most attention has been paid to candidates thought to have the best chances of nomination. By the same token, long-shots have gotten the least coverage. Since few votes are cast or delegates selected during the exhibition season, news organizations rely mainly on national poll standings to determine each candidate's coverage. According to television reporter Bill Plante, "the degree of scrutiny a candidate receives increases in direct proportion to his standing in the polls" (Robinson and Sheehan, 1983: 116). In his analysis of 1984 exhibition-season news, William C. Adams (1985) found a reciprocal relationship between a candidate's standing in the polls and coverage on television and in leading newspapers. High poll ratings attracted more press, and more press raised poll ratings even higher.

Very different pictures of the Democratic and Republican candidate fields emerged from polls taken during the 1988 exhibition season. Hart's departure in May 1987 left the Democrats without a genuine front-runner, and, though he quickly regained the lead upon rejoining the race in December, most pundits interpreted this as more indicative of a weak field than of solid support for him. The Republicans had a clear front-runner in Vice-President Bush, who topped the list in every poll of likely GOP voters nationwide. Dole always came in second, Kemp and Robertson alternated between third and fourth, du Pont and Haig swapped fifth and sixth. If poll standings had any significant influence on how much space these newspapers gave the candidates, then the resulting allocations of print lines should have reflected Democratic disorder and Republican hierarchy.

Looking first at the Democrats, table 6.2 presents exactly the picture expected of a field of candidates without a credible front-runner. With coverage defined as the number of print lines about each candidate, no Democrat consistently surpassed his rivals in all five newspapers.[4] Although Jackson nominally led in most Democratic polls until Hart returned, only the *Constitution* gave him more space than any other Democratic candidate. He was second in the *Tribune* and *New York Times*, third in the *Los*

Table 6.2 Print Lines about Candidates in Five Major Newspapers

	Atlanta Constitution	Boston Globe	Chicago Tribune	Los Angeles Times	New York Times	All Five Newspapers
Democrats						
Babbitt	2,161	2,967	589	1,876	2,183	9,776
Dukakis	4,580	17,581	1,689	3,947	4,436	32,233
Gephardt	3,199	4,694	1,604	4,657	3,382	17,536
Gore	4,286	4,141	1,224	2,411	3,301	15,363
Hart	3,889	6,905	3,185	5,191	6,077	25,247
Jackson	5,737	4,195	1,999	4,600	5,093	21,624
Simon	2,430	3,813	1,790	4,323	3,141	15,497
Democratic totals	26,282	44,296	12,080	27,005	27,613	137,276
Republicans						
Bush	6,338	11,818	5,545	12,258	10,573	46,532
Dole	4,582	7,842	3,607	7,648	9,151	32,830
du Pont	1,424	2,111	431	760	1,918	6,644
Haig	1,514	1,468	531	1,405	1,905	6,823
Kemp	2,543	3,682	1,354	2,455	3,079	13,113
Robertson	4,901	4,094	2,997	4,313	4,844	21,149
Republican totals	21,302	31,015	14,465	28,839	31,470	127,091
Candidate totals	47,584	75,311	26,545	55,844	59,083	264,367
Democratic percentage	55.2	58.8	45.5	48.4	46.7	51.9
Republican percentage	44.8	41.2	54.5	51.6	53.3	48.1
Total percentage	100.0	100.0	100.0	100.0	100.0	100.0

Angeles Times, and fourth in the *Globe*. Local interest no doubt accounted for much, if not most, of the *Globe*'s remarkable coverage of Dukakis, but, unaided in this way elsewhere, he got second billing in the *Constitution*, third in the *New York Times*, fourth in the *Tribune*, and fifth in the *Los Angeles Times*. Hart received more space than any other Democrat in three newspapers, but not in the *Constitution*, where Jackson, Dukakis, and Gore were the top three. Gephart did better than Jackson in the *Globe* and Dukakis in the *Los Angeles Times*. Senator Paul Simon got more *Tribune* and *Los Angeles Times* coverage than Dukakis. In short, the absence of a clear pecking order for most Democratic candidates showed up in major newspaper coverage as well as in the polls. The only exception was former Arizona Governor Bruce Babbitt, always last in the polls and least in coverage.

Coverage of the Republicans was no less reflective of national poll results. Except for Robertson overtaking Dole in *Constitution* coverage, there were no deviations from national poll standings. Each paper gave Bush substantially more lines than any other Republican—about sixteen times more in the *Los Angeles Times* than du Pont, eight times as many in the *Globe* as Haig, more than twice Kemp's total in the *Constitution,* more than twice Robertson's amount in the *New York Times,* and about half again as many lines as Dole in the *Globe, Tribune,* and *Los Angeles Times*. Dole was a solid second in four of the five newspapers, Robertson got more space than Kemp, and Kemp got more than Haig or du Pont.

Still another measure of unequal coverage is the frequency of candidates named in the headlines. An even more demanding standard is making the headlines on page one. Table 6.3 essentially repeats the patterns found in the data on print lines—no clear order among the Democrats and a well-established hierarchy for the Republicans.

Sparse Coverage of Formative Experiences and Family Life

Getting more space than other candidates is one concern, but what goes into this space is another. The general finding of previous research on coverage of presidential nominating races is that remarkably little is said about the private lives of most candidates. In their analysis of how CBS and UPI reported the 1980 preconvention campaigns, for example, Michael Robinson and Margaret Sheehan (1983: 55) found almost nothing about the upbringing, family relationships, or formative experiences of candidates. Such information was also rare in a study of 1984 New Hampshire primary coverage by national, regional, and local newspapers (Buell, 1987: 93).

There was no lack of potential background material in the lives of 1988 candidates. Babbitt, for example, had encountered third-world poverty

Table 6.3 **Candidates Named in Headlines of Five Newspapers**

	Atlanta Constitution	Boston Globe	Chicago Tribune	Los Angeles Times	New York Times	All Five Newspapers
Democrats						
Babbitt						
Front page	1	1	1	3	1	7
Other pages	7	20	1	5	14	47
Dukakis						
Front page	4	28	4	3	1	40
Other pages	39	140	4	21	28	232
Gephardt						
Front page	1	6	1	6	0	14
Other pages	21	24	3	12	21	81
Gore						
Front page	2	3	0	2	1	8
Other pages	42	37	8	17	22	126
Hart						
Front page	4	5	7	8	6	30
Other pages	43	50	19	30	39	181
Jackson						
Front page	4	6	6	4	0	20
Other pages	43	37	14	22	33	149
Simon						
Front page	1	5	2	2	1	11
Other pages	17	37	14	22	18	108
Republicans						
Bush						
Front page	7	21	8	18	9	63
Other pages	69	105	35	64	76	349
Dole						
Front page	3	11	5	15	5	39
Other pages	44	65	24	39	60	232
du Pont						
Front page	1	1	0	1	1	4
Other pages	5	21	1	4	7	38
Haig						
Front page	1	2	1	1	0	5
Other pages	8	6	2	5	13	34
Kemp						
Front page	1	3	0	1	0	5
Other pages	15	29	5	13	16	78
Robertson						
Front page	4	4	2	5	1	16
Other pages	41	40	13	24	36	154

firsthand while serving as a Peace Corps volunteer in Latin America. Gore was introduced to national politics at an early age while his father served in the Senate. Illegitimacy and racial segregation left their marks on Jackson. Bush piloted Navy dive-bombers in World War II and experienced combat before his twenty-first birthday. Dole knew Dust Bowl poverty during the Depression and spent years recuperating from war wounds received in Italy. And Robertson underwent a religious awakening in the late 1950s while scratching out a living in Bedford-Stuyvesant.

Aside from a few detailed biographical articles, information of this sort seldom appeared in the coverage of most candidates. Only 10 of 577 news items in all five newspapers referred to formative experiences in Babbitt's life. Such coverage was even thinner for Gephardt (5 of 721 items), du Pont (3 of 433), Haig (4 of 414), and Kemp (7 of 622). Front-runner status was no guarantee of more biographical coverage. Only 30 of 1,063 items about Bush mentioned important episodes in his earlier life, while 43 of Dole's 895 specifically noted his having been wounded in World War II. Jackson got more such coverage than any other Democrat, but "more" in this case was only 20 out of 734 items.

Given all the emphasis on marital fidelity during this particular exhibition season, one might have expected considerable coverage of relationships with wives and other family members. With few exceptions, this was not so. Again, items about Dole contained the most information of this sort, partly because he often spoke of his family's economic plight during the Depression, and because his wife played so prominent a part in his campaign. Ninety-three items about Dole mentioned relationship with family members. Hart was second, with 46 of 482 items, nearly all mentioning his wife, now a constant companion on the campaign trail. Gore got more family coverage than Bush, and the remaining candidates received still less in no discernible order.

Selective Coverage of the "Character Issue"

According to Jack W. Germond and Jules Witcover (1989), the so-called "character issue" is a relatively recent fashion in presidential campaign reporting. The general rule followed by journalists well into the 1960s was that "if personal conduct didn't affect the candidate's performance on the stump and wasn't a detriment to his conduct of the office he was seeking, it was his business" (Germond and Witcover, 1989: 58). A new rule has since evolved, in which nothing in a candidate's personal life is out of bounds. The *New York Times* evidently took this view when it asked the 1988 candidates to supply detailed financial statements, lists of close friends, copies of basic documents (college transcripts, marriage licenses, and medical records), and sign waivers of privacy rights. After dropping out of the Republican race in April 1988, Dole cited the *Times*'s request as proof that something was "out of whack" with contemporary campaign journalism (Molotsky, 1988). Even though the new rule hardly bars positive reporting, more intense media interest in a candidate's personal life usually spells bad news for the candidate.

Germond and Witcover (1989: 57 60) attribute the new rule to numerous developments in the 1960s and 1970s. First, the sweeping cultural changes of that time registered on the news media as on other institutions. Among the effects was a heightened cynicism about government and politics, a new candor in reporting the conduct of public officials, and an aggressive brand of investigative reporting. Second, the number of reporters regularly assigned to presidential campaigns grew "geometrically." With this increase, relationships between candidates and traveling press became more impersonal and rule-bound. Technology played an important part in these developments as well, with the advent of pocket tape recorders, computerized "campaign hot lines," laptop word processors, television satellites, and other innovations that not only increased the accuracy and speed of campaign reporting but helped alter press-campaign relationships as well. Reporters now judge the seriousness of a presidential campaign largely by how well it satisfies their many technological and logistical needs.

These changes became apparent on campaign airplanes and buses, where candidates and reporters spent considerable time in close proximity to one another. Larger numbers and the new rule of character reporting made candidates less willing to risk informal "off-the-record" chats with members of the traveling press, since an unwitting phrase or off-color remark might blow up into a campaign issue or "mediality."[5]

The new rule operated with a vengeance during the 1988 exhibition season when *Miami Herald* reporters staked out Hart's Washington, D.C., townhouse and observed his comings and goings with model and actress Donna Rice. The frenzy that followed swiftly destroyed Hart's credibility. It also prompted yet another debate over journalistic ethics, with typically inconclusive results. Some, like Anthony Lewis and A. M. Rosenthal of the *New York Times*, argued that candidates are entitled to a certain measure of privacy and criticized the *Herald*'s tactics. "I did not become a newspaperman to hide outside a politician's house trying to find out whether he was in bed with somebody," Rosenthal wrote (quoted in Germond and Witcover, 1989: 212). The more prevalent view was that journalistic competition justified pursuing such stories because other news organizations would do so in any event. Once a media frenzy began, collective obsession with the story obliterated individual reservations. Everyone in the pack had to know more about Hart's adultery and Biden's plagiarism. An embittered Hart likened the new rule to a hunt, in which candidates were the prey and reporters the hounds and hunters.

Hart and Biden were already out of the Democratic race by the time data collection began for this research, but Dukakis, Gore, Babbitt, Jackson, Bush, and Robertson would experience character scrutiny of varying intensity before the exhibition season ended. And, of course, the media spotlight once again settled on Hart when he rejoined the race in December.

Dukakis's character problem began with the discovery that his top aide, John Sasso, had played a leading role in the destruction of Biden's candidacy. The episode began when Sasso learned that the conclusion of a speech Biden delivered with great passion in Iowa had been taken almost word for word, without attribution, from an address by Neil Kinnock, the British Labor Party leader. Reportedly without notifying Dukakis, Sasso distributed a videotape of the two speeches to selected newspaper and television reporters. Their stories set in motion a chain of events that led to the collapse of Biden's candidacy within the month. By this time, news organizations not initially given the tape were going all out to uncover its source, which the original recipients refused to disclose. Suspicion at first fell on the White House and on the Gephardt campaign but soon shifted to Dukakis operatives. On September 28, Dukakis unwittingly trapped himself by publicly condemning whoever had supplied the tape and by avowing that such misbehavior by his aides would have been swiftly punished. Two days later, having learned the truth, a visibly distressed Dukakis accepted Sasso's resignation and that of another top aide who had helped distribute the tape. Dukakis also apologized publicly to Biden and his supporters.[6]

Some pundits argued that Sasso had done nothing wrong since Biden had indeed plagiarized the Kinnock speech. On the other hand, the whole affair tarnished Dukakis's claim of "competent leadership" and contradicted his high-sounding rhetoric about clean campaigning. With two Democrats already downed by character failings, some critics tried to tar Dukakis with the same brush. In Iowa, where Democrats were most upset with Dukakis, a principal Biden supporter told the *Globe* that this was "most definitely a character problem" for Dukakis because he had failed to meet his own high standard (Oliphant, 1987a).

After disclosures of sustained marijuana use undermined the nomination of Douglas Ginsburg to the Supreme Court, the press developed an interest in the possible drug habits of presidential candidates. Anticipating that the marijuana question would be asked of him, Gore and his advisors elected to make a statement before the press extracted an admission of past use. Though risking adverse reaction from voters, this strategy at least gave Gore some say in how the story would be framed. It also avoided any impression of evasion or dissembling. The moment of truth came at a November 7 press conference, when a clearly nervous Gore disclosed that he had smoked marijuana for several years as an undergraduate, serviceman, and graduate student. His wife had also tried it in her college years. Neither, he avowed, had used marijuana in the last fifteen years.

Gore's confession prompted telephone calls to the other candidates, and, when the Associated Press reached Babbitt in Des Moines, the former Arizona governor readily admitted to having smoked marijuana in the 1960s as a college student. Asked about the likely effect of this disclosure on his chances, Babbitt drolly expressed doubts that it would improve his poll standings (Hess and Sack, 1987).

No candidate appeared more vulnerable to tough character scrutiny than Jackson. Even supporters acknowledged his enormous ego and insatiable appetite for media attention. It was in this context that old charges of exploiting the assassination of Martin Luther King, Jr., still dogged his 1988 campaign. His claims of having heard King's last words and gotten King's blood on his shirt had been disputed by other witnesses to the shooting. Reportedly the widowed Coretta Scott King, Ralph Abernathy, and other King lieutenants in the civil rights movement had never forgiven Jackson, as evidenced by their refusal to endorse his 1984 and 1988 presidential candidacies.[7]

Another potential problem for Jackson in 1988 was his tense relationship with Jews. Many already regarded him with deep misgivings after embracing Yasir Arafat and the Palestinian cause in 1979, even though Jackson reportedly had urged Arafat to seek peace with Israel (Kaufman, 1988: 241). Much was also made of Jackson's earlier view that the Holocaust had been overly emphasized in comparison to the black slavery experience. He had begun to allay such concerns in 1984 when the *Washington Post* reported and then editorially condemned his "Hymie" remarks. More problems arose for Jackson's 1984 campaign when Louis Farrakhan, a Black Muslim minister and principal Jackson supporter in Chicago, threatened the black reporter who had tipped the *Post* to the Hymie story. Later in the campaign, Farrakhan denounced Judaism and decried the founding of Israel. Jackson ended his 1984 campaign on a more conciliatory note by eloquently apologizing for any offense he might have given. Still, many critics remained unconvinced, and their doubts remained when Jackson began his 1988 campaign. Though seldom a problem for Jackson during the exhibition season, these misgivings figured importantly in the New York primary.

Among his other soft spots was Jackson's reputation as womanizer. This old gossip took on new relevance with the Donna Rice hullabaloo, and Jackson's staffers fully expected a round of womanizing stories after he formally became a candidate (Associated Press, 1987).

Hart was even more vulnerable on this score, as the Donna Rice affair demonstrated. Moreover, in 1984 his explanations for changes in his name, signature, and date of birth had never satisfied the press. Like his 1984 campaign debts, these doubts still nagged assessments of his character three years later and were quickly revived when he reentered the race on December 15.

The spotlight of character coverage also fell on Republicans, and it lingered longest on Vice-President Bush. Following his loyal service to Reagan, Bush's chief character problem was an image of expediency and pliancy that fostered doubts about his capacity for leadership. The "wimp" insult condensed these reservations into a widely publicized symbol. Other reservations about Bush's leadership arose from questions about his part in the Iran-contra affair. Throughout the exhibition season, reporters tried unsuccessfully to get Bush to reveal the advice he gave Reagan on trading arms for hostages, and it was over Iran-contra that Bush and Dan Rather waged their fierce television debate. Though he never satisfied the press on this matter, Bush was able to turn the issue to his own advantage among Republican primary voters by emphasizing his loyalty to Reagan.

More so than any other candidate, Robertson campaigned on moral themes. In this vein he decried teenage pregnancies and called for a return to "the old-fashioned concept of moral restraint and abstinence before marriage" (Kranish, 1987: 12). Accordingly it was no small irony that Robertson's first character crisis in the campaign sprang from disclosures that his own marriage had occurred only ten weeks before the birth of his first child. When this was first revealed in the *Wall Street Journal* and the *Washington Post*, an angry Robertson lashed out at the press (Mashek and Harvey, 1987: 13A): "I think it is outrageous to pry into a man's past and try to do damage to a man's wife and children under the guise of journalism."

Robertson was also compelled to address several inaccuracies in his campaign literature. He had not served on the board of directors of a Virginia bank, as claimed, nor had he pursued graduate studies at the University of London. References to his "law career" were at best misleading since he had failed the New York bar examination after graduating from Yale Law School and had never actually practiced. Still another claim, that he had been a decorated combat veteran of the Korean war, was discredited by the revelation that his father, Senator A. Willis Robertson of Virginia, had intervened with the Pentagon to keep him out of the front lines.[8]

His 1988 campaign was also haunted by a long history of controversial claims and statements in his career as an ordained minister, author of numerous religious books, television faith-healer, and host of "The 700 Club" program on his own network. Among the statements preserved in print and on videotape were claims of having diverted a hurricane, cured all manner of physical ailments, and gotten God's approval of his candidacy. For many, Robertson's words gave rise to a fundamental issue indeed, whether "he could be trusted to behave rationally as President of the United States" (Harrell, 1987: 130).

Additional problems arose during the exhibition season when some of Robertson's verbal blasts damaged his own campaign more than the intended targets. Unaware that Nancy Reagan was undergoing surgery, Robertson outraged a gathering of Seattle Republicans by casting aspersions on the First Lady's anticommunism (Margolis, 1987a). In New Hampshire he avowed that medical authorities were concealing the true risk of contracting AIDS and maintained that it could be transmitted by breathing into the atmosphere of enclosed spaces (Ellement, 1987a). Testifying against the reduction of abortion restrictions, Robertson accused Planned Parenthood of wanting to create a "master race" (Political Notebook, 1988b).

Table 6.4 summarizes the coverage given each of these character issues in the five major newspapers. Here coverage is measured by counting the items about a candidate explicitly mentioning the episode in question. Two findings are especially apparent: some candidates got much more character scrutiny than others, and the five newspapers were remarkably uniform in the amount of coverage given each story. Every newspaper played up Dukakis's part in the Biden tape affair, Hart's association with Donna Rice, and the shadow cast by Iran-contra on Bush's candidacy. Each put comparatively little emphasis on the marijuana controversy, Jackson's assorted vulnerabilities, or the revelations about Robertson.

Before trying to explain why some character issues got so much more coverage than others, let us say more about the amount of coverage in each case, beginning with Dukakis. Altogether, the five newspapers published 143 news items associating Dukakis with the Biden-Kinnock tape. Sixty-five of these appeared in the *Globe*. Of 47 stories and feature articles mostly or wholly about the tape flap, 25 came out in the *Globe*. Although each paper continued coverage for a week or so after Sasso's resignation, the *Globe* kept it alive far longer with periodic updates and frequent salting of other Dukakis news.

When Hart rejoined the race on December 15, he reportedly expected to be hit with a "10,000-pound sledgehammer" (Dionne, 1987a). And so he was. Editorialists, columnists, and cartoonists subjected him to some of the most scathing commentary inflicted on any presidential candidate in this century.[9]

Hart's return was the biggest news story of the entire nineteen-week period observed in this research. In his first week back, December 15–21, Hart got more print lines in each newspaper than all other Democratic candidates combined. The *Tribune* and the *New York Times* gave him more space than all other candidates, Democratic and Republican com-

Table 6.4 Character Coverage of Selected Candidates

Items Mentioning	Atlanta Constitution	Boston Globe	Chicago Tribune	Los Angeles Times	New York Times	All Five Newspapers
Dukakis: Biden tape	24	65	10	24	20	143
Gore: marijuana	12	5	1	3	6	27
Babbitt: marijuana	4	2	0	2	5	13
Hart: Donna Rice	31	38	19	31	30	149
Hart: 1984 debts	10	15	5	15	25	70
Jackson: "hymie"	3	4	1	4	3	15
Jackson: 1987 problems with Jews	2	3	0	4	4	13
Bush: Iran-contra	31	56	18	45	43	193
Bush: "wimp"	13	13	6	9	12	53
Robertson: son's birth	6	5	5	5	5	26
Robertson: Korea	6	3	2	2	2	15
Robertson: prayers	6	4	2	4	3	19
Robertson: other flaps	8	4	2	6	8	28

NOTE: Cells refer to news items in each newspaper mentioning particular incident.

bined. Indeed, the volume of Hart coverage was so great in these weeks that it surpassed any other Democrat's for the entire October 1–February 8 period in the *Tribune, Los Angeles Times,* and *New York Times.*

The Donna Rice mentions noted in table 6.4 give some idea of how negative most of Hart's coverage was. Perhaps hoping that this issue would die if he refused to discuss it with the press, Hart on his first day back admonished reporters that his personal life was none of their business. Table 6.4 suggests that they saw matters differently. In the cyclone of publicity following his reentry, 149 news items explicitly mentioned the Rice affair. This coverage is even more astounding when put in proportion: Of 77 *Los Angeles Times* items about Hart, 31 (40.3 percent) referred to Donna Rice. The same linkage appeared almost as often in other newspapers — in 34.4 percent of all *Constitution* items about Hart, in 31.1 percent of the *Tribune*'s items about him, in 30.3 percent of all such *New York Times* items, and in 24.5 percent of all such *Globe* items. Newspaper coverage reached a saturation level during his first week back, when the five newspapers printed 55 news items associating Rice with Hart. Thereafter the flood receded a bit but never dried up, as 94 more such items followed in the next seven weeks.

Hart's leftover debts from the 1984 campaign also got considerable coverage, especially after the *Miami Herald* reported irregularities in his 1984 campaign fund-raising. Ironically, in view of all the press attention to his name, age, and signature changes in 1984, only 3 items out of 482 about Hart in all five newspapers mentioned these problems.

Iran-contra dogged Bush's coverage in every newspaper. He fared worst in the *Los Angeles Times,* where 23.2 percent of all the items explicitly linked him to the scandal. A high percentage of items in every other newspaper made the same connection: 19.7 in the *Globe,* 17.4 in the *New York Times,* 15.3 in the *Tribune,* and 14.1 in the *Constitution.* All told, 193 of 1,064 items about Bush, or 18.2 percent of his coverage, associated him with Iran-contra. Most of this coverage came out in the final five weeks of the exhibition season. Of the 18 *Tribune* items associating Bush with this affair, 15 appeared between January 5 and February 8. The same was true for 26 of the 31 items in the *Constitution,* 44 of 56 in the *Globe,* 35 of 45 in the *Los Angeles Times,* and 35 of 43 in the *New York Times.*

In contrast, Gore and Babbitt suffered about one week of marijuana coverage before the story petered out. Nearly half the Gore items appeared in the *Constitution,* no doubt a reflection of regional interest.

None of the previously recounted episodes in Jackson's life got much coverage. A few tough biographical articles (Painton, 1987; Vennochi, 1987; Shaw, 1987; Purnick and Oreskes, 1987) reviewed Jackson's behavior after the King assassination, discussed his continuing difficulties with Jews, and noted the womanizing rumors. Few straight-news items about Jackson mentioned these matters.

Though angered and embarrassed by the revelations about himself, Robertson got off lightly compared to Bush, Hart, and Dukakis. True, he came in for detailed scrutiny, as in a *Constitution* story (Sack, 1987a) detailing discrepancies in his campaign literature, but such damaging revelations were not often repeated. Again putting matters in proportion, between 3.3 and 6.2 percent of all the news items about Robertson in the five newspapers mentioned the circumstances of his son's birth. The dispute over his Korean War service and his prayers for assorted miracles received even fewer mentions.

Quite clearly, some character issues got much more coverage than others. Did Bush's wimp image really deserve more notice than Robertson's disputed war record? Did Gore's marijuana confession say more about his character than Jackson's perennial tensions with Jews, or Jackson's behavior after King was shot? Was Dukakis's role in the Biden tape flap truly more important than Robertson's apparent belief that he could harness nature's forces through prayer? Why do some character issues assume major proportions while others attract only brief notice?

One criterion often evident in such reporting is "magnification," or the context created by confirmation of prior suspicions or expectations. Thus the Donna Rice affair was especially newsworthy because it confirmed longstanding rumors of Hart's womanizing. Without this context, there would have been no reporters on his doorstep and no scandal. Bush's wimp and Iran-contra coverage can be understood in the same way after eight years of having served as Reagan's loyal subordinate.

Magnification can also occur when candidates act contrary to images previously projected. Much high-minded rhetoric on clean and constructive campaigning had issued from Dukakis by the time his top aide produced the Biden tape. The affair also contradicted Dukakis's theme of "hands-on" management. Biden's own character coverage can be understood in this context as well. He was supposed to be an eloquent and passionate orator, so why did he have to steal someone else's eloquence and passion?

But neither version of magnification accounts for the comparatively sparse coverage of Robertson's character. This is curious because, on the one hand, years of televised faith-healing and pronouncements mixing religion and politics had established a rich context for judging his statements as a candidate. And, on the other hand, the disclosures about his marriage, military service, and other claims contradicted his professed beliefs and image.

A second criterion is timeliness. The tape flap, Hart's reentry, and Iran-contra made news because they were brand-new events. Grumblings about Jackson were old, not new, hence not newsworthy. "Hymie" was news in 1984, not in 1987–88. Still, few members of the public knew anything about Robertson's marriage and war record.

A third consideration is the degree to which the news media take candidates seriously. Viewed from this perspective, numerous stories fall into place—the initial furor over Donna Rice that forced Hart out of the race, the Biden plagiarism story, the Sasso tape flap, and all the attention focused on Bush's role in Iran-contra. Since few reporters gave Robertson any chance of winning the GOP nomination, the same criterion helps explain why the press did not publicize his problems more. The seriousness criterion may also have been applied to the story of Hart's return. At first, no one could be certain what the impact of this extraordinary event would be, especially since Hart quickly regained the lead in national polls. By January, however, Hart's coverage had slackened as his Iowa poll ratings dropped.

The seriousness argument takes on a new twist with Jackson, whom most reporters gave little chance of winning the Democratic race, even though he ran first or second in many national polls. Jackson attributed this consensus more to racism than to typical journalistic handicapping of candidates early in the process. Race unquestionably complicated the coverage of his campaign and may well have induced reporters to avoid probing Jackson's character, as his former press secretary (Colton, 1989: 187–88) has claimed. On the other hand, Jackson gave the press no new "Hymie" or Farrakhan flap, no equivalent of the Donna Rice affair, nor any other genuine opening for fresh examination of his character. When it was disclosed that he had contracted to make television commercials for a chain of business and vocational schools, Jackson quickly terminated the arrangement. Nothing came of an allegation that he had plagiarized a term paper in college; Jackson vehemently denied the accusation, and it soon expired for lack of corroboration.

In summary, newspapers do not systematically or evenhandedly investigate the character of presidential aspirants. According to Germond and Witcover (1989: 238), the rules of such coverage are "written anew for each case." Apparently there are standard tests, but even candidates meeting one or two of these may suffer relatively little while others pay a considerable price. Being taken seriously evidently weighs more heavily on these scales than timeliness or magnification.

Public Office, Accomplishments, Issue Stands, and Campaign Themes

A stock criticism of preconvention coverage is the dearth of substance about candidate records and policy stands. Patterson (1980: 168) has characterized issue coverage during the entire nominating process as no more than a "rivulet" in the flow of news about campaign dynamics and hoopla. According to Patterson and Davis (1985), candidates fare no better in getting their main campaign themes publicized. On the other hand, newspapers make a greater attempt to publicize the issue stands and campaign themes of candidates during the exhibition season than during the primaries and caucuses.[10]

Tables 6.5 and 6.6 compare the Democratic and Republican candidates according to the percentage of items mentioning records of public service, stands on issues of public policy, and campaign themes. Items included in the public-service count had to mention specific efforts such as Gephardt's House sponsorship of trade legislation or Simon's Senate opposition to the 1986 tax reform law. To satisfy the code for specific issue stands, an item had to indicate what the candidate proposed to do about a problem, as in mentioning Bush's call for a cut in the capital gains tax or Dole's proposal to freeze most categories of federal spending. More general statements about issues, like Gore's characterization of himself as stronger on defense than his Democratic rivals, were categorized as campaign themes. Also classified as campaign themes were pronouncements about leadership and other character strengths, party loyalty, freedom, liberalism or conservatism, the national interest, the state of the economy, and visions of the future.

In addition to the three measures just described, table 6.5 reports the number of items about each candidate in each newspaper. This tabulation affirms previous findings based on print lines that some candidates got considerably more coverage than others and that no one Democrat enjoyed a consistent advantage over his rivals. As was not the case with the earlier comparison of print lines, however, Hart trailed all other Democrats in the number of items mentioning candidates. This simply demonstates that print lines and items about a candidate are not wholly equivalent indicators of coverage, owing to variation in item length. Even so, the results of using either measure reflected the absence of a clear Democratic front-runner.

Shifting from the volume of coverage to its content, table 6.5 shows that the five newspapers reported relatively little information about the records of most candidates. Only Gephardt and Dukakis received appreciable publicity in this regard, and the *Globe* provided most of Dukakis's coverage. Gephardt loomed so large in this comparison because of his sponsorship of trade and farm bills in Congress, while the *Globe* monitored Dukakis's problems as governor while running for president. All candidates fared considerably better in items mentioning their issue stands and campaign themes.

Table 6.6 repeats these comparisons for the Republican candidates. As in earlier print-line comparisons, the tally of Republican items reflected

Table 6.5 **Items Mentioning Accomplishments, Issue Stands, and Campaign Themes of Democratic Candidates**

	Atlanta Constitution	Boston Globe	Chicago Tribune	Los Angeles Times	New York Times	All Five Newspapers
Bases for Percentages						
Babbitt items	116	181	63	99	118	577
Dukakis items	182	391	86	137	166	962
Gephardt items	141	225	83	131	141	721
Gore items	164	190	64	100	124	642
Hart items	90	155	61	77	99	482
Jackson items	174	209	87	127	137	734
Simon items	142	226	96	131	143	738
Items Mentioning Accomplishments in Office (%)						
Babbitt	2.6	2.8	1.6	2.0	1.7	2.3
Dukakis	11.0	12.8	3.5	8.0	9.6	10.4
Gephardt	16.3	11.1	19.3	19.1	12.8	14.8
Gore	4.9	5.8	1.6	2.0	3.2	4.0
Hart	2.2	0.6	0.0	2.6	2.0	1.5
Simon	5.6	2.2	4.2	8.4	4.9	4.7
Items Mentioning Specific Stands on One or More Issues (%)						
Babbitt	18.1	26.0	25.4	37.4	16.1	24.3
Dukakis	18.8	16.9	12.8	25.5	19.3	18.5
Gephardt	21.4	19.6	24.1	33.6	19.9	23.1
Gore	13.5	14.2	7.8	21.2	10.5	13.8
Hart	10.0	10.3	9.8	13.0	6.0	9.7
Jackson	15.0	10.5	13.8	20.5	11.7	13.9
Simon	14.9	15.9	13.5	26.0	14.0	16.8
Items Mentioning One or More General Campaign Themes (%)						
Babbitt	19.8	17.1	20.6	31.3	19.5	21.0
Dukakis	18.7	21.2	18.6	20.4	24.7	21.0
Gephardt	24.8	22.2	20.5	30.5	17.0	23.0
Gore	20.7	22.1	17.2	31.0	26.6	23.5
Hart	23.3	21.3	19.7	28.6	21.2	22.6
Jackson	18.4	17.7	19.5	26.8	26.2	21.2
Simon	21.8	18.6	22.9	25.9	25.2	22.4

a clearly defined field in which front-runner Bush got the most coverage and Dole ranked second. On the other hand, both Dole and Kemp did better than Bush in the percentage of items mentioning records of public service, and Bush trailed several others in proportionate issue and theme coverage.

In summary, tables 6.5 and 6.6 are noteworthy because they demonstrate that sheer volume does not necessarily bestow a proportionate advantage in the coverage of accomplishments, issue stands, or campaign themes. Even though the most programmatic candidates got less publicity overall, their coverage still was more substantive than that of less-focused rivals standing higher in the polls.

Table 6.6 Items Mentioning Accomplishments, Issue Stands, and Campaign Themes of Republican Candidates

	Atlanta Constitution	Boston Globe	Chicago Tribune	Los Angeles Times	New York Times	All Five Newspapers
Bases for Percentages						
Bush items	220	284	118	194	247	1063
Dole items	188	231	107	164	205	895
du Pont items	87	131	45	84	86	433
Haig items	82	112	44	87	89	414
Kemp items	117	179	76	111	139	622
Robertson items	141	153	81	113	126	614
Items Mentioning Past or Present Accomplishments in Office (%)						
Bush	5.0	5.6	2.5	11.3	6.9	6.5
Dole	9.0	6.9	14.0	12.2	10.7	10.1
du Pont	4.6	3.8	2.2	2.4	3.5	3.5
Kemp	7.7	8.4	2.6	6.3	7.2	6.9
Items Mentioning Specific Stands on One or More Issues (%)						
Bush	18.2	16.5	14.4	25.3	21.9	19.5
Dole	21.8	18.2	16.8	25.6	20.5	20.7
du Pont	28.7	21.4	20.0	25.0	20.9	23.3
Haig	15.9	9.8	13.6	28.7	19.1	17.4
Kemp	23.3	17.9	18.4	21.6	23.0	20.8
Robertson	14.9	13.1	12.3	19.5	11.1	14.2
Items Mentioning One or More General Campaign Themes (%)						
Bush	12.7	12.3	11.0	22.2	15.4	14.8
Dole	17.6	17.7	16.8	28.7	22.9	20.8
du Pont	10.3	11.4	2.2	15.5	12.8	11.3
Haig	20.7	7.1	6.8	17.2	12.4	13.0
Kemp	21.4	14.0	9.2	23.4	13.6	16.4
Robertson	20.6	11.8	12.3	19.5	14.3	15.8

Table 6.7 points up the types of issues most mentioned in each candidate's coverage. Based on the combined totals for all five newspapers, the percentages in this table refer to items about each candidate mentioning at least one issue stand.[11] For example, 62.1 percent of all items mentioning one or more Babbitt stands noted his call for a 5 percent national consumption tax with proceeds earmarked for deficit reduction, or another proposal to reduce the deficit. Collapsing such particulars into more general categories did not mask major differences in newspaper coverage.[12]

Such differences are immediately evident among the Democrats. Table 6.7 shows that the issue coverage afforded Babbitt, Hart, and Simon focused on their tax and deficit ideas while Gore and Jackson coverage was oriented more toward foreign-policy pronouncements. Babbitt's oft-reported proposal to impose a tax on more affluent recipients of Social Security accounted for his proportionate lead in coverage of "social service" issues, and by the same token, Gephardt's frequent calls for farm production controls and retaliatory trade practices put him out front in coverage of "farm" and "trade" issues. There was very little coverage of whatever specific ideas the candidates may have offered on "social issues" like abortion, gay rights, and affirmative action. A typical reaction is to blame the press for not reporting such views, but a more likely explanation is that most candidates avoided these issues whenever possible. In any event, Democratic candidate coverage noted few specific ideas on dealing with AIDS and surprisingly little comment on Iran-contra or Reagan's Supreme Court nominees.

Republican candidate coverage also disclosed interesting variations in issue emphasis. Table 6.7 shows that Bush, Dole, and Kemp got the most press on issues related to the deficit and taxes. Virtually all Bush coverage in this connection mentioned his unequivocal vow not to raise taxes and a proposal to lower the capital gains tax. Bush's repeated endorsement of the INF treaty chiefly accounted for his defense and foreign-policy coverage. Enough du Pont items mentioned his ideas for an IRA-type alternative to Social Security, educational vouchers, and various welfare reforms to make his social-services coverage proportionately greater than any other candidate's. He also stood out on farm policy for his proposal to abolish crop subsidies. Stands on social issues were mentioned more often in Republican than Democratic candidate coverage, and Robertson's was particularly fulsome in this regard. Iran-contra surfaced more in items about Republican candidates, especially Haig and Dole, who implied that Bush knew more than he was telling and insisted that he tell all. No Republican's coverage indicated much attention to AIDS or to Supreme Court nominations.

Did the major newspapers in this study provide only a trickle of news about issue positions during the exhibition season? Since most references to candidate stands typically consisted of no more than a sentence or two, major newspaper coverage of the exhibition season was vulnerable to the standard complaint. On the other hand, a relatively large portion of each candidate's coverage contained such references. Simple fairness moreover requires acknowledgment of each newspaper's special efforts to inform their readers about leading issues of the preconvention campaign.

Studying UPI and CBS coverage of the 1980 presidential campaigns, Robinson and Sheehan (1983: 46) noted particular press reluctance to assess or evaluate issues. "For all practical purposes," they concluded, "whatever the candidates said about the issues served as issue coverage." While probably true of television and wire services even today, this generalization may not hold for major newspapers, which rely chiefly on their own reporters for stories on presidential nominating campaigns.

In any event, an occasional story line during the 1988 exhibition season was the reticence of candidates to speak out on certain controversial problems. Democratic candidates, for example, reportedly shunned discussion

Table 6.7 Policy Issues Most Emphasized in Candidate Coverage, Combined Percentages for All Five Newspapers

Democratic Candidates

	Babbitt (N = 140)	Dukakis (N = 179)	Gephardt (N = 165)	Gore (N = 89)	Hart (N = 46)	Jackson (N = 104)	Simon (N = 125)
Deficit/taxes	62.1	43.0	38.8	23.5	76.1	24.1	62.4
Defense/foreign policy	19.3	46.4	29.7	86.5	23.9	72.1	26.4
Social services	36.4	8.4	16.4	14.6	8.7	7.7	17.6
Social issues	3.6	7.3	9.7	6.7	0.0	7.7	9.6
Farm programs	5.0	2.8	21.2	5.6	13.0	4.8	9.6
Trade legislation	0.7	1.7	18.2	1.1	6.5	0.0	0.0
AIDS	1.4	1.1	3.0	3.4	4.3	4.8	4.0
Supreme Court	0.7	0.6	0.6	0.0	0.0	2.9	2.4
Iran-contra	0.0	2.2	1.2	1.1	4.3	0.0	0.8

Republican Candidates

	Bush (N = 205)	Dole (N = 185)	du Pont (N = 101)	Haig (N = 72)	Kemp (N = 128)	Robertson (N = 87)
Deficit/taxes	45.9	41.6	13.8	16.6	39.0	24.0
Defense/foreign policy	55.6	47.0	29.7	51.3	35.9	42.5
Social services	12.7	11.9	51.5	6.9	25.0	12.6
Social issues	12.6	9.2	21.7	15.3	21.9	43.6
Farm programs	2.4	4.3	2.0	1.4	0.8	0.0
Trade legislation	1.0	1.1	1.0	1.4	0.0	0.0
AIDS	1.9	2.7	2.0	4.2	3.1	4.6
Supreme Court	1.5	2.2	2.0	0.0	3.9	2.3
Iran-contra	N.A.	11.9	0.0	26.3	5.5	0.0

NOTE: Numbers in parentheses are total items mentioning one or more specific issue stands.

of the Israeli crackdown on rebellious Palestinians. Both the *Tribune* (Locin, 1987) and the *Globe* (Wilkie, 1988) noted that Jackson was the only Democrat willing to criticize the Israelis; the *Globe* even labeled Jackson's rivals as "the silent six." Other stories noted candidate inattention to rural poverty (Frisby, 1988), education (Cohen, 1987), farm policies (Tackett, 1988; Schmidt, 1988), the environment (Seabrook 1987), and national health care (King, 1988).

Additional signs of a critical press were stories noting lack of substance in candidate issue stands. The vehicle for most observations of this type was the "news analysis," a blend of fact and opinion printed in the news rather than the editorial section. A fairly typical example was the *Globe* (Oliphant, 1987b) article charging Democratic candidates with a dearth of ideas about how to prevent the next stock market crash. The *New York Times* (Rosenbaum, 1987) concluded that Babbitt was the only Democrat bemoaning the deficit to offer "clear prescriptions for solving the problem." The *Tribune* (Margolis, 1987b) pooh-poohed promises to cut the deficit without raising taxes. Another *Tribune* article (Lentz, 1987a) called attention to the lack of specifics in Dole's rhetoric about deficit reduction.

These newspapers were also willing to pinpoint factual errors in candidate pronouncements. The *Globe* was particularly aggressive in this way, especially when Dukakis was at fault. At least three stories (Black, 1987; Farrel, 1987a and 1987b) fastened on misleading estimates in the Dukakis proposal for deficit reduction through improved tax collection. When Jackson inaccurately likened New Hampshire voter registration rules to those of southern states in the 1960s, the *Globe* (Ellement, 1987b) effectively rebutted him by outlining the regulations and quoting the New Hampshire secretary of state. And no sooner did Robertson appear to change his stand on the INF treaty than the *Globe* noted his inconsistency (Marantz, 1987; Political Notebook, 1987).

In addition to critical reporting of the sort just noted, every newspaper ran a special series of feature articles detailing candidate positions on major policy questions. The *Constitution* was especially noteworthy for a ten-article "presidential campaign" series setting out candidate positions on defense policy (Stewart 1987a and 1987b), the stock market crash (Straus, 1987a), funding for public education (Mashek, 1987), the environment (Seabrook, 1987), tax increases (Harvey, 1988), and national health care (King, 1988). Other pieces in the same series looked at Gephardt's proposed Global Market Access Amendment (Straus, 1987b) and Hart's "new ideas" (Sack, 1987b) and deficit plan (Baxter, 1988). The *Constitution* also featured candidates' brief responses to questions of regional interest in a "Super Tuesday's Issues" series — rural and farm policy, job retraining, education, health care, and trade. Together these two series consumed 3,626 print lines, or 6.4 percent of the *Constitution*'s total volume of exhibition-season coverage.

The *Los Angeles Times* also made a major effort to inform its readers about candidate stands on major policy issues. In its "'88 Candidates and the Issues" series, the *Times* compared the views of all the candidates on policy towards Central America (McManus, 1987), the deficit (Redburn, 1987), AIDS (Cimons, 1987), trade (Rosenblatt, 1987), social programs (May, 1987), abortion and other social controversies (Houston, 1987). Like other newspapers in this sample, the *Los Angeles Times* published lengthy feature articles on policy stands as well. Four such articles published in the final weeks of the exhibition season detailed candidate positions on taxes and the deficit (Risen and Rosenblatt, 1988; Nelson, 1988; Rosenblatt, 1988), and defense policy after the Reagan-Gorbachev summit (Shogan, 1987). Another described at length how other Democratic candidates had embraced and refined Hart's "new ideas" (Risen, 1987).

The *New York Times* stood out for publishing transcripts of standard candidate speeches, and the *Tribune* concluded the exhibition season with five feature articles detailing candidate stands on farm issues (Orr, 1988a–e).

At least some candidates succeeded in getting major newspapers to report their campaign themes on a relatively frequent basis. Table 6.8 lists candidate appeals mentioned in at least twenty items in all five newspapers.[13] Tireless reiteration of the same slogans clearly shaped this coverage more than national poll standings since Babbitt and Gephardt led in coverage of single themes. Dole and Dukakis demonstrated that the same approach worked for four themes. Bush voiced many themes, only two of which got significant coverage. Hart belongs in a special category because his most-publicized themes were pleas for judgment on some basis other than the Donna Rice affair. Du Pont ran a campaign heavy with blunt specifics but almost devoid of themes, hence his omission from the table.

Handicapping the "Horse Race"

Usually the most criticized aspect of campaign journalism is its preoccupation with discovering "who is ahead, who is behind, who is gaining, who is losing, what campaign strategy is being followed, and what the impact of campaign activities is on the candidate's chance of winning" (Joslyn, 1984: 133). By definition, the exhibition season precedes most, if not all, caucus and primary voting. Even so, newspapers provide a form of horse-race coverage by repeatedly handicapping the contestants. According to F. Christopher Arterton (1984), the mainstays of horse-race reporting are scenarios, standards, and benchmarks.

"Scenarios" project how the expected outcome in one state might affect

Table 6.8 **Campaign Themes Most Mentioned in Newspaper Coverage of Candidates**

Candidate	Theme	N Items	Percentage
Babbitt	Deficit	65	11.3
Dukakis	"Massachusetts Miracle"	39	4.0
Dukakis	Leadership qualities	31	3.2
Dukakis	Deficit	25	2.6
Dukakis	Economic future	23	2.4
Gephardt	Trade	64	8.9
Gephardt	Anti-establishment, populist	41	5.7
Gore	Pro-defense	34	5.3
Gore	Iowa caucuses unrepresentative	28	4.4
Hart	Public and private morality	37	7.7
Hart	"Let the people decide"	23	4.8
Jackson	Leadership qualities	36	4.9
Jackson	Empowerment, populist	26	3.5
Jackson	Improve social services	21	2.9
Simon	Deficit	43	5.8
Simon	Integrity, honesty	42	5.7
Simon	Improve social services	27	3.7
Bush	Leadership qualities	52	4.9
Bush	Improve social services	22	2.1
Dole	Leadership qualities	56	6.3
Dole	"I'm one of you," roots	47	5.2
Dole	Deficit	34	5.8
Dole	Compassion for less fortunate	23	2.3
Haig	Leadership qualities	20	4.8
Kemp	Deficit, growth	45	7.2
Robertson	Immorality, social ills	33	5.4

NOTE: Percentages based on same Ns reported in tables 6.5 and 6.6

a candidate's chances in subsequent caucuses and primaries. Walter Robinson (1988) described Dole's scenario for *Globe* readers: "Dole, who holds a substantial lead over Bush in Iowa polls, is hoping a victory in Iowa will give him the boost he will need to overcome Bush's lead and organizational edge in New Hampshire, win the New Hampshire primary and establish himself as a candidate with appeal beyond his midwestern base."

"Standards," according to Arterton (1984: 144), are "the mileposts candidates pass along the way," or expectations necessarily satisfied if favorable horse-race coverage is to follow. A *New York Times* story by E. J. Dionne, Jr. (1987b), fairly brimmed with such expectations: "The Iowa caucuses, which are seen as crucial for Mr. Simon, Mr. Gephardt, and Mr. Babbitt — they must win or do exceedingly well here if their candidacies are to survive into the later primaries — are somewhat less important for Mr. Dukakis and much less so for Mr. Jackson."

"Benchmarks" are exact vote percentages that must be won to satisfy media expectations. Most front-runners assiduously avoid the "Muskie mistake" of accepting such estimates, for the penalty of failing to live up to expectations is needlessly negative press.[14] After Hart dropped out of the race, pundits settled on a New Hampshire standard for Dukakis—he had to win the primary to remain viable. Setting a benchmark proved more difficult, however, as Philip Lentz (1987b) informed *Tribune* readers:

> Dukakis needs a big victory to demonstrate his solid base in New England. But how big is big?
>
> Strategists in opposing camps, hoping to set expectations higher than Dukakis will be able to meet, say anything less than 50 percent would have to be considered a "defeat." Dukakis supporters contend that is unrealistically high, but they refuse to say what percentage of the vote would constitute a win.
>
> Charles Baker, the Dukakis campaign manager, points out that no candidate in a multicandidate field has ever won the primary with 50 percent and that regional candidates historically have not run well in New Hampshire. . . .

Scenarios, standards, and benchmarks pertain to particular primary and caucus states. Given the level of specificity demanded, one would expect more standards than benchmarks. Still other common measures of the horse race for particular states are "progress reports"—or terse notations of how well candidates are doing—and standings in state polls.[15] Tables 6.9 and 6.10 show how frequently such indicators appeared in candidate coverage.

Looking first at the Democrats, table 6.9 shows that only Gore's state coverage consistently contained many scenarios, a result of his unconventional plan to write off Iowa and concentrate on the Super Tuesday South. Gephardt and Dukakis were the only Democrats often held to standards—winning Iowa and New Hampshire, respectively. Benchmarks seldom appeared in more than one or two items about any candidate. On the other hand, everybody's coverage teemed with progress reports like "gaining," "closing the gap," "holding his own," "stalling," "scrambling," "hanging on," and "lagging." Poll standings were often cited as well.

Except for lack of a GOP counterpart to Gore on scenarios, table 6.10 reveals basically the same pattern for Republican candidates—relatively little mention of scenarios and standards, virtually no benchmarks, many progress reports, and frequent references to poll standings. As in the previous table, the five newspapers exhibited remarkable uniformity in their use of the conventions of horse-race reporting. Nobody's coverage in any newspaper contained many scenarios or standards, almost no benchmarks were to be found, and every candidate's coverage abounded with progress reports and polling news. Although some candidates got much more horse-race

Table 6.9 **Horse-Race Coverage of Democratic Candidates in Key State Campaigns**

	Atlanta Constitution	Boston Globe	Chicago Tribune	Los Angeles Times	New York Times	All Five Newspapers
Items Mentioning Scenarios (%)						
Babbitt	2.6	3.6	4.1	4.0	4.5	3.7
Dukakis	5.2	6.2	10.1	7.8	7.5	6.9
Gephardt	8.2	8.5	6.0	3.1	8.0	7.1
Gore	16.4	17.7	23.5	13.3	20.2	17.8
Hart	8.1	9.3	0.0	3.9	4.3	6.0
Jackson	4.5	5.0	4.8	6.3	12.9	6.5
Simon	4.0	4.0	8.3	4.8	4.7	4.8
Items Mentioning Standards (%)						
Babbitt	1.3	3.6	4.1	2.7	4.5	3.3
Dukakis	9.5	8.1	10.1	7.8	11.7	9.2
Gephardt	14.4	10.8	7.5	12.2	11.6	11.5
Gore	7.8	7.5	5.9	10.7	11.4	8.6
Hart	6.5	10.2	0.0	7.8	4.3	6.6
Jackson	7.3	5.0	6.3	3.8	4.7	5.4
Simon	2.0	9.0	12.7	3.3	6.6	6.8
Items Mentioning Benchmarks (%)						
Babbitt	0.0	0.7	0.0	0.0	0.0	0.2
Dukakis	0.9	1.2	1.4	0.0	0.0	0.7
Gephardt	1.0	0.0	0.0	0.0	6.5	1.5
Gore	0.0	0.0	2.0	0.0	1.1	0.4
Hart	1.6	0.0	0.0	0.0	0.0	0.3
Jackson	0.0	0.7	0.0	1.3	1.2	0.6
Simon	1.0	0.0	0.0	0.0	0.0	0.2
Items Indicating Progress of State Campaign (%)						
Babbitt	21.0	22.3	22.4	14.7	11.4	18.5
Dukakis	33.6	32.3	23.2	20.6	20.8	27.7
Gephardt	37.1	39.2	34.3	27.6	30.4	34.4
Gore	31.0	32.7	27.5	32.0	24.7	30.1
Hart	32.3	24.6	36.0	35.3	12.9	26.8
Jackson	29.1	20.6	19.0	7.6	18.8	19.9
Simon	22.8	37.9	36.1	34.3	29.2	32.6
Items Mentioning Standing in State Polls (%)						
Babbitt	25.0	25.9	24.5	20.0	19.8	23.2
Dukakis	25.9	20.5	26.6	26.4	24.2	23.4
Gephardt	29.9	25.1	25.4	28.7	21.7	25.9
Gore	20.0	25.5	21.6	23.8	20.4	22.5
Hart	25.8	28.8	22.4	35.3	19.7	26.5
Jackson	28.4	27.3	22.2	25.3	21.8	25.6
Simon	28.7	28.8	26.4	25.9	24.8	27.2

NOTE: Ns available on request from the author.

Table 6.10 Horse-Race Coverage of Republican Candidates in Key State Campaigns

	Atlanta Constitution	Boston Globe	Chicago Tribune	Los Angeles Times	New York Times	All Five Newspapers
Items Mentioning Scenarios (%)						
Bush	5.1	6.0	3.3	6.2	6.2	5.6
Dole	6.9	3.8	15.3	5.4	6.1	6.7
du Pont	6.3	1.9	5.6	3.4	7.6	4.5
Haig	5.1	1.1	2.9	3.5	1.8	3.3
Kemp	7.2	4.1	4.8	5.2	7.6	5.7
Robertson	9.6	5.7	7.9	7.0	5.6	7.1
Items Mentioning Standards (%)						
Bush	10.3	8.3	8.7	6.9	6.2	8.1
Dole	8.4	10.8	8.2	8.0	8.2	8.9
du Pont	6.7	1.0	0.0	5.1	7.6	4.0
Haig	10.2	8.6	2.9	5.3	6.5	7.2
Kemp	8.4	4.1	9.7	6.5	4.8	6.1
Robertson	8.6	9.1	12.7	5.7	5.7	8.3
Items Mentioning Benchmarks (%)						
Bush	0.6	0.0	0.0	0.8	1.2	0.5
Dole	0.0	0.0	1.2	0.0	0.0	0.2
du Pont	1.6	0.9	0.0	0.0	1.5	0.9
Haig	0.0	1.1	2.9	3.5	1.6	1.6
Kemp	0.0	0.0	1.6	0.0	1.0	0.4
Robertson	0.0	0.0	0.0	0.0	1.1	0.2
Items Indicating Progress of State Campaign (%)						
Bush	33.3	34.1	33.7	36.9	29.8	33.5
Dole	28.2	33.0	31.8	30.4	23.1	29.2
du Pont	20.6	25.0	30.6	25.4	15.2	22.9
Haig	27.1	23.7	31.4	29.8	20.6	25.7
Kemp	19.3	26.0	27.4	18.2	14.3	21.1
Robertson	27.7	28.7	25.4	39.4	29.2	29.8
Items Mentioning Standing in State Polls (%)						
Bush	27.9	25.6	20.9	25.4	24.7	25.3
Dole	35.4	29.7	23.8	28.6	23.3	28.5
du Pont	22.2	30.3	30.6	30.5	23.9	27.5
Haig	23.7	34.1	29.4	31.6	27.0	29.6
Kemp	20.5	24.1	21.3	27.3	20.4	22.8
Robertson	24.7	30.1	21.0	26.8	22.2	25.5

NOTE: Ns available on request from the author.

coverage than others, the proportion of coverage devoted to horse-race news was about the same for every candidate.

The most interesting thing about horse-race coverage is its "spin," or predominant direction. Since candidates are expected to do well or poorly in specific caucuses and primaries, it is imperative to note which states figure in spin descriptions. Candidates leading in Iowa may trail badly in New Hampshire or elsewhere. Table 6.11 demonstrates the importance of context by comparing each candidate's spin scores in Iowa, New Hampshire, and the Super Tuesday states. These scores vary from totally favorable (+100) to wholly unfavorable (-100), with 0 indicating completely offsetting amounts of positive and negative information about a candidate's horserace performance.[16] Enormous Iowa coverage made it possible to report each newspaper's Iowa spin scores for nearly every candidate while substantially less New Hampshire and Super Tuesday information in three of the newspapers necessitated computation of candidate scores for all five newspapers combined.[17]

Looking first at the Iowa scores of Democratic candidates, one quickly notes not only the enormous range of spin values but the generally uniform way in which all five newspapers reported the standing of most candidates. In keeping with conventional understanding of the race in Iowa, every newspaper reported favorable horse-race news for Dukakis, Gephardt, and Simon. All five depicted Gore's Iowa effort in wholly negative terms. Babbitt also got consistently negative press in this regard. The *Constitution* and *Tribune* coverage of Jackson's Iowa campaign contained too few references for computation of reliable spin scores, but the other newspapers gave Jackson negative horse-race coverage. Hart's feeble but favorable score in the *Tribune* contrasted with his negative ratings in the other newspapers, an unsurprising discovery given Hart's initially high poll ratings upon rejoining the race.

Summary Democratic scores for New Hampshire and Super Tuesday also comported with conventional wisdom about how these races shaped up. Dukakis was a prohibitive favorite in New Hampshire, as his +100 score indicates. Given no chance of winning in either Iowa or New Hampshire, both Jackson and Gore appeared more formidable in the South. Initially high poll standings boosted Hart's New Hampshire and Super Tuesday ratings. Gephardt's negative rating in New Hampshire and modestly favorable score for Super Tuesday reflected his preoccupation with Iowa. Simon got good horse-race coverage in New Hampshire but trailed every other Democrat except Babbitt in the South. Babbitt was a long-shot everywhere.

The Republican scores in table 6.11 are equally consistent with everything else we know about these campaigns. Bush's horse-race coverage in Iowa was decidedly less upbeat than Dole's and Robertson's in every newspaper, a hardly unexpected finding since he was expected to finish second there. In New Hampshire and the South, however, Bush got better spin than Dole or Robertson. Dole's Iowa coverage was uniformly excellent, but he suffered in comparison to Bush in New Hampshire and the South. Robertson was second only to Bush in Super Tuesday spin scores, but in New Hampshire, where he ran last in the polls, Robertson's overall spin score was dreadful. Haig got the worst horse-race spin of any candidate: -100 scores across the

Table 6.11 Spin Scores in Coverage of Iowa, New Hampshire, and Super Tuesday Campaigns

	Iowa Scores by Newspaper					Iowa, New Hampshire, and Super Tuesday Scores for All Five Newspapers		
	Atlanta Constitution	Boston Globe	Chicago Tribune	Los Angeles Times	New York Times	Iowa	New Hampshire	Super Tuesday
Babbitt	-50.0	-60.0	-42.9	-84.2	-80.0	-65.7	-42.5	-100.0
Dukakis	79.2	50.0	22.2	60.0	62.5	55.4	100.0	54.7
Gephardt	47.8	53.3	51.5	52.9	33.3	48.3	-52.4	22.1
Gore	-100.0	-100.0	-100.0	-100.0	-100.0	-100.0	-69.2	-29.0
Hart	-6.2	-39.4	10.0	-47.8	-20.0	-22.8	35.1	68.4
Jackson	a	-50.0	a	-84.6	-60.0	-65.2	-45.0	-95.5
Simon	58.8	37.7	83.3	68.9	68.2	58.0	74.1	-27.8
Bush	61.5	45.0	0.0	11.1	25.9	31.9	100.0	80.4
Dole	91.6	100.0	94.9	100.0	95.1	98.0	78.1	44.0
du Pont	a	-100.0	-80.0	-84.6	-84.6	-90.6	-22.8	-92.9
Haig	-100.0	-100.0	-100.0	-100.0	-100.0	-100.0	-100.0	-100.0
Kemp	-45.4	-53.3	-80.0	-7.7	a	-43.1	54.4	-93.7
Robertson	80.0	52.0	76.4	36.8	76.0	64.1	-77.8	63.2

NOTE: "a" indicates fewer than ten references. See note 18 for explanation of how these scores were computed.

board. Du Pont looked hopeless in all three contexts, though the *Manchester Union-Leader*'s tepid endorsement made his New Hampshire score less dire than elsewhere. Kemp's spin scores ranged from terrible to poor in Iowa, moderately favorable in New Hampshire, and truly dreadful in the Super Tuesday states.

Horse-race handicapping also goes on at the national level, albeit with different indicators. The two most prominent are national poll standings and fund-raising reports. Table 6.12 compares the frequency of such mentions in Democratic and Republican coverage. Poll standings figured more importantly in the coverage of GOP candidates, perhaps because their respective rankings were so fixed. All candidates got pretty much the same proportionate amount of fund-raising coverage.

Finally, based on these poll ratings and fund-raising news, table 6.13 reports spin scores for every candidate at the national level. Dukakis, Bush, and Dole got consistently favorable coverage in this regard while Babbitt, du Pont, Haig, and Kemp got unrelentingly negative press. Their national scores correlated reasonably well with those computed for Iowa, New Hampshire, and Super Tuesday—though Bush's wholly favorable national spin contrasted with middling or worse readings in Iowa. Except for a positive New Hampshire reading, Kemp's national coverage closely resembled his state spin. Gephardt, Simon, Hart, Jackson, and Robertson were less easily pigeonholed, as evidenced by inconsistent national spin scores in the five newspapers.[18]

Conclusion

Did major newspapers pay more attention to scandals and blunders than policy issues and campaign themes? Did the horse race eclipse substance in coverage of the 1988 exhibition season?

Table 6.14 compares the coverage of flaps, issue stands, themes, and horse-race particulars of the Democratic candidates.[19] Only news stories and feature articles were included in this analysis since much briefer news notes so seldom reported policy views. The table reports average flap, issue-stand, theme, and horse-race mentions per item. A score approximating 1.0, like the *Tribune's* horse-race score for Dukakis, indicates almost one mention per item. Conversely, zeroes indicate no coverage whatever.

The first noteworthy finding shown in this table is that most candidates got more issue or theme coverage than flap or scandal coverage. The main exception was Hart, who simply drowned in a deluge of Donna Rice publicity on rejoining the race. His most-publicized themes, moreover, were little more than pleas to be judged on some basis other than Donna Rice. Gephardt and Simon escaped flap coverage of any sort, and, on average,

Table 6.12 National Horse-Race Indicators in Newspaper Coverage of Candidates

	Atlanta Constitution	Boston Globe	Chicago Tribune	Los Angeles Times	New York Times	All Five Newspapers
Items Mentioning National Poll Standings (%)						
Babbitt	8.6	8.8	7.9	14.1	11.9	10.2
Dukakis	2.2	1.5	5.8	5.1	4.2	3.0
Gephardt	5.0	2.7	4.8	6.1	5.0	4.4
Gore	3.0	4.2	6.2	5.0	5.6	4.5
Hart	4.4	5.8	3.4	9.1	7.1	6.0
Jackson	15.0	6.7	5.7	9.4	11.7	8.4
Simon	2.1	1.8	4.2	3.8	4.9	3.1
Bush	15.8	16.2	25.4	27.8	25.9	21.5
Dole	12.8	10.4	19.6	23.2	19.6	16.4
du Pont	10.3	8.4	17.8	17.9	19.8	13.9
Haig	11.0	7.1	20.4	18.4	18.0	14.5
Kemp	8.5	5.6	9.2	14.4	11.5	9.5
Robertson	3.5	3.3	6.2	8.8	7.1	5.5
Items Comparing Fund-raising Success or Failure (%)						
Babbitt	7.8	4.4	3.2	7.1	6.8	5.9
Dukakis	6.1	6.7	9.4	9.6	9.6	7.7
Gephardt	5.0	2.7	3.6	4.6	5.7	4.2
Gore	3.1	2.1	3.0	5.0	4.8	3.6
Hart	2.2	3.1	1.7	1.2	2.9	2.4
Jackson	5.2	3.3	5.8	2.3	6.0	4.9
Simon	5.0	2.7	3.1	5.3	4.2	4.0
Bush	4.1	4.7	7.6	6.1	4.5	5.1
Dole	4.3	3.9	1.9	5.4	6.3	4.6
du Pont	5.7	5.3	2.2	4.7	6.7	5.2
Haig	7.4	7.3	4.5	6.7	7.4	6.9
Kemp	5.1	4.5	2.6	6.2	4.9	4.8
Robertson	5.0	3.9	6.2	7.0	7.7	5.8

NOTE: Percentages based on same Ns reported in tables 6.5 and 6.6

the issues and themes of Babbitt, Jackson, and Dukakis got substantially more press than their respective flaps and character crises.

More in keeping with conventional wisdom is the finding that horse-race news got mentioned more often than issue stands. Sometimes, however, this "substance gap" was not very large, as in Babbitt's case. Indeed Babbitt was the only candidate in either party to have a "horse-race gap," where, on average, the Los Angeles Times mentioned his policy views more often than his horse-race situation. Conversely, Gore had the worst substance gap of all the Democratic candidates in three of the five newspapers.

Still another noteworthy finding was the high degree of uniformity in major newspaper coverage. If a candidate's average flap score was low in one newspaper, it was equally low in the other four. This was also generally true for issues, themes, and horse-race particulars.

Table 6.13 **National Spin Scores for Democratic and Republican Candidates**

	Atlanta Constitution	*Boston Globe*	*Chicago Tribune*	*Los Angeles Times*	*New York Times*	*All Five Newspapers*
Babbitt	− 89.5	− 91.7	a	− 100.0	− 100.0	− 95.6
Dukakis	100.0	87.5	84.6	90.0	87.0	90.3
Gephardt	− 14.3	0.0	a	28.6	6.7	6.4
Gore	a	− 38.5	a	0.0	− 23.1	− 16.0
Hart	a	− 7.7	a	a	40.0	20.0
Jackson	62.5	5.3	− 20.0	46.6	− 8.3	16.7
Simon	40.0	80.0	a	− 33.3	− 23.1	16.0
Bush	100.0	100.0	100.0	100.0	100.0	100.0
Dole	93.7	100.0	100.0	100.0	100.0	95.7
du Pont	− 71.4	− 76.4	a	− 89.5	− 100.0	− 87.5
Haig	− 100.0	− 100.0	− 100.0	− 100.0	− 100.0	− 100.0
Kemp	− 71.4	− 66.7	a	− 47.8	− 73.9	− 63.2
Robertson	16.7	27.3	0.0	− 11.1	50.0	16.4

NOTE: "a" indicates fewer than ten references. See note 20 for explanation of how scores were computed.

Table 6.15 compares coverage of flaps, issue stands, themes, and horse-race news in stories and feature articles about the Republican candidates. The results closely resemble the findings for Democratic coverage. Substance outweighed scandals, even in stories about Bush and Robertson.[20] The horse race got more attention than policy views, hence a "substance gap" of varying magnitude for Republican candidates. The disparity was least for du Pont and Kemp, greatest for Bush, Haig, and Dole. As in Democratic coverage, these newspapers exhibited remarkable consistency in factors emphasized or de-emphasized. Bush's horse-race averages ranged from .807 in the *Constitution* to .923 in the *Los Angeles Times*, for example, while du Pont flap averages varied from .012 in the *Globe* to .028 in the *Constitution*.

In some ways, major newspapers lived up to expectations during the 1988 exhibition season. Consistent with the findings of previous studies, some candidates got much more press than others. As in earlier years, a strong relationship existed between the amount of coverage given a candidate and his national poll standings. When polls spoke clearly and consistently, as they did for the Republicans, the correspondence was nearly exact. When no clear front-runner emerged, as was the Democratic situation after Hart's withdrawal, erratic coverage resulted in which no one candidate enjoyed a clear advantage over all others. Conversely, Democratic polls pinpointed one true dark horse among the "seven dwarfs," and he consistently got the least coverage. In sum, these newspapers gave most space to candidates they took most seriously.

Seriousness was also a prime factor in the somewhat capricious coverage of character crises. Operating under the "new rule," reporters now are free

Table 6.14 Elements of Democratic Candidate Coverage: Flaps, Issue Stands, Campaign Themes, and the Horse Race in News Stories and Feature Articles

	Atlanta Constitution	Boston Globe	Chicago Tribune	Los Angeles Times	New York Times	All Five Newspapers
Babbitt						
N items	100	140	61	86	110	497
Mean flaps	.049	.021	.000	.035	.073	.038
Mean issues	.360	.507	.361	.744	.309	.457
Mean themes	.228	.229	.229	.407	.209	.255
Mean horse race	.535	.626	.557	.558	.495	.558
Dukakis						
N items	148	270	83	115	151	767
Mean flaps	.154	.253	.120	.200	.119	.185
Mean issues	.250	.352	.253	.461	.291	.326
Mean themes	.282	.395	.229	.296	.382	.322
Mean horse race	.649	.687	.805	.588	.624	.665
Gephardt						
N items	118	163	81	109	130	601
Mean flaps	.008	.006	.000	.000	.008	.005
Mean issues	.381	.485	.457	.697	.331	.466
Mean themes	.353	.356	.333	.505	.315	.370
Mean horse race	.788	.831	.687	.759	.708	.763
Gore						
N items	132	148	60	85	114	539
Mean flaps	.113	.054	.017	.058	.079	.070
Mean issues	.250	.392	.183	.482	.219	.312
Mean themes	.361	.432	.200	.391	.327	.360
Mean horse race	.641	.848	.833	.776	.699	.753
Hart						
N items	73	111	56	64	81	385
Mean Donna						
Rice	.397	.279	.304	.453	.321	.343
Mean issues	.233	.225	.161	.359	.123	.218
Mean themes	.225	.273	.318	.476	.240	.296
Mean horse race	.586	.694	.654	.698	.443	.616
Jackson						
N items	143	150	83	109	129	614
Mean flaps	.035	.027	.036	.055	.039	.037
Mean issues	.217	.313	.217	.349	.248	.270
Mean themes	.326	.287	.325	.391	.457	.355
Mean horse race	.613	.510	.469	.392	.540	.514
Simon						
N items	115	159	91	112	128	605
Mean flaps	.000	.013	.000	.000	.000	.003
Mean issues	.313	.396	.242	.562	.203	.347
Mean themes	.310	.228	.374	.369	.370	.322
Mean horse race	.556	.809	.822	.700	.625	.703

Table 6.15 **Elements of Republican Candidate Coverage: Flaps, Issue Stands, Campaign Themes, and the Horse Race in News Stories and Feature Articles**

	Atlanta Constitution	Boston Globe	Chicago Tribune	Los Angeles Times	New York Times	All Five Newspapers
Bush						
N items	179	184	113	168	215	859
Mean Iran-contra	.145	.245	.150	.262	.172	.197
Mean issues	.268	.342	.248	.500	.377	.354
Mean themes	.173	.272	.230	.292	.237	.241
Mean horse race	.807	.961	.911	.923	.829	.882
Dole						
N items	155	153	102	142	181	733
Mean flaps	.052	.086	.088	.106	.106	.088
Mean issues	.342	.405	.216	.472	.309	.355
Mean themes	.232	.288	.228	.394	.392	.314
Mean horse race	.756	1.001	.861	.873	.786	.856
du Pont						
N items	72	80	43	74	79	348
Mean flaps	.028	.012	.023	.013	.013	.017
Mean issues	.569	.512	.419	.500	.430	.491
Mean themes	.097	.160	.023	.162	.177	.135
Mean horse race	.648	.762	.809	.662	.721	.714
Haig						
N items	66	74	42	77	78	337
Mean flaps	.045	.027	.024	.013	.026	.027
Mean issues	.288	.257	.167	.442	.295	.303
Mean themes	.273	.108	.093	.299	.167	.195
Mean horse race	.661	.903	.829	.753	.750	.776
Kemp						
N items	96	109	73	98	124	500
Mean flaps	.000	.055	.014	.010	.000	.016
Mean issues	.448	.394	.288	.469	.306	.382
Mean themes	.289	.218	.123	.286	.164	.218
Mean horse race	.521	.729	.722	.663	.525	.624
Robertson						
N items	105	97	76	97	110	485
Mean flaps	.229	.124	.145	.175	.145	.165
Mean issues	.305	.371	.224	.371	.182	.291
Mean themes	.352	.350	.237	.330	.315	.321
Mean horse race	.641	.793	.757	.711	.771	.733

to follow the story of a candidate's imperfections anywhere it may lead. Whether it leads anywhere seems to depend on how seriously the candidate is regarded rather than how serious the candidate's problems may be.

Being taken seriously also counts for a great deal in the volume and spin of horse-race coverage. Genuine front-runners are much more favorably handicapped than dark horses during the exhibition season—consider the nearly perfect Bush and Dole spin scores and equally pathetic ratings for du Pont and Haig. When measuring spin, however, one must distinguish between national and state settings, and further, among different states. Recall the rather large differences in Gephardt, Hart, Jackson, Dole, Kemp, and Robertson spin scores as the setting shifted from Iowa to New Hampshire and Super Tuesday.

Sometimes exhibition-season coverage does not conform to conventional wisdom. Partly this is because conventional wisdom covers the whole nominating process right up to the conventions. It incorporates the caucus and primary season, when all media are preoccupied with the horse race. Clearly the best time to report candidate views on issues is before the race begins, not after the starting gun has been fired.

For the most part, the newspapers in this study endeavored to inform their readers about the policy views of candidates during the 1988 exhibition season. Every candidate willing to articulate clear positions got substantial issues coverage, albeit not in equal amounts, whatever his poll standings. Every newspaper offered its readers at least one series of articles on leading issues of the campaign. And, just as the "old rule" of character coverage has given way to a new one, so it appears that the rules of covering issues are also changing. Newspapers now seem more willing to point out the dubious premises, misleading statistics, outlandish claims, borrowed eloquence, superficiality, and hyperbole so typical of presidential campaign rhetoric. Like character coverage, however, only selected candidates may come under such scrutiny.

In conclusion, the perennial shortcomings of campaign journalism are too often discussed as if different news media—television, the wire services, newsmagazines, radio, and newspapers of varying prominence—are wholly alike. On balance, the evidence presented in this chapter indicates that major newspapers do a better job of informing the public, at least during the exhibition season, than most critics allow. Before rounding up the usual suspects the next time "the media" are accused of shallow campaign coverage, let us insist on two basic distinctions—among the different media and among phases of the presidential selection process.

Notes

The author gratefully acknowledges Denison University's generous support of this research, including a grant from the Denison University Research Foundation (DURF) to employ student coders during the summer of 1988. Nelson Fox, John Tucker, and Daniel Bibler provided invaluable assistance in coding and compiling the data. Of the 2,591 news items analyzed for this research, Tucker, Fox, and Bibler coded 38 percent, the author 62 percent. Repeated checks revealed a very high degree of reliability among coders.

1. Arthur T. Hadley (1976) was perhaps the first to give this important period a name, the "invisible primary." John H. Kessel (1988: 7–14) calls it the "early days" stage and identifies three successive, partly overlapping phases: (1) crucial "initial contests" in Iowa, New Hampshire, and several other states where a few candidates emerge from the pack: (2) later primaries and caucuses that "clear" away the "mists" by effectively picking the nominee of each party; and (3) the conventions where surviving candidates are officially nominated. I have adopted Rhodes Cook's term, the "exhibition season," because of its implications for news media coverage of candidates. Cook (1989: 31) sees five "unmistakable" stages in the 1988 cycle of presidential nominating politics: (1) the exhibition season, (2) the "media fishbowl" (corresponding to Kessel's "early days"), (3) Super Tuesday, (4) the "mop-up" stage after Super Tuesday, and (5) the conventions. Kessel's "mist clearing" occurred in both the third and fourth phases of Cook's scheme.

   Traditionally the exhibition season has ended on the day of the Iowa precinct caucuses. In 1988, however, one might argue that the race actually began in August 1986 with Republican caucuses in Michigan. Republican caucuses in Hawaii and Kansas also preceded Iowa in 1988. Still, Iowa marked the first time both parties held delegate-selection contests; it was also the first event in which every candidate seriously competed, although Gore and Haig eventually gave up. Clearly the media regarded the exhibition season as lasting until February 8, the day of the Iowa caucuses.

2. National editions of the *New York Times* and the *Chicago Tribune* were analyzed for this research.

3. These items constitute the totality of each newspaper's news coverage of the presidential nominating process for the October 1, 1987, to February 8, 1988, period. Most of the nineteen weeks dated from Tuesday to the next Monday and were defined as follows: October 1–5, October 6–12, October 13–19, October 20–26, October 27–November 2, November 3–9, November 10–16, November 17–23, November 24–30, December 1–7, December 8–14, December 15–21, December 22–28, December 29–January 4, January 5–11, January 12–18, January 19–25, January 26–February 1, and February 2–8.

4. To be coded "about" an aspirant, a print line had to mention a specific individual by name or make this connection clear by pronoun—"he" or "she," "his" or "her," "him" or "her." Statements by candidate surrogates were also counted if their comments directly related to the campaign, as in praising their man or attacking a rival. Statements of the latter sort also counted for the rival if clearly identified.

5. Germond and Witcover (1989: 60) nicely illustrate the decline of informality in this new era with the following anecdote: "In 1972, George McGovern on a flight from South Dakota to Washington sat down next to one of us to discuss the Eagleton controversy. The candidate had gotten only a few words out of his mouth in what was intended as a private conversation when we looked up and saw tape recorders being thrust in our faces. That ended the conversation."

6. See Black and Oliphant (1989: 59–75) for the most complete account of the Biden tape flap published to date.
7. Mrs. King reportedly reconciled with Jackson after the 1988 race.
8. This episode began when former Congressman Paul N. McCloskey disputed Robertson's claim of having been a combat veteran of the Korean War in a letter that found its way into print. According to McCloskey, who had served in the same Marine unit as Robertson, Robertson's father got him out of combat duty by pulling strings at the Pentagon. Avowing that his credibility as a future commander-in-chief would be ruined if he did not refute McCloskey, Robertson sued for libel. Robertson later dropped the suit.
9. See Buell and Maus (1988).
10. See Buell (1987: 86–91).
11. Up to two specific issue stands were allowed per candidate in the code. If more than two stands were reported, coders were instructed to note the two most-mentioned stands, and, if necessary, to make this determination by counting lines about each stand.
12. To illustrate the considerable variation within one category of issues, consider the different foreign-policy stands of Gore and Jackson. Gore emphasized aid for the Nicaraguan contras, Reagan administration policy in the Persian Gulf, and the INF treaty while Jackson stressed American policy in the Persian Gulf, the Israeli-Palestinian problem, and South African apartheid.
13. This tabulation is based on items mentioning one or more themes. Only one theme per item could be recorded, owing to space limitations in a code established for thirteen candidates. What results is a rough but still useful summary of each candidate's main themes.
14. In 1972 the Muskie campaign tacitly accepted 50 percent as a benchmark for its expected win in the New Hampshire primary. When Muskie fell short by several points, the press discounted his victory and hyped McGovern's better-than-expected second place.
15. The code included the same scenario variable for every candidate:

> Did this item describe how _____ could become the front-runner, knock others out, clinch nomination, block rivals, or hang on after defeats, by winning key state contests . . . ?

Various possibilities initially allowed by the code were collapsed into dichotomous yes-or-no mention of any scenario. The code also incorporated two measures of state standards:

> According to the item, how well is _____ expected to do in this . . . primary, caucus, or straw poll?
> 0 = no mention
> 1 = expected to win
> 2 = finish second
> 3 = finish third
> 4 = fourth or worse
> 5 = do generally well
> 6 = do poorly

and,

> Did this item say (or quote others as saying) that this contest was crucial for _____, or that he must win or do well here?

The benchmark variable for every candidate:

> Did this item cite a minimum percent of the vote _____ must get in this contest to meet expectations?

16. State spin scores were based on information obtained from the following variables:

> According to the item, how well is _____ expected to do in this . . . primary, caucus, or straw poll?
> 0 = no mention
> 1 = expected to win
> 2 = finish second
> 3 = finish third
> 4 = fourth or worse
> 5 = do generally well
> 6 = do badly
>
> How did the item describe the progress of _____'s campaign in this state?
> +1 = positively: much, some progress, holding steady
> −1 = negatively: scrambling, stalling, slipping, not making serious effort here
>
> What was _____'s standing in most recent state/regional poll mentioned in this item?
> 0 = no poll
> 1 = first
> 2 = second
> 3 = third
> 4 = fourth
> 5 = fifth
> 6 = sixth or seventh

The first and third variable classes were collapsed into dichotomous, positive and negative, categories. The resulting index allowed candidate scores to vary from −3 to +3 per state contest, with two separate contests possible for each item. Summary spin scores for the state were computed according to the formula $(P-N)/T \times 100$, where "P" indicated positive points, "N" negative points, and "T" total positive and negative points.

Some variation was necessary in determining positive and negative horse-race categories for different candidates and states. For Dole in Iowa, the expectations rule was +1 for winning or doing generally well and −1 for anything less than expected to win or do well; reports of his poll ratings in Iowa were recoded so that first came out as +1 and anything less as −1. The rule for Dukakis, Gephardt, Simon, and Bush's Iowa expectations was +1 for win, finish second, or do generally well, and −1 for do badly or finish third or worse. Poll standings were recoded as +1 for first or second and −1 for anything less. For all other candidates, the expectations variable was recoded +1 for win, finish second or third, or do well, and −1 for doing poorly or finishing fourth or worse. Their poll ratings were recoded +1 for first, second, or third, and −1 for anything lower.

Dukakis and Bush expectations were recoded anew for New Hampshire, where media expectations and polls projected a very different race: +1 for winning or doing generally well, −1 for finishing second or lower, or doing badly. Poll ratings were recoded as +1 for first, −1 for anything lower. Dole expectations were collapsed into +1 for winning, finishing second, or doing generally well, and −1 for all other references. By the same token, first or second in state polls earned Dole a +1, anything lower a -1. All other candidate expectations were recoded to make first, second, or third finishes, or doing generally well as +1, while finishing fourth or worse or expected to do badly were recoded as -1.

Bush's Super Tuesday expectations and poll variables were recoded in the same manner reported above for New Hampshire. For all other candidates, expectations were collapsed as follows: +1 for winning or finishing second or third, or for doing generally well, and −1 for doing badly, fourth or worse. Poll ratings were similarly recoded +1 for first, second, or third, and −1 for finishing fourth or worse.

17. Iowa received the lion's share of state contest coverage in four of the five newspapers: 44.8 percent of 41,805 print lines in the *Globe*, 51.4 percent of 17,239 lines in the *Tribune*, 58.9 percent of 25,830 lines in the *Los Angeles Times*, and 51.8 percent of 27,186 lines in the *New York Times*.

18. National spin scores were computed according to the same formula used for state horse-race readings, with adjustments again made for different candidates. The two variables comprising this measure were:

Did this item cite NATIONAL polls or otherwise say how well _____ is doing in the _____ race nationally?
0 = no
1 = front-runner
2 = second
3 = third
4 = fourth
5 = fifth
6 = part of pack
7 = dark horse/long-shot

Fund-raising progress: Did this item compare _____'s fund-raising success to that of his _____ rivals? If so, how did his money-raising efforts compare to theirs?
0 = no
1 = raising more than any other _____
2 = second or third
3 = doing generally well
4 = not doing well
5 = among least successful
6 = raising less than any other _____
7 = other

The decision rules for recoding national poll ratings were: Bush +1 for front-runner, −1 for anything less; Dole +1 for front-runner or second, −1 for anything less; and all others +1 for first, second, or third, −1 for fourth or worse. The fund-raising variable was recoded for all candidates as +1 for raising more than any rival, second, third, or doing generally well; −1 for not doing well, among the least successful, and raising less than rival. As before spin scores were determined using the formula $(P−N)/T \times 100$.

19. All horse-race mentions, state and national, were weighted equally and combined in a simple additive index of 0 to 11 points per item. The code also included a simple count of each candidate's specific issue stands and campaign themes mentioned in the item. The standard "flap" variable for candidates was: "Did this item mention misdeeds, verbal slips, inaccurate claims, or other indiscretions in 1987–88 (or earlier) by _____ or his aides?" Hart's code included specific variables for Donna Rice, 1984 campaign debts, changes in his name and birthdate.

20. Bush's code included a specific variable for Iran-contra references while Robertson's flap coverage consisted of four variables—mentions of his praying for miracles, the circumstances of his marriage, the disputed Korean War record, and assorted gaffes on the campaign trail.

References

Adams, William C. 1985. "Media Coverage of Campaign '84: A Preliminary Report." In *The Mass Media in Campaign '84: Articles from Public Opinion Magazine*, ed. Michael J. Robinson and Austin Ranney. Washington, D.C.: American Enterprise Institute for Public Policy Research.

Arterton, F. Christopher. 1984. *Media Politics: The News Strategies of Presidential Campaigns*. Lexington, Mass.: D.C. Heath.

Associated Press. 1987. "Jackson Dismisses Rumors of Troubles for His Campaign." *Atlanta Constitution* (October 12): 8A.

Bartels, Larry M. 1988. *Presidential Primaries and the Dynamics of Public Choice*. Princeton, N.J.: Princeton University Press.

Baxter, Tom. 1988. "Hart Offers Blueprint for Cutting Deficit." *Atlanta Constitution* (January 17): 8A.

Black, Christine M. 1987. "Dukakis Misused IRS Figures in Speeches." *Boston Globe* (November 20): 9.

Black, Christine M., and Thomas Oliphant. 1989. *All by Myself: The Unmaking of a Presidential Campaign*. Chester, Conn.: Globe-Pequot Press.

Blake, Andrew. 1988. "Scandal Draws More Media Attention Than Issues, Gephardt Says." *Boston Globe* (January 7): 7.

Broder, David S. 1987. *Behind the Front Page: A Candid Look at How the News Is Made*. New York: Simon and Schuster.

Buell, Emmett H., Jr. 1987. "'Locals' and 'Cosmopolitans': National, Regional, and State Newspaper Coverage of the New Hampshire Primary." In *Media and Momentum: The New Hampshire Primary and Nomination Politics*, ed. Gary R. Orren and Nelson W. Polsby. Chatham, N.J.: Chatham House.

Buell, Emmett H., Jr., and Mike Maus. 1988. "Is the Pen Mightier Than the Word? Editorial Cartoons and 1988 Presidential Nominating Politics." *PS* 21 (Fall): 847–58.

Cimons, Marlene. 1987. "Candidates Forced to Deal with AIDS Issue." *Los Angeles Times* (November 2): 1.

Cohen, Muriel. 1987. "Education Fades as Issue in Presidential Campaign." *Boston Globe* (December 1): 10.

Colton, Elizabeth O. 1989. *The Jackson Phenomenon: The Man, the Power, the Message*. New York: Doubleday.

Cook, Rhodes. 1989. "The Nominating Process." In *The Elections of 1988*, ed. Michael Nelson. Washington, D.C.: Congressional Quarterly Press.

Dionne, E. J., Jr. 1987a. "Hart Unsettles Democrats, Which Pleases Republicans." *New York Times* (December 16): 14.

———. 1987b. "In Iowa, Six Democrats Stress Their Differences." *New York Times* (November 8): 16.

Ellement, John. 1987a. "Robertson Says AIDS Easily Spread." *Boston Globe* (December 17): 37.

———. 1987b. "N.H. Official Rebuts Jackson on Criticism of Voter Rules." *Boston Globe* (November 25): 10.

Entman, Robert M. 1989. "How the Media Affect What People Think: An Information Processing Approach." *Journal of Politics* 51 (May): 347–70.

Farrell, John A. 1987a. "Memos Appear to Explain Dukakis Misuse of Tax Data." *Boston Globe* (November 21): 4.

———. 1987b. "Dukakis Tax Plan: Relief and Rhetoric." *Boston Globe* (December 6): 1.

Frisby, Michael K. 1988. "Deprivation in the Delta Draws Little Interest in '88." *Boston Globe* (January 18): 1.

Germond, Jack W., and Jules Witcover. 1989. *Whose Broad Stripes and Bright Stars? The Trivial Pursuit of the Presidency 1988*. New York: Warner Books.

Graber, Doris. 1989. *Mass Media and American Politics*. 3d. ed. Washington, D.C.: Congressional Quarterly Press.

Hadley, Arthur T. 1976. *The Invisible Primary*. Englewood Cliffs, N.J.: Prentice-Hall.

Harrell, David E. 1987. *Pat Robertson: A Personal, Political, and Religious Portrait*. New York: Harper and Row.

Harvey, Steve. 1988. "Democratic Candidates Bite Lip, Talk Taxes While GOP Holds Its Tongue." *Atlanta Constitution* (January 10): 11A.

Hess, Jennie, and Kevin Sack. 1987. "2 Candidates Admit Using Pot in Past." *Atlanta Journal-Constitution*. (November 8): 1A.

Houston, Paul. 1987. "Touchy Social Issues Split Candidates on Party Lines." *Los Angeles Times* (November 28): 1.

Iyengar, Shanto, and Donald R. Kinder. 1987. *News That Matters: Television and American Opinion*. Chicago: University of Chicago Press.

Joslyn, Richard. 1984. *Mass Media and Elections*. Reading, Mass.: Addison-Wesley.

Kaufman, Jonathan. 1988. *Broken Alliance: The Turbulent Times between Blacks and Jews in America*. New York: New American Library.

Kennedy, Edward M. 1987. "Hurrying History: How Not to Pick a President." Excepts from November 30 speech given at Kennedy School of Government. *Boston Globe* (December 7): 21.

Kessel, John H. 1988. *Presidential Campaign Politics,* 3d ed. Chicago: Dorsey Press.

King, Mike. 1988. "National Health Crisis Draws Few Words from Presidential Hopefuls." *Atlanta Constitution* (February 4): 29A.

Kranish, Michael. "Robertson Candidacy at Crucial Crossroad." *Boston Globe* (November 16): 1.

Lentz, Philip. 1987a. "Dole's 'Vision' for Country Still Seen as Rather Hazy." *Chicago Tribune* (December 14): 4A.

———. 1987b: "New Hampshire Voters in Hibernation until Iowa Caucuses." *Chicago Tribune* (December 13): 4A.

Locin, Michael. 1987. "Candidates Duck Debate on Israel." *Chicago Tribune* (December 25): 1A.

Marantz, Steven. 1987. "Robertson, Going against the Grain, Voices Support for Missile Accord." *Boston Globe* (December 14): 16.

Margolis, Jon. 1987a. "Robertson Stuns Republicans with Criticism of Nancy Reagan." *Chicago Tribune* (October 18): 19.

———. 1987b. "More Equals Less in Tax Math." *Chicago Tribune* (November 29): 4.

Marshall, Thomas R. 1983. "The News Verdict and Public Opinion during the Primaries." In *Television Coverage of the 1980 Campaign,* ed. William C. Adams. Norwood, N.J.: Ablex.

Mashek, John W. 1987. "Democratic Candidates Differ on Funding Education." *Atlanta Constitution (November* 6): 8A.

Mashek, John W., and Steve Harvey. 1987. "Robertson Relying on 'Forgiveness' in Disclosure." *Atlanta Constitution* (October 9): 1A.

May, Lee. 1987. "Reagan, Deficit Shape Debate on Social Issues." *Los Angeles Times* (November 16): 1.

McManus, Doyle. 1987. "Presidential Hopefuls Split on Central America Policy." *Los Angeles Times* (October 11): 1.

Molotsky, Irvin. 1988. "Dole Accuses Press and TV of Failing to Focus on Issues." *New York Times* (April 27): 12.

Nelson, Jack. 1988. "Parties at Odds on Use of Taxes to Fight Deficit." *Los Angeles Times* (January 10): 1.

Neuman, W. Russell. 1986. *The Paradox of Mass Politics: Knowledge and Opinion in the American Electorate.* Cambridge, Mass.: Harvard University Press.

Oliphant, Thomas. 1987a. "Dukakis Bent but Not Broken by Disclosure, Iowa Backers Say." *Boston Globe* (October 2): 9.

———. 1987b. "Democratic Fuzziness on the Economy." *Boston Globe* (November 2): 1.

Orr, Richard. 1988a. "In the Midwest: Presidential Hopeful Simon Says He'd Focus on Family Farms, Alcohol Fuel." *Chicago Tribune* (January 11): 3.

———. 1988b. "In the Midwest: Jackson Links Farm Aid, Controls." *Chicago Tribune* (January 14): 6.

———. 1988c. "In the Midwest: Bush Cites 3 Ways to Revive Farming." *Chicago Tribune* (January 25): 3.

———. 1988d. "In the Midwest: Democratic Presidential Candidates Go against the Grain in Iowa." *Chicago Tribune* (January 30): 3.

———. 1988e. "In the Midwest: Simon, Dole Push Ethanol Issue in Iowa." *Chicago Tribune* (February 1): 3.

Painton, Priscilla. 1987. "Jackson's Charisma, Principles Winning Converts, but Contradictions Linger." *Atlanta Constitution* (October 19): 1A.

Palmer, Thomas. 1987. "Press Gets Early Jump on Campaign." *Boston Globe* (November 28): 1.

Patterson, Thomas E. 1980. *The Mass Media Election: How Americans Choose Their President.* New York: Praeger.

———. 1989. "The Press and Its Missed Assignment." In *The Elections of 1988.* ed. Michael Nelson. Washington, D.C.: Congressional Quarterly Press.

Patterson, Thomas E., and Richard Davis. 1985. "The Media Campaign: Struggle for the Agenda." In *The Elections of 1984*, ed. Michael Nelson. Washington, D.C.: Congressional Quarterly Press.

Political Notebook. 1987. "Robertson Clarifies Position on Treaty." *Boston Globe* (December 15): 19.

———. 1988a. "Jackson Speaks about Drug Abuse." *Boston Globe* (January 5): 6.

———. 1988b. "Planned Parenthood Is Robertson Topic." *Boston Globe* (February 3): 14.

Purnick, Joyce, and Michael Oreskes. 1987. "Jesse Jackson Aims for the Mainstream." *New York Times Sunday Magazine* (November 29): 28.

Redburn, Tom. 1987. "Campaign Debate over Deficit Curiously Tame." *Los Angeles Times* (October 19): 1.

Risen, James. 1987. "Hart's 'New Ideas' Not So Different Anymore." *Los Angeles Times* (December 27): 1.

Risen, James, and Robert A. Rosenblatt. 1988. "Economists Like Babbitt Plan— But Few Others Do." *Los Angeles Times* (Janaury 25): 1.

Robinson, Michael J., and Margaret Sheehan. 1983. *Over the Wire and on T.V.: CBS and UPI in Campaign '80.* New York: Russell Sage.

Robinson, Walter V. 1988. "Dole Backers Hope Iowa Votes Rebound in N.H." *Boston Globe* (January 20): 16.

Rosenbaum, David E. 1987. "Experts Fault Democrats on Economic Platforms." *New York Times* (December 21): 1.

Rosenblatt, Robert A. 1987. "Candidates Differ Sharply on Answers to Trade Wars." *Los Angeles Times* (November 9): 1.

———. 1988. "GOP Candidates Share a Dilemma: How to Cope with Inherited Deficit." *Los Angeles Times* (February 8): 12.

Sack, Kevin. 1987a. "Robertson Newspaper Ad Exaggerated Qualifications." *Atlanta Constitution* (October 10): 1A.

———. 1987b. "Hart Holds No Monopoly on 'New Ideas.'" *Atlanta Constitution* (December 20): 37A.

Schmidt, William E. "Farm Upturn Clouds Issues in Campaign." *New York Times* (January 24): 1.

Seabrook, Charles. 1987. "Environment Issues Get Mostly Yawns, Token Talk from Presidential Hopefuls." *Atlanta Constitution* (December 6): 1A.

Shaw, Gaylord. 1987. "A Clash Within: The Mixed Blessings of Rev. Jackson." *Los Angeles Times* (December 16): 1A.

Shogan, Robert. 1987. "Summit Transforms Focus of Candidates on Defense." *Los Angeles Times* (December 13): 1A.

Stewart, Jim. 1987a. "Candidates Drawing Battle Lines on Defense." *Atlanta Constitution* (October 25): 1A.

———. 1987b. "Next President May Fight Crunch on Defense." *Atlanta Constitution* (October 26): 1A.

Straus, Hal. 1987a. "Market Turmoil Shifts Focus of GOP Presidential Race." *Atlanta Constitution* (November 1): 17A.

———. 1987b. "Gephardt Trade Proposal Increasingly under Fire since Stock Market Crash." *Atlanta Constitution* (December 12): 9A.

Tackett, Michael. 1988. "Candidates Are Forced to Face Farm Problems." *Chicago Tribune* (January 23): 1.

Vennochi, Joan. 1987. "Jackson: His Style Stirs Adoration and Antipathy." *Boston Globe* (December 28): 21.

Wilkie, Curtis. 1988. "Democrats Tiptoe around Israeli Issue." *Boston Globe* (January 24): A21.

7. "The More Things Change . . . ": Network News Coverage of the 1988 Presidential Nomination Races

Michael J. Robinson
S. Robert Lichter

In most respects, 1988 was a poor year for conventional wisdom about presidential campaigns. To be sure, the hoariest of such wisdom — that the in party wins during times of peace and prosperity — survived the year intact. But what about the notion that a fast start in Iowa was absolutely essential in order to establish a juggernaut of momentum? After carrying the Iowa caucuses, both Robert Dole and Richard Gephardt watched their campaigns fall apart over the next few weeks. And what about the old saw about vice-presidents being unable to win the presidency in their own right? After George Bush's victory, pundits are now pointing to the numerous advantages that sitting vice-presidents possess, enshrining a new conventional wisdom to replace the old.

Like so many other aspects of presidential campaigns, the performance of the press has spawned its own conventional wisdom — ideas so widely held that they have come to be accepted as truth. How well did the conventional wisdom concerning press coverage fare during the races for the 1988 Democratic and Republican presidential nominations?

The Conventional Wisdom about Press Performance

Political pundits, candidates and their staffers, social scientists, and other observers of presidential campaigns have frequently criticized the press for numerous objectionable practices. Amidst all the clamor about press performance, the following have risen to the top of the litany of questionable press practices, thereby achieving the status of conventional wisdom:

- *Horse-racism.* First, it is charged that the press can be counted on to ignore the "real issues" while emphasizing less important aspects of the nomination campaign. In particular, the campaign is said to be covered as if it were a horse race, with the media interested primarily in questions of interest to handicappers: who is ahead, who is behind, and what the prospects are for change in the current standings.

- *Early-bird news.* Second, the press is seen as paying inordinate attention to the Iowa caucuses and the New Hampshire primary while downplaying contests in states like New Jersey, Ohio, and especially California that involve far more delegates but appear later on the campaign calendar. Defying Yogi Berra's dictum that "it ain't over 'til it's over," the media have been criticized for losing interest in the campaign as it wears on.

- *Surprise journalism.* Third, the press is charged with gauging a candidate's actual performance according to its notion of how well the candidate was expected to do, hyping candidates who seem to be doing better than was expected of them.

- *Compensatory reporting.* Finally, the press is said to treat challengers less critically than front-runners, especially front-runners who represent the incumbent party.

We believe that these are not just four random components of the conventional wisdom about press coverage of presidential nomination campaigns. Rather, this *is* the conventional wisdom about press coverage of presidential nomination campaigns and has been at least since the 1968 campaign. As the nation headed into the 1988 campaign for the Democratic and Republican nominations, "horse-racism," "early-bird news," "surprise journalism," and "compensatory reporting" were viewed as the four primary principles of campaign coverage. But how did these "principles" pan out in 1988? Did they once again explain a great deal about how the races for the nominations were covered, or did the conventional wisdom about press coverage fare as poorly as the more general conventional wisdom about the campaigns?

Horse-Racism

In every presidential campaign during the television era, the "issue" that has received the greatest amount of coverage has been "who's ahead and who's behind?" It seemed virtually certain, then, that "horse-racism" would reign again in 1988, and data collected by the Washington-based Center for Media and Public Affairs (CMPA) indicate that the conventional wisdom was correct in this regard: in 1988 the network evening news programs were clearly "horse-racist" in their coverage of the nomination campaigns.

The CMPA analyzed 1,338 presidential campaign stories that were carried on the ABC, CBS, and NBC evening news shows between February 8, 1987, and June 7, 1988—a period that began a full year before the Iowa caucuses and ended with the last round of primaries. Dividing campaign stories into three basic types, the CMPA found 537 "horse-race" stories, 312 "campaign issues" stories, and 215 "policy issues" stories. Thus, horse-race reporting was far and away the predominant type of coverage, easily outdistancing policy news and campaign-issue news.

Horse-racism lived in the details, too. For example, six times as many news stories were devoted to expectations about winners and losers as to foreign policy issues. In fact, practically a third of all campaign stories included polling data about the progress of the horse race.

Even in 1987, when there was no "real" horse race to cover because no primaries or caucuses were yet being held, horse-race coverage finished several lengths ahead of policy coverage. During that pre-primary year, horse-race reporting received about twice as much attention as did all policy issues combined (86 versus 49 news stories).

Only once during the entire nomination campaign period did horse-race coverage lose out to issues as a news focus. After the New York primary, when the contest in each party was essentially concluded, the network news shows finally got around to devoting more attention to policy issues than to the horse race. Of course, a critic might note that by then it was too late for coverage of policy issues to play any meaningful role in helping people choose among presidential aspirants since the nominees had already been decided.

In any event, it is clear that in 1988, as in preceding presidential nomination campaigns, as long as there was a real horse race going on, it would constitute the top priority for news coverage. And even after there was no real horse race left to cover, horse-race coverage would still be a high priority. If there is one element of the conventional wisdom about campaign coverage that does not need to be revised before the 1992 campaign, it is that horse-racism remains the first principle of campaign journalism.

Campaign issues and the campaign-issues "issue." In 1988, policy news actually finished third, behind horse-race stories and coverage of campaign issues. The latter focus on controversies concerning the candidates or their campaigns. In 1988, the list of such issues was long and bizarre.

For one thing, there was the enormous brouhaha about Gary Hart's involvement with Donna Rice, along with revelations of Joseph Biden's plagiarism while in law school. There was also saturation coverage of Biden's plagiarism of campaign speeches, though when it turned out that this story had been planted by the Dukakis campaign, the story line was reconstituted as the treachery of Dukakis's staffers. There was coverage of the Dole campaign's financial problems. And, of course, there was Pat Robertson.

Long before the campaign got underway, Robertson's image in the press began to take on some loony aspects, and his problems escalated under the light of intense media scrutiny that accompanies a national campaign. His claim that he had received specific directives from God on various policy issues made him a figure of ridicule, as did his admission that his wife had been pregnant at the time of their marriage and charges that he had pulled strings to avoid military duty in Korea. Toward the middle of the primaries, Robertson faced rough coverage after he accused the Bush campaign of exposing Jimmy Swaggart's sexual escapades in order to undermine the credibility of religious broadcasters, and then he came in for more media criticism when he claimed that the Reagan administration knew where the American hostages in Lebanon were being held but refused to rescue them.

All in all, just under a dozen major campaign issues broke in the press during the eighteen months of the nomination campaigns. These campaign issues, large and small, accounted for more than 300 network news stories, according to CMPA—half again as much coverage as the networks devoted to policy issues.

There is no consensus as to whether campaign-issue reporting is of a higher or lower journalistic order than horse-racism. There is, however, growing anxiety that titillating campaign-issue coverage is increasing as a news focus. Since the Donna Rice story alone attracted 75 network evening news reports during the period between February 1987 and June 1988 (approximately a third of the total devoted to all policy issues during that period), this concern seems well founded.

The press itself began to have doubts in 1987 after the "Biden case" followed closely on the heels of the Hart affair. Indeed, ABC's "Nightline," something of a barometer of elite concerns, devoted several programs in 1987 to the "campaign issue" issue. Critics were particularly disparaging toward invasive "personality journalism," the target of which was not just the candidate but the candidate's character and, in some instances, his psyche.

According to the CMPA data, there was a heavy dose of such "character journalism" in coverage of the 1988 campaign. The CMPA divided campaign-issues stories into two types: those dealing specifically with "character" and those dealing mostly with "political" issues. Among the

312 campaign-issues stories, precisely half touched directly on the issue of candidate character.

Even though these concerns have been with us for some time, our reading of press history suggests greater media receptivity to character and personality issues in the 1988 campaign than had prevailed earlier. As evidence, we would cite the sheer volume of such coverage in 1988, its unprecedented pettiness and nastiness, and the retrospective character of a good deal of it.

"Retrospective" journalism is "news" that isn't new. Retrospective reporting looks backward in time, at how the candidate behaved before becoming a candidate — on occasion long before becoming a candidate or even a politician. Such coverage, like personality journalism in general, is nothing new; in 1979, for example, the press corps went retrospective to cover the Chappaquiddick incident as soon as Edward Kennedy announced his candidacy for president. But in the 1988 campaign the press was willing to go farther back than it had done in earlier campaigns — twenty-three years in the case of Biden's plagiarism case at Syracuse, thirty-six years in the case of Robertson's military record in Korea, and even farther with questions about the timing of Robertson's marriage. And these retrospectives were hardly about matters as serious as Kennedy's behavior at Chappaquiddick or Thomas Eagleton's bouts with clinical depression.

Finally, it is worth noting that the CMPA treated the Iran-contra affair as a policy issue, not a campaign issue or a character issue per se. If, instead, Iran-contra coverage were seen as an instance of character journalism, then there would be little question that character received greater attention in 1988 than in any other modern presidential campaign, including the Watergate election of 1972. And, since all three networks treated the "issue" more as a question of George Bush's integrity and competence than of whether the policy decisions were sound, we think that the appearance of 114 Iran-contra stories on network news during the campaign tells us a good deal about changing news values and practices.

The point is not to castigate the news organizations for looking back at what candidates have done in their recent or distant pasts. Rather, our points are these: that campaign issues are beginning to rival even horse-race coverage as a campaign news focus; that character journalism is becoming more and more prominent; and that coverage of substantive policy issues in the future will have to compete not just with old-fashioned horse-racism but with the press's enhanced interest in character as well. The press has now grown almost as disposed toward character issues as it is toward horse-race coverage.

Early-Bird News

The term "early-bird news" refers to a bias in coverage in favor of states that hold their caucuses or primaries toward the beginning of the campaign calendar. This does not necessarily mean that early states get "better press" (although as a rule they do) but that they get *more* press. Since 1976, when it was observed that each primary voter in early-bird New Hampshire got 180 times more news attention than a counterpart in late-in-the-calendar New York, the early-bird bias has been systematically monitored.

As the 1988 campaign approached, the early-bird news principle was accepted as political holy writ by pundits and campaign consultants alike. In fact, every candidate but one, Albert Gore of Tennessee, built his campaign with this bias in mind. Even Gore assumed that there was a news bias in favor of the early caucus and primary states, but because he gave himself no chance of winning in either Iowa or New Hampshire, he decided to focus on primaries and caucuses where he had a chance. He did assume that other early states—in this case, the Super Tuesday states—would get about as much attention as the very earliest states. The logical extension of the early-bird news principle, after all, is that, even though what happens in March may be less newsworthy than what transpires in February, what happens in March is still more newsworthy than what takes place in April or May.

But Gore miscalculated, for there is no general relationship between newsworthiness and voting early in the campaign calendar. William C. Adams (1987: 48) demonstrated this in his analysis of national news media coverage of the 1984 primaries and caucuses. True, the first two contests in 1984—the Iowa caucuses and the New Hampshire primary—got 19.2 and 12.8 percent of that year's national press coverage, respectively, even though a few delegates were at stake in the two states. However, when Adams dropped Iowa and New Hampshire from the analysis, he found that the number of delegates at issue was by far the best predictor of how much coverage a state contest received, whatever the timing.

In 1988, after years of catching up, Iowa finally surpassed New Hampshire. (See table 7.1.) Whereas the two states had attracted about equal television news coverage in 1980 and 1984, in 1988 Iowa surged ahead with a total of 285 stories on network evening news, a third more than New Hampshire. Indeed, Iowa alone received greater coverage than all the Super Tuesday states combined, which attracted "only" 228 stories.

New Hampshire still did very well for itself, collecting 210 evening news stories during the 1988 nomination campaign. New York, which had four times as many convention delegates assigned to it but held its primary two

Table 7.1 **Network News Coverage of Major Contests**

State Primary/Caucus	Mentions	Delegates	Ratio
Iowa	285	89	3:1
New Hampshire	210	41	5:1
New York	91	391	1:4
Illinois	66	265	1:4
Michigan	63	215	1:3
Wisconsin	51	128	1:3
Pennsylvania	45	274	1:6
California	41	389	1:9
Super Tuesday	228	2,056	1:9

SOURCE: S. Robert Lichter, Daniel Amundson, and Richard Noyes, *The Video Campaign: Network Coverage of the 1988 Primaries* (Washington, D.C.: American Enterprise Institute), 13.

NOTE: "Mentions" refers to number of times state primary or caucus was mentioned on network evening newscasts from February 8, 1987, through June 7, 1988. "Ratio" refers to the ratio of network news stories to delegates.

months after New Hampshire's, was deemed less than half as newsworthy as New Hampshire.

More generally, as it had in 1984, the early-bird news principle came up short in 1988. The earliness of a caucus or primary was a fairly good predictor of press coverage, but only as long as the calculations included Iowa and New Hampshire. Without those two states, there was simply no connection between coverage and a state's position on the campaign calendar (r=.03). On the other hand, aside from Iowa and New Hampshire there was a very strong connection between the number of delegates at stake in a state and the number of evening news stories about that state's contest (r=.72).

For 1992 and beyond, we presume that the news media will continue to make at least as much of Iowa and New Hampshire as they have always done in the recent past. Iowa will continue to "win" the competition for most newsworthy, and New Hampshire will continue to "place." After Iowa and New Hampshire, though, a new, unconventional wisdom needs to hold that press coverage will vary according to the size of a state rather than its position on the campaign calendar—a notion future campaign strategists will do well to take into account.

Surprise Journalism

"Surprise journalism" refers to the presumed tendency of the press corps to lavish coverage on any candidate who does "better than expected" at some point during the campaign. "Better than expected" has nothing to do with how earnestly the "surprise" candidate is addressing policy issues or public concerns, or even with a candidate's performance on the stump. What really defines "better than expected" is only how well the candidate does in the polls or at the polls. It makes little difference whether the poll is a tiny straw vote in Florida or a complicated pre-caucus in Michigan: if a candidate seems to have done better than expected in garnering support, then press attention will be showered on the candidate. So common has surprise journalism become that campaign strategists and the press itself have devised a new vocabulary to describe the phenomenon. The heightened coverage that the "better-than-expected" candidate receives is called a "press bounce." In order to maximize their "bounce," candidates "lowball" their prospects for victory beforehand. The machinations in which the candidates and the press engage before any caucus, primary, or new opinion poll constitute the "expectations game." And afterwards, each candidate's camp assigns someone to engage in "spin control"—to claim that, no matter how poorly the candidate has done, it was actually "better than expected."

Thus defined, "surprise journalism" has a history every bit as long as presidential campaigning, though criticism of this practice grew particularly acute during the late 1960s and early 1970s. In those years, the press (especially the television news organizations) sometimes went well beyond mere overcoverage of unexpectedly good performances by playing the "phantom victory" game of defining losers as winners. For example, several news organizations declared Eugene McCarthy to be the winner of the New Hampshire primary in 1968, and many crowned George McGovern the New Hampshire winner in 1972, even though both McCarthy and McGovern ran second in the New Hampshire vote counts. In 1976 and 1980, the news media continued to play up surprisingly strong showings (e.g., Jimmy Carter's Iowa surprise in 1976 and John Anderson's unexpected strength in early Republican primaries in 1980) but stopped short of reporting "phantom victories."

Through 1980, then, the press could typically be counted on to "hype" these "better-than-expected" performances through "news play," if not news "spin." In 1984, after Gary Hart finished a distant second behind Walter Mondale in the Iowa caucuses, the Hart campaign received a real news bounce. But what passed largely unnoticed at the time was that Hart's Iowa bounce was smaller than would have been predicted on the basis of coverage of earlier campaigns. This case should have suggested that campaign coverage was becoming less "elastic," but the various contenders approached the 1988 campaign still banking on surprise journalism.

If surprise journalism were going to crop up anywhere in the 1988 race, it certainly should have been after the Iowa caucuses—more specifically after Pat Robertson's second-place showing, ahead of George Bush, and Richard Gephardt's first-place showing on the Democratic side.

Following Robertson's "better-than-expected" showing in Iowa, where he took the second-place spot seemingly reserved for Bush, his share of network news coverage (based on the number of times he appeared on the evening news or was cited as a source) almost doubled in the week leading up to New Hampshire. (See table 7.2.) Though considerably less than the bounce some candidates got in earlier years, his was certainly greater than that of Dole, who won the Iowa caucuses but whose share of network news coverage actually dropped in the next week. Of course, Dole had been expected to win Iowa all along, but Robertson was not supposed to come in second. Robertson's share increased by another 38 percent in the two weeks following New Hampshire and leading into Super Tuesday, even though he came in last among the five active Republican candidates in the first primary. After he failed to win a single southern primary or caucus, Robertson essentially became a nonperson in coverage of the remainder of the Republican race.

Unlike Jimmy Carter in 1976 or Gary Hart in 1984, Gephardt failed to reap a press bonanza from his showing in Iowa. (See table 7.3) In fact, his win hardly affected network news coverage of his campaign. Like Dole, he had been expected to win. Thus his two-point bounce in the week following Iowa was actually less than that of Simon (who finished second), Dukakis (third), or even Gore (dead last). In modern press history, this was the poorest return on a political investment any Democrat has ever received for winning Iowa.

One could argue that, because Gephardt had received considerable attention in 1987, he had reached a "ceiling" in press coverage above which he could not go no matter how well he did in Iowa. Or, because Gephardt had come to be seen as a front-runner in Iowa before the voting, perhaps his victory there was not seen as sufficiently surprising to cause a bounce.

Table 7.2 **Bush, Dole, and Robertson Shares of Television News Coverage at Key Points in 1988 Republican Nomination Race**

	Bush (%)	Dole (%)	Robertson (%)
1987	30	22	13
1988:			
1/1–2/8 (up to Iowa)	33	31	14
2/9–2/16 (Iowa–New Hampshire)	27	23	26
2/17–3/8 (New Hampshire–Super Tuesday)	23	23	36
3/9–4/5 (after Super Tuesday)	29	57	10

SOURCE: S. Robert Lichter, "Misreading Momentum," *Public Opinion* 11 (May–June 1988): 16.
NOTE: Table based on number of times quoted as a percentage of all candidates.

One could even argue that, because Gephardt is a centrist Democrat, the "liberal" news media refused to give him the kind of bounce it would give to a liberal Republican like John Anderson or a liberal Democrat like Gary Hart.

Despite the enormous jump in coverage of Hart after the 1984 Iowa caucuses, there is some reason to believe that in 1992 the press will be less willing to hype surprise showings or victories to the same degree. Why? First, members of the fourth estate have become more sensitive to the criticism that they overreact. Second, candidates expected to do poorly in Iowa may follow Gore's example of denouncing the caucuses as unrepresentative. Note that Gore's press increased after Iowa despite his tie with Hart for last place there. Third, reporters have grown increasingly disdainful of "spin doctors" and other flacks peddling inflated scenarios. Yet it must also be said that surprise journalism depends on the circumstances of the year in question, beginning with the possible surprises and their magnitude. If Jackson were to win Iowa or New Hampshire in 1992, this feat surely would be hyped as a major surprise since in previous years his chances in these states have been minimized because so few blacks live in either. Other factors bearing on the recurrence of surprise journalism include who is running, who is expected to win, and what else happens in the other party's contest on the same day.

Compensatory Reporting

"Compensatory reporting" involves another double standard, a bias against front-runners and incumbents (especially front-running incumbents) and in favor of challengers, dark horses, and, on occasion, also-rans. Compensatory reporting goes beyond the question of how much coverage a candidate gets, all the way to the question of how much "good" or "bad" press the candidate gets.

In the 1980 nomination campaign, for example, Edward Kennedy received very negative coverage during the early months, when he held a big lead in the opinion polls over President Carter. But as soon as Carter became the odds-on favorite to win renomination, Carter's press "score" fell off a cliff. Similarly, during the final month of the 1984 general election campaign, the Mondale-Ferraro ticket, which had no chance of winning, enjoyed much more favorable coverage on network news than the unstoppable Reagan-Bush ticket.

Reporters themselves acknowledge that they practice "compensatory reporting." According to Bill Plante, a veteran CBS political correspondent, media scrutiny of a candidate increases proportionally with the candidate's poll standings. By the same token, losers and dropouts are given

Table 7.3 Democratic Candidate Shares of Television News Coverage at Key Points in 1988 Race

	Dukakis (%)	Gephardt (%)	Gore (%)	Hart (%)	Jackson (%)	Simon (%)
1987	10	12	10	22	13	12
1988:						
1/1–2/8 (up to Iowa)	15	21	6	16	8	19
2/9–2/16 (Iowa–New Hampshire)	21	23	12	6	8	19
2/17–3/8 (New Hampshire–Super Tuesday)	19	22	19	4	19	11
3/9–4/5 (after Super Tuesday)	26	14	15	2	34	9

SOURCE: See table 7.2.

gentle coverage because, as another CBS newsman indelicately puts it, "there's no point in picking on the dead" (Robinson and Sheehan, 1983: 116). Even so, compensatory reporting has never achieved full status as conventional wisdom. There is strong evidence that compensatory reporting was with us from the beginning to the end of the 1988 campaign.

At the beginning of the campaign, pundits and pollsters divided the Democratic field into the "plausibles" or possible winners, the "improbables," and the "unique." Biden, Dukakis, and Hart were regarded as plausibles; Babbitt, Gephardt, Gore, and Simon as improbables; and Jackson as unique. Setting Jackson aside for a moment, the compensatory-reporting principle suggests that likely losers enjoy more favorable press than possible winners. The CMPA's index of good press (simply the percentage of favorable assessments of each candidate aired on the evening news) suggests that this is exactly what happened during the 1987 exhibition season. (See table 7.4). The improbables did get more favorable coverage than the plausibles during this early period. This pattern held up for Babbitt as long as he stayed in the race. After his Iowa win, Gephardt's greater plausibility led to a sharp reduction in his favorability score. After a year of early campaigning, when the entire field was still intact, the "improbables" had an average press score of 85, while the "plausibles" had an average score of only 52.

Babbitt, by his own admission, was the press darling of 1988. During the six weeks between New Year's Day and the New Hampshire primary, his network spin score was 92, the best of any candidate in either party. Babbitt's case shows that candidates who somehow capture the imagination of the press but fail to capture the allegiance of the voting public still get favorable coverage.

Babbitt's deputy press secretary, John Russonello, says that it "wasn't automatic" that Babbitt would get good press. According to Russonello, it was Babbitt's very implausibility, plus "his having lots of ideas," that made him contrast with the rest of the Democratic field. Mimicking the infamous "farewell" Richard Nixon delivered to the press after losing his race for governor of California in 1962, Babbitt, bowing out of the presidential race, noted: "The press won't have Bruce Babbitt to puff up anymore."

As for Jackson, he finished the campaign with a spin score of 74, second only to Babbitt and well ahead of both Bush and Dukakis. He also stood outside the usual pattern of "compensatory reporting." After Jackson stunned the media by running second in Illinois and then stunned them again by winning in Michigan, he got increased attention *and* increasingly favorable press. In fact, the week after Michigan, Jackson's favorability on the evening news was 100 percent. Clearly, then, the news media violated

Table 7.4 **Percentage of Positive Coverage for Democratic Candidates in 1987–88**

	1987	1988			
	2/8–12/31	1/1–2/8	2/9–2/16	2/17–3/8	3/9–4/5
"Plausibles"					
Biden	54% (61)	–	–	–	–
Dukakis	64% (22)	53% (15)	45% (20)	42% (52)	63% (40)
Hart	38% (151)	34% (32)	0% (1)	0% (1)	–
Average	52%				
"Improbables"					
Babbitt	84% (19)	91% (11)	100% (1)	100% (2)	–
Gephardt	78% (23)	48% (48)	40% (25)	41% (49)	38% (16)
Gore	75% (4)	33% (3)	100% (3)	50% (14)	42% (12)
Simon	92% (13)	31% (16)	39% (23)	0% (1)	100% (4)
Averages	85%	57%	39%	45%	40%
"Unique"					
Jackson	84% (31)	86% (7)	100% (3)	73% (41)	79% (85)

SOURCE: Lichter, Amundson, and Noyes, *The Video Campaign*, 127.

NOTES: Table based on clearly positive and negative source assessments, excluding horse-race judgments. Ns (in parentheses) refer to number of each candidate's assessments on network evening newscasts. Percentages based on fewer than ten assessments excluded from computation of averages for "improbable" candidates.

their own modus operandi in covering Jackson: he did not "pay" very quickly for his early victories. In fact, he hardly had to pay at all until very late in the game.

Many different explanations of Jackson's special treatment could be offered, but in our view the key is that, since Jackson is black, it was obvious all along that the Democrats would not nominate him. The media never went negative with Jackson because there was no point in doing so. Jackson was "compensated" by the press because he had no chance of winning—the ultimate case of compensatory reporting.

Such "affirmative-action journalism" stems from the press corps's desire to level the political playing field for anybody who has a political disadvantage, particularly one as acute as race. Tellingly, in 1984 Geraldine Ferraro, the first woman to be major-party nominee for vice-president, finished the general election campaign with the most favorable press score among the final four contestants—another instance, we believe, of affirmative-action journalism.

Do the 1984 and 1988 experiences suggest that a candidate might be able to parlay affirmative-action journalism into a year-long press advantage? No one has yet successfully done so—not even Jesse Jackson. Once Jackson and Dukakis were the only Democrats left in the race (that is, once Jackson became a plausible candidate), his press advantage soured. By the New York primary, in fact, his spin score fell to 60, about average for the field. As for the future, we suspect that the advantages of affirmative-action journalism have run their course for Jackson. His next candidacy will be his third, and the novelty of being the first "serious" black presidential candidate will have worn off by then. So Jackson should not bank on special treatment the next time, especially if his rivals attack him as a spoiler and try to force him into an unequivocal pledge of support for the eventual nominee. A serious woman aspirant would be something new, as the flurry of interest in Congresswoman Patricia Schroeder and former U.N. Ambassador Jeane Kirkpatrick demonstrated in 1988. In this event, another round of affirmative-action press seems likely.

On the Republican side, the favorable press scores varied enormously and sometimes erratically. (See table 7.5). When the 1987 scores for Bush and Dole are averaged, the difference between them and the average for the less likely Republicans turns out to be less than two points (this excludes Haig's score, which is based on fewer than ten assessments). However, Dole's favorable press score was higher than that of any other Republican for whom a reliable score can be calculated. Still another anomaly was the truly awful press given du Pont, the longest shot in the Republican race. According to the principle of compensatory reporting, he should have been treated much more kindly in 1987.

Still, we should not be too quick to discard the principle as invalid. Recall that the basic idea is that a candidate's press gets worse as his or her chances of winning the nomination improve. The most consistent evidence for the principle is found in the roller-coaster course Bush's favora-

Table 7.5 **Percentage of Positive Coverage for Republican Candidates in 1987–88**

	1987	1988			
	2/8–12/31	1/1–2/8	2/9–2/16	2/17–3/8	3/9–4/5
"Plausibles"					
Bush	48% (89)	41% (98)	67% (64)	44% (55)	67% (15)
Dole	80% (35)	54% (61)	66% (38)	56% (27)	75% (20)
Averages	64%	47%	66%	50%	71%
"Improbables"					
Robertson	59% (29)	82% (11)	65% (26)	33% (52)	0% (4)
du Pont	40% (10)	75% (4)	–	–	–
Haig	85% (7)	60% (5)	33% (3)	–	–
Kemp	79% (19)	46% (24)	50% (2)	40% (5)	–
Averages	66%	59%	64%	–	–

SOURCE: Lichter, Amundson, and Noyes, *The Video Campaign,* 132.

NOTE: Table based on clearly positive and negative source assessments, excluding horse-race judgments. Ns (in parentheses) refer to number of each candidate's assessments on network evening newscasts. The 1987 "improbables" average included Haig; the first 1988 "improbables" average excluded Haig; the second 1988 "improbables" average for Kemp and Robertson only.

bility ratings followed as his electoral fortunes rose and fell. Heading into the Iowa caucuses, his press was dreadful—with an overall favorability score of 48 for 1987 and 41 for the weeks of 1988 leading up to the caucuses. (Indeed, before the campaign even formally began, he participated in the most hostile interview ever conducted between a network anchor and a national candidate, a live, ten-minute shouting match with Dan Rather just two weeks before the Iowa vote.) Thoroughly beaten in Iowa and regarded by many pundits as done for, Bush experienced a sudden press rebound in the week immediately following the Iowa debacle, when even the most hard-nosed network reporters suddenly found good things to say about him. But no sooner had he won the New Hampshire primary than his bad press reappeared. The only anomaly in Bush's pattern is the dramatic increase in press favorability after Super Tuesday, once it was clear that he would be the nominee.

On the other hand, Dole's coverage does not fit the compensatory-reporting principle so neatly. He finished 1987 with extraordinarily favorable coverage but dipped substantially during the run-up to Iowa, probably because of his clear lead there and his constant squabbling with Bush. In any event, his favorable press increased during the week after Iowa, when it looked as if he might win in New Hampshire. But then his favorability score fell off after losing New Hampshire. After Super Tuesday sealed his fate, Dole finally got the bump in kindly "death-watch" press predicted by the compensatory-reporting principle.

In short, compensatory reporting was much in evidence for Bush, but less so for the other Republican candidates. Favorability toward Robertson declined along with his chances, and the same was true for Kemp.

Conclusion: Back to the Future?

The conventional wisdom about television coverage of the nomination campaigns performed reasonably well in 1988. Horse-racism was very much in evidence throughout the campaign and seems quite likely to reappear again in 1992. Early-bird news was still a reality in 1988, but only because of the saturation coverage of Iowa and New Hampshire. We expect it to be more muted in 1992. The surprise-journalism principle, too, needs some modest revision in order to bring it into line with the realities of 1988 and the probabilities of the next campaign. But, whereas we are now seeing less early-bird news and surprise journalism, compensatory reporting (the tendency to employ a double standard against front-runners and incumbents and in favor of also-rans and challengers) seems to be growing more common. Of course, many counterinstances can be cited—most notably, perhaps, Dole's experience in the 1988 campaign. Still, the emergence of compensatory reporting may be the most important trend of all in building a new conventional wisdom about campaign coverage.

The extent to which the conventional wisdom still holds is due to the press following standard operating procedures that make it possible to predict with some accuracy how the typical news organization will cover a campaign. Even so, we may now be moving into a new era of campaign coverage—a period in which the media do less by doing more.

Out-and-out partisan bias is not a great problem in campaign coverage. The press, including the network news organizations, does not seek to elect Democrats or liberals by slanting its campaign stories. To be sure, in the last few campaigns, surprise journalism has helped upset those who began with an advantage: incumbents, front-runners, and the candidates preferred by the party organization. But the network news programs have now shifted away from surprise journalism. So surprise candidates no longer gain as much advantage, and the originally advantaged (incumbents, front-runners, and party favorites) are able to maintain a great deal of their advantage.

Thus, while news coverage pushes a campaign for the presidential nomination in many different directions, the campaign typically winds up about where it began: with the early favorites winning the nomination and with old-time political advantages mattering once again. In a strange way, then, the power of the media rebounds to the benefit of traditional political forces—the establishment candidate, the home-state son or daughter, the incumbent or the incumbent's political heir.

Does this mean that the media have succeeded largely in writing themselves out of the script? Not at all. It is the news media, and especially the television news organizations, that "decide," deliberately or not, whether the advantage goes to the surprise, media-created candidate or to the originally advantaged candidate. At this point, the media are seemingly content to cede some of their ability to create candidates, a "decision" that works to the great advantage of incumbents and front-runners, who re-emerge after the phantom candidates have appeared but then disappeared.

That is, the news media might help surprise candidates come forward to mount formidable-appearing challenges to the front-runner, though even this tendency is now less pronounced than it was in the recent past. But soon enough, reflecting the increasing power of compensatory journalism, the "other side of the story" will be presented. A challenger who, only a few weeks before, seemed an exciting hope for the future will be exposed, when subjected to the bright lights of intense press scrutiny, as a mere mortal, warts and all. At that point, the pendulum will swing back to the incumbent, the heir apparent, the original front-runner.

Overall, then, the new pattern is not simply for the front-runner or incumbent to win the nomination. Getting there is half the fun as the front-runner or incumbent falls behind, moves back in front, slides again, and finally emerges victorious. In the end, this new system leaves the advantage exactly where it was in the era of the "old" politics, before the advent of the "Big Media." So as we look forward to the future of campaign coverage in 1992 and beyond, we look back—back to the future.

References

Adams, William C. 1987. "As New Hampshire Goes . . . ." In *Media and Momentum: The New Hampshire Primary and Nomination Politics*, ed. Gary Orren and Nelson W. Polsby. Chatham, N.J.: Chatham House.

Lichter, S. Robert. 1988. "Misreading Momentum." *Public Opinion* 11 (May–June): 15–17, 57.

Lichter, S. Robert, Daniel Amundson, and Richard Noyes. 1988. *The Video Game: Network Coverage of the 1988 Primaries*. Washington, D.C.: American Enterprise Institute for Public Policy Research and Center for Media and Public Affairs.

Robinson, Michael J., and Margaret Sheehan. 1983. *Over the Wire and on T.V.: CBS and UPI in Campaign '80*. New York: Russell Sage.

8. The National Conventions: Diminished but Still Important in a Primary-Dominated Process

Emmett H. Buell, Jr.
John S. Jackson III

The final act in the long drama of presidential nominating politics is the official nomination itself. After two years of exhibition-season campaigning, and half a year more of contesting primaries and caucuses, the issue is finally and formally settled on the floor of the nominating convention by a roll-call vote of the states. In all probability, however, the outcome already will have been decided by voting in fifty state primaries and caucuses before the convention comes to order.

Nothing happened in 1988 to revise this description. Mathematically, George Bush won the GOP nomination on April 30 when victory in the Pennsylvania primary gave him more than enough delegates to claim the prize. Officially it was his on August 17 when the Texas delegation put him over the top at the New Orleans convention. Governor Michael Dukakis of Massachusetts cinched his nomination on June 7 by winning most of the delegates at stake in the California, Montana, New Jersey, and New Mexico primaries. The Atlanta convention made it official on July 20 when Dukakis received 2,876.25 votes to Jackson's 1,218.5 on the first and only ballot.

Loss of the principal reason for which it was created has truly reduced the importance of the national nominating convention. Yet even in its diminished capacity the convention still performs important functions for the party. It bridges the nominating and electing stages of the presidential selection process. In preparation for the fall campaign, the convention not only ratifies the ticket but adopts the platform and appeals to party unity. Moreover, all of this is done "with the whole world watching" on television.

How and when the nominating convention developed to the point of performing important but secondary functions for parties is the main topic of this chapter. The following pages sketch five stages in the history of presidential nominations—the original design of the Founders in 1787, the congressional caucuses of 1800 to 1824, a brief and overlapping period of nomination by state legislatures from 1824 to 1832, the "brokered" conventions and "smoke-filled rooms" of the 1832–1952 era, and the present system. Secondary functions are discussed in the context of the 1988 conventions.

This chapter also describes the socioeconomic characteristics and political views of delegates to the 1988 conventions. Repeated studies of convention delegates have found them considerably more affluent and more highly educated than ordinary voters. Moreover, delegates over the years have been more emotionally devoted to candidates, much more active in campaigns, and substantially more ideological than typical Democrats and Republicans. Thus something is gained in the translation when delegates speak for segments of the electorate (Baer and Bositis, 1988).

The chapter concludes with a brief discussion of what would probably happen to conventions if any of several proposed reforms were adopted. A national primary process would eliminate what remains of their presidential nominating function while regional primaries hold out at least the possibility of multiballot conventions actually selecting presidential nominees. Still other proposals would strengthen conventions by selecting delegates independently of any preference vote or by holding each party's convention before a national primary.

Evolution of Presidential Nominating Systems

The Original Design of 1787

When the Founders wrestled with presidential selection during the Constitutional Convention of 1787, they were obliged to consider both nomination and election, though the distinction often got lost in their deliberations. Most believed that political intrigue and factions should be kept out of the process as much as possible. Fearful of being overwhelmed in a new national government, representatives of the small states insisted that their interests be protected in selection of the executive. Still another goal was to preserve executive independence in a government most expected Congress to dominate (McCormick, 1982: 25).

This last objective proved particularly difficult for the Founders because they could think of no satisfactory alternative to nomination and election of the president by the national legislature. A key provision of the Virginia plan, which they quickly accepted for discussion purposes, was that both houses of a national legislature would select the executive. This provision was upheld in early procedural votes of the Philadelphia convention, but as the fateful summer of 1787 wore on, more and more delegates expressed reservations about legislative selection. Their concern was to prevent subordination and possible corruption of presidents by Congress. Was there no other way to select the executive? None recommended itself as the convention proceeded, certainly not direct popular election or selection by the state legislatures.

The eventual solution, as worked out by a select committee of eleven and revised further in the committee of the whole, consisted of five points. First, each state would receive as many electoral votes as it had representatives and senators in the national legislature, the electors to be chosen as each state legislature directed. Second, electors would meet in their respective states and vote for two persons, one of whom could not be a resident of the same state as themselves. Third, results of the balloting would be transmitted to the national capital, where the president of the Senate would count the votes in a public ceremony. Fourth, a majority of electoral votes would be required to elect the president while the person receiving the next most votes would become vice-president. Fifth, the House would make the final determination if no candidate won a majority or if two candidates tied for a majority. As a concession to the small states, each state delegation in the House would cast only one vote—regardless of the number of representatives comprising each delegation—and balloting would continue until one candidate won a majority of state delegations.

This was the scheme ratified along with the rest of the Constitution. Fortunately for the United States, George Washington was the universal choice for the first president and was duly chosen by unanimous vote of the electors in 1788. Even so, many expected the House routinely to choose his successors after these lesser figures failed to win an electoral majority. Under this scenario, the electors would nominate presidential candidates and the House would elect a president and vice-president from among the top five nominees. James Madison said as much in *Federalist Paper 39*, where he distinguished between the "immediate" and "eventual" elections of the president, the first by electors and the second by the House (Wills, 1982: 192).

As Richard McCormick (1982) has noted, the Founders devised rules for "a game never played." Politics figured in the very first election, when Alexander Hamilton took the lead in persuading some electors not to cast their second ballot for Adams. His goal was to avoid the risk of an electoral deadlock and the humiliation of a House contingent election. Hamilton succeeded more than perhaps intended, for Adams was elected vice-president with less than a majority of electoral votes.[1]

The Congressional Caucus, 1800–1824

The Founders also took a dim view of "parties," or factions. Yet these swiftly formed around competing personalities of Treasury Secretary Hamilton, Vice-President Adams, and Secretary of State Thomas Jefferson. After a confused contest in 1796, in which Adams was elected president and Jefferson vice-president, these factions congealed into two primitive political parties—the "Federalists" and the Jeffersonian "Democratic-Republicans"— chiefly based in Congress and linked to outside supporters through committees of correspondence and their own newspapers.

An electoral party's primary function is to nominate candidates for election to public office, and by 1800 the Federalists and Democratic-Republicans had become parties enough to pick their own presidential and vice-presidential candidates. Borrowing from the experience of state legislatures, where nominating caucuses had become common practice, Federalist members of the House and Senate met on May 3 to nominate John Adams and Charles Cotesworth Pinckney.[2] Eight days later, the Democratic-Republicans held their own conclave and secretly nominated Jefferson for president and Aaron Burr for vice-president. The era of presidential nominations by congressional caucuses had begun.

It was, for the most part, a troubled era. According to historian James Chase (1973: 25–28), the caucus failed three critical tests—representation of every part of the country, procedural stability, and uniting the party behind its nominees.

At first, representation in the Democratic-Republican caucuses was uneven because some districts and states had Federalist congressmen and senators. Even after the Federalist collapse, however, representation remained a problem because so many congressmen and senators refused to attend the caucuses. Some boycotted on grounds that the congressional caucus violated the separation of powers, others because they felt their votes did not matter, and still others to protest a likely but unacceptable nomination. Thus only 97 of 149 eligible members took part in the caucus that nominated Madison in 1808. Low turnout forced adjournment of the 1816 caucus; a second effort proved more successful later in the year. The 1820 caucus also adjourned for want of participants. Less than a third of all eligible members attended the final caucus of 1824.

Another problem plaguing the caucus was its procedural instability. Little is known about the 1800 Jeffersonian caucus because it was secret. The 1804 caucus was public, replete with an elected chairman and formal rules, but on whose authority it was convened remains a mystery. When the 1804 caucus chairman took it upon himself to summon the next meeting four years later, members were sufficiently outraged to discourage party leaders from calling another caucus on their own authority. Subsequent caucuses were announced by unsigned circulars. Some caucuses met as early as January, others as late as June. Early caucuses used committees of correspondence to maintain continuity between elections, but the practice was discontinued after 1812. Other procedures were similarly "in flux" (Chase, 1973: 26).

Finally, the congressional caucus became a focal point of conflict rather than the means of uniting Republicans behind a presidential ticket. Almost every caucus after 1804 bore the marks of factional strife, and by 1824, when a rump group nominated William Crawford, such tensions were palpable. Chase (1973: 60) reports that the last caucus met in the House chamber, its members outnumbered by hostile spectators in the gallery, who thumped the floor with walking sticks and chanted, "Adjourn! adjourn!" Only 66 of 240 eligible members took part, and of those showing up, 48 (73 percent) represented only four states—New York, Virginia, North Carolina, and Georgia. Ten states were not represented at all while five others had only one member present. Most spectators hissed as members of each delegation stepped forward to vote. Sixty-four voted for Crawford.

Nomination by State Legislatures, 1820–28

Adding to its other woes, the caucus was often accused of being unresponsive to popular preference. Of course, the Founders had disdained direct election of the president and contrived the electoral college instead. Their design allowed each state to decide whether its citizens would be allowed to vote for presidential electors. Until the 1820s most electors were chosen by state legislatures, thereafter by popular vote as the spirit of democracy spread.

These developments coincided with the breakup of the Democratic-Republican party into warring factions, each taking shape around such luminaries as Andrew Jackson of Tennessee, Henry Clay of Kentucky, John Quincy Adams of Massachusetts, and William Crawford of Georgia. Jackson's followers were especially likely to view the caucus as undemocratic.

Indeed, the congressional caucus had become so discredited by 1821 that no aspirant except possibly Crawford valued its nomination. Foreseeing that he would never prevail in the 1824 caucus, Jackson opened his presidential campaign two years earlier with a formal nomination by the Tennessee legislature. The Kentucky and Missouri legislatures soon responded by nominating Clay. Maine and Massachusetts followed in January 1823 with endorsements of John Quincy Adams. When the House of Representatives chose Adams over Jackson after an electoral college deadlock, Jackson cast himself as the victim of a "corrupt bargain" between Adams and Clay, and, again nominated by the Tennessee legislature, launched his ultimately successful 1828 campaign three years early.

At this point it is well to pause and note the indebtedness of national parties to the state practices. It is clear that the parties borrowed freely from state experience in devising methods of presidential nominations. The states had supplied the model for legislative caucuses, and their legislatures had stepped into the breach even before the final collapse of "King Caucus" in 1824. Now the states suggested yet another nominating method — a convention attended by delegates representing the people. In some states, according to McCormick (1982: 134), politicians hit upon conventions as an alternative when shut out of caucuses by their enemies. By the 1820s, conventions had become a common means of nominating state and local candidates. Thus ample precedent existed for the first presidential nominating convention, held by the Anti-Masonic party in 1831.

The Era of Brokered Conventions, 1832–1952

The Anti-Masons held the first of four national conventions preceding the 1832 election. After a preliminary meeting in 1830, they assembled in Baltimore on September 26, 1831, and nominated former Attorney General William Wirt for president and Amos Ellmaker of Pennsylvania as his running mate.

The National Republicans soon followed on December 12, 1831, also meeting in Baltimore. There 156 delegates from seventeen states nominated Clay for president and former Congressman John Sergeant of Pennsylania as his running mate on the first ballot (McCormick, 1982: 137). The convention also produced an "Address to the People," a forerunner of the party platform, which lavished praise on Clay and Sergeant and heaped scorn on Jackson.

Jackson's close advisers decided on a convention, not to renominate him (several state legislatures had already done that) but to unify most of the factions making up his support in the previous election. This coalition had come apart over sectional tensions, tariffs, internal improvements, the national bank, and the question of Jackson's eventual successor. The rupture could be seen in Jackson's cabinet, where Vice-President John C. Calhoun and Secretary of State Martin Van Buren became bitter foes. Eventually, Van Buren gained the upper hand, and, by 1831, Jackson was adamant that he replace Calhoun as vice-president in the next administration. Fearing that each faction would put up its own favorite for vice-president, Jackson allowed New Hampshire supporters to call for a convention to meet in Baltimore on May 21, 1832.

Approximately 320 delegates, representing every state except Missouri, attended.[3] Massachusetts, Rhode Island, and Connecticut sent as many delegates as they had presidential electors, but six other states, most notably Virginia and New Jersey, sent more than this standard allowed. Still other states were underrepresented. The delegates had been chosen in myriad ways — by legislative caucuses in three states, statewide conventions in seven states, county meetings in six other states, congressional-district conventions in Maryland, and by still other methods in Illinois, Alabama, Louisiana, and North Carolina (Chase, 1973: 263).

The overflow necessitated moving from the Athenaeum to the nearby Universalist Church. There three precedents for future Democratic conventions were established. First, each state delegation was to cast as many votes as it had presidential electors. This was an essential rule owing to the enormous variation in state delegations already noted. Second, a majority of each delegation would designate an individual to announce the state's vote. This meant voting by states rather than individuals, as had been the practice in congressional caucuses. Most delegations adopted a unit rule, under which a majority determined how all of the state's votes would be cast. Finally, to defend against criticisms that the convention did not represent national sentiment, the convention adopted a rule requiring two-thirds rather than a simple majority for nomination. (The Democrats kept the two-thirds rule until 1936 and did not do away with the unit rule until 1968.) The roll call of the states still survives as the most colorful moment in every convention, when reporting of delegate votes is accompanied by expressions of state pride.

Robert V. Remini (1981: 357) writes that the 1832 convention possibly gave birth to the "smoke-filled room" when a handful of Virginia delegates met in hopes of finding an alternative to Van Buren as Jackson's running mate. In any event, their efforts were to no avail, for Van Buren easily won the vice-presidential nomination on the following day. Congressman William Archer of Virginia, who had opposed Van Buren, then established yet another precedent by moving that the nomination be made unanimous.

Having unified the party, Jackson's advisers chose not to push their luck by drafting an address to the people. Such a document would have asked more than could be expected of Van Buren's enemies, and so the convention adjourned on the suggestion that state parties could formulate their own statements, if so inclined.

"Institutionalization" of the national nominating convention occurred throughout the next two decades. One such development was replacement of the address by a platform. Addresses contained little more than praise of the party's nominees and personal attacks on the opposition. Platforms described the party's policy views and offered proposals for the future.

The Democrats adopted the first platform in their 1840 convention, and the Whigs followed suit four years later. Until 1852, platforms were the final item of important business at conventions, adopted after nomination of the presidential and vice-presidential candidates. Both the Democratic and Whig conventions of that year changed their programs so that platform deliberations preceded the nominations, which is still the practice today.

Yet another important development was establishment of national party committees. The 1844 Democratic convention created a central committee and approved the idea of a permanent national committee to handle party affairs between elections, call the next convention, and wage the presidential campaign. In their next convention the Democrats formally established the Democratic National Committee (DNC). The Whigs created their own national committee in 1852.

The first instance of a brokered presidential nomination was the Whig convention of 1839, in which William Henry Harrison was chosen over Clay in complicated maneuvers engineered by New York and Pennsylvania leaders. The result was a victory for Harrison, first gained in a special committee operating much like a caucus, and then made unanimous on the convention floor. Another triumph of convention brokering was the 1844 Democratic convention's nomination of James K. Polk, the first "dark horse," after eight ballots had proven Van Buren's inability to win the necessary two-thirds.

The "brokers" of this era were state party leaders, who usually controlled their delegations and could bargain with candidates, extracting patronage and personal favors in return for their support. Under the unit rule one needed only a majority of a state's delegates to deliver the whole delegation, and a large delegation voting en bloc at the right moment could prove critical in the "bandwagon" psychology of multiballot conventions.

For good or ill, the art of coalition politics flourished during this period, especially in the Democratic convention, where the two-thirds rule required a concurrent majority for victory. Without this rule, Pomper (1966: 188) has noted, Stephen A. Douglas would have won nomination on the first ballot in 1860 rather than on the fifty-ninth, Franklin D. Roosevelt would have been nominated on the first rather than the fourth ballot in 1932, Polk would have lost to Van Buren in 1844, and House Speaker Champ Clark would have beaten Woodrow Wilson in 1912. The worst experience with the two-thirds rule was in 1924, when a showdown between Governor Alfred E. Smith and William Gibbs MacAdoo ended nine days and 103 ballots later with the nomination of a compromise candidate, John W. Davis of West Virginia.[4]

Analysis of convention balloting during the century of Democratic experience with the two-thirds rule indicates that it was a major factor in prolonging contested nominations. Of the twenty-six Democratic conventions held from 1832 through 1932, fourteen required two or more ballots to nominate, and seven necessitated more than ten ballots. The median number of Democratic ballots for this period was two, exactly double the Republican figure for 1856–1932.

Still, as the Republicans demonstrated in nine of their twenty-four conventions between 1856 and 1948, it was possible to have multiballoting without a two-thirds rule. The Republican counterpart to 1924 was 1880, when Senator James G. Blaine's forces checked former President Ulysses S. Grant's bid for a third term but could not put their own man over the top. On the thirty-sixth ballot the convention nominated Congressman James A. Garfield (the only sitting member of the House of Representatives to be elected president). Ten ballots were required for Warren G. Harding's nomination in 1920; eight to pick Benjamin Harrison in 1888; seven for Rutherford B. Hayes in 1876; six for Wendell L. Willkie in 1940; four for Blaine in 1884; and three each for Abraham Lincoln in 1860, Charles Evans Hughes in 1916, and Thomas E. Dewey in 1948.

The 1948 convention was the last time the Republicans needed more than one ballot to nominate a presidential standard-bearer. The last such convention for the Democrats took place in 1952 with a third-ballot nomination of the diffident Adlai Stevenson. In a remarkably prescient article written after the 1956 election, William G. Carleton (1957) predicted that future conventions would require only one ballot to select front-runners whose standing would accrue largely from national news media coverage. "The days of the favorite son, the dark horse, the stalking horse, the smoke-filled conference room, the senatorial and congressional cabal, and the decisive trading of votes by local bigwigs are numbered, if indeed they are not already finished," Carleton (1957: 224) wrote. Thirty years later, Byron Shafer (1988: 8) concluded that 1952 marked the end of the national convention's nominating function. Thereafter conventions would formally affirm, but not actually make, presidential nominations.

Table 8.1 lends support to such arguments by pointing up changing patterns in the types of nominations rendered by major party conventions. The table updates Gerald Pomper's 1966 typology of nominations through the 1988 conventions. The first Pomper type (1966: 182–83) is the "ratifying" nomination, where candidates win on the first ballot with two-thirds or more of the delegate votes. "Limited, but significant choice," occurs when the nominee wins on the first ballot with less than two-thirds. The third and fourth types occur only in multiballot conventions—when "major" (receiving more than 20 percent on the first ballot) and "minor" candidates (less than 20 percent on the first ballot) are eventually nominated.

Table 8.1 Patterns of Major Party Presidential Nominations, 1832–1988

	1832–1892		1896–1952		1956–1968		1972–1988	
	N	%	N	%	N	%	N	%
Single-ballot								
Ratification	12	39	16	53	5	62	6	60
Limited choice	2	6	4	13	3	38	4	40
Multiballot								
Major	11	36	5	17	0	0	0	0
Minor	6	19	5	17	0	0	0	0
Totals	31	100	30	100	8	100	10	100

SOURCES: Gerald Pomper, *Nominating the President: The Politics of Convention Choice* (New York: W. W. Norton, 1966), 196; for 1964–1984 data, *Congressional Quarterly's Guide to U.S. Elections,* 2d ed. (Washington, D.C.: Congressional Quarterly Press, 1985), 209–21; for 1988 data, Gerald M. Pomper, "The Presidential Nominations," in Gerald M. Pomper et al., *The Election of 1988: Reports and Interpretations* (Chatham N.J.: Chatham House, 1989), 54–55.

Sixteen "major" and eleven "minor" nominations occurred between 1832 and 1952; neither type has since been nominated by either major party. The last minor Republican nomination was in 1920, when a deadlocked convention eventually turned to Harding. Davis was the last such Democratic nominee, in 1924. Every nomination since 1952 has been of the "ratification" or "limited choice" type, and, as Howard Reiter (1985: 28) points out, the front-runner at convention time has won every time.

National Nominating Conventions and Presidential Primaries, 1908–68

National nominating conventions, no less than the congressional caucuses they replaced, have long been assailed as unrepresentative of popular choice. Critics first voiced this complaint after the 1832 conventions. The Democratic convention of 1835 took the issue seriously enough to draft a formal reply defending its delegates as popularly chosen (McCormick, 1982: 188).

Similar questions were raised again at the turn of the century when the Progressive movement unleashed an attack on "closed" party nominations at all levels of government. Among the most prominent critics of nominating conventions was Governor Robert La Follette of Wisconsin. "If the voter is competent to cast his ballot at the general election for the official of his choice," La Follette proclaimed, "he is equally competent to vote directly at the primary election for the nomination of the candidates of his party" (quoted in Ranney, 1975: 124). Reformers expected primaries to loosen the grip of party "bosses" on nominations and thereby produce better candidates while involving more people in politics.

According to Austin Ranney (1975: 121), party officials in Crawford County, Pennsylvania, invented the primary election in 1842 to nominate local officials. It was not until the Progressive Era, however, that states began enacting presidential primary laws. Florida was the first to act, in 1901, with a statute allowing the option of a presidential primary. Even so, Wisconsin is generally acknowledged to have begun the era of presidential primaries with a 1905 law providing for direct election of delegates to the 1908 conventions. Oregon took the next step in 1910 by creating a presidential preference primary. By 1916, more than half of all the states had experimented with presidential primaries of one type or another (Davis 1980: 41–43).

By the decade's end, however, eight states had abandoned their primaries after finding them too inconsequential to justify the expense. Democratic primaries yielded the poorest returns. In 1920, for example, the turnout for all twenty Democratic primaries was only 571,671 with 55.8 percent of all votes going to uncommitted delegates and favorite-son candidates. Only 763,858 voted in the seventeen Democratic primaries of 1924. Four years later, more than 60 percent of the 1,264,220 voters in eighteen Democratic primaries supported favorite sons or uncommitted slates. Republican turnout for the same years was consistently better—almost 3.2 million in 1920, just over 3.5 million in 1924, and 4.1 million in 1928—with much less support for uncommitted slates and favorite sons (cf. *Congressional Quarterly's Guide*, 1985: 391–97).

Interest in presidential primaries picked up again after World War II. Governor Harold E. Stassen of Minnesota made good use of the Wisconsin, Nebraska, Pennsylvania, and West Virginia primaries in his 1948 bid, before Dewey decisively defeated him in Oregon. Opposed by most state and national party leaders, Senator Estes Kefauver of Tennessee catapulted to front-runner status by winning state primaries in 1952. The Democratic convention rejected him all the same for Governor Stevenson of Illinois. Four years later, Stevenson and Kefauver fought it out in the primaries before Stevenson cinched renomination. General Dwight D. Eisenhower used the 1952 primaries to demonstrate his popular appeal to party elites. Senator John F. Kennedy deliberately chose the West Virginia primary in 1960 to show he could win Protestant votes. Victories in Wisconsin and West Virginia drove his main rival, Senator Hubert Humphrey, from the race well before the Los Angeles convention.

Despite the undeniably greater importance of primaries in the postwar period, the nomination still hinged on victory in the caucus-convention states. As already noted, Kefauver's string of primary victories did not win him the 1952 Democratic nomination. Senator Barry Goldwater won only five of seventeen Republican primaries in 1964 and often trailed his rivals in national polls. True, he eventually won the critical California primary that knocked Governor Nelson Rockefeller out of the race, but his nomination was mainly achieved by winning caucus-convention delegates (Novak, 1965). Four years later, Vice-President Humphrey won the Democratic nomination without formally entering a single primary. His majority chiefly resulted from the efforts of party regulars and organized labor in caucus-convention states and in primary states where the preference vote did not determine selection of delegates.

In any event, the nominees of both major parties in 1956, 1960, 1964, and 1968 arrived at their respective national conventions with their nominations already decided. Why had the conventions lost their principal function?

Having already perceived this development after the 1956 conventions, Carleton (1957: 233–35) viewed it as a response to "national and democratic forces outside the conventions." Among the most important in his estimation were the national news media, especially television and radio, which now had the power to transform politicians into national celebrities. Winning primaries had become a principal way to gain such exposure. Still another development in the transformation of national nominating conventions, according to Carleton (1957: 235), was the increasing importance of farm, labor, and other "mass pressure groups" in preconvention campaigns. A large turnout by labor or some other organized group could make the difference in state caucuses or boost a candidate's share of the primary vote.

Shafer takes a similar view in his more recent analysis of why presidential nominations have "departed" the national party conventions (1988: 17–39). Dramatic expansion of the federal government during the 1930s and rising affluence after World War II operate as the most basic causes in his account. Both trends contributed to the decline of political parties, as did the emergence of truly national news media. In turn, all of these developments accelerated the nationalization of American politics. As parochial politics counted for less and less, presidential candidates adjusted their strategies accordingly.

Conventions in a Primary-Dominated System, 1972–88

All these developments provided the background for more immediate tensions in 1968 when the Democrats met in Chicago for one of the most turbulent conventions in history. Delegates arrived at their heavily guarded hall divided by the Vietnam War and haunted by the killings of Martin Luther King, Jr., and Robert F. Kennedy. King's death had precipitated widespread rioting, and local officials feared more racial violence before the summer's end. Radicals of varying persuasions openly proclaimed their intention to disrupt the convention, thus provoking city authorities into a massive show of force. Delegates gained access to the convention hall only after passing through elaborate security checks. Symbolizing the old-fashioned politics that had steamrollered the McCarthy and Kennedy forces, Mayor Richard Daley packed part of the hall with city employees and surrounded himself with lieutenants in the Illinois delegation. Tensions arising from this volatile mixture of party regulars, antiwar dissidents, McCarthy and Kennedy delegates—as well as the risk of demonstrations inside as well as outside the convention hall—induced President Johnson to cancel an appearance coinciding with his birthday. On the night of Humphrey's nomination, the networks cut away from nominating speeches to cover fighting between the police and protestors on Michigan Avenue. It was in this context of bloodied heads and fractured party unity that Humphrey accepted a doomed nomination. Hoping to pacify opponents, he did not oppose convention votes creating commissions to review the rules of delegate selection and the proceedings of future conventions (Crotty, 1983; Polsby, 1983; Shafer, 1983.)

The more important body, the Commission on Party Structure and Delegate Selection, was quickly identified with its first chairman, Senator George McGovern of South Dakota, and with Congressman Donald Fraser of Minnesota, who succeeded him. As noted in chapter 1, state parties adopted the commission's edicts with remarkably little resistance. Other commissions refined national party rules in subsequent years. Under the new rules, a typical state party chair controlled only one vote at the convention, his or her own. Abolition of the unit rule in 1968 and adoption of proportional representation for many 1976 primaries dramatically reduced the unity of delegations at every Democratic convention after 1968 (Reiter, 1985: 74).

Apportionment of Delegates

Another concern much regulated by both parties has been apportionment of delegates. Both parties have wrestled with the following basic questions. On what basis should delegates be awarded? How much weight should be given to population relative to electoral behavior? Were party strongholds entitled to extra delegates? Should weakly performing states forfeit delegates?

In every Democratic convention from 1832 through 1940, "delegate votes" were apportioned on the basis of each state's strength in the electoral college, hence an advantage for the more populous states.[5] On the other hand, the two-thirds rule adopted in 1832 and sustained through the 1932 convention favored the less-populated but solidly Democratic South. As compensation for the rule's abolition, the 1940 Democratic convention voted to award two bonus delegate votes to each state won by the Democrats in the previous presidential election.[6] The DNC doubled the bonus in 1947. When the 1950 census foretold the loss of congressional districts in some states, the DNC ruled that no state would lose delegates at the next convention. In 1956 the DNC not only retained the no-loss rule but awarded additional bonus delegate votes to states either electing Democratic governors or senators or voting Democratic in recent presidential elections. The resulting distortions led DNC Chairman Paul M. Butler to call for an end to bonus delegate votes at the 1960 convention. Delegates were reapportioned on the basis of congressional and DNC representation, with the proviso that no state would have fewer votes than at the 1956 convention (Key, 1964: 407; David, et al., 1961: 170). Thus a bonus system of sorts was still operating when the Democrats held their fateful 1968 convention.

Naturally the McGovern-Fraser Commission took a long hard look at apportionment, and, after much discussion, settled on equal weight for total population and prior presidential voting (Shafer, 1983). This has been the basic method employed in every Democratic convention since 1972. In 1988, for example, the formula for apportioning 2,999 of 4,162 delegates among the fifty states and the District of Columbia took into account a state's Democratic presidential vote in 1976, 1980, and 1984, and its electoral college vote, as proportions of the total popular vote in all three presidential elections combined, and of all 538 electoral college votes, respectively.[7] Under reformed party rules, at least 75 percent of all pledged delegates were to be selected at the congressional-district level, the remainder at large. Each delegation also received a 15 percent "add-on" for pledged party and elected officials, and still more unpledged "super-delegates" consisting of DNC members, congressmen, senators, governors, and "distinguished former elected leaders."

Until the 1940s, apportionment was one of the few instances where Republicans had more complex rules than Democrats did. Beginning with their first convention in 1856, the Republicans awarded every state the same number of at-large delegates (six in 1856, four thereafter through the 1912 convention). Population differences were recognized by awarding extra delegates for each congressional district (three in 1856, two through 1912). Devised for a northern party, this scheme first came under question at the 1860 convention, when members objected to seating a delegation from Texas on grounds that it represented few Republican voters. Eventually the convention voted to seat a diminished Texas delegation, thus setting a precedent for taking party strength into account, even though it was not formally part of the apportionment formula (David, et al., 1961: 167–68; Davis, 1983: 56).

Reconstruction governments and black suffrage transformed the South into a Republican stronghold after the Civil War, and so southern states enjoyed full representation at GOP conventions for the rest of the century. The end of Reconstruction and subsequent disenfranchisement of blacks, however, soon transformed the South into a solidly Democratic region, thus once again posing a problem for Republican conventions. Some "rotten borough" delegates from the South represented few voters other than themselves and fellow federal appointees. The inevitable challenge came at the 1908 convention with a motion to reapportion delegates in accordance with past presidential voting. Had this resolution carried, the South would have lost half of its delegates at the next convention, and because it did not, William Howard Taft was able to overcome Theodore Roosevelt at the 1912 convention. After the election was lost to Woodrow Wilson, the Republican National Committee (RNC) joined with northern state parties to reapportion delegates so that Dixie lost seventy-eight delegates at the 1916 convention (David, et al., 1961: 168–69).

The plan adopted for 1916 and modified slightly for future conventions used three criteria for apportionment. First, each state received a fixed number of at-large delegates. Second, one delegate was awarded for each congressional district regardless of the district's previous electoral behavior. Finally, casting a minimum number of votes for a Republican presidential or congressional candidate entitled a district to one bonus delegate. In 1916 the minimum vote was 7,500; in 1920 it was 10,000 (Davis, 1983: 58).

Beginning with the 1924 convention, states voting Republican in the last presidential election received three additional, or bonus, at-large delegates. In 1940, effective for the 1944 convention, states were no longer entitled to one delegate per district regardless of electoral performance. Now only those districts casting a minimum number of Republican presidential votes (1,000 in 1944 and 2,000 after 1952) got even one delegate, while those casting 10,000 votes for the GOP presidential candidate earned a second or bonus delegate (Davis, 1983: 58).

After battles with the Ripon Society, a liberal Republican group, the GOP revised its apportionment rules again in 1972. Every state was now entitled to six at-large delegates, three delegates per congressional district, one delegate for each Republican senator elected, one delegate for election of a Republican governor, one delegate if the House delegation was half or more Republican, and extra delegates for voting Republican in the last presidential election (Davis, 1983: 59).[8]

By 1976 the new rules had facilitated a major power shift within the Republican party. Gerald Pomper (1979) called attention to this develop-

ment in explaining President Ford's narrow victory over Governor Reagan
in 1976. By Pomper's reckoning, southern and western states gained disproportionately while northeastern and midwestern states—the party's
traditional base—declined. Had 1976 delegates been apportioned under
the same crtieria used in 1952, Pomper estimates, Ford would have gotten
56 percent, rather than 51 percent, of the delegates from the forty-eight
states that participated in both nominations. Of the seventeen states that
had gained delegates over this time, sixteen were either south of the Mason-
Dixon line or west of the Mississippi River. Fifteen of the seventeen supported Reagan at the 1976 convention. Of the twenty-one state delegations
that had lost relative voting power over the same period, two-thirds voted
for Ford. "The rules reflected a geographical transfer of power," Pomper
(1979: 801–2) observed, "and almost promoted a personal transfer of power
as well."

The Delegates

Looking back at conventions of the late nineteenth and early twentieth cen-
turies, David and associates (1961: 245) concluded that the quality of
delegates had improved considerably over time. By this they meant that
delegates had become increasingly middle-class, progressively less "boss-
ridden," and more "trustworthy"—trends they attributed to such disparate
causes as women's suffrage, civil service reform, selection of delegates in
primaries, restrictions against participation of some federal officials in
electoral politics, and rising levels of education.

Whether the delegates were more demographically representative of
party identifiers or voters was altogether a different question. Every survey
of convention delegates since 1948 has revealed sharp socioeconomic disparities between delegates and ordinary partisans. Compared to their "constituents," delegates have always been more educated, wealthier, and more
concentrated in the most prestigious and best-paying careers. This was
even truer of the post-1968 reform era than before. Jeane Kirkpatrick (1976:
63) described delegates to the 1972 conventions in familiar terms: "As compared to most other people, delegates went to school longer, made more
money, and had better jobs. They were, in brief, an overwhelmingly middle-
class group, and they knew it."

For the most part, table 8.2 shows that the same was true of 1988 delegates. Based on *New York Times* telephone surveys conducted shortly
before each party's convention (*New York Times* 1988a and 1988b), the
table reveals that Democratic and Republican delegates resembled each
other more closely than the registered voters of their own parties with respect to education, income, and age.[9] More than two-thirds of the dele-

gates in either party possessed at least one college degree, compared to 16 percent of all registered Democrats and 26 percent of all registered Republicans also interviewed by the *Times*. Fifty-six percent of Democratic delegates and 66 percent of Republican delegates reported 1987 family incomes of $50,000 or more; indeed, more than a quarter of the Republicans disclosed incomes of at least $100,000. Among registered-voter samples, only 10 percent of the Democrats and 19 percent of the Republicans got into the $50,000-plus bracket. Finally, delegates were much more likely to be middle-aged than were registered voters.

In other demographic respects, however, delegates were closer to voters in their own party than to each other. This was especially evident in race and union-membership comparisons. Blacks and union labor constituted significant proportions of the Democratic rank and file in 1988, and they were an even larger presence among the Democratic delegates. *New York Times* surveys picked up no more than a trace of either element among the Republicans.[10] Interesting differences also turned up in the religious comparison. Whether delegates or ordinary voters, Republicans were more likely than Democrats to be Protestants. Conversely, Democratic delegates were twice as likely as Democratic voters to be Jewish, three times more likely than Republican delegates, and six times more than Republican voters.

Finally, Republican delegates stood apart from everybody else, including registered voters in their own party, as preponderantly male. Women in 1988 constituted only 37 percent of all delegates, a drop from 44 percent at the 1984 convention. Before the post-1968 reforms, however, women usually enjoyed more representation at Republican than Democratic conventions (Reiter, 1985: 61). Democratic quotas reversed this relationship between 1972 and 1984.[11]

Numerous studies have also uncovered major differences in political views between convention delegates and party identifiers in the "mass public." Here obeisance is due the classic study by Herbert McClosky and associates (1960), which has inspired a generation of research on the ideological representativeness of delegates. Based on interviews with delegates to the 1956 conventions and with ordinary citizens, this analysis uncovered similarities and differences among delegates, party identifiers, and the general public on selected issues of the day. The results located Democratic and Republican identifiers slightly to the left and right, respectively, of a centrist general public while Democratic delegates stood somewhat to the left of Democratic identifiers. Republican delegates, however, were so much more conservative than Republican identifiers that the latter more often agreed with Democratic delegates on the issues.

This view of Republican delegates as out in right field remained the con-

Table 8.2 Socioeconomic Comparison of 1988 Convention Delegates and Registered Voters, by Party

	Democrats		Republicans	
	Delegates (%)	Registered Voters (%)	Delegates (%)	Registered Voters (%)
Sex				
Male	48	44	63	51
Female	52	56	37	49
Race				
White	70	73	96	96
Black	21	20	3	3
Other	9	6	1	1
Education				
High school only	9	67	10	51
Some college	18	17	21	22
College graduate	21	16	26	26
Beyond college	52		42	
Annual income in 1987				
<$25,000	6	48	2	31
$25,000–$50,000	33	37	21	46
$50,000–$100,000	40	10	39	19
Over $100,000	16		27	

Union member	23	16	4	4
Age				
18–29	4	19	4	21
30–39	22	16	13	23
40–49	33	19	28	14
50–59	25	16	30	15
60 or older	16	29	25	25
Religion				
Protestant	51	59	70	67
Catholic	30	26	24	20
Jewish	6	3	2	1
Other	3	2	2	5
No religious faith	8	7	1	6

SOURCE: Summaries of the *New York Times* Democratic and Republican delegate surveys of June 20–July 12 and July 22–August 4, 1988, provided by the *New York Times*. Telephone-sample *N*s were 1,059 for the Democratic delegates and 739 for Republican delegates.

NOTE: The "high school only" category includes persons with less than a full high-school education. Income figures do not total 100% owing to respondent refusals to supply such information. Blanks indicate no data provided.

ventional wisdom until the post-1968 reforms inspired new investigations. According to a massive study of 1972 convention delegates and ordinary partisans (Kirkpatrick, 1976), the reforms had completely reversed the McClosky model. Now it was the Democratic delegates whose views isolated them from the general public and their own party in the electorate.

Subsequent studies of 1976 convention delegates (Ladd, 1977; Jackson, et al., 1978) and information released by the Winograd commission (Commission on Presidential Nominations, 1978) disagreed on whether the Democratic elites were still as isolated from the party's rank and file as they had been four years earlier. According to Everett C. Ladd (1977: 63), the 1976 Democratic delegates were no less leftist than their 1972 counterparts. But John S. Jackson III and his associates found evidence of moderation in 1976, as did the Winograd commission. Subsequent data gathered in 1980 by Warren E. Miller, M. Kent Jennings, and other scholars associated with the University of Michigan's Center for Political Studies (CPS), revealed that the general public and rank-and-file identifiers in both parties remained at or near the middle of the ideological spectrum, while Republican delegates had become notably more conservative than in 1972, and Democratic delegates had moved slightly towards the center. Shafer (1988: 104) depicts 1980 Democratic and Republican delegates as almost equally remote from their own rank-and-file identifiers.

In a replication of the McClosky study, Jackson and associates (1982: 166) classified 53 percent of all 1980 Democratic delegates as liberal, compared to 29 percent of the Democratic identifiers, 21 percent of the mass public, 15 percent of the Republican identifiers, and only 2 percent of 1980 Republican convention delegates. By the same token, 64 percent of the Republican delegates called themselves conservatives, compared to 67 percent of the Republican identifiers, 49 percent of the public, 42 percent of the Democratic identifiers, and only 4 percent of the Democratic delegates. Along with these divergences were major differences on most policy questions.

Indeed, the gulf was so wide in 1984 that terms like "conservative" and "liberal" had different meanings for Democratic and Republican delegates (Miller, 1988: 87–88). Compared on abortion, busing, and other social issues, so-called "moderate" Republicans were more conservative than "conservative" Democrats, and "liberal" Republicans held views similar to moderate Democrats. On domestic spending and foreign-policy questions, Republican liberals were more conservative than Democratic moderates, just as moderate Republicans were more conservative than conservative Democrats. There was no Republican group comparable to liberal Democrats.

Table 8.3 indicates that similarly great divides marked the political land-

Table 8.3 1988 Convention Delegates, Voters, and General Public Compared on Liberalism-Conservatism and Leading Issues

	Democratic Delegates (%)	Democratic Voters (%)	Total Public (%)	Republican Voters (%)	Republican Delegates (%)
Self-described outlook					
Liberal	39	25	20	12	1
Conservative	5	22	30	43	60
Domestic-policy views					
Prefer smaller government providing fewer services	16	33	43	59	87
Prefer bigger government providing more services	58	56	44	30	3
Favor more federal spending on education	90	76	71	67	41
Favor more federal spending on day care and after-school child care	87	56	52	44	36
Abortion should be legal as it is now	72	43	40	39	29
Government pays too little attention to black needs	68	45	34	19	14
Foreign-policy views					
Keep spending on military at least at current level	32	59	66	73	84
More worried about Communist takeover in Central America than U.S. involvement in a war there	12	25	37	55	80

SOURCE: "Convention Delegates and the Public on the Issues," *New York Times* (August 14, 1988): 14.

scape of 1988. Here delegates are compared with registered voters and a total adult sample in the New York Times surveys. Big differences are evident in every comparison, beginning with how delegates described their political philosophies. Thirty-nine percent of all Democratic delegates called themselves "liberals," compared to 1 percent of the Republican delegates, and 60 percent of the Republican delegates described their views as "conservative," compared to 5 percent of all Democratic delegates. Gaps between delegates and registered voters of the same party were of similar magnitude on both sides.

Comparisons on specific issues again revealed expectedly enormous differences between Democratic and Republican delegates. On day-care spending, legalized abortion, and defense spending, however, Democratic voters were closer to much more conservative Republican delegates than to their own, much more liberal delegates. Democratic delegates and Democratic voters exhibited the smallest differences on size of government and Central America; Republican delegates and Republican voters were closest on day-care spending, government attention to black needs, and levels of military spending; and the voters of both parties had the smallest differences of any two partisan groups on spending for education and abortion.

Additional data on the 1988 delegates from Jackson's research affirms the programmatic chasm dividing Democrats and Republicans.[12] As in the New York Times surveys, Democratic and Republican delegates in Jackson's survey stood remarkably far apart on such stock issues as federal responsibility for maintaining the standard of living, more or fewer government services, increasing the minimum wage, U.S. policy for Central America, relationships with the Soviets, and areas where federal spending should be cut.[13] Sixty-three percent of the Democratic delegates wanted to raise the minimum wage, for example, while 72 percent of their Republican counterparts did not. Seventy-nine percent of the Republicans said the United States should support anticommunists in Central America, while 68 percent of the Democrats wanted to limit U.S. involvement and promote regional cooperation. Ninety-three percent of the Democrats wanted to trim the defense budget, compared to 44 percent of the Republicans.

Are delegates so committed to their causes and candidates that they will sacrifice the election to win the nomination? Political scientists have investigated this possibility by applying James Q. Wilson's "amateur" and "professional" typology of political activists to national convention delegates (Wilson, 1962). "Amateurs" regard politics as a struggle to achieve principled goals while "professionals" are no less preoccupied with winning elections. Aaron Wildavsky (1965) similarly characterized most Goldwater delegates to the 1964 Republican convention as "purists" rather than "politicians." Purists admired Goldwater's unswerving conservatism and unwillingness to compromise for the sake of electoral victory. Purists and amateurs also turned up at the 1968 and 1972 Democratic conventions as McCarthy and McGovern supporters. Indeed, John W. Soule and Wilma McGrath (1975) estimated that amateurs constituted 51 percent of all 1972 delegates, up from 21 percent in 1968. Subsequent research, however, suggests that the notion of inflexible purists bent on nominating equally zealous candidates is overdrawn. According to Alan I. Abramowitz and Walter J. Stone (1985), who have extensively analyzed attitudes of activists in the caucus-convention process, ideology and issues certainly mattered, but so did winning the White House. (See also Stone and Abramowitz, 1983.) Indeed, winning mattered sufficiently for many activists to back a less desirable but more electable alternative. The upshot is that most caucus-convention activists—and possibly convention delegates as well—are not wholly purists or politicians but principled amateurs who want victory as much as any professional.

In sum, delegates stand apart from ordinary partisans in fundamental respects. No doubt they were more highly educated and affluent than the rank and file long before the first empirical studies established the now familiar socioeconomic disparities. Recent surveys show no break with this secular pattern of elite representation, though, in certain demographic respects, the delegates are fairly representative of their respective party electorates. The same studies show delegates often ideologically remote from ordinary partisans, sometimes exhibiting less in common with the great mass of party identifiers than most elites in the opposition party. Such findings raise basic questions about the meaning of "representation" as well as the latent functions of an "open" nominating process. Were the "boss-ridden" delegates of bygone brokered conventions less representative of ordinary voters than today's ideological elites? Has a reformed process of delegate selection improved the representative relationship? If so, for whom? These issues remain unresolved in the ongoing assessment of contemporary presidential nominating politics.

Secondary Functions

Ratifying the Vice-Presidential Choice

Valued for its runner-up status in the first four presidential elections, the vice-presidency lost most of its allure after ratification of the Twelfth Amendment in 1804. By 1840, when nominating conventions had taken firm root in American political soil, the vice-presidential nomination had become little more than a consolation prize for defeated factions. Tickets were often balanced with politically and personally incompatible nominees

(David, et al., 1961: 91). In some conventions, losing factions claimed the vice-presidential nomination as a matter of right (Pomper, 1966: 159). It was not until the 1940 Democratic convention that Franklin D. Roosevelt established the prerogative of presidential nominees to name their own running mates (Nelson, 1989: 186). Today vice-presidents are regarded as front-runners for their party's next presidential nomination. For most of the last century, however, the vice-presidency was a dead end. Since 1836 no sitting vice president had been elected president in his own right until Bush broke the spell in 1988. Moreover, no vice-president in the last century who sought a second consecutive term was renominated, and none who assumed the Oval Office on the demise of a president was nominated for a presidential term of his own (Pomper, 1966: 168; Nelson, 1989: 186).

Vice-presidents have fared considerably better in this century. Except for Henry Wallace in 1944, no sitting vice-president seeking a second consecutive term has been denied renomination since 1912. Moreover, the five vice-presidents in this century who became president upon the death or resignation of a predecessor won presidential nominations of their own. The vice-presidency has acquired considerable responsibility and prestige since World War II (Nelson, 1988), and most of the vice-presidential nominees in the postwar period have brought more governmental experience to the ticket than their running mates (Nelson, 1989: 186).

Today the vice-presidential nomination is decided by one vote, that of the presidential nominee (Wayne, 1980: 122). In 1988 Dukakis announced his choice of Senator Lloyd Bentsen of Texas five days before the Atlanta convention and one week before his own nomination. A poll released the previous day showed Bentsen trailing Jackson, Nunn, Glenn, and Gore in the preferences of Democratic delegates for second place on the ticket (*New York Times*, 1988a). The views of Republican delegates mattered even less in Bush's choice of Senator J. Danforth Quayle as his running mate. Bush revealed the choice only two days before his own nomination but nearly two weeks after a *New York Times* poll of Republican delegates (*New York Times*, 1988b), in which Quayle was not even listed as a possible choice.

It is doubtful, however, that such polls either reflect serious deliberation on the part of delegates or represent the full range of preference within a party. Pomper's case (1966: 166–67) against letting conventions select vice-presidential nominees has lost none of its force over the years:

> In regard to the vice-presidency, the convention is virtually unstructured.
> No primary contests or other significant measurements of public support
> are available and few delegates have given any prolonged thought to the ques-
> tion. A free choice in these circumstances cannot be described as truly dem-

ocratic or representative of the wishes of the party or the electorate. A free choice may be only the expression of a transient mood on the part of the delegates. The result may be unfortunate, bringing the nomination of a candidate who is repugnant to major factions in the party, adds little strength to the ticket, and disagrees with the presidential candidate on policy questions. There may be further unfortunate results if the ticket is elected. Then the new president will be in a situation where [the vice-president] owes no obligation to him for his nomination . . . [and] may therefore oppose the president's policies with relative impunity.

Thanks to the post-primaries campaign waged by Jesse Jackson in 1988, the Democratic vice-presidential nomination became a major issue well before the Atlanta convention. Immediately after the primaries ended, Jackson began hinting that he was entitled to second place on the ticket. Soon he was proclaiming his availability at every opportunity, exhorting supporters to "keep hope alive" and feeding the press warnings of convention floor fights unless given the nod. At one point Jackson even spoke of taking the platform debate outside the convention hall, where, he said, network cameras would surely follow (Dionne, 1988). And, in yet another turn of the media screw, Jackson proclaimed he would travel to Atlanta in a bus caravan packed with supporters and journalists. Of the seven buses eventually departing Chicago, six were filled with reporters and television crews (Germond and Witcover, 1989: 345).

Dukakis did not ask Jackson to be on the ticket, and, owing to a communications mishap, Jackson learned of Bentsen's designation from a reporter before Dukakis could reach him. A visibly miffed Jackson took his "Rainbow Express" to Atlanta, where his complaints preoccupied the press for the convention's first two days. At one point it was even suggested that former President Jimmy Carter mediate between Jackson and Dukakis, a proposal promptly rejected by Dukakis. Unity of a sort was attained when Dukakis and Jackson bypassed party officials to revise 1992 delegate-selection rules.[14]

In passing over Jackson, Dukakis eschewed a traditional strategy of vice-presidential selection—making peace with another faction in the same party (Pomper, 1966: 159). Picking Bentsen, however, comported with other stock stratagems. No Democrat has won the White House in this century without carrying Texas, and it was thought Bentsen might steal the Lone Star State away from Bush, having once beaten him in a Senate race there. Bentsen's positions on some issues were expected to increase the ticket's appeal to conservative Democrats, and his Senate service compensated for Dukakis's Washington inexperience.

The reasons behind Quayle's selection are less apparent. Indiana was dependably Republican without Quayle on the ticket, nobody viewed him as a surrogate for any of Bush's defeated rivals, GOP conservatives hardly regarded him as their spokesman, and he impressed few party insiders as ready to assume the awesome responsibilities of the presidency. According to Germond and Witcover (1989: 387), Bush picked Quayle mainly for his youth and congressional experience. It also appears that Quayle was the only finalist not to arouse strong opposition from one or more Bush advisors. Bush probably thought Quayle would be more of a "team player" than Dole or Kemp. In any event, the choice immediately came under intense media scrutiny, and initial doubts arising from all this publicity were compounded by Quayle's weaknesses as a campaigner and debater. Nelson (1989: 190) avows that Quayle cost Bush several million votes on election day.

Approving the Platform

According to Shafer (1988), the contemporary national convention has become an extension of the primaries, with defeated rivals fighting for their causes right through final votes on the platform. Thus was the struggle prolonged by Edward Kennedy in 1980, Jackson and Hart in 1984, and Jackson again in 1988, even though the nomination of Carter, Mondale, and Dukakis was certain in each instance. Each defeated rival demanded, and was granted, major rules and platform concessions. Each demanded, and got, prime time on television to repeat his campaign themes and promote his own future. Indeed, Hart and Jackson effectively launched their 1988 campaigns with their 1984 convention speeches. Finally, all three conventions were consumed by extensive negotiations between the victorious and defeated campaigns, thus reducing the time spent in celebrating party unity.

With only the pro forma trappings of nomination left to the national conventions, it may be true that losing candidates now compensate by contesting the platform or rules. On the other hand, it is well to remember that the most divisive platform battles in the history of either party occurred during the "brokered convention" era of 1832–1952. Indeed, no platform fight since 1968 has matched the ferocity or importance of Democratic clashes over slavery in 1860, a bi-metallic currency in 1896, or the Ku Klux Klan in 1924. Each struggle exposed deep divisions in the party and presaged disaster in the general election.

Reacting to stock complaints that the Democrats had become the party of "special interests," and hoping to forestall platform fights like those of the past two conventions, DNC Chairman Paul Kirk campaigned hard for an uncommonly brief and general 1988 platform. This strategy succeeded for the most part, though Jackson supporters were able to reword some planks during Platform Committee deliberations. Even so, the committee rebuffed Jackson language calling for higher taxes on corporations and the wealthy, a no-first-use pledge on nuclear weapons, and Palestinian self-determination (Elving, 1988: 1797). Jackson supporters moved the tax and no-first-use planks again at the convention but lost on both issues.[15] Jackson supporters then withdrew the Palestinian plank, as promised in previous negotiations with the Dukakis camp. Dukakis operatives won still another victory by holding the platform debate too early in the day for prime-time television.

In sharp contrast, the Republicans drafted and approved, with relatively little debate and dissension, 104 pages of highly specific proposals on everything from "the right of gun ownership" to energy policies for coal, oil, natural gas, and nuclear power. This document and the manner in which it was adopted attested to the GOP's unity in 1988.

Despite the varying length and specificity of the two platforms, differences were readily apparent on almost every issue where the Democrats took a clear stand. The Democratic position on abortion was that "the fundamental right of reproductive choice should be guaranteed regardless of ability to pay" (Kirk, 1988a: 3) while the Republicans stressed the "fundamental right to life" of the unborn child "which cannot be infringed" (Republican National Convention, hereafter cited as RNC, 1988: 31). The Democrats called for affirmative action to eradicate the "lingering effects of discrimination" through goals, timetables, and procurement set-asides (Kirk, 1988a: 4) while the Republicans promised equal opportunity without "dictating the results of fair competition" or resorting to "discriminatory quota systems and preferential treatment" (RNC, 1988: 31). The Democrats wanted to terminate contra aid (Kirk, 1988a: 7) while Republicans called for humanitarian and military assistance to help topple Nicaragua's "totalitarian regime" (RNC, 1988: 74). Finally, the Democrats branded South Africa "a uniquely repressive regime" and called for replacing the "failed policy of constructive engagement" with economic sanctions, including withdrawal of all American corporations (Kirk, 1988a: 7). The Republicans denounced apartheid as "evil" yet maintained that pressuring the South African government would not advance black economic progress. They also tacitly condemned the African National Congress by decrying violence against "innocent blacks and whites from whatever source" (RNC, 1988: 85–86).

Though not binding on presidents or members of Congress, platforms should not be dismissed as empty rhetoric. A careful study of every major party platform between 1944 and 1976 (Pomper and Lederman, 1980: 129–53) found them specific enough to guide citizens in casting rational votes. Moreover, both parties have tried to make good on their promises through legislation and executive orders (Fishel, 1985).

Lights, Cameras, Unity?

Hardly least important among the convention's secondary functions is celebrating party unity, especially after a divisive spring of primary and caucus battles. This ritual has steadily grown in importance since the advent of televised conventions and the emergence of the present nominating process.

Television was generally unappreciated in party circles when the networks won grudging permission to cover both conventions in 1952. According to a leading network executive of that time, only the Democrats allowed construction of floor platforms for head-on shots of the rostrum, and neither convention was willing to set aside much room for camera crews (Mickelson, 1989: 33). Attitudes quickly changed when party leaders learned that more than 55 million Americans had watched at least some convention coverage and that more than 60 percent of all television households had tuned in at peak periods. Moreover, the number of households with at least one television set increased from 34 percent in 1952 to 97 percent in 1976 (Kessel, 1988: 332–33). After 1952, conventions progressively became made-for-television events, with demonstrations and speeches abbreviated for the sake of easily bored audiences and with major speakers scheduled for prime time. A "bifurcated convention" has resulted, according to Shafer (1988: 297), "with one convention on site and another (via television) at home, each powerfully different from the other."

Perhaps the functional diminution of on-site conventions has carried over into a reduction of audience interest in the television spectacle. In any event, ABC, CBS, and NBC ended gavel-to-gavel coverage in the 1980s, and the percentage of voters deciding on presidential candidates at convention time consistently declined—from 35 percent in 1952 to less than 17 percent in 1984.[16]

Neither trend, however, has lessened the extraordinary efforts of victorious candidates to choreograph pageants of party unity for the millions still watching. No nominee-apparent wants another 1968 convention with its hours of prime-time fratricide. Such conflict, according to Martin P. Wattenberg (1988:27–28), swells the audience and extends broadcast time for conventions. In every instance between 1964 and 1984, whichever convention got the most television exposure also nominated the losing ticket.

The belated celebration of Democratic unity began in 1988 with Jackson's prime-time oration on July 19, when he spoke of finding common ground and briefly praised Dukakis. According to preliminary estimates, this speech attracted about half of that night's television audience, a very high rating (Boyer, 1988). Dukakis ended the convention on an upbeat note two nights later with probably the best speech of his career, and was promptly rewarded with a temporary seventeen-point lead over Bush in the CBS/*New York Times* poll (Farah and Klein, 1989: 105).

Though Quayle's problems dominated much of the GOP convention's television coverage, Republican unity was never in doubt. Though divisive, the primaries had produced a winner early enough for Bush's rivals to reconcile themselves to his nomination. However much they wanted to be on the ticket (Goldman and Mathews, 1989: 316–17), neither Dole nor Kemp publicly pressured Bush, nor did they demand concessions as the price of supporting him. Rather, in a carefully staged pageant of party unity, Bush's rivals endorsed the ticket with seeming enthusiasm, and the nominee polished off the event with a well-crafted acceptance speech. The traditional bounce in the polls soon followed, giving Bush a lead over Dukakis that he never relinquished.

Whither the Convention?

Whatever happens to the national convention depends on what happens to the rest of the presidential nominating process. If reforms were left to ordinary voters, recently published survey data indicate that most features of the present process, including conventions, would be retained.

One study in this vein found relatively little dissatisfaction with the current primary system except for concerns about the costs of campaigning and media influence on public perceptions of candidates and outcomes. Using Gallup survey data collected in January 1988 for the Times Mirror Company, Michael Traugott and Margaret Petrella (1989: 347) concluded that, overall, "the population feels that primaries are a good way of choosing the best-qualified nominees." Approval, moreover, increases with political activism and partisanship.

Satisfaction was somewhat less pronounced in the results of a post election poll of 1988 voters and nonvoters by the *New York Times* and CBS News, but the most serious complaints in this survey pertained to the length of the nominating process. Huge majorities of Bush voters, Dukakis voters, and nonvoters wanted nominations decided in less time. Thus 73 percent of all respondents wanted to shorten the process "to just a *few* [emphasis in original] days." Seventy-two percent of all Bush voters preferred regional or other grouped mega-primaries, as compared to 78 percent of all Dukakis voters. Similarly, when requested to choose between "one single national primary day" and the present system of "many different primary days," 70 percent picked the former. Bush and Dukakis voters differed by only one percent—71 to 72—on this issue. However, when asked to choose between "electing delegates to a national convention, as we do now," and a "single national primary for each party to pick its presidential candidate with *no* [emphasis in original] convention," the total subsample of voters divided evenly—47 percent for convention and 47 percent for national primaries. This breakdown masked substantial differences between Bush and Dukakis voters: 52 percent of the Bush group favored conventions while the same percentage of Dukakis voters preferred national primaries (CBS News/*New York Times,* 1988: 24–25). Evidently millions of Americans still perceive a useful purpose in presidential nominating conventions, however diminished.

If elites are to force major changes in the nominating process, such reforms are unlikely to come from Congress, which has become a veritable cemetery for national and regional primary schemes. Between 1911 and 1980, according to James W. Ceaser (1982: 118), more than 275 such bills were introduced in Congress; few got out of committee, and none came close to passing either house.[17]

No measure took deadlier aim at the nominating convention than the national direct primary. First proposed in Congress in 1911, advocated by Woodrow Wilson in 1913, and overwhelmingly supported in polls since, national primary proposals would vest the choice of presidential nominees directly in each party's registered electorate. Depending on the particular bill, any candidate winning a plurality or majority of the primary vote would become the nominee. If no candidate won enough votes for outright nomination, the race would be resolved in a runoff between the two leading contestants. Under legislation sponsored by Congressman Albert Quie of Minnesota in 1977, the same method would be used to choose vice-presidential nominees.

Once championed as the best way of wresting presidential nominations from party bosses, the national primary idea lost most of its fervor with the reforms of the 1970s. Experience with the present, primary-driven system has left many a pundit unreceptive to another massive dose of democracy in presidential nominating politics. No one disputes that a national direct primary system would have momentous consequences for both major parties.[18] It would reduce conventions to televised pep rallies, hardly worth the trouble and expense of selecting delegates.

Less drastic consequences for conventions would follow enactment of any of the bills introduced in Congress to create a process of regional or grouped primaries. Like national direct primary legislation, such measures have quietly expired in committee. The 1977 bill cosponsored by Republican Senators Robert Packwood of Oregon, Mark Hatfield of Oregon, and Ted Stevens of Alaska, for example, was a reincarnation of similar bills killed in 1972, 1973, and 1975 (Ranney, 1978: 5–6).

No more successful in 1977, the Packwood bill allowed each state to decide whether to participate in one of five regional primaries. The Federal Election Commission (FEC) would set the date for each event, in which only a party's registered voters would take part. Delegates in each participating state would be allocated proportionally to every candidate winning at least 5 percent of the preference vote. All delegates chosen in this manner would be bound to vote for their candidates on the first two convention ballots, unless their candidate received less than 20 percent on the first ballot, or they were released. Each convention would decide its own procedure for vice-presidential nominations (Ranney, 1978: 6).

Other proposals, like that sponsored in 1977 by Congressman Richard Ottinger of New York, would require every state to participate in one of five regional primaries scheduled by the FEC. The other main provisions in Ottinger's bill were identical to those in the Packwood-Hatfield-Stevens measure.

Ranney (1978: 23) argues that the probability of the convention's actually selecting the nominee would be higher under a voluntary than a mandatory regional-primary plan. In neither instance, however, does he regard the failure of regional primaries to pick a winner as very likely. Conversely, James W. Davis (1983: 230) warns that even a voluntary system with nearly full state participation could lead to convention deadlock, which the absence of brokers would make difficult to resolve. Presumably the only brokers at the convention would be the candidates themselves, at least until the second ballot, and, given the low threshold in either plan's allocation of delegates, the number of candidates still in contention might be considerable. The upshot, in Davis's opinion, would be a return of divisive, multiballot conventions. Much would obviously depend on how many states took part in a voluntary plan, how many delegates were at stake in each regional primary, the generosity of FEC financing, and on myriad other factors peculiar to each race.

Such scenarios are almost certain to remain speculative since the enactment of any regional primary scheme is most unlikely. Too many interests and traditions are offended. On the other hand, a grouped primary process may well evolve out of the independent decisions of state legislatures and party organizations. The close cooperation among southern states in building their 1988 regional primary on Super Tuesday is perhaps a harbinger of future events. A midwestern primary held later in the spring is still another possibility. Clustering of primaries to this extent would not shorten exhibition seasons, but it would bring swifter closure to nominating races, especially on the Republican side. And, in the improbable event of no clear winner emerging from such mega-events, existing rules allow either party's delegates sufficient discretion to choose a nominee on the second or third ballot.

In contrast to the evolution sketched just above, several sweeping plans recently offered by academics and scholarly politicians seemingly have little chance of adoption. The least likely is a 1980 plan drafted by former North Carolina Governor (now U.S. Senator) Terry Sanford, which calls for selection of uncommitted delegates without regard to voting in non-binding presidential "beauty contests." Sanford's objective is not so much to turn back the clock as to create Burkean trustees, a role few delegates enjoyed during the brokered-convention era. As Davis (1983: 241–42) rightly points out, Sanford makes impossible demands on too many players—candidates (who would pressure delegates mercilessly), delegates (who could not ignore polls and primary results), and parties (which probably would not scrap state and national rules).

Similarly, a proposal to hold national nominating conventions before national direct primaries (Cronin and Loevy, 1983) has attracted little interest outside academic circles. Like all other radical plans, this one would require every state to alter its presidential contest and possibly the timing of other nominating races as well. Though it would indeed restore the nominating function of conventions, the plan is predicated on an assumption that this is what most party leaders want. Conventional wisdom holds that most party leaders are dissatisfied with the present process, and so they may be, but are they agreed on what should replace it? More to the point, is there strong support in either party for strengthening conventions? Our best guess is that most party elites regard Sanford's approach as both infeasible and undesirable. Even the Cronin-Loevy plan, which might interest some Democrats, probably would be unacceptable to Republicans.

For better or worse, the present system of direct democracy, leavened with state tradition, is likely to remain relatively intact, with continued tinkering by state and national parties. If Democrats truly regard the present system as too protracted and divisive, they can abandon proportional representation for winner-take-all rules and encourage state parties to participate in several mega-primaries. If, however, they adhere to the Dukakis-Jackson agreement and make their process even more proportionally representative, then the contemporary belief that conventions no longer matter may be proven wrong. Republicans at this writing appear more satisfied with their process. Thus conventions are likely to survive into the next century, at the very least performing important albeit secondary functions in the presidential nominating process.

Notes

1. The problem Hamilton had helped avert in 1788 occurred in 1800, when Jefferson and Aaron Burr received the same number of electoral votes, thus necessitating the first House contingent election. The Twelfth Amendment, ratified in 1804, eliminated the chance of a recurrence by separating balloting for president and vice-president. It also required a majority of electoral votes for vice-president and applied the same age and citizenship restrictions to the vice-president as required of the president.

2. The caucus infuriated Adams by nominating Charles Cotesworth Pinckney and himself for president without giving preference to one or the other. See McCormick (1982: 63–64).

3. Chase and McCormick put the number of delegates attending the 1832 convention at 320 while Remini reports 334.

4. For detailed accounts of the 1924 Democratic convention, see Burner (1975: 103–41) and Murray (1976).

5. The cumbersome term "delegate votes" must be used for the Democrats because their state parties traditionally sent more delegates than they had votes to cast at the convention. Something of a precedent had been established at the first Democratic convention in 1832, and in any event, a handsome way of rewarding party service was to make the stalwart a delegate to the national convention. Thus Democratic conventions adapted to fractional voting. In 1940, however, Mississippi pushed tradition to its limit by sending fifty-four delegates to cast two votes. The convention responded by ruling that no future delegate could cast less than a half vote (Key, 1964: 405).

6. We are indebted to James W. Davis for making this point in correspondence with the authors, December 14, 1989.

7. The Democratic formula for 1988, as described in Kirk (1988b: 1):

$$A = 1/2 \left(\frac{SDV\ '76 + SDV\ '80 + SDV\ '84}{113,889,380} + \frac{SEV}{538} \right) \times 3,000$$

where "A" = Allocation factor, "SDV" = State Democratic Vote, and "SEV" = State Electoral Vote. Fractions of .5 or higher were rounded up to the next highest integer.

8. According to Davis (1983: 58–59), on whom this account chiefly relies, each state won by the GOP in the preceding presidential election received 4.5 delegates plus 60 percent of the state's electoral vote total, rounded upward if necessary.

9. The *New York Times* delegate surveys, on which table 8.2 is based, did not provide occupational information for the registered-voter samples. The occupational data for delegates, however, affirm the preponderance of lawyers, other professionals, executives, and managers one would expect. In 1988, 58

and 63 percent respectively of the Democratic and Republican delegates fit into the above groups.

10. See Reiter (1985: 62) for the percentage of black delegates participating in Democratic and Republican conventions from 1952 through 1984. Reiter shows that the proportion of black Democratic delegates doubled between 1964 and 1968 and tripled between 1968 and 1972, from 5 to 15 percent. In 1984, 18 percent of all Democratic delegates were black. At no point during this period did the percentage of black Democratic delegates match or exceed the percentage of black Democratic identifiers in the electorate. Blacks never made up more than 4 percent of the delegates at Republican conventions during the same period. If the standard for representation is the percentage of black identifiers in the electorate, however, blacks were overrepresented at every Republican convention after 1964.

11. Gender quotas did not originate with the national party. As early as 1952, Florida law required that half of all delegates selected in its presidential primaries be women (David, et al., 1961: 232–33).

12. These preliminary data are part of an ongoing study of party elites that began with the 1974 Democratic midterm conference, and, since 1980, has included samples of delegates to both national conventions. In 1988, as in past years, questionnaires were mailed to systematic random samples of delegates immediately after their respective conventions in July and August. One follow-up was done in the fall. Ultimately, questionnaires were returned by 260 Democrats and 212 Republicans, for response rates of 35 and 32 percent, respectively.

13. All differences were statistically significant at <.001, and Cramer's V coeffiicients ranged from .44 to .75.

14. Asked about his role in the negotiations over 1992 rules changes, DNC Chairman Kirk disclosed that he had been excluded from the session at Jackson's insistence and had learned of the agreement only after it had been concluded. Kirk decided not to protest formally after being informed by Dukakis operatives that both sides had instructed their delegates to approve the abolition of bonus and loophole primaries and the reduction of the number of super-delegates. Kirk disclosed this information at a conference on presidential selection at the College of William and Mary on November 10, 1989.

15. Pearsonian correlations indicate that the delegates were highly consistent in their voting on the two contested planks and in supporting Dukakis or Jackson for the nomination. The correlation between opposing a tax increase and voting for Dukakis was .965; it was .970 between opposing a no-first-use pledge and Dukakis support. Almost all Jackson supporters voted for the tax increase and no-first-use planks, hence Pearsonian coefficients of .977 and .985. All relationships were significant at <.001.

16. National Election Study (NES) data for 1952–80 are reported in Davis (1983: 197); 1984 percentage calculated from the NES 1984 codebook.

17. Earlier, Ranney (1978: 1) noted that only 3 of more than 250 measures introduced between 1911 and 1977 ever got to the floor for a vote — in 1947, 1950, and 1952 — and that none came close to passing.

18. The consequences of a national direct primary process for both major parties would be enormous. See Ranney (1978), Ceaser (1982: 113–53), and Davis (1983: 216–44) for assessments for the strengths and shortcomings of numerous reform proposals, including national direct primaries.

References

Abramowitz, Alan I., and Walter J. Stone. 1985. *Nomination Politics: Party Activists and Presidential Choice*. New York: Praeger.

Baer, Denise L., and David A. Bositis. 1988. *Elite Cadres and Party Coalitions: Representing the Public in Party Politics*. Westport, Conn.: Greenwood Press.

Boyer, Peter J. 1988. "Convention Is Big TV Hit, with Jackson High Point." *New York Times* (July 21): 10.

Burner, David. 1975. *The Politics of Provincialism: The Democratic Party in Transition 1918–1932*. New York: W. W. Norton.

Carleton, William G. 1957. "The Revolution in the Presidential Nominating Convention." *Political Science Quarterly* 72 (June): 224–40.

———. 1988b. Republican Delegate Survey. July 22–August 4 summary (offset).

CBS/*New York Times* News. Post-Election Survey, November 10–16, summary (offset).

Ceaser, James W. 1982. *Reforming the Reforms: A Critical Analysis of the Presidential Selection Process*. Cambridge, Mass.: Ballinger.

Chase, James S. 1973. *Emergence of the Presidential Nominating Convention 1789–1832*. Urbana: University of Illinois Press.

Commission on Presidential Nominations and Party Structure. 1978. *Openness, Participation, and Party-Building: Reforms for a Stronger Democratic Party*. Washington, D.C.: Democratic National Committee.

Congressional Quarterly's Guide to U.S. Elections. 2d ed. 1985. Washington, D.C.: Congressional Quarterly Press.

Cronin, Thomas, and Robert Loevy. 1983. "The Case for a National Pre Primary Convention Plan." *Public Opinion* 5 (December–January). Reprinted in *Analyzing the Presidency*, ed. Robert E. DiClerico. 2d ed. Guilford, Conn.: Dushkin Publishing Group, 1989.

Crotty, William. 1983. *Party Reform*. New York: Longman.

David, Paul T., Ralph M. Goldman, and Richard C. Bain. 1964. *The Politics of National Party Conventions*. Rev. ed. New York: Vintage Books.

Davis, James W. 1980. *Presidential Primaries: Road to the White House*. Westport, Conn.: Greenwood Press.

———. 1983. *National Conventions in an Age of Party Reform*. Westport, Conn.: Greenwood Press.

Dionne, E. J. 1988. "Jackson Says He May Leave Hall to Speak Outside the Convention." *New York Times* (July 9): 1.

Elving, Ronald D. 1988. "Hoping to Attract More Voters, Democrats Offer Fewer Words." *Congressional Quarterly Weekly Report* 46 (July 2): 1797–98.

Farah, Barbara G., and Ethel Klein. 1989. "Public Opinion Trends." In Gerald L. Pomper et al., *The Election of 1988: Reports and Interpretations*. Chatham, N.J.: Chatham House.

Fishel, Jeff. 1985. *Presidents and Promises*. Washington, D.C.: Congressional Quarterly Press.

Gallup, George, Jr. 1989. *The Gallup Poll: Public Opinion 1988*. Wilmington, Del.: Scholarly Resources.

Germond, Jack W., and Jules Witcover. 1989. *Whose Broad Stripes and Bright Stars? The Trivial Pursuit of the Presidency 1988*. New York: Warner Books,

Goldman, Peter, and Tom Mathews. 1989. *The Quest for the Presidency*. New York: Touchstone Books.

Jackson, John S., III, Barbara L. Brown, and David Bositis. 1982. "Herbert McClosky and Friends Revisited: 1980 Democratic and Republican Party Elites Compared to the Mass Public." *American Politics Quarterly* 10 (April): 158–80.

Jackson, John S., III, Jesse C. Brown, and Barbara L. Brown. 1978. "Recruitment, Representation, and Political Values: The 1976 Democratic Convention Delegates." *American Politics Quarterly* 6 (April): 187–212.

Kessel, John H. 1988. *Presidential Campaign Politics*. 3d. ed. Chicago: Dorsey Press.

Key, V. O., Jr. 1964. *Politics, Parties, and Pressure Groups*. 5th ed. New York: Thomas Y. Crowell.

Kirk, Paul G., Jr. 1988a. *The 1988 Democratic National Platform*. Washington, D.C.: Democratic National Committee.

———. 1988b. *Final Call for the 1988 Democratic National Convention*. Washington, D.C.: Democratic National Committee.

Kirkpatrick, Jeane. 1976. *The New Presidential Elite: Men and Women in National Politics*. New York: Russell Sage Foundation.

Ladd, Everett C. 1977. *Where Have All the Voters Gone?* New York: W. W. Norton.

McClosky, Herbert, Paul J. Hoffman, and Rosemary O'Hara. 1960. "Issue Conflict and Consensus among Party Leaders and Followers." *American Political Science Review* 54 (June): 406–27.

McCormick, Richard P. 1982. *The Presidential Game: The Origins of American Presidential Politics*. New York: Oxford University Press.

Mickelson, Sig. 1989. *From Whistle Stop to Sound Bite: Four Decades of Politics and Television*. New York: Praeger.

Miller, Warren E. 1988. *Without Consent: Mass-Elite Linkages in Presidential Politics*. Lexington, Ky.: University Press of Kentucky.

Murray, Robert K. 1976. *The 103rd Ballot: Democrats and the Disaster in Madison Square Garden*. New York: Harper & Row.

Nelson, Michael. 1988. *A Heartbeat Away*. New York: Priority Press.

———. 1989. "Constitutional Aspects of the Elections." In *The Elections of 1988*, ed. Michael Nelson. Washington, D.C.: Congressional Quarterly Press.

New York Times. 1988a. Democratic Delegate Survey. June 20–July 12 summary (offset).

Novak, Robert D. 1965. *The Agony of the G.O.P. 1964*. New York: Macmillan.

Polsby, Nelson W. 1983. *Consequences of Party Reform*. New York: Oxford University Press.

Pomper, Gerald. 1966. *Nominating the President: The Politics of Convention Choice.* New York: W. W. Norton.

———. 1979. "New Rules and New Games in Presidential Nominations." *Journal of Politics* 41 (August): 784–805.

———. 1988. "The Presidential Nominations." In Gerald M. Pomper et al., *The Election of 1988*: Reports and Interpretations. Chatham, N.J.: Chatham House.

Pomper, Gerald M., and Susan S. Lederman. 1980. *Elections in America: Control and Influence in Democratic Politics.* 2d. ed. New York: Longman.

Ranney, Austin, 1975. *Curing the Mischiefs of Faction: Party Reform in America.* Berkeley: University of California Press.

———. 1978. *The Federalization of Presidential Primaries.* Washington, D.C.: American Enterprise Institute for Public Policy Research.

Reiter, Howard. 1985. *Selecting the President: The Nominating Process in Transition.* Philadelphia: University of Pennsylvania Press.

Remini, Robert V. 1981. *Andrew Jackson and the Course of American Freedom, 1822–1832.* New York: Harper & Row.

Republican National Convention. 1988. *Republican Platform: An American Vision for Our Children and Our Future.* Washington, D.C.: Republican National Committee.

Shafer, Bryon E. 1983. *Quiet Revolution: The Struggle for the Democratic Party and the Shaping of Post-Reform Politics.* New York: Russell Sage Foundation.

———. 1988. *Bifurcated Politics: Evolution and Reform in the National Party Convention.* Cambridge, Mass.: Harvard University Press.

Soule, John W., and Wilma E. McGrath. 1975. "A Comparative Study of Presidential Nomination Conventions: The Democrats of 1968 and 1972." *American Journal of Political Science* 19 (August): 501–19.

Stone, Walter J., and Alan I. Abramowitz. 1983. "Winning May Not Be Everything, But It's More Than We Thought: Presidential Party Activists in 1980." *American Political Science Review* 77 (December): 945–56.

Traugott, Michael W., and Margaret Petrella. 1989. "Public Evaluations of the Presidential Nominating Process." *Political Behavior* 11 (December): 335–52.

Wattenberg, Martin P. 1988. "The 1988 and 1960 Elections Compared: What a Difference Candidate-Centered Politics Makes." Unpublished paper presented at Annual Meeting of American Political Science Association, Washington, D.C. (September 1–4).

Wayne, Stephen J. 1980. *The Road to the White House.* New York: St. Martin's Press.

Wildavsky, Aaron. 1965. "The Goldwater Phenomenon: Purists, Politicians, and the Two-Party System." *Review of Politics* 27 (July): 386–413.

Wills, Gary, ed. 1982. *The Federalist Papers*, by Alexander Hamilton, James Madison, and John Jay. New York: Bantam.

Wilson, James Q. 1962. *The Amateur Democrat.* Chicago: University of Chicago Press.

9. Evaluating the New Nominating System: Thoughts after 1988 from a Governance Perspective

W. Wayne Shannon

There is no better way to grasp the extent to which the American presidential nominating system has been transformed over the last quarter century than to consult V. O. Key, Jr.'s *Politics, Parties and Pressure Groups* (1964). Key was the foremost student of American parties and elections in his time, and his text dominated the field. Here, as in all of his work, he was concerned not only with what political scientists today call empirical theory but with the quality of governance and the achievement of institutional arrangements that permit ordinary citizens to understand and influence the public order.

Key's account of the nominating system was not idiosyncratic. So many political scientists taught it to students all over the country precisely because it was the best available summary of a vast monographic literature on presidential nominations. Now, it will be immediately apparent to everyone that it is hopelessly outdated. As a basis for developing a contemporary nomination strategy, it would be a prescription for disaster.

"The convention," Key tells us, "operates flexibly with a range of freedom that enables it to elevate to leadership men it judges to be suited to the needs of the time . . . " (Key, 1964: 433). He describes the convention as a meeting of professional state and local party leaders largely motivated to select candidates who will promote party unity and maximize the chance of victory in the general election. Key, along with most other students of American political parties in his time, saw the presidential nominating convention as a highly important centripetal force in American politics. Fortunately, he thought, a method congenial

to the separation-of-powers system had been found "through which party leaders, dispersed over a nation of continental proportions, could negotiate sufficient agreement to *maintain parties capable of governing* through the presidential system" (Key, 1964: 398 [emphasis added]).

In the party of the reeligible incumbent there is little need for preconvention activity, for "by custom a president is entitled to a second nomination. . . . [I]t is quixotic to challenge him" (Key, 1964:399). Candidates need not announce early, or in many cases announce at all; there is no need for a public preconvention campaign because their managers can quietly seek support from party leaders throughout the nation. Winning primaries is by no means an essential element of successful candidacy. Whether to enter them at all is a "vexing question" for campaign managers since candidates must weigh the risk of antagonizing numerous "favorite sons" of the various states and regions of a sectionally divided polity. "Dark horses" may emerge at the convention, if the supporters of rival front-runners deadlock the convention (Key, 1964: 402–4). Key's summary of the role of the primaries is particularly noteworthy:

> While the primary has modified nominating practices, it has not produced conventions of automata that mechanically record the preferences expressed by the voters at home. Party organizations in many states retain a fairly high degree of autonomy despite the primaries. Candidates for the presidency choose not to enter many primaries. State delegations often retain their freedom of choice by commitment to favorite sons through the primary as before; the voters may even vote for uncommitted delegations. Indeed, for the convention to be capable of achieving its broad objective of developing party consensus on a candidate, delegations must retain a range of discretion. (1964: 411–12)

Although it now seems clear that the old nominating politics was undergoing subtle transformation long before Key prepared the last edition of his classic text (e.g., Reiter, 1985), it is an indisputable fact that as recently as 1968 the presidential nomination *could* still be won by the rules of the game that Key described. Although there would soon be a heavy price to pay for it, Hubert Humphrey's managers gathered enough delegates to give him a first-ballot victory at the Democratic convention without entering so much as a single primary. Nothing of the sort could possibly happen today, nor could it have happened in any one of the five nominating rounds since 1968.

Although the exact rules of the game have varied in every election cycle since 1968, there is an essential underlying structure to the new system

that stands in sharp contrast to the old system described by Key. The new system dictates that delegates to the national conventions be won in a long string of primaries and caucuses open to wide participation. Key could argue that the advent of primary elections in the early 1900s had not essentially changed the old nominating system because primaries had not (despite the hopes of progressive reformers) eliminated the central role of traditional partisan elites at the convention. The elimination of this role is surely the essential result of the changes made after 1968. New party rules, changes in federal and state election laws, and new norms surrounding the nominating process have fundamentally altered the delegate-selection process, displacing the leaders of traditional party organizations and allowing individual candidates to win large majorities of bound delegates to every subsequent convention.

Whatever else the functions of convention delegates may be in the new system, selecting the party's standard-bearer for the presidential race is not among them. There is nothing for the convention to do but legitimize the outcome of the preconvention campaign. In the new system, for better or worse, nothing remains of the "range of discretion" Key considered so important in 1964.

What we have here is a familiar story. Just as we think we have understood something, it changes. As we step back to gain some perspective on this transformation of the nominating phase of the presidential selection process, we should now be able to see that the process that Key and others (e.g., Rossiter, 1960a, 1960b) understood as a fixed feature of the American party system only a few years ago was part of a much more dynamic picture. We should now view it as part of what Richard P. McCormick has called "The Party Game" (1982), a distinct method of presidential selection that best operated in the hundred or so years between Polk and Truman. The old system of nomination by powerful state and local traditional party organizations that was the essence of "The Party Game" lasted a long time, but as Howard Reiter (1985) and others (e.g., Shafer, 1988) have shown, it was being eroded by social and technological changes well before its final delegitimization at the disastrous Democratic convention of 1968. The current game, which I shall call "The Primary Game," is its successor, and its rules as of 1988 are examined in detail in the foregoing chapters of this volume.

My purpose in this chapter is not to contribute new data on the workings of the new nominating system since 1972 but to consider how well it has served in our continuing national quest for successful democratic governance. I will provide a normative perspective on what has been gained and lost in the move from the old to the new system. Such an exercise will,

I hope, be useful in bringing the discussion of American nominating politics up to date and in clarifying options for the future.

Functions of the Nominating System

What should we expect from a good nomination system? What criteria can we employ to evaluate the performance of the old system as it worked under the rules of "The Party Game" and the new system as it has operated since 1972? I propose five criteria:

1. Insofar as possible, the system should produce candidates whose experience and temperament equip them to fulfill the high expectations of the modern presidency. The imperatives of the presidency call for extraordinary personal performance. We should expect the nominating system to put forward those who are best qualified to do the job.

2. The system should promote coalition building in the parties rather than magnifying existing intraparty divisions or creating divisions that otherwise would not exist. It should encourage a view of national governance as cooperative rather than individualistic.

3. The system should assist the parties' aggregation or "packaging" functions so voters better understand the broad options offered for future policy. The system should help to lower the information costs that citizens have to pay in order to link their preferences to decision-making in Washington.

4. The system should encourage the selection of candidates in both parties who can make a broad appeal to the national electorate.

5. The system should encourage participation in party affairs at all levels. It should certainly not discourage or foreclose participation on the part of any class or category of citizens. But it should not contribute independently to the weakening of political parties as organizations.

Are these the right criteria? The honest answer is that no criteria command general agreement. The best we can do is to state our argument as clearly as possible and try to persuade others to adopt our point of view.

The practiced eye will see that my criteria are greatly influenced by the arguments of those who favor a strong role for political parties in American politics. These arguments were classically stated by such students of American political parties as E. E. Schattschneider (1942), V. O. Key (1964), and Clinton Rossiter (1960a, 1960b), and they continue to influence many contemporary discussions of the nominating system (e.g., Ranney, 1975; Polsby, 1983).[1] True, many other models could be used to evaluate the nominating system, such as the classical republican determination of the framers of the U.S. Constitution to create a "partyless" politics. We could choose the Progressive model with its emphasis above all else on electoral participation intended to limit the role of elected representatives and extragovernmental party organizations. Or we could adopt the "strong democracy" model advocated by Benjamin Barber (1984) and others with its deemphasis of electoral politics and representative government in favor of continual face-to-face activity. In fact, it would not be difficult to demonstrate that each of these models, often without formal articulation, has contributed to the transformation of the presidential nominating process and the larger American party system in recent years. That, however, is not my purpose. It goes without saying that readers in various degrees committed to one or more of these models will find my approach wanting (Crotty, 1983; Nelson, 1987).

My criteria for evaluating the nominating process assume that political parties must play a strong role in the democratic process and that they must be understood as organizations of activists who perform specific political functions, such as formulation of programs, selection of candidates, and conduct of election campaigns. Two lines of reasoning underlie this perspective. The first involves the realistic limits on citizen participation in a large-scale polity. The second stems from the problem of generating leadership and support for national governance through the presidency—a unique American problem posed by the architectural features of our Madisonian Constitution.

Clearly, the criteria I have proposed are premised on a "realist" understanding of large-scale democracy as a process of electoral competition in which voters choose between broad alternatives offered by political parties. Schattschneider argues (and there is a wealth of evidence in subsequent empirical studies of participation in the United States and other Western democracies to back him up) that citizens have neither the time nor the inclination to govern directly. The "zone between the sovereign people and the government . . . is the habitat of political parties" (1942: 15). From this point of view, parties as organizations are useful precisely because they offer alternatives to, and channel information for, citizens who are unable or unwilling to participate constantly at a high level in public affairs.

The thrust of this argument is not that party organizations need to be "machines," or that they must be motivated principally by patronage considerations, but rather that they are organizations with specific functions to perform. Insistence on very high levels of citizen participation in candidate selection and on procedures designed to make all party organizational activities internally democratic in effect denies this functional specificity and raises the danger that the parties' unique contribution to the democratic process will be weakened or lost. It was part of Schattschneider's argument that the virtues of strong parties were not sufficiently appreciated in America. That these virtues are even less apparent to Americans today does not diminish the power of his argument.

The second line of reasoning underlying the criteria proposed here concerns a specifically American problem—how leadership, direction, and coherence can be generated, given the unique Madisonian architecture of the Constitution. It is commonplace for students of comparative government to observe that no other democratic constitution so divides, checks, balances, and fractures the authority of government. This constitutional design, derived from the framers' desire to limit and control the dangerous power of the state, has proved itself a superb instrument for accomplishing that purpose, but it has always begged the question of how a national government so divided could achieve the direction or coherence required to govern.

As the functions of national government have expanded exponentially in this century, we have constantly inflated our expectations of presidential leadership, but in recent years "The Party Game" on which we have relied to support it has seemingly come apart. Key, Rossiter, Schattschneider, and other students of the American party system thought a generation ago that presidential selection provided the "glue" or centripetal force necessary to counter the conflict and stasis inherent in our constitutional design. All saw the nominating convention as a central element of this process. Perhaps they were mistaken. At any rate, we need now to reconsider their logic. The criteria that I propose for evaluating the nominating system are meant to encourage a concern with governance. We should look at the nominating system in terms of its ability to bring direction, coherence, and accountability to national government.

Getting the Right Person: Experience and Personality

A frequent criticism of the present nominating system is that it does not bring forward the most qualified candidates. In every election since 1972 the complaint that "surely we can do better than this" has been widely voiced with respect to the nominees of one or both of the parties. Throughout the 1988 nomination cycle, the press called attention to the "lightweight" quality of the Democratic contenders by dubbing them "the seven dwarfs."

Is there merit to this argument? If it is possible to demonstrate that the nomination system in place since 1972, "The Primary Game," has systematically put forward candidates less fit for the presidency by their experience and personalities than one or more of the earlier systems, there would be good reason to condemn it on this ground. What does the evidence suggest?

The expectations inherent in the modern presidential job description demand an extraordinary combination of skills and personal attributes. Once we understand this, we see where a good many of the conundrums of modern presidential selection originate. We are alone among the world's democracies in demanding so much capacity for leadership from an individual. If, as we expect, the president is to be the symbol of the nation, chief executive, major formulator of foreign and defense policies, party leader, leader of public opinion, chief legislator, economic manager, and so on (Rossiter, 1960b), what manner of person is required? The answer, according to the presidential literature, is that we must have "experienced politicians of extraordinary temperament" (Neustadt, 1960). The skills required to maintain the high "professional reputation" with Washingtonians and popularity with the public that presidents need in order to be successful are inescapably personal, and may even be largely a function of the deep structure of the individual's personality. Since this is fixed by young adulthood and cannot be changed once a president is in office, the right kind of person has to be identified in the process of nomination and election while the wrong kind of person is screened out (Barber, 1985).

If "experienced politicians" are wanted, what is the exact nature of the experience that teaches the skills the presidency requires? What is the right kind of "apprenticeship" for the office? Here, the problem is greatly complicated by basic features of the U.S. Constitution—separation of powers and federalism—and by our uniquely open party system. Whereas parliamentary institutions demand more or less the same apprenticeship from all who hope to ascend to the top (long service in close quarters with partisan colleagues in the national legislature and ministerial experience in the government or the opposition), presidential candidates can come from many different backgrounds—the vice-presidency, either house of Congress, state governorships, the cabinet, or a number of other backgrounds, e.g., the military, national or state courts, or even careers in the private sector (Rose, 1988: 94–102). Does presidential success seem to be correlated with any particular kind of experience? If personality is a key variable in determining presidential performance, can we state with any precision just how it is related to presidential success? If we are unable to provide clear answers to these questions, comparing the performance of our historical nominating systems in finding "the right people" for the presidency cannot produce a very satisfactory result.

Let us look first at the question of experience. We possess little if any reliable knowledge about the relationship of experience or apprenticeship to presidential success. However much we may wish otherwise, we recognize presidential success best *after* the fact, and the modern presidency is so new that we have very few cases to go on. Eliminating Bush because of insufficient evidence, we have nine cases, three of whom were accidental successors to the office. The evidence provided by the ten presidents who have served since 1933 seems baffling. If we assume that Franklin Roosevelt, Truman, Eisenhower, Kennedy, and Reagan were relative successes and that Johnson, Nixon, Ford, and Carter were relative failures, it is certainly not clear what their experience or apprenticeships contributed to their performance in office.

Aside from Bush, the new nominating system has produced only two individuals who have become president, Carter and Reagan. Most presidential scholars would pronounce one a relative failure and the other a success (Jones, 1988), but they had identical apprenticeships—late entry to politics in midlife and service as governor. Were we to go back farther in time for data bearing on experience and presidential success, the picture, I suspect, would not become clearer. There is no evidence that those regarded as "great" presidents have come from any particular background. Nor do the clearest cases of failure or those in-between fit any clear pattern of experience or apprenticeship.

Nevertheless, it is still possible to ask whether our nominating systems have systematically produced candidates with different kinds of experience or apprenticeship for the presidency. The answer is that only the system of congressional caucus nomination used from 1800 to 1824 has reliably produced candidates with a particular kind of background. That system, the only one that has operated more or less like the candidate selection procedures of the world's parliamentary democracies, chose insiders with predictable apprenticeships in national government. In an almost British way, that system chose eminent party men who had "ministerial" experience. Perhaps it is no accident that the congressional system fit poorly with the emerging political culture of American democracy. To a growing host of critics it seemed elitist and class-tinged, and for that reason it lost its legitimacy well before its demise in 1824. Oddly enough, it was the only American nominating system that would require presidential candidates to have national executive experience. The lack of such a requirement has always seemed curious to European observers of presidential selection (King, 1985), but the American presidency is a unique institution, very different from its prime-ministerial counterparts throughout the world. Ronald Reagan is only the most recent in a long string of relatively successful presidents who have done without it.

The evidence seems quite clear that the nomination system of "The Party Game" from the 1840s to the late 1960s and its successor, "The Primary Game," have brought forth candidates from a much wider range of backgrounds than the caucus system, but in general there does not seem to be any pronounced difference in the qualifications of the candidates they have produced. John Aldrich, who has done a careful analysis of the period between 1876 and 1984, concludes that "presidential candidates look remarkably similar" over this period (Aldrich, 1987: 156). Again, I would argue, comparisons are best made inside the period of the modern presidency on the grounds that the extraordinary demands for personal performance characteristic of this period are unique. Looking just at those nominated in their own right (without prior accidental succession) since 1945, it is not apparent that those nominated under the new system (McGovern, Carter, Mondale, Reagan, Dukakis, and Bush) are inferior in experience to those nominated in the last decades of the old system (Dewey, Stevenson, Eisenhower, Kennedy, Nixon, Goldwater, and Humphrey). All the latter but Eisenhower are stock characters from the familiar political backgrounds from which presidential nominees have been drawn since the demise of the caucus system in 1824—senators, governors, or, more recently, vice-presidents. It is difficult to conclude that the present nominating system has systematically produced candidates who are dwarfed by comparison with those nominated before 1972. The same holds for the "also-rans" of the two periods. There is nothing more dwarflike about Paul Simon or Albert Gore in 1988 than about Estes Kefauver in 1952 or Stuart Symington in 1960.

Going back farther in time would seem, if anything, to make a stronger case on the average for the apprenticeship qualifications of candidates nominated in recent years, but that would hold for both nominating systems that have operated since World War II. Anyone nostalgic for the remote past should be reminded of the harsh judgment rendered by two of our best historians on the nominees of the old "Party Game:"

> Since 1840 successful presidential candidates have not been prominent and experienced statesmen, but military heroes or relatively obscure men who have not had time to make enemies. Only by inadvertence, as in the case of Lincoln or the Roosevelts, did the president prove to be a man of outstanding ability. (Morrison and Commager, 1930)

After the demise of the congressional caucus, when the requirement of inside apprenticeship was abandoned, party leaders who controlled the nominating convention chose presidential candidates from many backgrounds, often with little thought to how they might perform if elected. Virtuoso performances simply were not expected. Only in the last fifty years, as the presidency was becoming the focal point of national governance, have we sought seriously to identify the proper qualifications for so demanding a performance. We have not succeeded in doing so.

The best conclusion from the evidence of long experience is that we cannot identify any ideal experiential background for the presidency. The awesome combination of skills that the presidential literature identifies as important in fulfilling the role expectations of the modern office cannot, it seems, be reliably learned in any of the political roles from which presidential candidates are drawn.

Oddly enough, the present system, which is often accused of bringing forth "outsiders" with little or no political apprenticeship, has not yet nominated any such person. In the convention system many outsiders were selected in the hundred years between William Henry Harrison and Wendell Willkie. Our conclusion must be that, whatever else may be the shortcomings of the new nominating system, it cannot fairly be faulted for producing candidates less experienced than those produced in the hundred or so years of "The Party Game."

This brings us to the question of personality, character, or temperament. There is much to be said for the argument that, however conceptualized, presidents' psychological attributes influence their behavior in office. Because the presidency is uniquely personal and comparatively uninstitutionalized, personality conditions any incumbent's relationships with the public, subordinates, adversaries, and the press. It is far from clear, however, that we have the ability to *predict* presidential performance from what we can observe about individuals before they become president. That, of course, is the aim of such students of presidential personality as James David Barber. For such an applied psychology of presidential selection to work, we would have to have, at minimum, a reliable analytical scheme, sufficient information to assess the personality characteristics of individual candidates, and awareness of both among those who are to play key roles in the nominating process—partisan elites in the old system, voters and caucus participants in the new. In fact, we have none of these requisites.

Moreover, chapters 6 and 7 show that there is simply not enough information generated by the press during the campaign to sustain serious analysis of the personalities of the many candidates in the field. And, even if we had a perfect knowledge system and reams of "serious" personality data on all the candidates in the field, ordinary citizens could not possibly assimilate them and do the kind of analysis that would be required to reach reliable conclusions about candidates' personalities and their import for future presidential behavior. Here we run up against what Schattschneider (1942: 14) identified as "difficulties arising from the numbers, preoccupation, immobility, and indifference of the people." No mass electorate should ever be assigned such a task. It is simply beyond the realm of possibility.

Of course, there is little or no evidence that the nomination system in place from the 1840s to the late 1960s—a much more elite-dominated system—could do personality or character analysis any better. Many presidents produced by the old nominating system were "wrong" for the office, according to Barber: Wilson, Hoover, Eisenhower, Johnson, and Nixon. The best conclusion is not that one nomination system has performed better than the other in this respect but that we have found no reliable way to produce candidates of "extraordinary temperament."

It is sobering indeed to be reminded of the judgments that leading pundits of the time rendered on Franklin Roosevelt, the very model of "first-class temperament" in the presidential literature, when he was a candidate in 1932. Walter Lippmann, for example, thought him "a pleasant man who, without any important qualifications for the office, would very much like to be president" (Schlesinger, 1957: 291). Lippman was not alone. Very few saw the great man coming on. My own conclusion is that our ability to identify the personal qualities of a Roosevelt before the fact is probably no greater now than it was in 1932. It is not fair to ask any nominating system to do what we do not know how to do.

The conclusion must be that "The Primary Game" cannot be fairly faulted on the grounds that is has produced candidates less qualified for the presidency than its predecessors. On the whole, the candidates nominated under the present system and the old convention system look remarkably similar. If they fall short of the ideal qualifications called for in the presidential literature, the fault would seem to lie more in our unrealistic expectations than in failures of the nominating system.

One final point on experience and personality criteria needs to be made. Although it is often said that "The Primary Game" discourages the best-qualified candidates from running, it seems far from clear that this is so. To be sure, the new system requires early entry in the campaign and bars the convention from drafting a reluctant candidate. From my perspective, there are unfortunate features of the new system, but it is not easy to believe that those who have held back since 1972 are cut from essentially different cloth than those who have entered the race. If, indeed, such potential Democratic candidates in 1988 as Sam Nunn and Mario Cuomo stayed out of a race they saw as too long, expensive, punishing to their families, subject to unfair media scrutiny, or whatever, it is not clear that they would have seemed better qualified than the "seven dwarfs" had they decided to run. They would almost certainly have been revealed to be ordinary mortals if they had joined the others in the field.

Something about the dynamic of the new system makes people look better simply by virtue of their not being candidates. If "The Primary Game" does not actually produce inferior candidates, it does seem often to diminish the stature of those who choose to run—to make them *seem* less able than they are. Accordingly, the system can at the same time produce nominees who are capable individuals but fail to generate support for them. The problem, then, would not be that we have a faulty mechanism for selecting individuals but that the nominating system is no longer capable of generating the support on which successful governance depends.

Coalition-building and Cooperation

A governance perspective directs our attention to how the nominating process, other things being equal, promotes or hinders the development of a sense of common purpose inside each of the parties and an understanding that governing the nation is a cooperative enterprise. It calls attention to the difficult problem of generating support for presidents and their programs. Key, Schattschneider, Rossiter, and most other students of the American party system a generation ago, just before the old nominating system was swept away, considered the national convention of state and local party leaders as attractive for precisely this reason; it operated, they thought, as a unifying, centralizing force in a policy characterized by extremely divided formal authority and decentralized political parties. It served as a mechanism to mediate the internal quarrels among the parties' heterogeneous sectional and social followings and the diverse policy perspectives to which they gave rise.

When Rossiter wrote *The American Presidency,* he warned against tampering with the system for this reason. The convention, as he saw it, had served for more than a century as the major unifying influence on "political parties that are decentralized to the point of anarchy" (Rossiter, 1960b: 187). Primaries, he thought (agreeing with Adlai Stevenson, whose words he quoted), were "a very questionable means of selecting presidential candidates" (1960a: 186). They should certainly not be extended or made binding on convention delegates. He warned would-be reformers against upsetting "the nice balance between the hard responsibilities of the professionals at the convention and the vague wishes of the voters at home"(1960a: 186). Unless it could be demonstrated that the presidency, the one American office capable of generating national leadership, would not be damaged by altering the nomination process, "we ought to stand fast on tradition and prescription" and leave it alone (1960a: 192). Little could Rossiter have guessed how soon this sensible perspective would fall victim to the passions produced by unforeseen events in the strange new world of the late 1960s.

What Americans, then and now, have had trouble seeing is that primaries as a normal system of presidential nomination are *by definition* divisive and individualistic. Clearly they appeal to deep individualistic and participatory strains in American political culture, or else we alone among the world's democracies would not have come to rely on them so extensively. Nevertheless, we ought to see more clearly than we do the dangers they pose for the party system. Everywhere else in the world it is regarded as obvious that inviting a large number of copartisans to compete with one another over a long period of time in public over whose personal qualifications and ideas are best is divisive and potentially threatening to a party's ability to unite in the general election and function afterward as a more-or-less cooperative entity in government. Parties everywhere have leadership-selection fights arising from ideological and policy disagreements and personal rivalries. Mainly, however, they deal with them as quickly and quietly as possible behind closed doors. The American system of selecting presidential candidates by national nominating convention after the 1840s was always recognized by European observers as an unusually open and participative system. The addition of "advisory" presidential primaries in the early 1900s made it much more so. "The Primary Game" in place since 1972 has institutionalized openness to an extreme degree. It virtually requires that intraparty policy disputes and personal nomination campaigns be fought out under the glare of the communications media's lights over a period of more than two years. The nominating system as it now operates literally manufactures personal rivalries and individualistic policy positions among copartisans. It inevitably encourages a candidate-based rather than a party-based politics.

In following this line of reasoning we need not idealize the old convention system. The historical evidence is clear that it was sometimes a forum for bruising intraparty battles over both policy differences and personal rivalries. When either party was severely split on policy grounds, the convention offered no guarantee of successful compromise. Hopelessly divided parties are incapable of pulling themselves together, winning elections, and governing under any nominating system.

The question of what kind of nominating system *best* facilitates intraparty agreement and cooperation in the ongoing contest for national power is better put when the parties have real but less severe internal policy differences and when several candidates want a nomination that can go only to one. In this situation, the preponderance of the evidence favors a convention of party leaders and officeholders over the present primary-dominated system of party activists bound to particular candidates. Ironically, the Democrats seem to have been most adversely affected by the new system — one that would not have been invented in the first place had it not been for their bitter internal divisions in the late 1960s. But the system has had negative governance-related effects on the Republicans as well, despite their much greater unity in recent years.

The Democrats' problems since 1968, to be sure, have not been *caused* by the new nominating system. They are rooted in the nature of the party's electoral coalition. The party has always been an odd coalitional beast, hard to hold together at best—the classic illustration of Rossiter's party "decentralized to the point of anarchy." Franklin Roosevelt's New Deal coalition strengthened the party's hold on the odd bedfellows of the 1920s—the nativist white South and the immigrant, largely Catholic, urban North, and, for good measure, added blacks in both sections (a contingent that would be vastly expanded over the next generation) and the new legions of organized labor. From the beginning, this coalition contained the seeds that would later grow into major divisions over questions of racial, social, and foreign and defense policies. As we all know, since 1964 it has taken more than a little imagination to formulate policies and find presidential candidates appealing to these disparate elements.

This tricky task has surely been rendered more difficult by the new nominating system. The new system highlights and magnifies the Democrats' bedeviling internal divisions. Why would it not? What could be less promising for such a coalitional party than to set its disparate elements against one another in a long public argument among various candidates, unmediated by anyone with an institutional interest in finding middle ground?

Looking back over the five nominating rounds of the new system, it is difficult not to believe that a delegate-selection system much less radically altered after 1968 (and one that would not have triggered a sudden state legislative movement to create new primaries) would have better served the Democrats as a presidential party. Someone more like Muskie than McGovern would have been nominated in 1972; the election would most likely have been lost in any case, but it would have been more strongly contested. Someone other than Jimmy Carter would probably have been selected in 1976, and would have had a good chance to win the presidency with or without Watergate. Whoever had won as a Democrat would have been better off in those difficult years by virtue of having a greater measure of respect and support from other Democrats in Washington. No Democratic president would have had to fight off a strong primary challenge to renomination. Whatever would have happened after 1980, it would not have been likely that a Gary Hart would ever have so effectively labeled a Democratic front-runner as the "candidate of special interests" or that any other candidate would have depicted a Gephardt as a flip-flopping waffler in negative television ads. Women and blacks would surely have come to play a greater role in party affairs, although a less dramatic one without *de facto* quotas in national party rules. Jesse Jackson, of course, would have had no opportunity to run his long campaigns of 1984 and 1988, but other black politicians with more party and electoral experience would have staked their claims to power in a more traditional and less party-dividing manner.

Pure nostalgia? No. All of the above, as much as it may run against the grain of contemporary sensibilities, would be preferable to what actually happened from a viewpoint seriously concerned with political parties' ability to build and maintain coalitions, generate support for their office-holders, and promote cooperation in their ranks.

There is no such persuasive evidence that the Republicans have been adversely affected by changes in the nominating system, but that is not to say that they will always be so fortunate. Less coalitional than the Democrats, normally more orderly, and much more unified at both the elite and mass levels in recent years, the Republicans have been less likely to suffer damage during the long, public nomination campaign. And, of course, except for the Carter years, they have been the "in" party, much less vulnerable to internal squabbles. Nevertheless, other things being equal, they would have been still better off under the previous nominating system—one with which they had no serious discontents.

It was certainly not helpful to Gerald Ford's presidency and his uphill struggle for a term of his own to have been set upon by Ronald Reagan in 1976. There can be no doubt that his reelection prospects were seriously damaged by Reagan's nearly successful challenge, which persisted right down to the convention. No such damaging attack on a president from the ranks of his own party had been launched since Theodore Roosevelt's assault on Taft in 1912, and it is difficult to believe that it would have occurred had the inviting new machinery of "The Primary Game" not been in place.

In 1980, the strongly fought campaign between Reagan and Bush in the early primary season established "voodoo economics" as a household expression and thereby made it more difficult for Reagan to convince the general electorate that he was not an extremist. In 1988, the personal, negative attacks that Bush and Dole inflicted on one another in the first weeks of the primaries left wounds that were very difficult to heal on two rivals who would subsequently need to cooperate as president and leader of the president's party in the Senate. Nowhere else in the world is there anything remotely comparable to the present nominating system's propensity to set copartisans against one another. The system is *inherently* subversive of party unity. Even the Republicans, now perhaps more unified ideologically than any other major American party has ever been, are divided by it.

To make matters worse, it seems abundantly clear after five rounds of the new nominating system that what the primaries take apart the convention cannot put back together. The convention in the age of "The Primary

Game" is a nearly hollow shell of its former self—an institution ill equipped to perform *any* of the functions once thought so important in achieving party unity and generating support for presidential candidates. This is nicely illustrated by the account in chapter 8 of the "secondary functions" of the contemporary convention. Not only is the candidate-selection function gone, there is little left of even the "secondary" functions. While it is doubtful that anyone intended the result, the potent combination of new technologies, social change, and reformed delegate-selection rules has utterly transformed the party convention.

Aside from the carefully staged acceptance speeches of the victorious candidates, the nominating convention is now little more than an expensively produced television show with a problematic rating. In 1988, the networks wondered whether there was much left that was worth covering. Only C-SPAN served up the full show for the small audience that cared to watch it. The essence of the convention's transformation, as chapter 1 has shown, is that the vast majority of delegates are now won by candidates' campaigns in primaries and caucuses open to wide participation. As individuals, the delegates have about as much importance as members of the electoral college. Most delegates today are not institutional party actors but activists who have enlisted in support of an individual candidate. Delegates who are selected to nominate particular candidates write platforms and make rules to suit particular candidates as well. The real action ends when the delegates are chosen.

This has been all too apparent at Democratic conventions in recent years. In 1984, as Buell and Jackson show in chapter 8, both Hart and Jackson insisted on and got concessions on platform planks and delegate-selection rules for the next round that party "professionals," a dwindling breed, would never have made. In that year, both Hart and Jackson virtually began their 1988 campaigns from the convention podium, while Walter Mondale, who had won the nomination, nervously looked on. Jackson, in a much stronger position in 1988, having won nearly 30 percent of the primary vote, insisted on critically important delegate-selection concessions for 1992 (requiring proportional representation in all primaries and caucuses and abolishing all of the Democratic National Committee superdelegates).[2] And again, of course, he got the most valuable concession of all, the right to address a national audience. It was not so much a party speech as a personal one, which no nominee would have wanted made on the eve of his or her own acceptance speech. Again, it gave every impression of being the launch of a 1992 campaign from the podium of the 1988 convention.[3]

The candidates, not institutional party actors, now control the delegates. Whatever deals are struck are determined by the candidates and their campaign staffs. If the long, public campaign has created hard feelings among them (as it has for the Democrats for years), party officials and officeholders have little capacity to provide conciliation. That being the case, the enthusiastic symbolic showing of partisan spirit and unity at the start of the general-election campaign—the "rallying" function for which the old convention was often notable—is now feebly performed at best. Since 1976 the Republicans have not needed much conciliation, but given what we know about American parties over the long run, their current state of ideological bliss is unlikely to long outlive the Reagan era. If and when the Republicans are again subject to serious internal divisions, it will become clear that their convention provides no assistance.

In general, the conclusion must be that the basic structure of "The Primary Game" is deficient as a mechanism for promoting the capacity of the American party system to build and maintain presidential coalitions. It detracts from the parties' ability to generate support for candidates and for presidents, who must rely on the cooperation of copartisans in order to govern. It has encouraged assaults on two presidents from the ranks of their own party. By requiring that copartisans engage in long campaigns against one another, the system serves to magnify existing intraparty divisions and to generate divisions and antagonisms that would not otherwise exist. No one would intentionally create such a system with governance ends in mind.

Clarifying Options: Helping Voters to Understand

A few years ago, ordinary Americans needed to pay scant attention to presidential politics until after the conventions met in the summer of the election year. The presidential campaign, already long, took place between the conventions and the election in November. The voter's job was relatively simple—to choose between the Democratic and Republican "packages" of candidates and issues, both independently important in the American presidential system. Even so, the American system of divided powers and federalism made demands on citizens that ran well in excess of those in parliamentary systems, in which voters could opt for one or another broad direction in national government by simply voting for a member of parliament, and that mainly on the grounds of party preference. Even in the much simpler world of the late nineteenth century, European observers like Lord Bryce thought American elections demanded too much of ordinary citizens. In more modern language, Bryce thought the information costs facing American voters were too high; voters were expected to know too much about too many things. In this context we need to ask whether we are better or worse off for having decided, in effect, that functions formerly performed by party organizational elites and officeholders ought to be performed directly by the electorate.

The foregoing chapters in this volume collectively make clear that the tasks facing ordinary voters in the new system are formidable indeed. First, the presidential campaign has been greatly lengthened. By the most conservative definition, the nomination phase alone now runs for well over a year. Unless they are to abandon what the new system expects them to do—directly select the presidential nominees and determine the issue orientation of the parties in the general election—voters are required to be attentive during a much longer campaign. Second is the much larger roster of players in the new game, perhaps as many as twenty on both sides in a year like 1988, when both parties' nominations are open. Every candidate on both sides is a potential personality and issue conundrum for voters. Since intraparty processes cannot be structured for voters according to partisan symbols, the candidates have to be understood as individuals—not as Democrats or Republicans. We have seen that the 1988 nomination campaigns, like others under the new system, were subject to intense press coverage. From the "exhibition season" through the election, a massive new "elections industry" churns out coverage of virtually every aspect of the presidential race—the candidates, their organizations, fundraising, strategies, personalities, issues, poll standings, predictions, and so on. It is asking a great deal to expect ordinary voters to cope with such a barrage of information and somehow to sift out of it the essentials for making informed decisions on candidates and issues.

Buell's content analysis of national newspaper coverage during the "invisible primary" phase of the 1988 elections in chapter 6 shows that there is a great deal of good reporting on the nomination campaigns in this period. Although the candidates did not receive equal coverage and there was relatively little treatment of a sort that advocates of formal personality analysis call for, there was more coverage of issues and campaign themes than we might have anticipated. A citizen who had carefully read any one of these papers throughout the early stages of the 1988 nomination process would have been very well informed about the many candidates and their policy positions. Yet we know that relatively few voters did that. The vast majority of Americans have neither the opportunity nor the inclination to digest all the information that is taken so seriously by the candidates themselves and by the new "elections industry" elites who follow the candidates around. Most voters do not begin to learn much about the candidates until the beginning of the actual primary season, and by then the press is much more interested in the "horse race." There is simply no way that the mass electorate can master the complex information necessary for the active role that ordinary citizens are expected to play in the new system. It is hopelessly inaccessible for reasons Schattschneider identified many years ago—"the numbers, preoccupation, immobility and indifference of the people."

Robinson and Lichter's account in chapter 7 of television coverage of nominating politics in 1988 confirms the worst suspicions we might have had about the limitations of the informational source on which most Americans now depend for whatever understanding they get of the doings and pronouncements of the candidates active during the long nominating campaign. While there is no evidence that television plays a primary causal role in the selection process, the medium simply does not provide the kinds of information citizens need to understand the candidates in any serious sense. Television, as we should all know by now, is interested in the high drama of the horse race. Who will leap from the pack in Iowa? Who will slip on the icy terrain of New Hampshire? Be with us tonight or you may miss a major development in this exciting struggle! While the networks now seem more careful about interpreting "surprises" and putting expectational spin on outcomes in the early events, "horserace" stories clearly predominated again in 1988. According to Robinson and Lichter, it was not until after New York, when both nominations were clinched, that television coverage shifted predominantly to questions of issues and policies. Putting this together with Buell's findings, we might reach the conclusion that a voter wanting to know mainly about issues would do best to avoid following the nomination contest during the peak of the primary season!

Most citizens pass through the long nominating season without knowing or caring much about intraparty confrontations. Even on the eve of the 1988 Democratic convention, Michael Dukakis, who had been on the campaign trail for more than a year, remained unknown to roughly half of the electorate (Farah and Klein, 1989: 106). Most voters are not sufficiently interested in what is going on to pay the high information costs necessary to find out. Strong interest in the nomination campaign is restricted to a relatively small portion of the electorate. Why, after all, would the electorate be expected to sustain interest in what Buell aptly calls "the dubious premises, misleading statistics, outlandish claims, borrowed eloquence, superficiality, and hyperbole so typical of presidential campaign rhetoric"? During the general election, strong partisans, at least, can be expected to attend to such stuff with a certain amount of satisfaction. During a long nomination contest, though, it is simply too much of a bad thing. Most people tune it out.

The new nominating system does little to help citizens understand broad options for the future direction of public policy. Ideas and claims of leadership ability are a dime a dozen inside both parties as candidates have at one another, but few of these ideas and claims help ordinary citizens link their private concerns to the world of national politics. In this partyless politics the voter is in the position of the southerner in the erstwhile one-party Democratic primaries described by Key (1949). The candidates were so numerous, the gimmicks so outlandish, and the rhetoric so cacophon-ous that the voter had little chance of making any sense of it all. This, of course, was why Key and others of his era considered *party* politics so important. It had a capacity to clarify, instruct, and mobilize — to create effective linkages between the private concerns of everyday life and the public order. It would be absurd to lay the entire blame for the weakening of this linkage on "The Primary Game," but it should certainly be seen as a significant part of the problem.

Strong Candidates and Broad Electoral Appeal

The traditional logic of the American party system is that two moderate parties, operating in the centrist space of our unique political spectrum, compete for control of the White House by making as broad as possible an appeal to their own partisans, independents, and some of the opposi-tion's partisan followers as well. My fourth standard for evaluating the new nominating system incorporates this majority-seeking logic. It says that, when we structure the nominating system to achieve such values as open-ness, representativeness, and popular participation, we should take care not to hinder the parties' ability to produce strong, attractive candidates with broad appeal to voters across the nation.

While the old convention system did not always produce such candi-dates, most often the party leaders who dominated it tried to find presiden-tial nominees who had the best chance to win the election. How does the new system fare by this standard? The evidence after five nominating rounds is that it comes off much better than we might have supposed after 1972. There is no good reason to fear now that the system is loaded to produce Democrats so far to the left or Republicans so far to the right that presidential politics will become ideologically polarized. No candi-date nominated since 1972 except George McGovern has been so ideo-logically removed from the center of the American spectrum that his de-feat was a foregone conclusion. Carter would almost certainly have failed to win the Democratic nomination under a convention system, but not for reasons of ideology. He artfully staked out a centrist position that served him well with the national electorate in 1976. He simply would not have seemed a proper choice to party regulars and office holders. Mondale and Dukakis, on the other hand, are exactly the sort who appeal to "profes-sional" party peers. Both came to be seen as liberal ideologues by a large portion of the electorate, but, of course, they were not; both were experienced politicians, medially located in their party. Ford—an accidental president who finally patched together the delegates he needed in 1976—as well as Reagan and Bush are all garden-variety Republicans. Reagan, although he seemed somewhat too far to the right to many voters in 1980, had been a successful two-term governor of California, no mean accomplishment. There is no good reason to doubt that he would eventually have been nominated, no matter what system of nomination the Republicans used. And, of course, he has been the main actor in creating the most formidable Republican presidential coalition the party has known since the 1920s. None of this merits an indictment of the new system on the grounds that it has produced candidates ill equipped to make a strong national appeal.

Still, it is interesting to ask why, as long as the new system has been in operation, we have so often heard the lament, "Surely, we can do better than this!" To return to a point discussed earlier, there is something about the new nominating system that makes people who are well suited to carry their party's standard in the presidential election *seem* lacking. It is especially curious that people like Mondale, Dukakis, Dole, and Bush—who are as smart, well apprenticed in government, and seasoned in party politics as the best people put forth in the era of the modern presidency by the old nominating convention—now seem so unimpressive. Why do those who stay out of the race nearly always seem to be better? Although there is no way to prove the proposition, I suspect that the culprit is the long intraparty squabble that lies at the heart of the new system. It requires candidates to toot their own horns endlessly and to undermine their partisan colleagues at every turn by hook or by crook. Much of this activity is inherently demeaning. The rules of this game virtually guarantee that the stature of the players will be diminished. Although it was not designed to do so, it seems to dwarf even those of substantial accomplishment.

In the old convention system, and especially in the more remote days of "The Party Game," presidential candidates suddenly emerged from the nomination process clothed in the robes of partisan symbolism. The victorious individual could not but look more impressive than the ordinary run of mere mortals for having been anointed by one of the tribes to which most people belonged. The candidates in the new system, by contrast, undergo a long and demanding process of public scrutiny during which they face the constant glare of the electronic media and their inherently skeptical commentaries on the "horse race." There is no way to win in this system, except by advancing themselves and creating all manner of doubts about their opponents. No candidate can be expected to emerge from this process unscathed. Someone will always win in such a system, but it is not a system likely to ennoble the nominee. Even the moment of victory does little to magnify the nominee's stature, since, as we have seen, the functionally hollow modern convention has little partisan glory to bestow. In an atmosphere of weakened partisanship, the nominee in the new system seems less the leader of invigorated party legions than a mere individual who has won the game. For this, again, we must not indict the nominating system alone; nevertheless, we should recognize it as an important component of an institutional setting that has weakened partisan linkages that once bonded us more effectively to presidents and thereby generated the support that successful governance in our system of divided powers requires.

Participation, Representativeness, and Party Organizations

The final standard for evaluating the nominating system holds that it should encourage participation by citizens in party affairs, and that the parties' activities should be open to all who desire to participate, but that it should not weaken parties as institutions. Broad participation in party affairs is a worthy goal. It is not, however, one that ought to be pursued single-mindedly without consideration for other goals, such as maintaining the health of institutional partisan organizations at the state and local levels. Here we need to recognize the strong possibility of trade-offs. As we seek greater participation and representativeness, we are likely to diminish the ability of party organizations to perform their traditional structuring functions for the electorate.

Most of the impetus to create a more participatory and socially representative party system has come from the Democrats. After the debacle in Chicago in 1968, the McGovern-Fraser Commission drafted rules designed to open decision-making at all levels to rank-and-file Democrats, to increase representation of blacks, women, and other underrepresented categories of Democratic followers, and to guarantee wide participation in the delegate-selection process (Shafer, 1983). These requirements in turn led state legislatures to alter the statutory arrangements governing delegate selection in favor of primaries and other more participatory procedures. The Republicans, who otherwise almost certainly would have left their delegate-selection procedures alone, were carried along in this process. Even so, as Buell and Davis note in chapter 1, the Republicans have continued, wherever possible, to allow their state parties to craft their own delegate-selection rules. As things now stand, paradoxically, the Democrats, a party of highly disparate local followings, have nationalized their rules to an unprecedented degree while the Republicans, a much more socially homogeneous party with impressive national organizational unity, have allowed their state and local organizations much more freedom to make their own rules.

What has been gained since 1968 by way of participation and representativeness? Chapter 8 provides an interesting perspective on representation at the 1988 conventions. We can be certain that the Democrats' rules changes have made their convention much more representative of two groups of their identifiers in the electorate, blacks and women. It is much less clear what effect the new delegate-selection procedures have had on the social-class composition of the conventions. Chapter 8 shows that both parties' delegates are now much more educated and affluent than their followers in the electorate, but it is very likely that this has always been the case. American party organizations have probably had a middle-class bias from the beginning. Although earlier data are lacking, few close observers of the new nominating system would argue that it is *more* representative in class terms than the one it replaced.

The gender, racial, and social-class composition of the convention delegates is important but is much less closely related to the functional performance of the party system than the delegates' ideological and policy orientation. Before the post-1968 reforms, survey data indicated that both parties' convention delegates were more ideological than their followers or the general public. In the 1950s the Republican delegates were the ones who seemed to be out of step. They were so far to the right that Republican followers were much closer to Democratic activists than to activists in their own party. Studies done after the reforms suggest a general pattern in which both parties' delegates have become consistently much more ideological than their followers in the electorate. The main change since 1968 seems to be that the Democratic delegates have moved sharply to the left to mirror the position that the Republican delegates had earlier occupied at the other end of the political spectrum.

Is this amount of ideological polarization excessive? The answer is not clear, but from the perspective of this chapter, it must depend largely on whether the "principled amateurs" of the new system have the ability to package candidates and issues in such a manner that presidential majorities can be constructed and maintained. Both parties' convention delegates now seem to need the counsel that institutional party leaders on both sides often gave their more ideological colleagues in the old convention system. The party leaders' function was to keep them from becoming too unrepresentative of the parties' identifiers in the electorate and the broader electorate from which support was needed if elections were to be won. Buell and Jackson's conclusion that the delegates of the primary-dominated era want to win as well as achieve their ideological goals may be correct, but it is hard to believe that they are as well equipped to pursue electoral victory as the state and local leaders who dominated the action under the convention system.

While no one clearly intended the result, the movement to primaries between 1968 and 1972 created a presidential nominating politics largely unmediated by those with the greatest interest in the long-term ability of the parties to compete successfully for the presidency. The "principled amateurs" who in the new system have to do the job that party organizations used to do are certainly not pure ideologues, but they are much less skilled than the organization leaders they have supplanted in framing the essential structure of the presidential race. Both parties still need an institutional concern with "electability" that cannot be provided by citizen activists motivated by personal attachments to particular candidates or by policy or ideological preferences. Such concern is sorely lacking in the current nominating system.

Conclusion: A Flawed System

By the evaluative standards introduced above, "The Primary Game" does not fare well. The problem is not that it puts forth individual candidates less well suited by virtue of their experience or personal attributes than prior nominating systems did. Nevertheless, the system generates less support for nominees than they need in order to contest national elections vigorously and govern effectively if they win. In several ways it has contributed to the weakening of political parties in the presidential election, the central electoral drama of American democracy. The system magnifies existing intraparty cleavages, and—worse still—contributes to the creation of new ones in the course of its normal operation. It has not helped the parties perform the important function of clarifying broad policy options for the electorate. Rather, it has made matters worse by confusing and boring voters for months on end. It has little of the capacity of the old convention system to forge party unity and create enthusiasm before the general-election campaign. The new system has needlessly weakened state and local party organizations. Since 1968 they have been almost entirely displaced from the central action in selecting the party's presidential nominee and shaping the issues on which the campaign is to be fought.

Would anyone with the benefit of what we now know about this system of nomination have chosen to create it? I do not think so.[4] Had the events of 1968 not generated such uncontrollable passions, we would not likely have set in motion the forces that transformed a central part of the venerable machinery of American government. Nominating politics might well have continued in the form we knew in the mid-1960s—the convention of delegates selected state by state in many different ways, with the primaries playing a very strong role in an age of national electronic communi-cation. Would we be better off if that were the case? I think so. Why, in the face of the accumulated evidence, would we want to continue year after year to employ such a flawed nominating system? It is not easy to see why we continue to tolerate it. Yet another round of its mischief is al-ready well under way.

The greatest problem we face in getting out of the lock-hold "The Pri-mary Game" now has on us is a shallow realism that says, in effect, that this is the only kind of system we can have in an era of party decomposi-tion driven by social and technological forces beyond our control. In this scenario, parties are simply the victims of postindustrial society. We must see that there is nothing inevitable about this progression. In fact, parties as organizations continue to play a strong structuring role in most of the world's democracies. The real problem is the one to which E. E. Schatt-schneider devoted his academic career—the intellectual problem of con-vincing Americans, against the grain of much of our ideological heritage, that strong political parties are essential to healthy democratic government.

Our flawed nomination system is only a part of a broader trend toward party decomposition in this country that has undermined the governance capacity of the contemporary Washington community. Weaker presidents, a more individualistic Congress, divided government, and a House of Representatives all but divorced from the issue-related dynamic of the na-tional election process are all parts of the big picture. Very few whose ex-perience in Washington goes back to the period before Vietnam think we are better off now than we were then. Most believe that we now have less ability to sustain a more-or-less coherent process of national governance, and a wealth of evidence indicates that citizens are less effectively linked to national government than they were then. Electoral participation has fallen off sharply. For an alarmingly large segment of the public, Washing-ton is out of sight and out of mind. The underlying dynamic seems to be a general weakening of political parties in American politics. The welcome evidence of the Reagan years that this process is not inevitable should not lull us into complacency but should encourage us to do whatever we can to re-create a vigorous party system.

Could "The Primary Game" be changed if we wanted to change it? Of course it could. The first steps are to understand that it does not work well and to understand that incremental tinkering with it (superdelegates, Super Tuesdays, and so on) will not help. From there, many other steps are possible. It is often said that we "can't go back to the smoke-filled room." That is true. But we could go back to selecting convention delegates as Democratic and Republican state organizations would wish if they wanted to make a larger role for themselves in the nomination process. Both national parties could encourage state parties to alter state statutes again in order to regain their place in the selection process. Or, if we wish to retain elements of "The Primary Game," we might design a preprimary convention system that would allow institutional party actors to play a larger role in candidate selection subject to review by party followers in later elections.[5] Perhaps there are other means to the end, but whatever we do, we should now try to find a way to restore the ability of state and local organizations to influence both candidate selection and the platform on which the national election is fought. A political science of the sort that Key practiced would not assume that what is is immutable. It would turn its hand toward the hard job of reestablishing the partisan links between citizens and government.

National governance has always been difficult to attain in the United States for reasons that have been present since the founding: our extremely partitioned system of separated powers with its Madisonian logic of "ambition against ambition," the deep distrust of central government from which this system was derived, the centrifugal tendencies of a vast and heterogeneous nation, and political parties "decentralized to the point of anarchy." Decomposition of the party system in recent years has made our ongoing quest for national leadership and accountability through our unique formula of presidential government more difficult. A good first step toward arresting this ominous trend would be to repair the flaws in the unfortunate nominating system that we stumbled into after the disasters of 1968.

Notes

1. I do not mean to suggest that these advocates of a strong role for political parties in American government were in agreement about all aspects of the party system. They were not. Schattschneider favored "responsible party government," an arrangement whereby nationally unified parties take full responsibility for the conduct of government (as in British parliamentary practice). Key and Rossiter generally took a position more congenial to the American parties as they actually were — decentralized, ideologically heterogeneous, and organizationally weak at the national level. Rossiter did acknowledge in *Parties and Politics in America* that "modest steps" toward Schattschneider's ideal were in order. Ever the centrist, he took a position somewhere between "the present world of Lyndon Johnson and the future world of E. E. Schattschneider" (Rossiter, 1960a: 181). Looking back from the perspective we have on parties in the 1980s, one is more struck by the similarities than the differences in the perspectives of the three men. None foresaw the decomposition of the party system that would occur in the next generation. All would have been deeply disappointed by this turn of events.

2. In September 1989 the DNC voted to reverse the pact between Jackson and Dukakis on eliminating superdelegate status for members of the committee at the 1992 convention. Ironically, Ronald H. Brown, who had been Jackson's main negotiator with the Dukakis campaign on this issue at Atlanta, as chairman of the Democratic party backed the repudiation of the deal he had earlier negotiated. I take this as a good illustration of my point that the party needs institutional perspective. Things look very different from where Mr. Brown now sits. Perhaps the proportional representation concession will also be repudiated at a later time. Few with an institutional interest in the Democratic party would wish to preserve it.

3. Gerald Pomper has a much more sanguine interpretation of the events of the 1988 Democratic Convention. Although he continues to see the new nominating system as problematic on a number of grounds, he cites the 1988 nominating round as a textbook example of the parties' achieving "unity among all factions." If the Atlanta convention was an example of unity in the new system, we have surely lowered our expectations by a good deal as we have gotten used to the new system. The Jackson phenomenon would have looked strange indeed to traditional party professionals (see Pomper, 1989: 33–34).

4. Even Benjamin Barber agrees that the new nominating system is no improvement over the old (Barber, 1984: 206).

5. My colleague at the University of Connecticut, David RePass, a thoughtful student of American elections, has drawn up a preliminary plan for a national preconvention system.

References

Aldrich, John H. 1987. "Methods and Actors: The Relationship of Processes to Candidates." In *Presidential Selection*, ed. Alexander Heard and Michael Nelson. Durham, N.C.: Duke University Press.

Barber, Benjamin. 1984. *Strong Democracy: Participatory Politics for a New Age.* Berkeley: University of California Press.

Barber, James David. 1985. *The Presidential Character: Predicting Presidential Performance in the White House.* 3d ed. Englewood Cliffs, N.J.: Prentice Hall.

Crotty, William. 1983. *Party Reform.* New York: Longman.

Farah, Barbara G., and Ethel Klein. 1989. "Public Opinion Trends." In Gerald M. Pomper et al. *The Elections of 1988.* Chatham, N.J.: Chatham House.

Jones, Charles, ed. 1988. *The Reagan Legacy: Promise and Performance.* Chatham, N.J.: Chatham House.

Key, V. O., Jr. 1949. *Southern Politics.* New York: Alfred A. Knopf.

———. 1964. *Politics, Parties and Pressure Groups.* 5th ed. New York: Crowell.

King, Anthony. 1985. "How Not to Select Presidential Candidates: A View from Europe." In *Analyzing the Presidency*, ed. Robert E. DiClerico. Guilford, Conn.: Dushkin.

McCormick, Richard P. 1982. *The Presidential Game.* New York: Oxford University Press.

Morrison, Samuel Eliot, and Henry Steele Commager. 1930. *The Growth of the American Republic* 1. New York: Oxford University Press.

Nelson, Michael. 1987. "Who Vies for President?" In *Presidential Selection*, ed. Alexander Heard and Michael Nelson. Durham, N.C.: Duke University Press.

Neustadt, Richard E. 1960. *Presidential Power*. New York: Wiley.

Polsby, Nelson W. 1983. *Consequences of Party Reform*. New York: Oxford University Press.

Pomper, Gerald M. 1989. "The Presidential Nominations." In Gerald M. Pomper et al., *The Election of 1988*. Chatham, N.J.: Chatham House.

Ranney, Austin. 1975. *Curing the Mischief of Faction: Party Reform in America*. Berkeley, Calif.: University of California Press.

Reiter, Howard. 1985. *Selecting the President: The Nominating Process in Transition*. Philadelphia: University of Pennsylvania Press.

Rose, Richard. 1988. *The Postmodern President: The White House Meets the World*. Chatham, N.J.: Chatham House.

Rossiter, Clinton. 1960a. *Parties and Politics in America*. Ithaca, N.Y.: Cornell University Press.

———. 1960b. *The American Presidency*. New York: Mentor.

Schattschneider, Elmer E. 1942. *Party Government*. New York: Rinehart.

Schlesinger, Arthur M., Jr. 1957. *The Age of Roosevelt: The Crisis of the Old Order*. Boston: Houghton Mifflin.

Shafer, Byron E. 1983. *Quiet Revolution: The Struggle for the Democratic Party and the Shaping of Post-Reform Politics*. New York: Russell Sage.

———. 1988. *Bifurcated Politics: Evolution and Reform in the National Party Convention*. Cambridge, Mass.: Harvard University Press.

Selected Bibliography

Abramowitz, Alan I., John McGlennon, and Ronald Rapoport. 1983. "The Party Isn't Over: Incentives for Activism in the 1980 Presidential Nominating Campaign." *Journal of Politics* 45 (November): 1006–15.

Abramowitz, Alan I., and Walter J. Stone. 1984. *Nomination Politics: Party Activists and Presidential Choice.* New York: Praeger.

Abramson, Paul R., John H. Aldrich, and David Rohde. 1990. *Change and Continuity in the 1988 Elections.* Washington, D.C.: Congressional Quarterly Press. See especially pp. 11–40 for an overview of the 1988 nominating races.

Adams, William C. 1985. "Media Coverage of Campaign '84: A Preliminary Report." In *The Mass Media in Campaign '84: Articles from Public Opinion Magazine,* ed. Michael J. Robinson and Austin Ranney. Washington, D.C.: American Institute for Public Policy Research.

Aldrich, John H. 1980. *Before the Convention: Strategies and Choices in Presidential Nomination Campaigns.* Chicago: University of Chicago Press.

Alexander, Herbert E., and Brian A. Haggerty. 1987. *Financing the 1984 Election.* Lexington, Mass.: Lexington Books.

Arterton, F. Christopher. 1984. *Media Politics: The News Strategies of Presidential Campaigns.* Lexington, Mass.: Lexington Books.

Baer, Denise L., and David A. Bositis. 1988. *Elite Cadres and Party Coalitions: Representing the Public in Party Politics.* Westport, Conn.: Greenwood Press.

Barber, James David, ed. 1974. *Choosing the President.* Englewood Cliffs, N.J.: Prentice-Hall.

———. 1978. *Race for the Presidency: The Media and the Nominating Process.* Englewood Cliffs, N.J.: Prentice-Hall.

Barker, Lucius J. 1988. *Our Time Has Come: A Delegate's Diary of Jesse Jackson's 1984 Presidential Campaign.* Urbana: University of Illinois Press.

Barker, Lucius J., and Ronald W. Walters, eds. 1989. *Jesse Jackson's 1984 Presidential Campaign.* Urbana: University of Illinois Press.

Bartels, Larry M. 1988. *Presidential Primaries and the Dynamics of Public Choice.* Princeton, N.J.: Princeton University Press.

Black, Christine M., and Thomas Oliphant. 1989. *All by Myself: The Unmaking of a Presidential Campaign.* Chester, Conn.: Globe-Pequot Press.

Brereton, Charles. 1987. *First in the Nation: New Hampshire and the Premier Presidential Primary.* Portsmouth, N.H.: Peter E. Randall.

Broder, David S. 1987. *Behind the Front Page: A Candid Look at How the News Is Made.* New York: Simon and Schuster.

Broh, C. Anthony. 1987. *A Horse of a Different Color: Television's Treatment of Jesse Jackson's 1984 Presidential Campaign.* Washington, D.C.: Joint Center for Political Studies.

Buell, Emmett H., Jr. 1986. "Divisive Primaries and Participation in Fall Presidential Campaigns: A Study of 1984 New Hampshire Primary Activists." *American Politics Quarterly* 14 (October): 376–90.

———. 1987. "First-in-the-Nation: Disputes over the Timing of Early Democratic Presidential Primaries and Caucuses in 1984 and 1988." *Journal of Law & Politics* 4 (Fall): 311–42.

Carleton, William G. 1957. "The Revolution in the Presidential Nominating Convention." *Political Science Quarterly* 72 (June): 224–40.

Ceaser, James W. 1979. *Presidential Selection: Theory and Development.* Princeton, N.J.: Princeton University Press.

———. 1982. *Reforming the Reforms: A Critical Analysis of the Presidential Selection Process.* Cambridge, Mass.: Ballinger.

Chase, James S. 1973. *Emergence of the Presidential Nominating Convention 1789–1832.* Urbana: University of Illinois Press.

Clemente, Frank, and Frank Watkins, eds. 1989. *Keep Hope Alive: Jesse Jackson's 1988 Presidential Campaign.* Boston: South End Press.

Collat, Donald S., Stanley Kelly, Jr., and Ronald Rogowski. 1981. "The End Game in Presidential Nominations." *American Political Science Review* 75 (June): 426–35.

Colton, Elizabeth O. 1989. *The Jackson Phenomenon: The Man, the Power, the Message.* New York: Doubleday.

Cook, Rhodes, 1987. *Race for the Presidency: Winning the 1988 Nomination.* Washington, D.C.: Congressional Quarterly Press.

———. 1989. "The Nominating Process." In *The Elections of 1988*, ed. Michael Nelson. Washington, D.C.: Congressional Quarterly Press.

Crotty, William. 1983. *Party Reform.* New York: Longman.

Crotty, William, and John S. Jackson III. 1985. *Presidential Primaries and Nominations.* Washington, D.C.: Congressional Quarterly Press.

David, Paul T., Ralph M. Goldman, and Richard C. Bain. 1960. *The Politics of National Party Conventions.* Washington, D.C.: Brookings.

Davis, James W. 1980. *Presidential Primaries: Road to the White House.* Westport, Conn.: Greenwood Press.

———. 1983. *National Conventions in an Age of Party Reform.* Westport, Conn.: Greenwood Press.

Drew, Elizabeth. 1989. *Election Journal: Political Events of 1987–1988.* New York: William Morrow and Company.

Entman, Robert M. 1989. *Democracy without Citizens: Media and the Decay of American Politics.* New York: Oxford University Press.

Farah, Barbara G., and Ethel Klein. 1989. "Public Opinion Trends." In Gerald M. Pomper et al., *The Election of 1988: Reports and Interpretations*, Chatham, N.J.: Chatham House.

Fenno, Richard F., Jr. 1990. *The Presidential Odyssey of John Glenn.* Washington, D.C.: Congressional Quarterly Press.

Geer, John G. 1986. "Rules Governing Presidential Primaries." *Journal of Politics* 48 (November): 1006–25.

———. 1989. *Nominating Presidents: An Evaluation of Voters and Primaries.* Westport, Conn.: Greenwood Press.

Germond, Jack W., and Jules Witcover. 1989. *Whose Broad Stripes and Bright Stars: The Trivial Pursuit of the Presidency 1988.* New York: Warner Books.

Goldman, Peter, and Tom Matthews. 1989. *The Quest for the Presidency: The 1988 Campaign.* New York: Touchstone Books.

Gopoian, J. David. 1982. "Issue Preferences and Candidate Choice in Presidential Primaries." *American Journal of Political Science* 26 (August): 523–46.

Graber, Doris A. 1989. *Mass Media and American Politics.* 3d. ed. Washington, D.C.: Congressional Quarterly Press. See especially pp. 193–234.

Grassmuck, George, ed. 1985. *Before Nomination: Our Primary Problems.* Washington, D.C.: American Enterprise Institute for Public Policy Research.

Green, John C., and James L. Guth. 1988. "The Christian Right in the Republican Party: The Case of Pat Robertson's Supporters." *Journal of Politics* 50 (February): 150–68.

Hadley, Arthur T. 1976. *The Invisible Primary.* Englewood Cliffs, N.J.: Prentice-Hall.

Hammond, Jack H. 1980. "Another Look at the Role of 'The Rules' in the 1972 Democratic Presidential Primaries." *Western Political Quarterly* 33 (March): 50–72.

Harrell, David Edwin, Jr. 1987. *Pat Robertson: A Personal, Political and Religious Portrait.* New York: Harper & Row.

Hatch, Roger D. 1989. "Jesse Jackson in Two Worlds." In *Religion in American Politics,* ed. Charles W. Dunn. Washington, D. C.: Congressional Quarterly.

Heard, Alexander, and Michael Nelson, eds. 1987. *Presidential Selection.* Durham, N.C.: Duke University Press.

Hedlund, Ronald D., Meredith W. Watts, and David M. Hedge. 1982. "Voting in an Open Primary." *American Politics Quarterly* 10 (April): 197–218.

Hess, Stephen. 1988. *The Presidential Campaign.* 3d ed. Washington, D.C.: Brookings.

House, Ernest R. 1988. *Jesse Jackson and the Politics of Charisma.* Boulder, Colo.: Westview Press.

Hutter, James L., and Steven E. Schier. 1984. "Representativeness: From Caucus to Convention in Iowa." *American Politics Quarterly* 12 (October): 431–48.

Iyengar, Shanto, and Donald R. Kinder. 1987. *News that Matters: Television and American Opinion.* Chicago: University of Chicago Press.

Jackson, Jesse L. 1987. *Straight from the Heart.* Philadelphia: Fortress Press.

Jackson, John S., III., Barbara L. Brown, and David Bositis. 1982. "Herbert McClosky and Friends Revisited: 1980 Democratic and Republican Party Elites Compared to the Mass Public." *American Politics Quarterly* 10 (April): 187–212.

Jackson, John S., III, Jesse C. Brown, and Barbara L. Brown. 1978. "Recruitment,

Representation, and Political Values: The 1976 Democratic Convention Delegates." *American Politics Quarterly* 6 (April): 187–212.

John, Kenneth E. 1989. "The Polls—A Report: 1980–1988 New Hampshire Presidential Primary Polls." *Public Opinion Quarterly* 53 (Winter): 590–605.

Johnson, Loch K., and Harlan Hahn. 1973. "Delegate Turnover at National Party Conventions, 1944–68." In *Perspectives on Presidential Selection*, ed. Donald R. Matthews. Washington, D.C.: Brookings.

Joslyn, Richard. 1984. *Mass Media and Elections*. Reading, Mass.: Addison-Wesley.

Kalb, Marvin, and Hendrik Hertzberg, eds. 1988. *Candidates '88*. Dover, Mass.: Auburn House.

Kamarck, Elaine C. 1987. "Delegate Allocation Rules in Presidential Nomination Systems: A Comparison between the Democrats and Republicans." *Journal of Law & Politics* 4 (Fall): 275–310.

Keech, William R., and Donald R. Matthews. 1976. *The Party's Choice*. Washington, D.C.: Brookings.

Keeter, Scott, and Cliff Zukin. 1983. *Uninformed Choice: The Failure of the New Presidential Nominating System*. New York: Praeger.

Kenney, Charles, and Robert L. Turner. 1988. *Dukakis: An American Odyssey*. Boston: Houghton-Mifflin.

Kenney, Patrick J., and Tom W. Rice. 1987. "The Relationship between Divisive Primaries and General Election Outcomes." *American Journal of Political Science* 31 (February): 31–44.

Kessel, John H. 1988. *Presidential Campaign Politics: Coalition Strategies and Citizen Response*. 3d ed. Chicago: Dorsey Press.

Key, V. O., Jr. 1964. *Politics, Parties, and Pressure Groups*. 5th ed. New York: Thomas Y. Crowell.

Kirkpatrick, Jeane. 1976. *The New Presidential Elite: Men and Women in National Politics*. New York: Russell Sage.

Ladd, Everett C. 1977. *Where Have All the Voters Gone?* New York: W. W. Norton.

Lengle, James I. 1981. *Representation and Presidential Primaries: The Democratic Party in the Post-Reform Era*. Westport, Conn.: Greenwood Press.

———. 1987. "Democratic Party Reforms: The Past as Prologue to the 1988 Campaign." *Journal of Law & Politics* 4 (Fall): 233–74.

Lengle, James I., and Byron Shafer. 1976. "Primary Rules, Political Power, and Social Change." *American Political Science Review* 70 (March): 25–40.

Lichter, S. Robert. 1988. "Misreading Momentum." *Public Opinion* 11 (May–June).

Lichter, S. Robert, Daniel Amundson, and Richard Noyes. 1988. *The Video Campaign: Network Coverage of the 1988 Primaries*. Washington, D.C.: American Enterprise Institute for Public Policy Research and the Center for Media and Public Affairs.

Mann, Thomas E. 1985. "Elected Officials and the Politics of Presidential Selection." In *The American Elections of 1984*, ed. Austin Ranney. Durham, N.C.: Duke University Press.

Marshall, Thomas R. 1981. *Presidential Nominations in a Reform Age*. New York: Praeger.

McClosky, Herbert, Paul J. Hoffman, and Rosemary O'Hara. 1960. "Issue Conflict and Consensus among Party Leaders and Followers." *American Political Science Review* 54 (June): 406–27.

McCormick, Richard P. 1982. *The Presidential Game: The Origins of American Presidential Politics.* New York: Oxford University Press.

Mickelson, Sig. 1989. *From Whistle Stop to Sound Bite: Four Decades of Politics and Television.* New York: Praeger.

Miller, Warren E. 1988. *Without Consent: Mass-Elite Linkages in Presidential Politics.* Lexington: University Press of Kentucky.

Miller, Warren E., and M. Kent Jennings. 1986. *Parties in Transition: A Longitudinal Study of Party Elites and Party Supporters.* New York: Russell Sage.

Moran, Jack, and Mark Fenster. 1982. "Voter Turnout in Presidential Primaries: A Diachronic Analysis." *American Politics Quarterly* 10 (October): 453–76.

Murray, Robert K. 1976. *The 103rd Ballot: Democrats and the Disaster in Madison Square Garden.* New York: Harper & Row.

Norrander, Barbara. 1986. "Measuring Primary Turnout in Aggregate Analysis." *Political Behavior* 8: 356–73.

———. 1989. "Ideological Representativeness of Presidential Party Voters." *American Journal of Political Science* 33 (August): 570–87.

Orren, Gary R. 1985. "The Nomination Process: Vicissitudes of Candidate Selection." In *The Elections of 1984*, ed. Michael Nelson. Washington, D.C.: Congressional Quarterly Press.

Orren, Gary R., and Nelson W. Polsby, eds. 1987. *Media and Momentum: The New Hampshire Primary and Nomination Politics.* Chatham, N.J.: Chatham House.

Patterson, Thomas E. 1980. *The Mass Media Election: How Americans Choose Their President.* New York: Praeger.

———. 1989. "The Press and Its Missed Assignment." In *The Elections of 1988*, ed. Michael Nelson. Washington, D.C.: Congressional Quarterly Press.

Patterson, Thomas E., and Richard Davis. 1985. "The Media Campaign: Struggle for the Agenda." In *The Elections of 1984*, ed. Michael Nelson. Washington, D.C.: Congressional Quarterly Press.

Polsby, Nelson W. 1983. *Consequences of Party Reform.* New York: Oxford University Press.

———. 1985. "The Democratic Nomination and the Evolution of the Party System." In *The American Elections of 1984*, ed. Austin Ranney. Durham, N.C.: Duke University Press.

Polsby, Nelson W., and Aaron Wildavsky. 1988. *Presidential Elections: Contemporary Strategies of American Electoral Politics.* 7th ed. New York: Free Press. See especially pp. 88–161.

Pomper, Gerald M. 1966. *Nominating the President: The Politics of Convention Choice.* New York: W. W. Norton.

———. 1979. "New Rules and New Games in Presidential Nominations." *Journal of Politics* 41 (August): 784–805.

———. 1989. "The Presidential Nominations." In Gerald M. Pomper et al., *The Election of 1988: Reports and Interpretations.* Chatham, N.J.: Chatham House.

Pomper, Gerald M., with Susan S. Lederman. 1980. *Elections in America: Control and Influence in Democratic Politics.* 2d ed. New York: Longman. See especially pp. 128–55.

Rae, Nicol C. 1989. *The Decline and Fall of the Liberal Republicans from 1952 to the Present.* New York: Oxford Univerity Press.

Ranney, Austin. 1972. "Turnout and Representation in Presidential Primary Elections." *American Political Science Review* 66 (March): 21–37.

———. 1975. *Curing the Mischiefs of Faction: Party Reform in America.* Berkeley: University of California Press.

———. 1977. *Participation in American Presidential Nominations.* Washington, D.C.: American Enterprise Institute for Public Policy Research.

———. 1978. *The Federalization of Presidential Primaries.* Washington, D.C.: American Enterprise Institute for Public Policy Research.

Rapoport, Ronald B., Alan I. Abramowitz, and John McGlennon, eds. 1986. *The Life of the Parties: Activists in Presidential Politics.* Lexington: University Press of Kentucky.

Reichley, A. James, ed. 1987. *Elections American Style.* Washington, D.C.: Brookings.

Reiter, Howard L. 1985. *Selecting the President: The Nominating Process in Transition.* Philadelphia: University of Pennsylvania Press.

Robertson, Pat. 1984. *Beyond Reason: How Miracles Can Change Your Life.* New York: Bantam.

———. 1986. *America's Dates with Destiny.* Nashville, Tenn.: Thomas Nelson.

Robinson, Michael J. 1984. "The Power of the Primary Purse: Money in 1984." In *The Mass Media in Campaign '84: Articles from Public Opinion Magazine,* ed. Michael J. Robinson and Austin Ranney. Washington, D.C.: American Enterprise Institute for Public Policy.

———. 1985. "Where's the Beef? Media and Media Elites in 1984." *The American Elections of 1984,* ed. Austin Ranney. Durham, N.C.: Duke University Press.

Robinson, Michael J., and Margaret Sheehan. 1983. *Over the Wire and on T.V.: CBS and UPI in Campaign '80.* New York: Russell Sage.

Rose, Richard. 1988. *The Postmodern President: The White House Meets the World.* Chatham, N.J.: Chatham House.

Rossiter, Clinton. 1960a. *Parties and Politics in America.* Ithaca, N.Y.: Cornell University Press.

———. 1960b. *The American Presidency.* New York: Mentor.

Rothenberg, Lawrence, and Richard A. Brody. 1988. "Participation in Presidential Primaries." *Western Political Quarterly* 41 (June): 253–72.

Rubin, Richard. 1980. "Presidential Primaries: Continuities, Dimensions of Change, and Political Implications." In *The Party Symbol: Readings on Political Parties,* ed. William Crotty. San Francisco: W. H. Freeman.

Runkel, David R., ed. 1989. *Campaign for President: The Managers Look at '88.* Dover, Mass.: Auburn House.

Schattschneider, Elmer E. 1942. *Party Government.* New York: Rinehart.

Schier, Steven E. 1980. *The Rules of the Game: Democratic National Convention Delegate Selection in Iowa and Wisconsin.* Washington, D.C.: University Press of America.

———. 1982. "Turnout Choice in Presidential Nominations: A Case Study." *American Politics Quarterly* 10 (April): 231–45.

Schlesinger, Joseph A. 1966. *Ambition and Politics: Political Careers in the United States.* Chicago: Rand McNally.

Shafer, Byron E. 1983. *The Quiet Revolution: The Struggle for the Democratic Party and the Shaping of Post-Reform Politics.* New York: Russell Sage.

———. 1988. *Bifurcated Politics: Evolution and Reform in the National Party Convention.* Cambridge, Mass.: Harvard University Press.

Sheehy, Gail. 1988. *Character: America's Search for Leadership.* New York: William Morrow and Company.

Simon, Paul. 1989. *Winners and Losers: The 1988 Race for the Presidency—One Candidate's Perspective.* New York: Continuum Press.

Sorauf, Frank J. 1988. *Money in American Elections.* Glenview, Ill.: Scott, Foresman and Company. See especially pp. 186–221.

Soule, John W., and Wilma E. McGrath. 1975. "A Comparative Study of Presidential Nomination Conventions: The Democrats of 1968 and *1972.*" *American Journal of Political Science* 19 (August): 501–19.

Southwell, Priscilla L. 1986. "The Politics of Disgruntlement: Nonvoting and Defection among Supporters of Nomination Losers, 1968–1984." *Political Behavior* 8: 81–95.

———. 1988. "Open versus Closed Primaries and Candidate Fortunes, 1972–1984." *American Politics Quarterly* 16 (July): 280–95.

Squire, Peverill, ed. 1989. *The Iowa Caucuses and the Presidential Nominating Process.* Boulder, Colo.: Westview Press.

Stanley, Harold W., and Charles D. Hadley. 1987. "The Southern Presidential Primary: Regional Intentions with National Implications." *Publius* 1 (Summer): 83–100.

Stone, Walter J. 1984. "Prenomination Candidate Choice and General Election Behavior: Iowa Presidential Activists in 1980." *American Journal of Political Science* 28 (March): 361–78.

Stone, Walter J., and Alan I. Abramowitz. 1983. "Winning May Not Be Everything, But It's More than We Thought: Presidential Party Activists in 1980." *American Political Science Review* 77 (December): 945–56.

Traugott, Michael W., and Margaret Petrella. 1989. "Public Evaluations of the Presidential Nominating Process." *Political Behavior* 11 (December): 335–52.

Wald, Kenneth D. 1987. *Religion and Politics in the United States.* New York: St. Martin's Press.

Wald, Kenneth D., Dennis E. Owen, and Samuel S. Hill, Jr. 1988. "Churches as Political Communities." *American Political Science Review* 82 (June): 531–48.

———. 1989. "Evangelical Politics and Status Issues." *Journal for the Scientific Study of Religion* 28 (March): 1–16.

Washington, James M. 1985. "Jesse Jackson and the Symbolic Politics of Black Christendom." *Annals of the American Academy of Political and Social Science* 480 (July): 89–105.

Wattenberg, Martin P. 1990. "From a Partisan to a Candidate-Centered Electorate."

In *The New American Political System*, ed. Anthony King. Washington, D.C.: AEI Press.

Wattier, Mark J. 1983. "The Simple Act of Voting in 1980 Democratic Primaries." *American Politics Quarterly* 11 (July): 267–92.

———. 1983. "Ideological Voting in 1980 Republican Presidential Primaries." *Journal of Politics* 45 (November): 1016–26.

Wekkin, Gary D. 1984. *Democrat versus Democrat: The National Party's Campaign to Close the Wisconsin Primary.* Columbia: University of Missouri Press.

Wildavsky, Aaron. 1965. "The Goldwater Phenomenon: Purists, Politicians, and the Two-Party System." *Review of Politics* 27 (July): 386–413.

Wilson, James Q. 1962. *The Amateur Democrat.* Chicago: University of Chicago Press.

———. 1985. "Realignment at the Top, Dealignment at the Bottom." In *The American Elections of 1984*, ed. Austin Ranney. Durham, N.C.: Duke University Press.

Winebrenner, Hugh. 1987. *The Iowa Precinct Caucuses: The Making of a Media Event.* Ames: Iowa State University Press.

Contributors

Alan I. Abramowitz is Professor of Political Science at Emory University, coauthor of *Nomination Politics: Party Activists and Presidential Choice* (with Walter J. Stone), coeditor of *The Life of the Parties: A Study of Presidential Activists* (with Ronald B. Rapoport and J. McGlennon), and author or coauthor of numerous chapters in edited collections and articles in the *American Political Science Review, American Journal of Political Science*, and other scholarly journals.

Emmett H. Buell, Jr., is Professor of Political Science at Denison University and the author of *School Desegregation and Defended Neighborhoods: The Boston Controversy* as well as articles in the *American Politics Quarterly, Social Science Quarterly*, and other scholarly journals.

James W. Davis, recently retired as Professor of Political Science at Western Washington University, is the author of *The American Presidency: A New Perspective, National Conventions in an Age of Party Reform, Presidential Primaries: Road to the White House, National Conventions: Nominations Under the Big Top,* and coauthor of *The President and Congress: Toward a New Power Balance* (with Delbert Rinquist).

John S. Jackson III is Dean of the College of Liberal Arts and Professor of Political Science at Southern Illinois University in Carbondale as well as coauthor of *Presidential Nominations and Primaries* (with William Crotty), and the author or coauthor of numerous articles in *American Politics Quarterly*, the *Journal of Politics*, and other scholarly journals.

S. Robert Lichter is Codirector of the Center for Media and Public Affairs in Washington, D.C., and coauthor of *America on Television, The Video Campaign: TV News Coverage of the 1988 Primaries, The Media Elite: America's New Power Brokers,* and *Roots of Radicalism: Jews, Christians, and the New Left,* as well as the author or coauthor of numerous monographs, book chapters, and articles in scholarly journals and magazines.

Barbara K. Norrander is Associate Professor of Political Science at the University of Arizona and the author or coauthor of numerous articles in the *American Journal of Political Science, Journal of Politics*, and other scholarly journals.

Ronald B. Rapoport is Associate Professor of Government at the College of William and Mary, coeditor of *The Life of the Parties: A Study of Presidential Activists* with (Alan I. Abramowitz and J. McGlennon), and the author or coauthor of articles in the *American Journal of Political Science, Comparative Political Studies*, and other scholarly journals.

Michael J. Robinson is Associate Professor of Government at Georgetown University, coauthor of *Over the Wire and on TV: CBS and UPI in Campaign '80*, and author or coauthor of numerous chapters in edited collections, scholarly journals, and magazines.

W. Wayne Shannon is Professor of Political Science at the University of Connecticut, author of *Party, Constituency and Congressional Voting*, coeditor of *The American Polity Reader* (with Ann G. Serow and Everett C. Ladd), and author of chapters in edited collections and articles in the *Journal of Politics, Polity*, and other scholarly journals.

Lee Sigelman is Dean of the Faculty of Social and Behavioral Sciences as well as Professor of Political Science, Public Administration, and Communication at the University of Arizona, coauthor of *Blacks' Views of Racial Inequality: The Dream Deferred* (with Susan Welch), and the author or coauthor of numerous chapters in edited collections and many articles in the *American Political Science Review, British Journal of Political Science*, and other scholarly journals.

Walter J. Stone is Associate Professor of Political Science at the University of Colorado in Boulder, author of *Republic at Risk*, coauthor of *Nomination Politics* (with Alan I. Abramowitz), and the author or coauthor of chapters in edited collections and articles in the *American Political Science Review, American Journal of Political Science*, and other scholarly journals.

Kenneth D. Wald is Associate Professor of Political Science at the University of Florida; author of *Religion and Politics in the United States, Crosses on the Ballot: Patterns of British Voter Alignment Since 1885*, and *Shall the People Rule? The Democrats in Nebraska Politics*; and the author of numerous chapters in edited collections as well as articles in the *American Political Science Review, Journal of Politics*, and other scholarly journals.

Clyde Wilcox is Assistant Professor of Government at Georgetown University and the author or coauthor of numerous articles in the *Journal of Politics, American Politics Quarterly*, and other scholarly journals. He worked as a statistician for the Federal Election Commission in 1984–86.

Index